Gabriel García Moreno and Conservative State Formation in the Andes

LLILAS New Interpretations of Latin America Series

GABRIEL GARCÍA MORENO and Conservative State Formation in the Andes

Peter V. N. Henderson

UNIVERSITY OF TEXAS PRESS, AUSTIN
Teresa Lozano Long Institute of Latin American Studies

FRONTISPIECE: Portrait of Gabriel García Moreno, personal collection of the author.

Printed in the United States of America

First edition, 2008

∞ The paper used in this book meets the minimum requirements of ANSI/NISO Z39.48-1992 (R1997) (Permanence of Paper).

LIBRARY OF CONGRESS CATALOGING-IN-PUBLICATION DATA

Henderson, Peter V. N., 1947–
Gabriel García Moreno and conservative state formation in the Andes / Peter V. N. Henderson. — 1st ed.
p. cm. — (LLILAS new interpretations of Latin America series)
Includes bibliographical references and index.
ISBN 978-0-292-72152-4
1. García Moreno, Gabriel, 1821–1875. 2. Ecuador—History—1830–1895. 3. Presidents—Ecuador—Biography. I. Title.
F3736.G3H46 2008
986.6'06092—dc22
[B] 2008025960

Contents

List of Illustrations

Acknowledgments

During the many years it has taken me to conceptualize, research, and write this book, I have incurred numerous debts. First and foremost I want to thank those who made the time and effort to read the entire rough draft: Kris Lane, Ronn Pineo, Marc Becker, George Lauderbaugh, and especially my undergraduate mentor, J. León Helguera of Vanderbilt University, who worked through the draft four times. They uncovered various errors and significantly improved the final product. I am solely responsible for any mistakes that remain. Winona State University and the National Endowment for the Humanities provided funding to broaden my experiences as an Andeanist and to underwrite several research trips. Other friends—including Jaime and Linda Rodríguez, Derek Williams, Guillermo Bustos, and again Kris Lane—provided me with encouragement early in the project and helped this transplanted Mexicanist find basic information about Ecuador and its archives.

My colleagues at Winona State University—Seymour and Marianna Byman, Greg Schmidt, Alex Yard, John Campbell, Aimee Dobbs, Norm Sobiesk, Troy Paino (now dean), and Colette Hyman—have been supportive of my scholarly efforts for years, as have my friends Doug and Nancy Brown, who shared their great humor with a sometimes too serious historian. Fellow Andeanists such as Michael Moseley, Tom Cummins, Mark Thurner, Jorge Salvador Lara, Vinicio Sosa, Alegría Rivadeneira, Michelle Wibbelsbaum, and Ernie Capello taught me much about Ecuador and its past. My friends at the University of Texas at Austin—Ann Twinam, Seth Garfield, Jonathan Brown, Virginia Burnett, and Jorge Cañizares-Esguerra—helped clarify many of the ideas contained herein. Among my students, Kari Aanensen, Jenise Doty, Keary Dennison, Megan Zeilinger, Ellie Nowicki, and Cristen Marish have worked on theses about Ecuadorian history over the last decade that have helped me think about important themes.

Ecuadorian archivists in Quito proved uniformly helpful, finding materials and making available uncatalogued documents. I especially want to thank for their assistance Grecia Vasco Escudero and her aides Margarita Tufiño and Cecilia Caceres at the Archivo Nacional de Historia for granting me access to the Ministerio del Gobierno materials, as well as to the better-known portions of the collection. Germán Solano de la Sala, Honorio Granja Azanza, and Eduardo Proaño generously helped me work through the Jacinto Caamaño y Jijón materials, the Treasury Department's documents, and the photographic collection at the Archive of the Banco Central del Ecuador. María Elena Porras opened up materials at the Archivo Histórico del Ministerio de Relaciones Exteriores so that I could grapple with the diplomatic issues facing García Moreno in the 1860s. At the Archivo General del Ministerio de Defensa, I must thank my friend, Colonel Fausto Flores, and the director, Colonel Galo Chacón, for granting me full access to this important documentary source. Padre Skiper allowed me to study at the Archivo Arzobispal. Finally, Father Jorge Villalba at the Catholic University granted me access to the Flores family papers.

Librarians also provided invaluable assistance, both in the United States and in Ecuador. In Quito Father Iván Lucero supplied insights while his staff at the Biblioteca Aurelio Espinosa Pólit photocopied many rare items for me—always with a smile. In the United States, Richard Phillips of the University of Florida's George A. Smathers Library; Ann Hartness, Margo Gutiérrez, and Michael Hironymous of the Nettie Lee Benson Latin American Collection at the University of Texas at Austin; and Joe Mount, Vernon Leighton, and Susan Krage of Winona State University all helped me to obtain useful materials. At Indiana University, the staffs at the Lilly Library and the Herman B. Wells Library, especially Andrea Singer, made my one-month visit very productive, sharing with me their incredibly rich government documents and microfiched rare books collection. Finally, the librarians at the Ohio Historical Society, the Kentucky State Historical Society, and the Morris Library at Southern Illinois University in Carbondale provided me with access to many informative items.

I especially want to thank Virginia Hagerty, managing editor of the Teresa Lozano Long Institute of Latin American Studies at the University of Texas at Austin, for her guidance throughout the production of this book. Thanks also to Elaine F. Tankard for her attentive copyediting, and to Anne Finucane and Sydney Henderson, who proofread the manuscript and drew the maps. Most of all I would like to thank Shirley Wheat and Lisa Hessel, our office administrators in the History Department at Winona State University, who faced the unenviable task of turning my chicken scratching into typed prose.

Introduction

Well beyond a century and a quarter following his death, Gabriel García Moreno remains "the most argued about personality in the history of Ecuador."[1] His importance as Ecuador's leading political figure from 1859 to 1875, however, extended far beyond the borders of this small (about the size of Colorado) Andean nation, as his actions and ideas resonated throughout Latin America and Europe. Not surprisingly, then, writers in multiple languages have penned more than thirty full-length biographies of the man, although none in English since 1914.

Not only Ecuadorian intellectuals but also average citizens still hold strong opinions about García Moreno, as a personal anecdote will illustrate. I was sitting at a rooftop café in the town of Otavalo, awaiting the beginning of the San Juan Festival (also called *Inti raimi*), which thanks the deities for a good harvest while parading under the guise of a Catholic celebration. Some Ecuadorian acquaintances asked me why I was spending so much time in their country, and I mentioned my interest in writing a book about García Moreno. Almost immediately a good-natured domestic tiff ensued between a fellow who liked García Moreno because he wielded a strong hand and brought progress to the country, and his girlfriend who despised García Moreno for suppressing liberty and being so pro-Catholic. So right there we see part of the paradox that is García Moreno.

With this book, I aspire to tell much more than the tale of the life of an important historical personage or the history of Ecuador in the mid-nineteenth century. The book operates at the intersection of two other topics of scholarly interest: state formation and the "new political history." State formation, the process of creating a modern nation, saw some of its first experimental efforts in the Western Hemisphere during the postindependence era. As "imagined political communities," the new South American nations had difficulty seeking their identities in distinctive cultural roots—unlike England, for example, where national precepts had developed over centuries.[2]

For many Andean nations, particularly Ecuador, cultural uniqueness proved a puzzling concept, for they shared with neighbors a common language (at least among the elite and middle classes), common historical experiences, and ill-defined boundaries. During the first few decades after independence, the new states waffled among regimes that sought to recreate Spanish colonial institutions, those that attempted state formation based on liberal ideals modified to fit local circumstances, or (worse yet) governments founded on the whims of self-identified military heroes.

García Moreno offered a thoughtful conservative alternative containing both ideological and pragmatic elements. Understanding the culture of highland Ecuador (as did Simón Bolívar, the great liberator), García Moreno argued that the common heritage of the Catholic faith could unite a nation divided by geography and ethnicity. Catholic education and a moral crusade would, he believed, bind Ecuador together culturally. At the same time, he undertook the development of transportation and communication networks that would literally tie the country together and modernize it. So successful was the Garcian experiment that conservatives throughout Europe in the late nineteenth century held up his state as a shining beacon for other would-be Catholic rulers.

García Moreno's state also succeeded, albeit temporarily, because his extensive powers of patronage—especially after 1869—allowed him to impose greater unity on Ecuador than had existed previously. Although the genre of biography tends to attribute earthshaking events to a single heroic individual, the "new political history" has emphasized the importance of networks of supporters and the use of patronage as key factors contributing to the durability of regimes.[3] Like many Latin American political leaders, García Moreno drew upon resources provided by friends and family. To a degree never before realized, his brothers helped him immeasurably in one geographical region, the coast, where his ideas met with much skepticism. Successive marriages into two interrelated and powerful families from the northern and central highlands enabled him to engender the support of many landlords from that region. While attending the university and later serving in the Senate, García Moreno acquired a network of friends throughout the highlands, including the south, who would serve in many roles during his administration—from cabinet officers to church employees to governors. As a result, in 1869 when García Moreno wrote a new constitution, he used the document to control patronage throughout the country even down to the local level, a change that left liberals howling at the tyranny of this "Black Charter" (so nicknamed because of its highly centralized and authoritarian nature).

The implications of the state-formation process and the scholarship about patronage networks have restored the art of biography to respectability. A spate of biographies about the U.S. founding fathers has also rekindled public interest in the genre. The critical literature about biography, meanwhile, suggests a deep theoretical division about its purpose, dating back more than two thousand years to the time of Plutarch. One school contends that famous lives must serve a didactic rationale, whether good or evil. In the medieval period, the lives of saints fulfilled this purpose, as did much of the moralistic biographical literature produced in the Victorian era. A second school of biographers asserts that the life of any individual is worthy of study in and of itself because the reader comes to understand more about the human condition by learning about interesting and significant people. A third school began with Sigmund Freud's unfortunately error-prone psychobiography of Leonardo da Vinci.[4] All three types of biographies have been represented in previous studies of García Moreno, along with a fourth school justifying the inclusion of descriptive fiction to spice up the narrative.

Unfortunately almost all of the García Moreno biographies fall into the first and least satisfactory category. The frenzy of early biographies began in the 1880s with the work of Father Augustine Berthe, which became the source for biographies in many languages because conservative European writers saw García Moreno's Ecuador as the ideal Catholic state. These authors portrayed García Moreno as a secular saint who saved his country and led it to progress, only to be treacherously slain in his prime by liberals.[5] García Moreno's contemporary political enemies—led by Antonio Borrero, Pedro Moncayo, and Roberto Andrade—responded in kind, drawing portraits of García Moreno as a ruthless tyrant who snuffed out liberty and tried to return the nation to the sixteenth century.[6]

Both types of polemical biographies continue to be published up to the present, adding to the quantity of materials but rarely contributing any new interpretation.[7] Due to the polemical nature of these works, his second term ends up being underrepresented because few, if any, of the controversial events occurred during that time. The present study will also redress this imbalance. Only two works, produced in the 1940s, qualify as reasonably equitable accounts belonging to the second category of biographies, the humanistic genre—and neither, of course, had the advantage of sixty years of subsequent research, the new theoretical literature, or access to the recently available archives (both public and private).[8] Hence another purpose here is to rewrite the life and times of García Moreno in a more measured way.

This book consists of eight chapters of nearly equal length. The first describes García Moreno's early years from his birth in 1821 to his involvement in national politics in 1859. This chapter examines the origins and development of García Moreno's national network of friends made during these decades. Chapter 2 covers the years of the civil war from 1859 to 1861, when the country nearly disintegrated. Here the focus shifts to the issue of regionalism, in part the result of topography, which divided the nation into four nearly irreconcilable sections.

Chapter 3 looks at the domestic side of García Moreno's first presidency from 1861 to 1865. Although members of his network (especially from the coast and the south) favored a federalistic system of government to protect their regional interests, García Moreno quickly became disillusioned with this model and sought greater central authority. Thus this chapter examines the rich intellectual debate between liberals and conservatives at midcentury about the nature of the state, a quarrel so bitter it led to conflicts in every Latin American nation. Chapter 4 studies García Moreno's foreign policy failures during the first term: two unsuccessful wars against Colombia and tension with Peru. While foreign wars promoted national identity elsewhere in South America, the case in Ecuador is more debatable. Chapter 5 discusses the interim regimes of Jerónimo Carrión from 1865 to 1867 and Javier Espinosa to 1869, focusing on the theme of *caudillismo*, a quintessentially nineteenth-century Latin American form of government. García Moreno's emergence as a caudillo in 1868 offended many of his moderate friends and splintered the coalition that had brought him to power in 1860.

The next two chapters concern themselves with García Moreno's final term in office, from 1869 to 1875, and the policies of conservative state formation for which he became famous (or infamous). Because religion and morality were so important to García Moreno's state-building project, chapter 6 details his attempts to introduce European monks and nuns into Ecuador to staff the schools (primary, secondary, and university), and also examines his attempt to create a moral nation by force of law. Chapter 7 explores the Garcian system of development: encouraging export earnings by diversifying agricultural production and allowing entrepreneurs full rein to exploit resources, and constructing modern systems of transportation connecting various regions of the country in hopes of unifying it politically and economically. The final chapter relates the dissent against the "perpetual dictatorship" and considers the gory events of August 6, 1875, as well as the aftermath of that day. This section also analyzes García Moreno's significance, both for Ecuador and the Catholic world, to determine why he is still such a controversial figure, even in the twenty-first century.

In short the book devotes attention to "high politics," but these last three chapters also examine the social, economic, and racial issues that hindered García Moreno's attempt to create a viable nation state. The conclusion places García Moreno within the broader context of state-formation theory and illustrates why his life provides a deeper understanding of the critical issues facing nineteenth-century Latin America.

Ecuador during García Moreno's presidencies

Gabriel García Moreno and
Conservative State Formation in the Andes

Chapter One

Preparing for National Leadership, 1821–1859

Although it was the morning of Christmas Eve, one of the holiest days of the religious calendar, Doña Mercedes Moreno de García decided not to attend Mass. She felt a stirring in her womb and, having given birth ten times previously (with eight children still living), she knew her time was near. A joyful mood filled the household, even though the family fortunes had declined recently. The new arrival's imminent birth would coincide with the holiday season, a good omen for the very devout family. And that evening—December 24, 1821—Gabriel García Moreno made his appearance.[1]

The father, Gabriel García Gómez (after whom the baby was named), had emigrated to Guayaquil in the 1790s. Raised in Spain he spent much of his early life in the port city of Cádiz, where his uncle worked for King Charles IV as a scrivener. García Gómez followed suit in this moderately important role during an era when relatively few people could read or write and the Spanish bureaucracy produced countless documents. Because the position paid poorly, he decided to make his fortune in the Indies.

Taking advantage of the free trade laws, García Gómez invested his meager savings in a substantial quantity of goods. Then in 1793 he shipped both them and himself to Callao, Peru's principal port. He quickly sold the merchandise, making a handsome profit, and took up residence in Lima. There fellow Spaniards, or *peninsulares*, convinced him that would-be entrepreneurs could better increase their modest fortunes in a city such as Guayaquil. In addition he knew that as a *peninsular* he would enjoy a certain cachet and therefore could acquire a well-to-do wife from among the upper crust of the local *criollo* (Spaniards born in the New World) elite, as many of his compatriots had done.

Mercedes Moreno, who became García Gómez's bride, had been born in Guayaquil, although both her parents emigrated from Spain. Her father owned an import-export business as well as a profitable cacao plantation.

The fact that Mercedes was apparently no beauty and thus perhaps less marriageable did not hurt Gabriel's chances. The Moreno family considered itself quite pious, as a number of family members held high positions in the Catholic Church. In 1869 her nephew was the first person born in the Americas to be elevated to cardinal (although the seat itself was in Spain). When she met Gabriel in 1794, Mercedes was only 17. The couple married in 1797 and produced a large family, as was commonplace in those times.[2]

As a son-in-law, Gabriel García Gómez did not disappoint—at least initially. Apparently he enjoyed modest success as a merchant and, because of his relations with both *peninsulares* and *criollos*, won election to local political office in the critical year of 1820. Although some writers have attributed his family's decline in fortune in the 1820s and 1830s to their "royalist attitudes," the evidence suggests otherwise. As a member of the city's governing council (*ayuntamiento*), García Gómez signed the Acts of Independence in October 1820, contributing 650 pesos (not an inconsequential sum) to the maintenance of its army. Three years later, while still a city council member, he supervised the collection of local funds to help pay for Simón Bolívar's final campaign against the Spanish in Peru.[3] The family's diminished income was more likely a consequence of the general economic malaise that impoverished Ecuador in the 1820s, resulting from the maritime disruptions accompanying the Napoleonic conflict in Europe and the struggle for independence in Latin America.

The marriage proved prolific. Five boys and three girls were already living when Gabriel, the youngest, first opened his eyes. The family dynamics are interesting in light of one of García Moreno's most memorable quotations: "Only two worthwhile things ever came from Guayaquil, bananas and my mother." This comment is often interpreted to mean that he despised his siblings and his father. Yet detractors claim he was not even close to his mother, pointing to sparse correspondence between them and the terms of her last testament, which left the family home to his sisters. One should note (parenthetically, since the sisters never married) that it was reasonable to provide for them in this way.[4] The evidence further suggests that García Moreno relied on three of his brothers much more than has been previously realized.

Certainly the family had its share of strong personalities, young Gabriel's not the least among them. As sometimes happens when a significant age gap exists between the youngest son and the nearest older brother, Gabriel displayed many of the characteristics associated with first-borns: He was conservative, aggressive, ambitious, jealous, militant, moralistic, and domineering. Because the parents expected their older boys to enter the priesthood or business, their wishes left political leadership as a niche open to Gabriel—one suited to his temperament. Established in the church, in business, and in coastal society, the brothers helped García Moreno build a patronage network along the coast even while he resided elsewhere. Beginning in the 1830s, he would extend this network to all regions of the country, as described in later sections of this book.

The five brothers were Manuel, José (called Pepe), Pedro Pablo, Miguel, and Fernando. The eldest, Manuel, followed his mother's wishes and became the parish priest for Jipijapa, a town in Manabí that manufactured so-called Panama hats, and later held a sinecure in the Guayaquil Cathedral. Manuel and Fernando fell out with Gabriel in the 1850s over political issues described later in this chapter. Manuel's career came to an abrupt halt in the 1860s, and Fernando eventually became so estranged that he had to ask others to help him curry favor with his youngest brother.[5] The remaining three, however, remained close to Gabriel.

The next brother, José, briefly experimented with the priesthood. He had an even more explosive temper than did Gabriel (as revealed in some vituperative letters scattered among the Treasury documents of the 1860s), but his stints in local government showed him to be capable. José took over the troubled cacao tax registry, which oversaw the government's primary revenue source, and tried to end its corruption. Gabriel was probably closest to Pedro Pablo, who made a fortune as a merchant and cacao planter. Pedro Pablo let Gabriel work in his business at various times. Eventually Pedro Pablo married the daughter of former president and independence hero Juan José Flores in the 1850s, which proved a turning point for Gabriel in terms of acquired networks. The third "good" brother, Miguel, served twice as governor of Guayas, the province including Guayaquil—once in the 1850s, when he protected Gabriel from almost certain arrest (and possibly worse), and once in the 1860s. All three helped Gabriel maintain relationships with coastal bankers, merchants, and planters. The three sisters who lived to adulthood (Josefa, Carmen, and Rosario) unfortunately inherited neither good looks nor money, and so grew old to spinsterhood together, taking care of their long-lived mother. In any event, Gabriel wrote all but the estranged brothers frequently and always stayed at his mother's house when he came to Guayaquil.[6]

EARLY CHILDHOOD IN GUAYAQUIL

Today bustling Guayaquil is Ecuador's largest city, but in the 1820s a population of about 20,000 people ranked it only third in size, behind

Quito and Cuenca. Even then, however, because of its location on the broad estuary forty miles up the Guayas River from the Pacific, the city was Ecuador's commercial hub, a vibrant port handling shipping from all over the Pacific coast of South America. Oceangoing ships found the city an ideal place to undergo repairs, as the Pacific coast's most active shipyard had long operated along the banks of the Guayas. Approaching Guayaquil from the sea, foreign visitors were impressed with what seemed to be shimmering white stucco homes and public buildings of marble lining the river. Upon landing, travelers discovered the illusion—the whitewashed fronts on wooden buildings with thatched roofs only lent the appearance of stucco and marble. Oppressive heat and humidity plagued Guayaquil during the rainy season from January to May, along with disease and filth.

The pride of the city was its boardwalk, the Malecón, which stretched along the river for about a mile and served not only as a walkway but also as a dock and a barrier against rising waters. In the 1800s Guayaquil's most respected families lived within a block or two of the Malecón, as did García Moreno's parents. Usually these elite homes rose two or three stories, often with a shop occupying the ground floor and the family living on the highest floor. Homes had ample windows with wooden shutters, which let in fresh air and tried to screen out as many insects as possible. Typically such homes also had balconies where families could enjoy breezes on sultry evenings.[7] These wooden structures proved very vulnerable to fires that regularly incinerated whole blocks at a time.

Inside the homes, travelers remarked upon the numerous hammocks in which upper-class women rested even during the day. The ordinary people of Guayaquil were stereotyped as being hard-working, hard-drinking, irreligious, secular, rough-and-tumble sorts—typical of active seaports. Consequently, few travelers had positive comments about the people of the coastal lowlands. One adventurous German lady traveling alone (a cultural sin in nineteenth-century Ecuador) was furious about being constantly cheated out of money. She stated that the hospitality she encountered in Ecuador was "far below what I have experienced among the Arabs, the Bedouins, or even the savages of Borneo." When she accidentally fell out of her boat on the Guayas, not one of the oarsmen moved to help her. She was saved by a fellow passenger![8]

Of course the vast majority of visitors to Guayaquil in the 1820s were not tourists but rather ship captains and businesspeople. Beginning in the latter part of the eighteenth century, Guayaquil had become the principal port for cacao exportation, which for more than a century would dominate

Guayaquil, Ecuador's foremost port and García Moreno's birthplace, ca. 1870 (Courtesy of Library of Congress LC USZ 62-94524)

the country's commerce. This plant, which grew luxuriantly in the rich soils of the plains around Guayaquil, produced a bean that was the source of chocolate, a favorite drink of royalty and, in the nineteenth century, upper- and middle-class Europeans. Despite market fluctuations, cacao generally commanded a high price, so its production brought wealth to Ecuador. Poor peasants left their homes in the highlands to work at better-paying jobs on cacao plantations, beginning a demographic shift that has continued to the present.[9] This dynamic economy meant that fortunes could be both won and lost, however.

For the García Gómez family, finances worsened after independence. Gabriel Sr. apparently never held office again. Because manual labor was socially unacceptable for an upper-class Spaniard, he had only his accumulated capital left for sustenance after his business failures. Pesos became increasingly hard to find. One story, probably specious, claims that the father was reduced to lurking in hotel doorways to beg cigarettes from passersby. By all accounts Gabriel Sr. was intelligent and a gifted conversationalist, but as the years passed he gradually spent not only the profits he had earned in Peru but also his wife's dowry. Although all the biographies agree about the straitened circumstances, the family remained part of the social elite.[10] With a house one block from the Malecón, Doña Mercedes continued to have household servants (who have been notoriously inexpensive at all times in Ecuador).

Although some biographies describe Doña Mercedes as meek and demure, others speculate that she became the dominant parental force as the family fortune dwindled. She certainly ran a highly moral ship, encouraging three of her five sons to seek careers in the church. When Pedro Pablo's wife complained to Mercedes that he had a "second home" and an established mistress, she gave her son a tongue-lashing and boxed his ears—all when he was a middle-aged millionaire and a leading light of society. Mercedes has also been criticized for refusing to allow Gabriel to romp with the urchins who played along the Malecón and swam in the river like youthful Huck Finns.[11] Such social intermingling would have been unthinkable, of course, in the formal and traditional household that Mercedes ran, but it hardly meant that young Gabriel was repressed and cut off from the world.

Although strict, Mercedes clearly loved her son, protecting him and imbuing him with strong religious values. A sickly child in his early years, he did not readily gain weight. He was also timid—excessively so, in his father's opinion. To toughen him up, Gabriel Sr. attempted to teach him bravery. On one occasion the father locked Gabriel out of the house on a balcony during a lightning storm. Tropical Guayaquil has horrific storms, so the deafening thunder, flashes of lightning, and downpour of water must have terrified the six-year-old. On a second occasion, upon hearing that Gabriel feared the idea of death, the father locked the boy alone in a room with a corpse for a whole night with only a single candle for company.

These anecdotes bear further examination because they are the only stories about García Moreno's childhood that he later recounted to his friends. Writers who find García Moreno to be an outstanding statesperson and a great leader claim that García Moreno learned about courage as a result of the experiences. According to a story still circulating today, García Moreno boasted that the episodes strengthened him. "Now I have no reason to fear a bolt of lightning." (The Spanish word for lightning bolt is *rayo*—an ironic statement in light of the events of August 6, 1875, discussed in chapter 8.)[12] Writers critical of García Moreno attribute much of his subsequent cruelty and harshness to his father's actions. According to these interpretations, the incidents contributed to García Moreno's mercurial and contradictory nature, which worsened when he reached puberty and discovered his sex drive.[13] Of course both of these interpretations require conjecture, yet are typical of the debates contained in almost all the García Moreno biographical literature. This book will try to refrain from engaging in these quarrels except where they inform the narrative.

Because of the family's penury, Gabriel's mother and sisters home-schooled him. He proved an academic prodigy, reading and writing by the age of seven and rapidly outstripping the family's ability to teach him. Although the family's poverty had forced other siblings to drop out of school, Gabriel showed such promise that his mother searched for a way to continue his education and enter the church. The family priest, Father Miguel Betancourt, offered Doña Mercedes a solution: He volunteered to tutor the boy. Father Betancourt was astonished by Gabriel's ability, teaching him Latin in a space of ten months. Because Guayaquil had no secondary schools, the family decided to send Gabriel to be educated in Quito, the nation's capital. In 1834 Gabriel Sr. died of an unknown illness, but this loss did not deter the plans of Doña Mercedes for her son's future. With Father Betancourt's help, she petitioned the government for a scholarship that would pay tuition and provide a very modest cost-of-living subsidy. Still she hesitated to send the lad until Father Betancourt offered one more inducement. He persuaded his two sisters, who lived very near the school in Quito, to provide Gabriel with room and board at no cost to Doña Mercedes. Although poor, these pious women were more than willing to accede to their brother's wishes. And so, at the age of 15, Gabriel García Moreno was sent off alone to Quito.[14]

SECONDARY SCHOOL DAYS

Riding on a horse from Guayaquil to Quito was not exactly a pleasant experience in the 1830s. Although horse and mule trains regularly plied the so-called "Royal Road" once every two weeks (less frequently during the rainy season), the 320-mile, 21-day journey entailed considerable hardships. Every traveler to Ecuador before the 1870s complained about the condition of the roads, which frequently featured potholes so deep that mules actually disappeared in them, bridges so untrustworthy that streams had to be forded, and seas of mud so endless they bespattered a traveler's clothing. Because the trip required many overnight stays, the government continued to rely on the old pre-Hispanic system of *tambos*, or inns, to provide refuge for the weary traveler in rural areas. These hostels, however, lacked the basic sanitation and comforts that Europeans expected. When a *tambo* did offer bedding, the traveler shared a woven mat with an abundance of fleas. The food was no better. If lucky, one might get a decent *locro*, a kind of creamy potato soup that was the national dish of the highlands. Often *tambos* were unprepared for visitors and simply had no provisions to offer. Travelers hoped and prayed to get to towns where they could find better accommodations and decent meals.

Gabriel's horse and the mule train made good time over the flat plains and low hills of what are today Guayas and Los Ríos provinces, and then began to climb into the foothills of the Andes towards the town of Guaranda, where they had to hire new animals. Along this trek, temperatures dropped significantly (especially at night) and the air became perceptibly thinner. Compensating for all these difficulties were spectacular views of the mountains, and on rare days, of the coast itself shimmering in the distance. After crossing a portion of the base of towering Mt. Chimborazo, long thought to be the tallest mountain in the world at around 20,700 feet, weary travelers stumbled into what famed explorer Alexander von Humboldt had nicknamed the Avenue of the Volcanoes, a series of basins between the eastern and western ranges of the Andes that arguably made up the heartland of Ecuador until the early twentieth century.[15]

Once in the Avenue, the journey became less arduous, passing through Ambato, the city of fruits and flowers, and Latacunga, in the shadow of the perfectly shaped volcanic cone of Mt. Cotopaxi. Within a few days Gabriel entered Quito, then a city of about 35,000. He immediately went to find the Betancourt sisters' home. María Betancourt and her married sister, Josefa Espinosa, welcomed young Gabriel and soon introduced him to their friends and relatives. Their nephew, Javier Espinosa, about the same age as Gabriel, and Francisco Javier León, another boy who lived nearby, both later served in government with García Moreno for many years and became important participants in his political network. By all accounts Gabriel's first impressions of Quito were extremely positive. As a very religious youth, he could not help but be impressed with the architecture of what is now called Quito's Historic District, with monasteries such as San Francisco, the magnificent golden-altared Jesuit church of La Compañía, and the cathedral itself. As an administrative rather than a commercial city, Quito lacked the hustle and bustle of Guayaquil. On the narrow and hilly streets, adobe homes with tile roofs mirrored traditional Spanish architecture and helped to fend off cold highland evenings and torrential rains. Quito's life centered around churches and Sunday visits in the main plaza. In terms of climate, topography, ethnicity, and culture, the city could not have been more different from Guayaquil. The sharp contrast between the

Quito, the capital and García Moreno's residence after 1836 (Courtesy of the Benson Latin American Collection, University of Texas at Austin)

two has led more than one commentator to oversimplify the country's history as "the tale of two cities."[16]

Soon Gabriel began his studies at the Colegio San Fernando, a preparatory school for the University of Quito. Under the traditional Hispanic educational system, students pursued essentially a secondary-school degree at the *colegio*, and then advanced to the university to specialize in philosophy, law, theology, or medicine (the latter being unavailable at the University of Quito then). Because of his own interests, as well as the urging of his mother and Father Betancourt, Gabriel followed a preparatory course leading to a career in theology. He again excelled at his schoolwork, and on his own learned English, French, and Italian. While classmates enjoyed parties and social events, he pushed himself hard, spending long hours over his books. When he felt drowsy, he would put his feet in a pan of cold water to jolt himself back to a state of wakefulness.[17] In other words, because he had a remarkable work ethic as well as intelligence, he did extremely well in school.

At the age of 17, he took minor orders and received the tonsure, or haircut of a young acolyte. At this point, he was still destined for the priesthood. But in 1839 García Moreno experienced a change of heart and decided not to become a priest, much to the disappointment of his mother and Father Betancourt. Gabriel's misgivings have been reasonably explained and should not be construed as a crisis of faith; he simply doubted that he had the calling. Most biographers, in fact, suggest an intellectual reason for the change. García Moreno, recently fascinated with science, had started to study with an émigré French scientist, Sebastián Wisse, recruited by President Juan José Flores to engineer the road between Quito and Guayaquil. Other accounts suggest that the young man discovered women at this time and the temptations of the flesh were simply too great.[18] These two theories are not mutually exclusive, especially since García Moreno disdained corrupt priests who violated their vows. In any case, when it came time to enter the University of Quito, García Moreno decided to pursue a degree in law rather than theology.

UNIVERSITY AND SOCIAL LIFE

In October 1840, García Moreno began his legal education at the University of Quito. In addition to courses on law, he pursued classes in language, literature, and particularly mathematics and science. His reputation for academic brilliance grew when he challenged a math professor's error and proved him wrong.[19] He continued to work very hard at his studies, memorizing legal codes as law students were required to do. García Moreno did not seem to have a burning desire to practice law, though. Instead he saw the degree as an avenue to a political career.

In the 1840s, as now, Ecuadorians viewed the university as a training ground for the next generation's political leadership. Students tended to be critical of the status quo, and campus politics provided leadership opportunities. In addition student leaders often formed *camarillas*, or coteries that followed a leader from university days through political office. Such was the case with García Moreno. During his time at the University of Quito, he made friends with Rafael Carvajal, Manuel Gómez de la Torre (later governor of Imbabura), Roberto de Ascásubi, José Javier Eguiguren (treasury minister in the 1870s), Daniel Salvador (later minister of war), Manuel Vega (a future governor from Cuenca), and many other sons of important families.[20]

García Moreno also blossomed socially. As a student from an elite Guayaquil family, he gained easy entry into Quito's inner circles. No doubt his university friends facilitated his introduction to the upper echelons of the community. García Moreno accepted invitations to spend time on some of the great estates, or *haciendas*, in the surrounding valleys. He also participated in *tertulias*, or coffee clubs, which met at fashionable people's homes. Some of these gatherings (such as dinners at the house of his friend Carlos Aguirre) were elegant affairs indeed, combining pleasantries and gossip with serious political and philosophical discussions. As one of the best and brightest in Ecuador, García Moreno was welcomed, probably because of his maternal relatives and despite his comparative poverty. Quickly assimilating into Quito society, he considered himself a *quiteño* at heart, thinking disdainfully of other regions. Quiteños refer to those from the coast as *monos* (monkeys) for several reasons, while people from other highland towns are often denigrated as *chagras* (rubes).

At the same time, García Moreno discovered women. Great license was permissible with women from the lower class. Supposedly as a result of one of these unions, a son was born on July 27, 1841. García Moreno never mentioned or acknowledged this boy, who allegedly entered the military, captained the firing squad that executed General Manuel Tomás Maldonado described in chapter 4, and died in Quito shortly after 1900.[21] Of course, such youthful escapades were both possible and acceptable for elite men, but there is no firm evidence that García Moreno fathered a child out of wedlock.

He did, however, fall seriously in love in 1842. The object of his affections, Juanita Jijón, was the sister-in-law of President Juan José Flores, whose wife, Sra. Mercedes Jijón de Flores, held some of the most glamorous *tertulias* in all of Quito. García Moreno eventually received an invitation to attend one of these gatherings. Within a short time he began to court Juanita, who besides being very well connected was young and pretty. She, too, apparently had feelings for the young man, allowing him to write a love poem in her album—the first extant piece of writing by García Moreno. Their love, however, did not prosper, as General Flores found the impoverished García Moreno to be an inappropriate suitor and ordered him to stay away.[22] As a result, García Moreno turned his attention back to his studies and politics, as described in the next section.

After completing his studies, García Moreno apprenticed with Joaquín Enríquez and practiced law off and on for the next four years, becoming licensed in 1848. Allegedly he took on poor clients pro bono. In one of his most notable cases, he represented a priest who (supposedly) had been wrongfully disciplined by the archbishop of Quito. Upon discovering that the archbishop had acted properly and that his client had lied to him, García Moreno withdrew his representation. But Gabriel García Moreno did not seek to make a mark on the nation's history because of his courtroom prowess or his romantic poetry. As he told one of his friends who suggested at this time that he write the history of Ecuador: "I prefer to make it."[23] Consequently, even before he had completed his degree, he threw himself into national politics.

ECUADORIAN POLITICS, 1809 TO 1845

Ecuador's quest for independence began in 1809 when a group of *quiteño* aristocrats, some belonging to the Ascásubi and Jijón families, rose up and replaced the colonial government on August 10, now commemorated as Independence Day. Enlightenment notions of liberty, ideas of anticolonialism, disrupting consequences of the Napoleonic Wars in Europe, and general discontent with the Bourbon reforms motivated the patriots to seek autonomy from French-dominated Spain. Their success proved short-lived. Within three months the ousted head of the colonial government retook Quito and imprisoned the conspirators for nearly a year before putting them to death. A second attempt at independence in 1810 fared no better. With the cream of Quito's elite decimated, foreigners would liberate Ecuador a decade later—such as Simón Bolívar and his lieutenant, the great Ecuadorian national hero Antonio José de Sucre (also a Venezuelan). Eventually Sucre secured independence at the battle of Pichincha on May 24, 1822.[24]

Bolívar had a grand vision for the northern part of South America after liberation from Spain. He hoped to unify what are the present-day countries of Venezuela, Colombia, Panama, and Ecuador into a single government, the Republic of Gran Colombia. Until his death in 1830, Bolívar managed to hold his dream together despite constant revolts and economic problems that dimmed prospects for the unwieldy state. The Gran Colombian experiment proved a disaster for Ecuador. As the smallest and least influential of the three larger regions, since Panama was attached to Colombia, it received the fewest benefits. When the dust settled from the burial of Bolívar and Gran Colombia, Ecuador was saddled with a $7-million-peso debt primarily owed to Great Britain as its proportionate-by-population share of Gran Colombia's obligations—a burden disrupting finances even in the 1870s.[25]

Thus Ecuador began its life as a nation in 1830, with Juan José Flores, a lieutenant of Bolívar's and a midlevel hero of the independence struggle, as president. The country's difficulty in achieving a national identity manifested itself from the outset, when its founders chose to name it after a meridian line rather than the more obvious but politically divisive historical name derived from the Kingdom of Quito. Furthermore, Flores also was Venezuelan, although he had married into the cream of Quito aristocracy, the Jijón family, and acquired vast estates in the lowlands near Guayaquil. Ecuador's situation was not unique. Many Latin Americans (except Brazilians) in that era had little sense of national identity, and for at least a few decades, tended to think of themselves as Spanish-Americans at one extreme, or natives of a particular province at the other—rather than citizens of a particular country. Flores' successor to the presidency in 1835, Vicente Rocafuerte, fit into this category. Rocafuerte, celebrated by patriots today as the country's first real president, had held important posts in the Mexican government. Both men offered nation-building projects. Flores hoped to modernize the economy and construct a road linking Quito to Guayaquil; Rocafuerte also wanted to increase the availability of elementary education. Both presidents failed to accomplish their goals, largely because debts and salaries ate up almost all of Ecuador's tax receipts.[26]

Ecuadorian history proved turbulent in the 1830s and 1840s. The economy remained weak: No European government would lend Ecuador a peso because of its poor credit rating, and the military and civilian bureaucracies were expensive burdens. Matters worsened in 1843 when Flores revoked the bargain he and Rocafuerte had made to alternate presidential terms. Ecuadorians fought long and hard against Flores' so-called Charter of Slavery, which allowed his reelection, and by 1845 drove him from power. García Moreno played a minimal role in this struggle, although clearly he sided with the anti-Flores forces. Apparently the Flores government detained García Moreno briefly for making a critical speech, suspended him from the university, and tried to exile him—after which García Moreno fled to the northern province of Imbabura, where he joined the rebels.[27] He saw no real military action. Before long Flores agreed to sign the Treaty of Virginia, under which he would receive his full military pension in exchange for going into exile. Shortly thereafter Rocafuerte died, ending the era of political dominance by independence leaders. Now a new generation of men slightly older than García Moreno appeared ready to take a turn at managing the government.

FROM POLITICS TO SCIENCE TO MATRIMONY TO EUROPEAN TRAVEL

Meanwhile García Moreno served his apprenticeship at law and dabbled with his avocations—mountain climbing, politics, and, yes, women.

Before him few people in his country had expressed scientific curiosity about the natural wonders surrounding them in the Avenue of the Volcanoes. Teaming up with his science mentor, Sebastián Wisse, and an Indian guide, García Moreno descended into the active crater of Mt. Pichincha, the volcano that abuts Quito. Pichincha actually had two craters: an old inactive one directly overlooking the city (Rucu Pichincha), and a younger active crater (Guagua Pichincha), which occasionally erupts even today. The explorers took scientific instruments with them intended for measuring the depth of the crater, analyzing the types of gases emitted, and chipping away rock samples to bring back for analysis. After descending about 1,300 feet, the explorers decided to stay for several days despite noxious gases, taking observations and admiring the unusual landscape. At one point, García Moreno and the guide were nearly crushed to death beneath an avalanche. With their scientific curiosity slaked, the three men climbed out of the crater and returned to Quito. García Moreno would repeat this journey twice during his career. Also, just before Christmas in 1849, he and Wisse attempted to reach the summit of Mt. Sangay, a volcano over 17,000 feet high. As they ascended, Sangay erupted four times, sending dust down over the slopes, but García Moreno continued to climb and nearly reached the summit before beating a hasty retreat.[28] He found the world of scientific exploration a welcome respite from national politics.

During these years, García Moreno also settled down and began raising a family. Although rumors linked his marriage prospects briefly with a beauty from Guayaquil, he soon proposed to the sister of one of his closest friends, Roberto de Ascásubi. Gabriel and Rosa de Ascásubi were married on August 4, 1846. The marriage proved controversial, for Gabriel was 24 and Rosa 36. In the nineteenth century, she was considered near the end of her childbearing years. Not only did the age disparity cause tongues to wag, but also all reports indicate she was quite homely—which no doubt contributed to the reason she was unmarried despite wealth and family connections.

Her older brother, Manuel de Ascásubi, was an important politician who served both as vice president and secretary of the treasury at different times in the 1840s. Apparently opposing the marriage on grounds that García Moreno was a gold digger, he probably did not like the prospect of another alpha male in the family either. Like many upper-class families in the sierra, the Ascásubis did not have much spare cash on hand but did own a number of haciendas, including historic La Ciénega, scattered around the northern and central highlands.

Weighing in on Gabriel's behalf, however, was Roberto, who led a rather monastic life and never married. He had joined the liberal anti-Flores opposition in 1843 and knew García Moreno well from their days at the university. Ultimately Roberto persuaded his brother that García, as they called him, loved their sister, and the wedding went forward. The other Ascásubi sisters—Rosario, Dolores, and María Josefa—soon embraced García Moreno as a brother.

García Moreno biographers have naturally been divided in their treatment of the marriage. His friends suggest not only that he loved Rosa, but also that he offered her a very distinguished family name. Enemies, on the other hand, view the marriage as a self-serving attempt for García Moreno to grasp at power and prestige, which had seemed to be his motivation when he courted Flores' sister-in-law.[29] Logic suggests that the critics' argument makes a great deal of sense. García Moreno desperately wanted acceptance and entry into *quiteño* society, which this advantageous marriage would provide—as well as monetary assets sufficient to pursue his political career. Regardless of the initial motivation, García Moreno's letters over the years suggest that he came to love his wife. Looking at the matter dispassionately, García Moreno's advantageous marriage provided him with an important network of friends and relatives in the center-north highlands.

Despite her age, Rosa was almost constantly pregnant during the early years of their marriage. Their first child, a daughter, was stillborn. On February 11, 1849, Rosa gave birth to a live daughter, who died in May from a tumor on her chest. Following a miscarriage in the fall of 1849, she bore a second living daughter at the end of July 1850, who also died in a matter of months. Both were named María del Rosario. In 1851 a son who lived but five months compounded the tragedy.[30] At this point, Rosa was 41 years old, and it became clear she would never provide García Moreno with an heir. Nevertheless from the tone of many letters exchanged over the years, the union remained a close one, as Gabriel always worried about her fragile state of health and told her frequently how much he missed her. Rosa adored her husband, even though he espoused some views that modern women would find offensive. In particular during Rosa's pregnancies, García Moreno harped on the idea that she must produce a son in part because of what he termed women's difficult role in this life, filled with hardship and despair.[31] Also, of course, García Moreno preferred to have a son to carry on his line.

Another test of a happy marriage is whether it can withstand the stresses of infidelity. Almost every Ecuadorian that you meet today will tell you that in the 1850s García Moreno had an affair with Virginia Klinger, who was married to one of García Moreno's best friends, Carlos Aguirre. She was a beautiful, polished, and well-educated daughter of another prominent *quiteño* family. Some go so far as to claim they had a daughter together, although friendly biographers say the affair was never consummated and that she was just a family friend. Although possible, the legend of García Moreno's unfaithfulness seems unlikely. Despite the undoubted stress of the failure to have children, as well as the cultural tradition of machismo permitting men to stray, two reasons would suggest García Moreno and Virginia Klinger never had a sexual relationship. First, García Moreno remained a friend of her husband through the 1870s, after the alleged affair; and second, García Moreno, at least later in life, vehemently opposed adultery.[32]

In any event, young Gabriel's connections with the Klingers, the Ascásubis, and other elite families enabled him to enter the world he coveted, the national political scene. Historian Lewis Namier's characterization of eighteenth-century English politics as a struggle between "the ins and the outs" of the elite Tory and Whig families is instructive for viewing the nineteenth-century Ecuadorian situation.[33] García Moreno's alliances tied him to a number of the large landowning families of the north-central sierra. Given the surplus of men with law or philosophy degrees and the lack of meaningful employment opportunities for them, they naturally looked at office-holding as a suitable career. Namier's thesis also explains the remarkable persistence of "outs" trying to get back "in" through rebellions. For example, after Juan José Flores was forced from the presidency in 1845, he spent fifteen years trying to recover both his position and his confiscated properties. Similarly exiles like José María Urbina would seek to restore their positions from 1860 to 1876.

With his new extended family connections, García Moreno began his political career in earnest in 1846. Those who had deposed General Flores drafted a new constitution, but divided over whom to select as president. García Moreno, on the sidelines, was disappointed when his preference lost to Vicente Ramón Roca. García Moreno never approved of *any* of the chief executives of the 1840s and 1850s, so it is not surprising that he launched his career by publishing a series of newspapers commenting critically on events of the day.[34] These were the same sorts of no-holds-barred broadsheets that would anger him when he was president. García Moreno's commentaries, funded no doubt by Ascásubi family monies, made contemporaries notice him. As a result, Roca appointed him first as a judge for

Quito and then, because of his opposition to Flores and his family connections, dispatched García Moreno in December 1847 to head the provincial interior department (*gobernación*) that oversaw the police in Guayas Province to prevent subversion.[35] García Moreno acted energetically, effecting the arrest of several suspects and also collecting tax revenues for the government—making sure they did not fall into Flores' hands during his invasion.[36]

García Moreno's reconciliation with the Roca government did not last long. During a debate in the Chamber of Deputies in October 1848, charges about misappropriated funds flew around the room. Roberto de Ascásubi laid the malfeasance at the door of Secretary of the Treasury Manuel Bustamante, who responded by blaming the previous two secretaries—the Ascásubi brothers. The discussion became quite heated, with news of the debate spilling outside the chamber's halls. On the evening of October 30, García Moreno confronted Bustamante and told him that he must retract the "insulting, discourteous, and infamous lies" that he had uttered. Bustamante refused. The next day García Moreno, accompanied by General Fernando Ayarza and Manuel de Ascásubi, publicly repeated the demand for an apology and, failing that, a duel. When Bustamante again refused, García Moreno slapped him hard across the face. The quarrel demonstrated two of García Moreno's personal characteristics. First, he defended his family's honor and would go to extremes to do so; second, he possessed an irascible temper.

Bustamante could not back down in the face of this very public insult and, within a few days, had convinced the city prosecutors to charge García Moreno not only with assault and battery but also with intent to murder. (Apparently García Moreno had a pistol with him during the episode, although he never drew it.) García Moreno insisted on defending himself in court, forgetting the adage that whenever a lawyer represents himself, he has a fool for a client. He tried to argue that the law only criminalized acts of violence committed against public officials in their public persona ("while in the actual exercise of his official functions"), whereas he had slapped Bustamante as the result of a private quarrel. The trial court found against García Moreno and ordered him to prison. He filed an appeal, which stayed the judgment, and fled to Guayaquil to go into hiding. A friend, Manuel Gómez de la Torre, represented him before the Supreme Court, but in March 1849 García Moreno lost his appeal.[37]

While Rosa remained in the highlands with the Ascásubis for various reasons such as being fairly well advanced in a pregnancy, García Moreno found refuge with his mother and sisters. Meanwhile the governor of Guayas province privately assured García Moreno that he would not be arrested. As he wrote to his brother-in-law Roberto, he found life in Guayaquil "sad and tiring. I never see anybody, and I leave the house only when I must have activity. I have no distractions." Even occasional trips to Pedro Pablo's estate in Vinces did not cheer him up much. While in Guayaquil, Tuesdays were the high point of his week; the mail came from Quito and he would hurry to the post office to pick it up. But on February 20, 1849, while the population celebrated Carnaval by soaking each other with water in the Ecuadorian tradition, the mail brought a warrant for García Moreno's arrest, and a judge ordered a process server and four police officers to seize the fugitive. When the squad arrived at Doña Mercedes' home, García Moreno convinced the process server to send the police away and to seek further orders from the governor—who allowed the fugitive to find refuge with Pedro Pablo in Vinces.[38]

Assuming that going home to the sierra would cure his malaise, García Moreno took that opportunity in July 1849. He hoped that a new president would facilitate a pardon. Prospects seemed particularly bright when congress could not agree on Roca's successor, and Manuel de Ascásubi stepped into the void. Loading the pack train with gifts requested by the family, as well as some of the marvelous local fruits for which Ecuador is known, García Moreno mounted his horse and returned home.[39] Although he had successfully eluded incarceration for seven months, his hopes of returning to a normal life did not come to fruition because congress did not pass an amnesty bill nor did acting President Manuel de Ascásubi help him. Not surprisingly García Moreno continued to show antipathy for his brother-in-law, saying that Manuel deserved a nickname that evidenced his "vile character." García Moreno added that Manuel was credulous and naïve,[40] a characterization that seemed accurate when the military rose against Manuel and deposed him—but by that time García Moreno and Pedro Pablo were in Europe.

As a successful entrepreneur in the 1840s, Pedro Pablo García Moreno had traveled extensively in Peru and Chile, establishing business connections and buying property, as his first wife was Chilean. Given Gabriel's stalemated political career, Pedro Pablo probably thought this moment opportune, either to bring his brother into the business or provide him with the distraction of a grand excursion to Europe. In addition to exporting cacao, Pedro Pablo also imported goods. On this journey he negotiated contracts with British and continental companies with which he wanted to do business. García Moreno's letters do not mention his role in these business meetings; instead they convey a sense of haste to be done with the journey and return home. He commented at some length on the long winter in Hamburg: In April it was still snowing and the canals were frozen. The brothers did take time for cultural activities. With the assistance of the brother of Britain's consul in Guayaquil, they gained entry into some private British art collections and also attended the Paris theatre and opera.[41] This hasty journey had little effect on the development of García Moreno's political thought, however. Less than two months after their arrival on the continent, Gabriel and Pedro Pablo boarded a ship and headed back to Guayaquil, where they landed on August 4, 1850.

Ecuadorian politics had taken another murky turn while they were gone. The military revolt that had tumbled Manuel de Ascásubi from power replaced him with Diego Noboa, a weak elderly man from Guayaquil. Two of García Moreno's brothers, Miguel and Fernando, formed part of the successful civilian team that the military and Noboa appointed to office. As usual Gabriel thought very little of the new government and with small charity described his brothers' roles as an "infamous blot" that would "disgrace" their mother. Nonetheless Miguel became governor of Guayas, enabling him to extricate brother Gabriel from the next political morass the latter created for himself.

Meanwhile García Moreno and Noboa did agree on one issue, the importance of restoring the Jesuit order to Ecuador. Despite giving up his theological studies, García Moreno remained very spiritual. On their return trip, he and Pedro Pablo met a party of Jesuits in Panama who had once again been expelled from New Granada, or present-day Colombia. (This text will use "Colombia" hereafter.) Although the Jesuits had planned to return to continental Europe, García Moreno convinced them to come to Ecuador, where he promised that a sober and Catholic people awaited their ministry. Lobbying the devoutly Catholic Noboa, García Moreno secured permission for them to land in Guayaquil and travel to Quito and other highland locations—one of the first concrete, if fleeting, accomplishments of his early career.[42]

Otherwise Gabriel objected to the new government, saying Noboa was a mere figurehead for the military despite amnesty legislation that saved García Moreno from jail. As he warned his brother-in-law Roberto, "the appearance that all is orderly will last only as long as the military wants it to. The day they grow weary of the fiction, they will defeat the government . . . and will dispose of the country at their whim."[43] García

Moreno's words proved prophetic as General José María Urbina, the most influential general from the campaign against Flores in 1845, assumed the presidency in 1851.

A DEFINING MOMENT: THE DEFENSE OF THE JESUITS

Although most Ecuadorians accepted the arrival of the Jesuits, some with great enthusiasm, their presence soon provoked an international incident. Colombia objected strenuously to their finding refuge so close to the border and blustered about invading in the hopes of reversing Ecuador's policy. Despite the weak logic of their position, the Colombian "Reds," as the anticlerical liberals were known, pressed the issue. Even Ecuadorian liberals like Pedro Moncayo spoke defiantly in response, defending the "national honor." García Moreno was entrusted with the task of discussing the issue with the Colombian envoy, who talked about friendly relations but who held anticlerical opinions.[44]

Having brought the Jesuits to Ecuador, García Moreno believed that he had a duty to support them, so he published his lengthiest political tract at the end of 1851, entitled *Defensa de los Jesuitas*. He argued that the Jesuits had undeservedly become the targets of reformers in the latter years of the Spanish empire for basically two reasons. First, the wealthy order was rumored to have hidden caches of gold and precious stones. (Looking at the fabulous gold remaining today in Quito's Jesuit church, La Compañía, one can see why tales of Jesuit wealth enjoyed such credibility.) Second, unlike any other colonial monastic order, the Jesuits reported directly to the Pope and thus had no national allegiance such as characterized the Franciscans, Dominicans, and Augustinians—their principal rivals. Yet the internationalism of the Jesuits also constituted one of the order's great strengths, as it attracted highly intelligent and well-educated men from all over Europe to its ranks. Because of their erudition and discipline, García Moreno argued that the order would benefit Ecuador's educational system. Furthermore, he pointed out their willingness to undertake missionary work in undesirable areas, such as among the hostile Indians living in the Amazonian region of the country.[45] Despite his strong arguments, the case in favor of the Jesuits ultimately fell victim to external pressures.

Meanwhile Urbina's military regime did little for almost a year, hoping to build popular support by defining its program and preparing defenses against Flores, who threatened to launch another expedition from Peruvian soil. By 1852 García Moreno found himself siding with his network of friends, the landlords of the center-north sierra, against the new government. He spoke out when authorities detained Vicente Aguirre (Carlos' father) and later helped the younger Aguirre wives (Virginia Klinger and her sister, Leonor) go into hiding at Roberto de Ascásubi's house. Other friends and colleagues were jailed or exiled to Colombia.[46] García Moreno's family urged him to come to Guayaquil, not only to get out of the public eye but also to allow the three brothers connected to the Urbina regime (Miguel, Fernando, and José) to protect him. As the animosity between factions heightened, the government cracked down harder. García Moreno remarked about Urbina, "the wolf begins to show his ears."[47] The rumors that disturbed him most involved the fate of the Jesuits, who, gossipmongers had it, would be secretly expelled at night. García Moreno lamented this turn of events: "the worst thing for this country will be the departure of these virtuous and learned men who so effectively have contributed to bettering the education of youth."[48]

Just as García Moreno spoke out in favor of his beloved Jesuits, he suffered a serious accident. Apparently he was cleaning his pistol on the afternoon of August 6, 1852, when it accidentally discharged, wounding him in the leg. Although the bone did not break, García Moreno's clothing became deeply embedded in the injury, causing an infection. Doctors cleaned out the wound and prescribed bed rest to heal it. Well into October, however, he remained bedridden, even though surgeons had drained the sore twice. Decrying their lack of skill and general ignorance, García Moreno railed at his physicians. By November he could take only a few hesitant steps with the aid of crutches, and was clearly in a dark mood. His older brother José (Pepe) offered a homeopathic cure: washing the wound with *cascarilla* bark—from which quinine is derived—and then drying it with a linen cloth before applying balsam oil. "Watch your diet," Pepe wrote, "no heavy meat like hen, no hot drinks [García Moreno liked his daily cup of cocoa], and a steady intake of dry rice, roast meat, and plain bread."[49]

Other personal issues kept him away from politics as well. He confessed to his brother-in-law that "I have debts I cannot cover" and lamented his misfortunes in the world of business. Whether he had no aptitude, no luck, or no interest is hard to tell. During the remainder of his life, he would dabble with moneymaking, largely through running a rented estate efficiently, but unlike many other politicians he would never become wealthy. Fortunately his relationship with the Ascásubi family meant he never had to worry about money. He remained solicitous of the family these days, particularly for his two sisters-in-law who had gone with Roberto to Piura, Peru, to partake of the curative waters. Meanwhile Rosa miscarried again in October, apparently losing a boy in her fourth or fifth month. His only aunt, his mother's closest companion, also died at the same time.[50] This compounding of personal tragedies no doubt contributed to his foul mood, so certainly he was in no frame of mind to hear about Urbina's constitutional convention tampering with his Jesuit project.

Whether because of diplomatic pressure or the liberal antipathy for Jesuits, the government expelled the order. Quito reacted violently. A large crowd rioted on the streets surrounding La Compañía Church, shouting, "Death to the Reds and to the government!" Although some of García Moreno's friends hoped that President Urbina would bow to pressure from the highlands and not enforce the decree, the rest were less optimistic. In a fit of pique, however, García Moreno allegedly told his friends: "Ten years from now we will sing the 'Te Deum' [a solemn mass reserved for very special occasions] celebrating their return."[51] García Moreno's defense of the Jesuits catapulted him into national prominence and made him the logical spokesperson for conservative religious people.

The expulsion of the Jesuits turned García Moreno openly against the Urbina government. He chose a time-tested means, the publication of essays, to attack the regime. First he wrote "Adiós a los Jesuitas" (A Farewell to the Jesuits). A short poem, "Al General Urbina" (To General Urbina), quickly followed. These writings were reminiscent of the tone García Moreno had taken in his earlier anti-Flores writings: vituperative, mean spirited, and totally uncompromising. He believed, however, that he had to unveil the truth (as he saw it) and reveal Urbina as a monster—a military tyrant who repressed the liberties of the people. He coined his own slogan: "Liberty for all except the evildoers."[52] Despite these attacks, Urbina remained popular because he had protected Ecuador against another Flores invasion and had averted a conflict with Colombia.

García Moreno's family had little patience with him. Brother José was the most critical: "I don't approve of your conduct. I believe that when you get help like Urbina gave you in 1849, . . . you have no right to defame him in public." José reminded Gabriel that their mother was now 73 years old, and added, "You will be the cause of her death." Brother Manuel also reported that Mercedes was upset with her son because she feared what would happen to him.[53] Due to Gabriel's writings, Urbina had begun to question the loyalty of the other brothers to the administration. Pedro Pablo heard that Urbina had called Gabriel a "retrograde, a Jesuit, and a Flores supporter" (which he was not), and wrote to José asking whether Gabriel planned a revolution to bring back the Jesuits.[54] One could consider Gabriel to be either very foolish, as his politically active brothers clearly did, or else very principled—someone who would not compromise his position simply because the object of his criticism had once done him a favor.

And so he continued to write. On March 8, 1853, he published the first issue of *La Nación* in Quito, a newspaper filled with harsh criticism of the Urbina administration. In it he argued that Urbina intended not only to serve out his full term, but also to rig the elections of 1856 in favor of one of his military cohorts—either General Francisco Robles or General Guillermo Franco. Concerned about the loss of republican freedoms, García Moreno continued to sound the alarm. The issue of *La Nación* dated March 15 had the same tone to it.[55] Urbina's response was swift. Fed up with this journalistic sniping, he sent troops to arrest García Moreno and his two friends who worked with him on the paper.

EXILE AND THE GENESIS OF A POLITICAL PHILOSOPHY

Defying a military government such as Urbina's had swifter consequences than even García Moreno had imagined. Seized in the middle of the day, he and his two friends were hustled northward toward the border. Within two days they had crossed into Colombia, and were confined just north of Tulcán. García Moreno's usual hot temper flared at what he regarded as a great injustice. "I am now dedicated to doing that which I had not wanted to do up to now, to make war on our ridiculous 'sultan.'"[56] Filled with umbrage against Urbina, he and his colleagues decided to return home surreptitiously. Playing on the sympathies of one of their Colombian guards, the three men slipped out of their house arrest one evening. With a Colombian priest acting as their guide, the refugees traveled at night, arriving in Quito sometime in mid-May 1853. García Moreno feared that the Ascásubi family might face repercussions if he hid with them, so he decided to seek protection in Guayaquil, as he had done before.

Meanwhile friends had nominated him for one of the open senatorial seats from Guayas province. If elected, he in theory would enjoy immunity and hence might be able to return to Quito. The elections went as García Moreno hoped. Foreign diplomats noted that Urbina's party was an unpopular despotism that lost in provinces like Guayas, where ballots were freely counted.[57] (Ironically, the coast would later become Urbina's *patria chica*, his base of support.) A battle of wills ensued. Urbina determined to overturn the election, while the stubborn García Moreno filed a petition with the governor, his brother Miguel, demanding that he be seated in congress—a struggle the president won. Both General Robles and General Guillermo Franco, who commanded another army corps in Guayaquil, told Miguel that they had "specific orders to make [Gabriel] leave the country."[58]

So in September 1853, García Moreno left Guayaquil by ship, beginning a period of exile that would last until November 1856. He spent nearly a year and a half in Paita, Peru, a seaport fairly close to the Ecuadorian border described by contemporaries as a pestilent hellhole. Joining him in exile were Rafael Pólit, his companion from the Colombian imprisonment who had recently been recaptured in Quito, and Rafael Carvajal, his old neighborhood chum who would become minister of foreign relations in the early 1860s. The exiles soon settled down to a humdrum life, which consisted mainly of writing and reading letters and conversing with other expatriates—including three Jesuit fathers and Paita's most famous resident, Manuela Sáenz de Thorne (best known as Simón Bolívar's mistress).[59] Time weighed heavily on their hands. Roberto de Ascásubi suggested that the entire family could relocate to the United States, but García Moreno vetoed the plan: "Rosa moves like a tortoise and would bring the whole house with her." The family would not like the United States, he asserted, because of "its different customs, climate, food, and way of life."[60]

Still, during his Peruvian exile García Moreno added to the network of friends that would fight for him in 1859: Joaquín Eguiguren and, most importantly, José and Ignacio de Veintemilla (experienced military men related by marriage to the Ascásubis), joined the exiles after Urbina expelled them from the country.[61] Because President Urbina showed no signs of weakening politically, García Moreno allowed his brother-in-law, Roberto de Ascásubi, to persuade him in April 1855 to take a trip to Europe to broaden his education and work on scientific projects related to the family business of distilling *aguardiente* (sugarcane alcohol).

Once in Paris, García Moreno was extremely impressed by the accomplishments of French Emperor Napoleon III, who had built many roads and railroads and modernized Paris by constructing grand boulevards like the Champs Elysées. García Moreno also noted France's modern system of education.[62] Napoleon III was hardly alone among his contemporaries in promoting modernization. Throughout Europe, North America, and Latin America (with the possible exception of Paraguay before 1840, where José Gaspar Rodríguez de Francia created a "hermit" nation), modernization was in vogue. Nations sought to emulate Great Britain and other industrializing societies exhibiting their wares in the great international exposition held in Paris during the summer and fall of 1855.

Certainly García Moreno attended the exposition. He praised one of his future political enemies, Pedro Carbo (now also in exile), for the piece he wrote about the Paris fair, bemoaning the fact that Ecuador had sent no exhibits—therefore going unmentioned in the Palace of Industry.[63] The fair must have made an impression on him because in the 1860s he was determined that Ecuador would participate in the next exposition. World fairs provided an opportunity for nations to advertise and promote their riches in a relatively inexpensive way, thereby attracting foreign investment and showcasing their national identities.

With the world's fair concluded, García Moreno launched himself into a heavy load of classes: physics, inorganic and organic chemistry, zoology, advanced algebra, calculus, and mechanics. In sum he received an excellent semester of scientific training, culminating in a minor paper his professor submitted to the French Academy of Science. Although he felt honored by the publication of this article, García Moreno candidly admitted that his work was only that of a talented amateur.[64] During his coursework in organic chemistry, he focused his research on the complex distillation process. Finally he spent an inordinate amount of time helping Roberto purchase some modern distilling equipment. After reviewing the specifications of the competing manufacturers, consulting back and forth, and arranging for the transfer of funds and shipping through Pedro Pablo's company, García Moreno finally consummated the transaction just before he left France. He also demonstrated his sincerity and gratitude to the family by working extremely long hours. "In working hard and learning I will be repaying you for the expenses you made, and the family will gain."[65]

Rather surprisingly, García Moreno's letters never mentioned the other major experience that he had in Paris, a spiritual reawakening. According to his first biographer, Augustine Berthe, García Moreno was walking with friends in a park discussing religion when they began to tease him because he was not going to confession. Realizing the hypocrisy of his ways, García Moreno began attending Mass daily. In addition he read and reread a twenty-nine-volume work called *Histoire Universale de l'Eglise Catolique*, and met a Chilean Jesuit, José Ignacio Eyzaguirre Portales, whose views profoundly influenced him. Although they talked only briefly in Paris, later their extended conversations would consolidate García Moreno's ideas about church policy. The interest in the history of the Catholic Church and the new papal doctrine of ultramontanism was scarcely a passing fancy for García Moreno; he would incorporate these ideas into his governing philosophy in the 1860s and 1870s.[66]

Ultramontanism divided the Catholic world in the mid-nineteenth and early twentieth centuries, having an especially strong following in northern Europe and Italy, as well as in South America. Essentially, the movement called for the reformation of the Catholic Church by emphasizing the primacy of the pope and the clerical hierarchy. To underscore his new role, Pope Pius IX proclaimed the doctrine of papal infallibility in 1870. The reformed clergy, which included new socially active monastic orders, created a reinvigorated Catholic community. García Moreno also saw in ultramontanism an opportunity to provide national unity based on faith, an alternative to the doctrinaire Enlightenment liberalism that had become standard political fare in Latin America since independence. For the moment García Moreno's ideas were not fully formed, but they would be refined during his first presidential term.[67] By now he had fixed plans for his return at the end of November 1856. He missed many things about Ecuador, particularly, he said, hunting turkeys and rabbits on the Ascásubi hacienda of Mindo.[68]

While García Moreno was in exile, Urbina and his colleagues wrestled with one of the nineteenth century's key questions: how to transform the segregated colonial system of two republics, one for whites and one for Indians, into a nation where all could enjoy citizenship. As a result a spate of legislation in the 1850s changed the legal status of Ecuador's lower class: the abolition of slavery (1854), the *Ley de Indigenas* that curtailed some aspects of debt peonage (1854), and the abolition of Indian tribute (1857). Despite the change of legal status for Indians and Afro-Ecuadorians, the underlying reality of who performed manual labor remained the same. Interestingly, landlords as well as liberals supported most of this legislation. Manumission passed congress nearly unanimously because slave owners received compensation.[69] Despite some agreement on principles, most highland estate owners had no love for the coastal military regime that continued after the election of General Francisco Robles, Urbina's close friend, as president in 1856. Recognizing these feelings, the general began his presidency with a gesture of reconciliation welcoming all exiles home (except the ever-dangerous General Flores).

GROOMING FOR LEADERSHIP, 1857–1859

Fortune, or more probably a network of family and university connections, smiled on García Moreno upon his return to Ecuador in November 1856. Within a short period of time, he had been elected as the *alcalde*, or mayor, of Quito, and as the president, or rector, of the University of Quito. Ably qualified for the latter position because of his academic degrees and his recent training abroad, he performed capably if controversially in that role. (There is no evidence one way or another about his success or failure as mayor.) As rector García Moreno was expected to manage the institution, provide academic leadership, and oversee open competition among candidates for teaching positions at the *colegios*, or secondary schools.[70]

Running the business affairs of the university helped to form his ideas about higher education. Demonstrating little patience or tolerance for the incompetent, García Moreno requested that the secretary of the interior fire the university's bursars, who were apparently not billing students for their tuition. He also proposed some improvements to the university building and set up a lecture hall for teaching chemistry. He had personally donated to the university chemistry equipment purchased while in Paris. His own foray into the world of scientific publication continued with an article based on the explorations of Pichincha that he and Sebastián Wisse had made.[71]

García Moreno also critiqued Urbina's Educational Reform Act of October 28, 1853 (copied from Colombia's) that had radically transformed the university. Under this statute, students were relieved from the "tyranny of faculty" and no longer required to attend classes, a philosophy still in vogue in many European universities. One of Ecuador's greatest intellectuals and García Moreno's enemy, Juan Montalvo, who received his degree under this system, by his own admission never attended a class but nevertheless ultimately produced high-quality essays and poetry. García Moreno argued, however, that most students who had no guidance, no standards, and no discernment could scarcely educate themselves.[72] Thus he begged for a repeal of this legislation, which would happen in the 1860s.

His growing stature, along with his family and personal connections, made García Moreno a logical candidate for the upcoming congressional elections. Thus in the summer of 1857 he won a seat in the Senate representing the interests of the estate owners of the center and north. Two sierra provinces elected him as senator; his friend Rafael Carvajal, elected as alternate, took the other seat. (As in Great Britain, at this time a legislator did not need to live in the represented province.) When the Senate met that fall, García Moreno found he had to interact frequently with his old enemy Manuel Bustamante, "who treats me with such deference it makes him look timid."[73] Already García Moreno had voiced his opposition to the Robles government in typical fashion. Founding a new periodical called *La Unión Nacional*, he lashed out at the military regime and its policies. He and his editorial assistants, Rafael Carvajal and Pablo Herrera (later minister of foreign relations), advocated passage of the university reform bill and legislation outlawing secret societies—more specifically, the anticlerical Masonic lodges.[74] Both of these issues raised his profile within the loose coalition of people who opposed the Robles government and generally agreed on conservative principles philosophically.

Family matters also occupied García Moreno at this time. After Pedro Pablo's Chilean-born wife died, García Moreno's brother married Virginia Flores Jijón, the daughter of General Juan José Flores. Gabriel acted as best man at the wedding and stated that he was very pleased by the marriage, as was all the García Moreno clan.[75] Through this new extended family, García Moreno's political network broadened considerably, as the general still had many friends among the military. The family changed in a second important way. By then everyone knew that Rosa, almost 50 years old, would never have children. Her sister Rosario and husband Manuel del Alcázar agreed to let Rosa and Gabriel adopt their five daughters. (One of those daughters, Mariana, would become García Moreno's second wife—see chapter 5.) García Moreno took the adoption very seriously and decided that he had to earn money to provide for the girls' future. As he told his brother-in-law Roberto, he was tired of being a financial burden on the family. "Although I never wanted to be rich, being content with a modest existence, I am very concerned for the future of my five adopted daughters." As a result, he agreed to work in Pedro Pablo's business. The brothers were planning to travel to Lima in early 1859 to liquidate an operation there, and then go on to Chile. García Moreno promised to visit his wife and stepdaughters at an Ascásubi family estate every summer; otherwise he thought they could get on well enough without him.[76] García Moreno's concerns about his daughters' future seem heartfelt, but an international crisis offered him a moment for decisive leadership and changed his plans.

PORTRAIT OF GARCÍA MORENO IN 1859

What portrait can we now draw of this complex man on the brink of political power? In physical terms, García Moreno was a striking but hardly handsome man. His time in exile had not improved his physical appearance but had made it even more unusual. During his exile in Peru, García Moreno reported that he looked like a man of 70 instead of only

42. By now his hairline had receded rapidly and a bald spot appeared.[77] He was extremely thin, but his height and piercing gaze gave him a physical appearance fitting for a leader. His degrees, his journalistic work, and his intellectual curiosity spoke volumes about his competence. The only question was whether he had the appropriate character to become a good president.

On the negative side, he was hot-tempered, quick to judge, and ready to condemn even friends. To date, his quick temper had caused little harm because he had not held positions of authority that would permit him to make life-and-death decisions. As president in the 1860s, however, the authority to act on his rash judgments would almost inevitably land him in hot water, as chapters 3, 4, and 5 will show. He was also totally unforgiving towards his enemies. His brother Manuel, the priest, chided Gabriel for his intemperate writings against Urbina and Robles. "You are a sincere Christian and must pardon those who caused you ill." Likewise he harshly criticized those friends he thought had slighted him. For example, when he learned that his old and dear friend Sebastián Wisse had published a paper about their expedition up Mt. Sangay without his permission or input, he exploded. "Without me, Sr. Wisse would never have made this excursion." Further, he railed that Wisse knew no biology and little chemistry and therefore the scientific credit for the expedition belonged to him (García Moreno) alone.[78] Fortunately he later reconciled with Wisse and they continued their scientific work together, but Wisse was hardly alone in receiving García Moreno's angry comments when the latter was crossed.

Perhaps he was so dogmatic because he was secure in his faith. Although, like many believers, he had gone through a youthful period of questioning, by 1859 he stood firmly on principle as a true believer in Roman Catholicism. Not only in his defense of the Jesuits, but also in a very revealing letter to his wife, he displayed the intensity of his beliefs. Chiding her and her sisters for their fears about his future, he called her weak, asserting she was not a true believer. He urged her to study the articles of faith to achieve peace of mind. In contrast, García Moreno said he himself believed in an omnipotent and merciful God who would always protect him. In short, the Catholic faith would in large part govern García Moreno's life. Once he held a belief, he grasped it firmly, as he himself admitted. "It is impossible for me to do anything halfway; my character won't permit it."[79]

In addition to his strong personality (for good and ill), García Moreno had accumulated two additional assets that would contribute to his success. First, through marriage, university friendships, and alliances made as a senator in the late 1850s, he had built a network of like-minded colleagues who would help him administer the country in the 1860s and 1870s. In the absence of formal political parties, these networks made a national political following possible.[80] At the same time, he began to formulate specific ideas about state formation based on conservative, Catholic principles. Clearly impressed by the modernization he observed in Napoleon III's France, he wanted to achieve similar objectives for Ecuador. Like virtually all Latin American national politicians of his time, he believed in development: roads, railroads, modern communications, urban improvements, and, above all else, a modern educational system that would promote universal (or at least greatly expanded) literacy. At the same time, as someone who had spent much of the decade in exile for "political" crimes and been forced from home by a "tyrant" (Urbina) who did not even bother to bring him to trial, he claimed to believe that the protection of liberties was important. Therefore in 1859 García Moreno conceived of himself as a moderate who would be willing to participate in a government that would eliminate or reduce tyranny. These ideas would be tested, however, as García Moreno and Ecuador embarked on an exhausting civil war that threatened the very existence of the nation.

Chapter Two

Regionalism and Civil War, 1859–1860

When Gabriel García Moreno was courting his future bride in 1846, one of his good friends from Quito wrote him: "Now we have the good fortune of seeing you completely established in *our country* [*nuestro país*, meaning Quito and the northern and central sierra] and united with one of the most distinguished señoritas we have."[1] Certainly as of the 1860s, most Ecuadorians conceived of "my country" as the region in which they had been born and were living. Very few Ecuadorians traveled—García Moreno being a clear exception. The state of the country's roads was abysmal, but additionally most people felt loyalty to the regions where their families resided. In many ways regionalism was a state of mind as well as a practical reality in the mid-nineteenth century. Political traditions furthered the sense of regionalism. When Ecuador separated from Gran Colombia in 1830, the founding fathers structured the nation around the three established colonial departments: Quito, Azuay (Cuenca), and Guayaquil. Each of these districts received equal representation in congress and each had an equal voice in the electoral college. As a result most Ecuadorians in 1859 thought of themselves as regional rather than national citizens[2] (and there are still vestiges of this sentiment today).

Nor were Ecuadorians alone in feeling this way during the nineteenth century. The regional impulse had a long and storied tradition. Catholic southern Germans, for example, felt distinct from northern Germans in both culture and religion. Regionalism destroyed the Central American federation, dividing a historically unified area into five individual countries in the 1830s.[3] In the Andean nations the mountainous topography exacerbated regionalism. North of Ecuador, Colombians consciously divided themselves into separate regions and attributed racial identities to those regions. As noted in chapter 1, Ecuadorians' regional views also combined racial characteristics with derogatory epithets: *monos* (monkeys) for the coast, *chagras* (rubes) for the Azuay area, and *longos* (servile Indians) for the central and north sierra. But the latter part of the nineteenth century, both in Europe and Latin America, became the age of nationalism—the antithesis of regionalism—exemplified best by the creation of new nation states like Italy and Germany. The Ecuadorian state also developed in the 1860s, as García Moreno began the process of state formation under his conservative program, which was both practical and visionary.

The role of regionalism in Latin America has been the subject of considerable historiographical debate. Despite a centralist tradition dating from the colonial regime, regionalism dominated political thinking on occasion (such as in the postindependence era). Part of the controversy centers around the notion of "state" and when Latin American countries effectively created the mechanism known as the state.[4] As we shall see in chapter 3, before García Moreno the Ecuadorian political leadership (with the possible exceptions of Flores and Rocufuerte discussed in chapter 1) had no clear definition of Ecuador in mind. The seeming lack of patriotism of the important players in 1859 becomes explicable only when one realizes that these men were, as García Moreno's friend indicated, loyal to their own regional "*país*" rather than to any larger notion of national interests. In fact no better case study exists to demonstrate the destructiveness of regionalism than the Ecuadorian civil war of 1859 through 1860. That experience, however, allowed García Moreno to hone his leadership skills and to reach a greater understanding about how to create a nation, as this chapter will show.

ECUADOR'S REGIONS

Obviously Ecuador's four primary geographical regions did not fit neatly into the country's three major political subdivisions. Writers describe the four topographical regions as: the coast, including the areas north and south of Guayaquil; the sierra (highlands), comprising the Avenue of the Volcanoes from the Colombian to the Peruvian border; the Oriente, consisting of the tropical area east of the Andes Mountains including tributaries of the Amazon; and the Galápagos Islands, separated from the mainland by more than 600 miles of open sea. Even this delineation may be an oversimplification. As a case in point: During the civil war of 1859, the highlands fragmented into three distinct subregions—the central-north, the southern highlands (Azuay), and the far south (Loja).[5] Geologists confirm these finer distinctions, contrasting the low, older, contiguous, and less volatile volcanic region of the south with the region of more rugged and active isolated volcanoes in the north. To minimize complexities, however, this text will adhere to the standard view that Ecuador contains four distinct regions—only two of which (the highlands and the coast) mattered much in García Moreno's time.

The coast remained the heart of Ecuador's export economy, as it had been since the middle of the eighteenth century. The climate (hot, humid, and unpleasant for much of the year) and the terrain (ranging from flat grasslands to gently rolling hills) remained unchanged, of course. The population of the region had increased, however, beginning in the late eighteenth century as workers migrated from the highlands to labor on the cacao plantations, the coast's principal source of wealth. Despite García Moreno's coastal origins, he remained wary of most *guayaquileños*, except those among his family network and allies, because he viewed the majority of people who lived there as corrupt and dissolute. Once in power, he developed a political strategy of trying to neutralize Guayaquil.

The highlands had become, as noted in chapter 1, the core of García Moreno's support or, in nineteenth-century terms, his *patria chica* (regional base)—particularly the north and central highlands. He knew the southern sierra (Cuenca and Loja) much less well, although at the university he made several good friends from that part of the country who became political allies. Humboldt's tag, the Avenue of the Volcanoes, remained the popular description for the terrain—the highlands resembling a ladder laid flat on the ground.[6] That is, two chains of high volcanoes run vertically north and south (called the Eastern Range and the Western Range) from the Colombian border to southern Ecuador (here including both northern and southern highlands), while horizontal hills subdivide the "avenue" into a number of small basins. Each of these basins, in essence, made up a province after the 1860s. People in the region tended to be *mestizo* (about 40 percent of the population today), although a number of indigenous groups (perhaps another 40 percent of the population) lived in the higher, and hence poorer, elevations. The white upper class—most of the actors in this drama—tended to live in the cities even while owning much of the countryside and deriving a living as absentee landowners. The highlands had been in economic decline since the middle of the eighteenth century, as cheap imported textiles eroded their traditional markets for hand-crafted woolen textiles in Colombia and Peru. Although some people had migrated towards the coast, the highlands still retained the majority of the population, and until 1895 would remain the dominant political center of the nation.[7]

To the east, the wilds of the Oriente beckoned only to the most hardy. After sixteenth-century conquistadors explored the Oriente, the region had largely been ignored except by missionaries. Only the tiny town of Macas evidenced Ecuador's presence there. Most literate Ecuadorians had heard frightening tales of the Shuar or Jívaro (as they were known in the nineteenth century), peoples of the Oriente who felled their game and their adversaries with poisoned blow darts and engaged in the ancient Andean practice of shrinking heads, *tsantsas*, long abandoned elsewhere.[8] The fourth region, the remote and rocky Galápagos Islands, had been claimed by Ecuador in 1833 and served primarily as a prison colony for the worst, most hardened criminals (yet, despite García Moreno's fulminations, no political prisoners in his time—as far as can be established). Catapulted into international fame by Charles Darwin, the islands, like the Oriente, remained undeveloped until the 1960s.[9]

These four regions were even more distinctive and isolated in 1859 than they are today. As demonstrated in chapter 1 during the story of García Moreno's first journey, Ecuadorian roads made travel nearly impossible, especially to the Oriente. Ships rarely traveled to the Galápagos, and foreigners were more likely to bring news of events on the islands to the mainland than were Ecuadorian officials. Like most of his compatriots, García Moreno never visited the Galápagos or the Oriente because they were places where undesirables were sent. Even putting aside these marginal areas, García Moreno faced a nearly insurmountable task when he attempted to overcome the regionalism dominating the country in 1859.

BACKGROUND TO THE CIVIL WAR

The great civil war that nearly splintered Ecuador began innocently enough when President Francisco Robles (1856–1859) decided upon what seemed like a perfect solution to one of the country's longstanding problems. Saddled with a huge debt to the British Baring Brothers' bondholders from the 1820s, Ecuador's governments had enjoyed almost no disposable income for public works. With 50 percent of the budget spent on military salaries and another 25 percent on bureaucratic salaries, the remainder scarcely paid the interest on the foreign debt—much less diminished the principal. Naturally every administration since 1830 felt pressure to accomplish domestic objectives. Therefore those projects (education and roads, for example, and repayment of internal loans) further lessened the monies available to pay the foreign bondholders, creating diplomatic tensions. No wonder Ecuador frequently defaulted on its payments. Defaults further complicated the country's financial status because its poor credit rating prevented the foreign borrowing necessary to accomplish any modernization projects. In 1857 Robles hit on a scheme that he hoped would resolve the debt issue and lead to development.

Simply stated, Robles planned to sell land in the Oriente region to the bondholders to satisfy a large portion of the debt. From the bondholders' perspective, the scheme made some sense, because after years of negotiation and multiple defaults, the likelihood of full payment seemed slight. Besides, British naturalists such as Richard Spruce had recently explored the Amazon basin, circulating tales of tropical lushness.[10] For Robles the plan had two advantages. Not only would it successfully resolve the treasury's unmet obligations, but the English settlers with their values of thrift, hard work, and industriousness would also develop the jungle. The U.S. minister, Philo White, offered a more realistic evaluation of Robles' proposal. He described the area as "not habitable," in part because of an absence of roads and the prevalence of disease. In addition he noted that hostile Indians shot poisoned arrows at intruders, although other Indians were "tractable and submissive" because of the "tyranny and paternalism" of the Jesuits. Neither group of indigenous peoples would labor well for others, he predicted.[11]

Unfortunately Robles' plan ran afoul of international complications. Peru's president, Marshall Ramón Castilla, asserted that the territory Ecuador sought to sell to the British bondholders actually belonged to Peru. Truthfully neither side knew; the border between Peru and Ecuador had never been clearly drawn. Peru cited an 1802 decree, in which the Spanish colonial government severely reduced the size of the Quito district and added territory onto Peru. For its part Ecuador pointed to an 1829 treaty greatly enlarging Gran Colombia's borders (and hence Ecuador's) at the expense of Peru. Indeed this border dispute was not fully resolved until 1998.[12]

In 1858, however, the proposed sale of land to British bondholders for $3 million pesos provided an excuse for Castilla to meddle in Ecuador's affairs. His diplomatic representative to Ecuador, Juan Celestino Cavero, protested the bondholders' deal and made bombastic demands telling Ecuador that it must cede to Peru all territory just east of Quito, all of the Oriente, and land in the south of the country.[13] In response to this outburst, Robles handed Cavero his passport at the end of July 1858. The Spanish consul related how the streets of Guayaquil were abuzz with gossip about this event. Castilla blustered, informed Ecuador that it must readmit Cavero (which as a matter of pride Robles refused to do), and blockaded Guayaquil in late October. Congress responded immediately to the threat, granting Robles emergency powers to run the government as he saw fit, to move the capital if necessary to the city of Riobamba, and to negotiate a foreign loan of $3 million pesos. Although initially supportive, Senator García Moreno ultimately delivered an impassioned speech opposing the grant of extraordinary powers. He and others suspected that Robles and Urbina intended to sell the Galápagos to the United States to raise the money, just as they had tried to do in 1854.[14]

In addition to concern about the sale of national territory, congress complained that Robles moved the capital to Guayaquil without authorization. García Moreno queried the reason for this action and suggested that Robles and Urbina had transferred the capital to the coast to abscond more easily with the $3 million pesos once the sale of the Galápagos was consummated. Led by García Moreno and liberal politician Pedro Moncayo, congress stripped Robles of his extraordinary power to raise a foreign loan, setting the stage for the civil war.[15]

As the new year dawned, Peru reinforced the blockade and ordered a few soldiers to occupy Puná Island in the Gulf of Guayaquil, where they skirmished briefly with Ecuadorian troops. The country braced itself for a full-scale invasion. In the highlands, believers took the Virgin of Quinche, the national religious symbol, from her normal home to the Cathedral in Quito, a distance of about 30 miles, to plead for divine intervention.[16] More concrete assistance came from foreign powers, especially Chile, which offered to mediate the conflict. Castilla agreed to hold talks, but stubbornly demanded that Ecuador accept the return of Minister Cavero as a non-negotiable item. Undoubtedly Castilla did not want a peaceful solution, but rather an opportunity to impose on Ecuador the 1802 border, although he had to be somewhat cautious because the British threatened Peru's credit if he acted too aggressively. The Robles government sent Benigno Malo, a wealthy Cuencan and later an occasional García Moreno colleague, to Lima in March to negotiate, but nothing came of these talks.[17]

By now García Moreno had risen through the ranks of the congressional opposition and become one of its principal speakers protesting against Robles' coastal-dominated military government. Sensitive to landlord issues, García Moreno talked about the need to protect the interests of the interior (the highland core), demonstrating that at this point he too wore regional lenses. "I see the extremes to which the interior is reduced, and I deplore it." In this crisis, he gave up all thoughts of a business career, especially when the Robles regime turned repressive. Jailings were bad enough, but in late January 1859 the government allegedly assassinated one of García

Moreno's acquaintances, sending him into a rage: "When will God permit the overthrow of the evil ones?"[18] Suspecting his involvement in the "subversive" publications circulating in Quito, the Robles government unleashed its police on him, and in early March 1859 ordered him arrested. (Pedro Pablo was jailed shortly thereafter, as was García Moreno's friend Pablo Herrera.) García Moreno was captured on the streets of Guayaquil, where the military held him incommunicado for a week before allowing him to write his family to tell them he was being exiled from the country. He felt his reputation sullied: "That incurable liar Urbina has invented lies about conspiracy, and worse, about treachery." When the boat to Panama failed to arrive, the local general in the port decided to exile García Moreno to Paita, Peru, instead.[19]

Meanwhile religious-minded people saw the earthquake that shook Quito in March 1859 as a portent of the end of the Robles government. Other more secular observers noted disunity within the military government. One day, for example, Colonel Secundino Darquea took his troops on maneuvers in the city of Guayaquil and happened to stop in front of ex-President Urbina's house. Urbina stepped out on the balcony and the troops, instead of saluting him with honors, just marched away. Infuriated, Urbina demanded Darquea's arrest. Darquea explained his behavior by arguing that the event had occurred after 6 p.m. and military regulations did not require formal salutes after that hour. (Darquea would eventually become fast friends with García Moreno.) Undoubtedly Urbina's pique resulted from something more significant than a petty breach of protocol. In any event, the arrest of Colonel Darquea had repercussions when one of his friends, General Manuel Tomás Maldonado, rebelled in April. Maldonado's revolt marked an open division within the national army, part of which would eventually follow García Moreno. Quickly captured, Maldonado was cashiered and placed under house arrest in the interior. Later in the month, soldiers in Quito left their barracks without permission and marched on the Government Palace, demanding their pay.[20]

Blockaded by a foreign power and its commerce in disarray, Ecuador faced grave difficulties in May 1859. One might question whether this moment was an appropriate one in which to unleash a civil war. García Moreno's friendly biographers assert that because the military had so angered Peru's Castilla, only García Moreno could be trusted to negotiate with the Peruvians. These same sources point out that Marshall Castilla initially claimed to be hostile only to the Robles regime, not the Ecuadorian people, and that he had no territorial ambitions. (This naïve conclusion is hardly borne out by Castilla's later acts.) On the other hand, García Moreno's enemies see his actions in 1859 as a great betrayal of the country.[21] Nevertheless, several members of García Moreno's network led a rebellion at the very moment when Ecuadorians most needed unity. Whether García Moreno himself was involved in the May 1 Quito uprising described below is impossible to tell.

THE MAY 1859 UPRISING: OPTIMISM IN THE SIERRA

The uprising of May 1, 1859, surprised President Robles and began Ecuador's descent into near chaos. Beginning as either a patriotic struggle to expel the militarists and the foreign invader (as García Moreno's friends would argue), or alternatively as a selfish grab for power in the midst of a national crisis (as the Robles government asserted), the civil war that lasted from 1859 until September 1860 represented a key moment in García Moreno's career. From this point forward, politics and public service became his life. Initially these were heady optimistic days, as the rebels believed that the Robles government would quickly collapse. A euphoria swept over the sierra as news spread about a triumvirate that would lead the provisional government: García Moreno representing the church (who better could argue its position after his *Defense of the Jesuits*?); Jerónimo Carrión, the current vice-president, representing the legitimate constitutional succession; and Pacífico Chiriboga, Urbina's former governor of Pichincha, representing the landlords.[22]

Persuading others to follow proved more difficult than anticipated. Not only did the pro-Robles governors of the highland provinces refuse to support the new government, but so did General Manuel Tomás Maldonado as well. (Months later he would join, but he always remained unpredictable.) Vice President Carrión also refused initially, although he too would later change his mind.[23] Nevertheless the north and central highland provinces, district by district, soon rallied behind Quito's provisional government, in part because Robles had taken much of the army with him to Guayaquil to face the Peruvians. In the north, Ibarra, capital of Imbabura province, created a popular assembly that named a new governor and military commander. Other major cities like Latacunga, Riobamba, and Ambato quickly threw their support behind the provisional government, with smaller towns like Baños following suit later in the month. By the end of May, then, the north and central sierra had firmly adhered to the provisional government in Quito, probably because its decrees promised municipal autonomy and more personal liberty than had been the case under the military.[24]

In the meantime, where was García Moreno? From exile in Paita, he rushed back to Quito, arriving on May 25. He had loaded his pockets with chocolate, an energy-boosting trick he had learned years ago, and made his way home (some accounts say through Guayaquil, while others say overland through the south). In either event, he had to walk a portion of the way when his mule died. As usual he took charge once he arrived in Quito. After being named Supreme Director of the War, he and his principal commander, Bernardo Dávalos, began to organize an army to confront Robles' forces.[25]

As military preparations progressed, significant political changes occurred in the rebel-held areas. The provisional government replaced the *jefes políticos*, local officials in charge of cantons (the largest subdivision of provinces), in accordance with "the will of the people" (a liberal phrase emanating from the French Revolution of 1789). In Riobamba, for example, the "odious conduct" of Robles' appointee provided sufficient grounds to have him replaced by a new *jefe político* who represented the "will of the people," and who, not surprisingly, favored the provisional government. Roberto de Ascásubi told the *jefe político* in Ambato: "As the program of the revolution . . . is principally to comply with the sovereign will of the people, you will replace the city council's secretary with the popular choice."[26] According to the provisional government, the will of the people included protecting the rights of the church and the Catholic faith. Liberal language also protected regional interests. The military government, however, employed similar words as its justification, absent the discussion of religion, for ending the revolt and presenting a united front in the face of the Peruvian threat.[27] Because the provisional government held elections and created popular assemblies throughout the sierra in May 1859, its claim to represent the popular will, at least of the highland region, seems more legitimate.

Soon García Moreno poised his army to do battle against Robles' troops, who had marched upland from Guayaquil to the hill of Tumbuco, just south of the city of Guaranda. As always García Moreno was supremely optimistic. Marching through the sierra and hearing the heady applause of crowds shouting support for the provisional government must have been very encouraging. In this supremely confident vein, he wrote his wife and the government on the night before the battle. He said that there were about 500 enemy soldiers at Tumbuco and that "I will attack

Roberto de Ascásubi, García Moreno's brother-in-law (Permission of the Banco Central del Ecuador)

tomorrow [June 2, 1859] and tomorrow I will write you about the victory," adding, "in around 16 hours, Ecuador will be free." But he had miscalculated. While he had enthusiastic but green volunteers, his army lacked arms, gunpowder, uniforms, and pack animals. Instead of the 500 soldiers he expected to face, he found almost 2,000 battle-hardened veterans led by Urbina himself, who had taken commanding positions on the hill. Advancing from two leagues away through corn and alfalfa fields, García Moreno's outnumbered force of 500 volunteers fought hard for hours but suffered many casualties. García Moreno had his horse shot out from under him and allegedly was rescued when Colonel Ignacio de Veintemilla gave García Moreno his mount, thereby avoiding capture by Urbina's army.[28] Urbina took the field, dashing the provisional government's hopes for a quick victory. Its army had been routed, the sierra was in danger of being conquered, and García Moreno would for years be saddled with the derisive nickname Hero of Tumbuco.

Understandably the crushing defeat demoralized the volunteer army.

García Moreno tried to rally his forces, encouraging them to stick with the provisional government and drafting peons into the army, to no avail. With the rainy season over, Urbina and his men took the sierra. Pro-Robles factions now felt emboldened and regained power locally. The provisional government's forces deserted and fled to their homes. Meanwhile its leadership—Chiriboga, Manuel Gómez de la Torre, and José María Avilés—left Quito for the north, as Urbina's soldiers moved into the capital without firing a shot by the middle of June. In exchange for an amnesty, the provisional government agreed to lay down its arms in July 1859. Chiriboga, Gómez de la Torre, and Avilés simply retired to their estates, while a few of García Moreno's other friends, like Rafael Carvajal, fled across the border to Colombia.[29] Meanwhile García Moreno sought reinforcements. As the provisional government collapsed it conveyed extraordinary powers to him, authorizing him to negotiate with Castilla for assistance. So García Moreno dashed down to Guayaquil and boarded a ship for Peru. In his spare time, he allegedly began to read about the art of war, a subject in which he had been too overconfident to study up to that time.[30] Negotiations with Castilla would prove difficult, however, because the provisional government had been badly defeated and had nothing to offer him.

A DIFFICULT INTERLUDE: BEGINNING THE WAR ANEW

For the next few months, García Moreno would be the guest of Peru and of Ramón Castilla, the lone voice of the provisional government—which no longer enjoyed even a foothold in the sierra. In July he issued a proclamation, described by his enemies as the Pact of Infamy, which optimistically predicted the "fall of the barbarians." He asserted that Robles had trampled on the constitution and that therefore he (García Moreno) had no choice but to turn to the Peruvians. "The Peruvian army and naval squadron are our allies, and not our enemies," he claimed. He ultimately consummated a deal in Lima (an offer of weapons and cash with "no strings attached") over the opposition of his liberal ally Pedro Moncayo, who attended the secret meeting between Castilla and García Moreno and argued against the Peruvian promises. When García Moreno accused Moncayo of being fearful, the latter allegedly said, "I am afraid of staining my name with an abominable betrayal" and broke with García Moreno forever. Robles denounced García Moreno's pact, and at the same time vowed to defend the nation's independence against Peru.[31]

Then Robles overreached himself. Although in June he had initially proclaimed a generous amnesty and forgiven the people associated with the provisional government, by the end of July he took umbrage at García Moreno's dealings with Peru, voided the amnesty, and began persecuting García Moreno's adherents—levying forced contributions on Pacífico Chiriboga, José María Avilés, Benigno Malo, and the like. Others, like Roberto de Ascásubi, who could not pay their levy were exiled.[32] Popular sentiment in the northern sierra shifted back to the side of the provisional government. This explanation is not to suggest that ordinary folk cared particularly about the outcome of the struggle, but rather that the politically aware landlord class—as well as the bureaucrats and professional men who constituted García Moreno's network and the real body politic in the nineteenth century—again favored García Moreno.

Robles' governor in the northernmost province of Imbabura had been warning all summer about a possible insurgency from across the Colombian border. García Moreno's friend Rafael Carvajal took the lead. Borrowing money from landlord allies, he rounded up volunteers and attacked Robles' forces on the border. Carvajal enjoyed success in recruiting because he came from Imbabura, and a number of his fellow citizens (that is, people from the north and central sierras) had fled with him from the military regime. Although the Robles government sought cooperation from its Colombian counterpart in suppressing Carvajal's recruiting, the southern part of Colombia (Pasto and Túquerres) was itself in turmoil and ready to rebel against Bogotá, making effective policing of the frontier impossible. The Robles government did manage to beat back the initial Carvajal invasion, but could spare only 55 soldiers to guard the frontier. With about 600 volunteers, Carvajal took Tulcán early in September 1859 and then marched to Ibarra, capital of the province.[33] A few days later Quito rebelled under the leadership of Colonel Daniel Salvador, a key military figure related to the important Gómez de la Torre family. All up and down the northern and central sierra, cities followed suit: Ambato, Riobamba, and Latacunga. As one of Robles' commanders astutely noted, "the owners of the estates [throughout the sierra] are the enemies of the government." Or as the leaders of the reconstituted provisional government preferred to say, the will of the people had triumphed. As the provisional government reasserted itself and drove out the unpopular Robles officials, more volunteers came forward to join García Moreno's forces.[34]

Meanwhile García Moreno had pursued negotiations with Robles' commander in Guayaquil, General Guillermo Franco, arguing that the Peruvian government was not making war on Ecuador but rather on Generals Robles and Urbina. "I have found in Castilla's guarantees a desire for honor and patriotism." García Moreno assured General Franco that Castilla had promised to let Ecuadorians freely choose their own government. The above-quoted letter led to a shipboard meeting, where allegedly the two Ecuadorians discussed a compromise government in which General Franco would play a military role. García Moreno exulted to his wife that he had succeeded in separating the powerful General Franco from Robles and Urbina. He optimistically predicted that Franco would rebel in favor of the provisional government, and that by the end of the week he would be ensconced safely in his mother's house, with the civil war nearly over. Looking over the national scene, he wrote, "Each uprising will shorten the misfortune of the republic, and bring closer the fall of the bandits. My faith in Providence is as fixed and unmovable as Chimborazo."[35]

Rather than lining up behind García Moreno and the provisional government, however, General Franco decided to depose President Robles and seize the presidency himself. Not long thereafter, Urbina resigned from the army and also boarded a ship for Chile. The motive behind Franco's coup has been much debated. Perhaps Robles' inability to talk peace with Peru angered Franco. Described as a rough-hewn soldier, Franco certainly had no political experience, nor did he know much about foreign affairs. Perhaps he believed he would be more successful than the other two generals, who had recently lost major battles in the sierra. More likely, Franco fell victim to raw ambition, as did many military leaders in nineteenth-century Latin America. In any event, he would be difficult to dislodge from his firm base in Guayaquil. Although Franco held the upper hand militarily, he could never make a plausible argument that his government was legitimate.[36]

Complicated as Ecuador's situation seemed at this juncture, it would continue to disintegrate further, as the lack of central authority encouraged other regions like Cuenca and Loja to seek autonomy in the fall of 1859. In Cuenca, for example, the small garrison stationed in the provincial capital responded to the internecine squabble between the generals by declaring for General Urbina on September 13. After Urbina's exile, however, the garrison retreated and left the government in the hands of Ramón Borrero (whose brother Antonio had befriended García Moreno at the university years before) and his associates, who dictated the terms of the province's relationship to the national government.[37]

Philosophically the new Cuenca regime supported the provisional government in Quito, as Governor Ramón Borrero stated. Cuenca would even send troops to assist Quito in the struggle against General Franco. The leadership particularly favored the principal of "the sovereignty of the people." It agreed to organize a military force that would "preserve order and defend *our territory* if necessary." Given the hardships and anti-landlord reforms wrought by Urbina's military regime in the 1850s, naturally *hacendados* like those dominating Azuay's new government favored a decentralized system with greater regional autonomy.[38] Leaders of the provisional government, especially García Moreno, were less enthusiastic about Cuenca's declaration of autonomy. As a key military commander suggested, provincial sovereignty presented a danger when faced by a dictator like General Franco, a prophecy that proved accurate when pro-Franco forces retook Cuenca in November.[39]

At the same time, the southernmost province of Loja also considered the possibility of recasting itself as an autonomous region. As the leader of the Loja movement stated, "When we obtain a triumph over tyranny, we will want to exercise the rights of sovereignty under our provincial government." Hence Governor Manuel Carrión Pinzano decided to proclaim Loja's separation as the fourth regional state in the fall of 1859. Carrión Pinzano's government cooperated initially with Franco's regime. Carrión Pinzano wrote Franco, "I offer you my most active cooperation and whatever I can contribute to the peace, order, and prosperity of the nation."[40] Thus, by the fall of 1859, Ecuador had divided itself into four autonomous regions: the north-central sierra, held by García Moreno and the provisional government; the coast, controlled by General Franco and his well-supplied army; the southern sierra, dominated by Cuenca's state government; and the far south, held by Carrión Pinzano trumpeting the cause of local rule. García Moreno faced a formidable task in trying to weld these four regions into a nation.

This description could leave the impression that Ecuador in the fall of 1859 consisted of four regions, each with firm goals and objectives. Actually the situation was more volatile, with both of the major factions enjoying considerable support even in the other regions. For example, García Moreno, visiting Riobamba on November 9, was jailed by a disgruntled commander who informed the former that he would be hanged in the morning. The officer and his troops then proceeded to loot and pillage the city, complaining that they had not been adequately provisioned. Next they engaged in a drunken orgy. During the night, García Moreno persuaded his lone jailor to release him. Then he made his way to the nearby town of Mocha, where he rounded up a few friends. They returned and fell upon the sleeping drunks, killing several who fought and taking the remainder prisoner.[41]

Thus even in the relatively safely held home regions, pockets of opposition existed. All parties held their respective regions tenuously, and the vicissitudes of war could change fortunes quickly. Even Quito's garrison rebelled briefly in early December, before officials restored order. The coastal provinces of Manabí and Esmeraldas, ostensibly firm in Franco's camp, hosted sporadic pro–provisional government revolts in the fall of 1859. There General Franco's brother Juan mounted a campaign and retook Esmeraldas, "freeing [its people] from the oppression [of the provisional government] they suffered in November and December."[42]

THE INVOLVEMENT OF FOREIGNERS AND THE PURLOINED LETTERS

Given the stalemate that García Moreno and Franco had reached on the battlefield, it is not surprising that each sought a trump card that would provide the winning hand. Each thought that a foreign ally might well turn the situation in his favor. Meanwhile President Castilla believed he could take advantage of Ecuador's civil war for his own ends. Loading about 5,000 troops onto naval vessels, he set sail from northern Peru to reinforce the blockade. As the convoy moved north, Castilla reassured Ecuadorians that his motives were peaceful and pure. He claimed that he only wanted reparations for "the grave and scandalous offenses the Robles government committed" (expelling Minister Cavero) and "I desire only to see Ecuador prosper under a just government *that is satisfactory to Peru*" (my emphasis). In reality Castilla wanted to impose quickly a favorable border settlement, his legacy to Peru.[43]

By November 1859, the Peruvian-sponsored negotiations between García Moreno and Franco had stalled. Castilla fastened the blame on García Moreno's dilatory tactics. "There is no other recourse," he stated. "I am forced to continue my military operations which were briefly suspended as a concession to the patriotism of Ecuadorians." Castilla had more mischief in mind than the Ecuadorians realized. In September he had inked a secret treaty with the strongman of southern Colombia, General Tomás Cipriano de Mosquera (governor of Cauca state), under the terms of which Ecuador would be truncated—with Peru receiving Guayaquil and the southern sierra region, and Mosquera the northern coast and much of the northern sierra—to create a new state (or a greater Colombia, should his revolt against the national government succeed). As one author creatively commented, the implementation of this treaty would have resulted in the "polandization" of Ecuador.[44]

Observers on the scene in Guayaquil, including José García Moreno, noted that Franco and Castilla seemed increasingly friendly. Franco and Castilla agreed that the 5,000 Peruvians would camp at the hacienda called Mapasingue, about a half hour from Guayaquil on the Daule River. Now Castilla demanded that all four of Ecuador's governments (those of Franco, García Moreno, Azuay, and Loja) parley. Believing that his military could force a boundary settlement on Ecuador if all else failed, Castilla dictated an ultimatum giving the four warring factions forty days to reach an agreement with Peru.[45] García Moreno, however, had no intention of agreeing to Castilla's proposal.

Instead the provisional government engaged in more dilatory tactics. García Moreno disavowed the idea of a convention, claiming that only he could sign such a protocol. Then he sent his other two triumvirs, Manuel Gómez de la Torre and José María Avilés, to the meeting. Privately, García Moreno told the French minister that the envoys were going "more to gain time than in the hopes of forming a national government."[46] Then the two rejected the proposed agreement. Azuay and Loja proved uncooperative as well. Azuay's representative favored leaving the border issue unresolved and demanded that Franco leave Cuenca alone. Loja also insisted on autonomy.[47] Hence the resulting treaty, whereby Castilla recognized Franco as the sole legal government of Ecuador, would not resonate in the interior. The treaty even caused rumblings in Guayaquil, where the locals disliked it, because according to the U.S. consul, the white elite feared the "colored" General Franco, the "sworn enemy of the white population." (The so-called *tauras* in the army of Urbina, Robles, and Franco contained a high percentage of recently freed slaves.)[48]

On January 25, 1860, Franco signed the Treaty of Mapasingue, in which he apologized for the expulsion of Minister Cavero and settled the boundary dispute by agreeing to the 1802 royal *cédula* that gave almost all of the disputed territory to Peru, declaring void the land sale to the British bondholders. In return, Article 29 of the agreement obliged Castilla to assist Franco in quelling the rebellion in the interior. Franco offered the provisional government the opportunity to surrender peacefully, but Quito responded directly to Castilla, justifying its resistance and encouraging him to take his army home.[49] Although Castilla initially refused, troubles in Peru soon forced him to withdraw his brigades from Mapasingue.

Written complaints about the treaty deluged the provisional government. Individuals, groups of notable personages, and towns all forwarded their "solemn protests" negating the treaty. Wisely the provisional government disavowed it, arguing that Quito represented the majority of Ecuadorians, that no congress had approved the agreement, and that its tenets violated international law requiring a state to act to preserve itself. García Moreno had already made up his mind to resist, and he had plenty of legal provocation. His fellow triumvirs, who had been treated badly while they were in Guayaquil, deserved better, he said. García Moreno informed the nation he was prepared to continue the battle,[50] even though to outsiders the odds did not look good. At least García Moreno and the provisional government could claim to be the patriots in the battle because they had not openly sided with a foreign power and sold out Ecuador to others. Or could they?

Unbeknownst to the Ecuadorian public, García Moreno had also sought external assistance. Broaching the subject of a European (French and possibly Spanish) protectorate in a series of secret letters to the French minister to Ecuador (Emile Trinité), García Moreno—apparently with the knowledge if not the approval of the other leaders of the provisional government—proposed in December 1859 that Ecuador assume a status much like that of Canada in the British Empire, whereby Canada controlled internal domestic affairs and enjoyed what the British referred to as "responsible government" while England directed its foreign policy.[51] García Moreno believed that a majority of Ecuadorians, at least in the sierra, would support his position. His motives were simple, if not pure. "We are tired of struggling with the licentiousness of the soldiery and the turbulence of demagogues." Instead of anarchy, "we would find ourselves under the auspices of France, the civilization of peace, liberty, and order." García Moreno begged Trinité to keep the letters secret. He did so until 1861 when his mistress gave them to General Franco—who promptly published them for political reasons in a Lima newspaper. In 1859 Trinité sidestepped García Moreno's offer by simply not forwarding the letters to France.[52]

Just as García Moreno and the provisional government condemned General Franco for selling out national interests to Peru, so too did García Moreno's enemies rightly excoriate him for the Trinité letters. His supporters today defend him by arguing that the Peruvian threat outweighed the loss of sovereignty implicit in the protectorate and that other heroes like Bolívar and José de San Martín (the leader of independence in Argentina and Chile) discussed the necessity for protectorates, but this argument holds little water.[53] Neither García Moreno nor Franco behaved well at the end of 1859, certainly not in the national interests. Both murmured meaningless sentiments of patriotism, which bring to mind Dr. Samuel Johnson's quip, "Patriotism is the last refuge of a scoundrel." Like Franco, García Moreno seemed more interested in winning the civil war than protecting Ecuador's sovereignty. As this chapter has argued, however, Ecuador was not really a nation in 1860, but rather an artificial construct composed of distinct regions. At this juncture, few Ecuadorians "imagined" their nation because their vision remained regional for the most part.

Without foreign intervention, the outcome of the civil war would depend solely on domestic factors. Franco enjoyed military superiority because he controlled most of the trained army.[54] The winner, however, would also need to claim the hearts and minds of the local leadership from the various regions: Quito, Guayaquil, Cuenca, and (to a lesser degree) Loja. Here García Moreno clearly held the advantage, as even some *guayaquileños* were put off by Franco's subservience to Peru and Castilla. The next few months would tell which side would prevail.

ADVANTAGE GARCÍA MORENO: THE REGIONS COALESCE

In the aftermath of Marshall Castilla's departure from Guayaquil, the battle for Ecuador began anew. Franco hoped that a quick strike would enable him to overrun the mostly volunteer forces of the provisional government and seize control of the entire country. Without Peruvian allies, though, the task was more difficult. Nevertheless, Franco went on the offensive, marching his men up to Guaranda. On January 25, 1860, a heated battle broke out in a muddy pasture outside the city, with General Manuel Tomás Maldonado in command of the provisional government's troops and García Moreno's friends Daniel Salvador and Secundino Darquea playing lesser roles. Another García Moreno ally, Bernardo Dávalos, led a lancer division of men who fought from horseback with pikes. As Maldonado reported, "our soldiers possessed the ardor of the French and the cold blood of the Spanish." When the smoke finally cleared, Franco had retreated, leaving behind not only wounded and dead but also many deserters.[55] Mass desertions should not have surprised Franco. Because the Treaty of Mapasingue had made his cause increasingly unpopular, Franco had to draft the poor of Guayaquil into his ranks. Lack of supplies, a rigorous campaign in bad weather, and bouts of illness also caused desertions.[56]

García Moreno now controlled four of the eight provinces. Loja was leaning in his direction, while Franco held on in Azuay, Manabí, and of course Guayas. Cuenca became the provisional government's next objective. There General Maldonado began conversations with the garrison's commander, Fernando Ayarza, encouraging him to switch sides because of the treaty. In early March, General Maldonado's forces menaced Ayarza's garrison of 50 soldiers in Cuenca, as districts within Azuay declared for García Moreno. A small battle took place and General Ayarza surrendered. After the battle, General Maldonado praised Secundino Darquea's "military genius, patriotism, and enthusiasm" as well as the important assistance of volunteers such as Carlos Ordóñez, a member of one of Cuenca's most important families. The provisional government quickly sent its congratulations to the new governor, Ramón Borrero, for having regained its rights and formed a government consistent with the "will of the people."[57] García Moreno went one step further: He mounted a horse and rode to Cuenca to congratulate the new governor in person.

García Moreno saw this visit not only as a chance to solidify his influence over the situation in Cuenca, but also to parley with the government of Loja. He seized the moment, even giving up Holy Week with his family. Already his now-and-then ally, Jerónimo Carrión, had started to Loja "with the goal of seeing whether this *little republic* will join us" (my emphasis). Initially Loja's governor, Manuel Carrión Pinzano, stood aloof, offering only to provide 3,000 pesos a month to the provisional government for the war effort. García Moreno recognized Loja's geographical separateness, comparing the land with its twists and turns to a crumpled piece of paper.[58] Nevertheless the provisional government could not afford to let Loja go its own way, so García Moreno began to coax (or coerce) it into a closer union.

Hence García Moreno's quick ride to the city of Loja in mid-March enabled him to use his network with a prominent local family, the Eguigurens, to full advantage. García Moreno employed veiled threats of military action, but Carrión Pinzano countered that Loja, like Quito and Cuenca, wanted a government that respected regionalism and federalism, "the natural system and the only reasonable and just one." García Moreno agreed but warned Carrión Pinzano: "there cannot be neutrality for Ecuadorians in this moment of conflict . . . . there is no middle ground—you are for the country or against it," and the governor agreed to "make common cause with our brothers of the interior."[59]

Although prospects now looked favorable for the provisional government, García Moreno experienced a fright in April 1860. Captured correspondence uncovered a plot led by General Fernando Ayarza. After the battle of Cuenca in March, Ayarza had lived in Quito under one of the casual house-arrest arrangements so typical of the time. The government quickly seized the conspirators. While García Moreno exiled others, he decided to punish General Ayarza by having him whipped, a decision that raised an uproar both then and now. Essentially his critics charge that the punishment (500 lashes) and the victim (a 70-year-old independence hero of African ancestry) demonstrate both García Moreno's cruel streak and his racism. Defenders claim that Ayarza had committed treason—that the punishment of whipping often occurred within the military, and therefore Ayarza received justice.[60]

As usual, the most logical explanation lies somewhere in between the two extreme claims, although García Moreno's detractors make several strong points. First, the punishment was not as harsh as usually reported. No one could physically survive 500 stripes, no matter how lightly stroked—40 was the actual punishment. Even this number could have proven life threatening for an elderly man, though, so one of García Moreno's fellow triumvirs lessened the punishment even further. Two doctors attested to General Ayarza's good health before a soldier administered the punishment. Nor did Ayarza die within three days from the pain and humiliation, as most accounts (even friendly ones) have indicated. More thorough scholarship revealed that Ayarza died in early August while walking down San Roque Street in Quito, when he fell and struck his head on the stone pavement. While García Moreno may not have exercised "cruel" punishment in Ayarza's case, he certainly employed "unusual" punishment. Other high-ranking officers, lawyers, and writers who betrayed his government were exiled, shot (in a few instances), or jailed. Ayarza received a unique punishment, one undoubtedly based on race.[61]

The Ayarza whipping did have serious consequences for García Moreno and the provisional government. His two best officers, General Manuel Tomás Maldonado and Colonel Secundino Darquea, protested loudly about the proposed punishment. Darquea tried to educate García Moreno about the honor of the military. "For a general, his crimes must be judged and punished by four shots or by exile but by no means by an infamous punishment like whipping." General Maldonado wrote a long letter protesting the punishment, making a similar argument. But García Moreno underestimated this sense of comradeship, focusing instead on the need to crush the rebellious spirit of the officer corps. As he told Maldonado, his goal was to save the nation from traitors, while you [Maldonado] "believe the uniform is sullied by the punishment and not the crime."[62] Immediately Maldonado and Darquea both resigned their commissions. Both would return to the field before the civil war ended, but clearly felt that García Moreno had besmirched the military's honor. Nevertheless García Moreno recognized that the unruly military was an impediment to a stable government, and he would try to reform it.

Maldonado and Darquea's temporary defections heightened García Moreno's concerns about finding the right person to lead the army to victory. The provisional government's leading cavalry officer, Bernardo Dávalos (a friend of García Moreno since the 1840s), wrote that "our forces are not working in a unified manner because we lack a commander-in-chief." Luckily the Hero of Tumbuco displayed enough wisdom not to offer himself in that capacity. Eventually the provisional government acquired the services of none other than General Juan José Flores, a first-class military strategist whose name appealed to many in the volunteer army. Initially García Moreno had qualms. After all, fifteen years previously he had participated in the coup against Flores as his first political act. Even in late 1859, he wanted nothing to do with Flores, explaining to Rosa that he would resist the "stupid people" who wanted Flores to reassert control over Ecuador.[63]

In 1860 Flores and García Moreno exchanged a number of letters and, like reluctant suitors, gradually warmed to each other. In his first letter, García Moreno admitted that for years he had been Flores' political enemy out of conviction, "but from the moment that you decided to help us in the glorious struggle to sustain our independence and the integrity of the Republic, I have considered you a friend." García Moreno added that he looked forward to Flores' "wise counsel" on the prosecution of the war and his assistance in procuring guns and ammunition from foreign sources. Not all of García Moreno's allies responded favorably to the news of the alliance with Flores. Some clearly feared in the ambitious general the sort of machinations that had made him unpopular in the 1840s. Eventually, however, the vast majority of the leadership in the sierra acquiesced with García Moreno's decision to include Flores in the war plans.[64]

The narrative of the civil war thus far presents a rather orderly progression of events leading to an inevitable conclusion, yet such an impression would be overly simplistic. Even as the provisional government prepared for the final showdown, events demonstrated its hold to be tenuous. Endemic regionalism still prevailed, including an indigenous revolt in Chimborazo over tax collection and an antiprovisional government uprising occurring in one of the districts of Azuay called Cañar. There, in June 1860, a local landlord and *jefe político* named José Alejandro Espinosa rebelled, espousing Franco's cause and raising about 70 soldiers and a larger number of indigenous people to do the fighting. Espinosa kidnapped former governor Borrero before finally being killed in a decisive battle on August 14, in which García Moreno's friend Carlos Ordóñez played a major role.[65]

While these revolts flared up, Flores wasted time in northern Ecuador, at least in García Moreno's opinion. He begged Flores to drop everything and head south to the battlefront. Flores decided he needed to resolve a potential crisis with Colombia, however, knowing that Peru's Castilla and Colombia's Tomás Cipriano de Mosquera had signed the previously mentioned secret agreement in 1859. Flores and Mosquera were old friends from the War of Independence, and Flores begged the latter to forego his ambitions for the moment.[66] Finally Flores arrived in Guaranda. "His presence has increased the enthusiasm of the valiant army that defends the honor and integrity of the Republic,"[67] said García Moreno. For the first time, he could concentrate his energies on a task in which he excelled—serving as the quartermaster for the army.

Because of General Franco's control of Guayaquil, García Moreno had to obtain weaponry internally. Thus the government first decreed that any individual who possessed a gun must present it to local officials within three days and receive ten pesos in compensation, but the measure was ignored. García Moreno then decided to manufacture the weapons the army needed, asking his friend Carlos Aguirre to convert the textile mill on his hacienda, Los Chillos, into a munitions plant. Soon Aguirre was melting down lead and fashioning bullets. By the end of the war, the provisional government even seized bronze church bells to melt down into cannons, an old colonial practice. Likewise García Moreno resorted to homespun cloth to provide uniforms for the soldiers. Adequate meals of fresh beef heightened soldiers' enthusiasm for the rigors of the battlefield. By July 1860 García Moreno felt confident for the first time that he and his colleagues were providing sufficient munitions, clothing, and food to meet the army's needs.[68] As important as warm clothing, a full stomach, and a functioning weapon were, the soldiers also needed to be paid. Cash ensured loyalty, and as the civil war wound down, both sides became strapped for hard currency. Although initially General Franco enjoyed customs revenues and Peruvian loans, by July 1860 he was without funds.[69] García Moreno did better under the trying circumstances.

The provisional government tapped municipal taxes and resurrected an old colonial practice, the *donativo gracioso* (forced loans), to help with the funding. Although the first loans looked like voluntary campaign contributions, by the time the civil war reached its critical phase in 1860, forced loans lived up to their name and became an impromptu emergency tax. A decree required that payments be made on the first of the month, that property owners pay 1 peso in taxes for every 4,000 pesos of appraised property, that priests and teachers surrender one-quarter of their salaries, and that people engaged in commerce pay between 1 peso and 25 pesos monthly, depending on their income. Decrees established quotas for each province.[70] By the end of the war, these forced loans totaled 545,000 pesos. Some of García Moreno's socialite friends from Quito contributed as much as 10,000 pesos each. Government employees sacrificed their entire salaries. One member of the provisional government told the governor of Pichincha to make certain that he was "not paying anything to the civil servants. . . . and that you are only giving credit for military expenses."[71] By July 1860 the provisional government, thanks to García Moreno's leadership, had adequate revenues for its military purposes.

THE BATTLE FOR GUAYAQUIL AND ITS AFTERMATH

As General Flores geared up his talents to lead the army, he and García Moreno focused their attention on the final objective of the civil war, the capture of Guayaquil. Absent Peruvian interference, the goal looked achievable in August, so García Moreno urged Flores to hasten his preparations. Already García Moreno had come to trust his commander in chief. He gave Flores a free hand, telling him, "You resolve to do what seems most wise depending on the circumstances. . . . I can offer only zeal and activity."[72] García Moreno recognized his strengths (incredible energy and charisma) and his weaknesses (a lack of knowledge of military tactics). Methodically General Flores implemented his plan to isolate Guayaquil by capturing all of its hinterlands and then laying siege to the city.

As the first step in the process, Flores fought the battle of Babahoyo, a city that serves today as the capital of the province of Los Ríos. Babahoyo lies on the banks of two streams, and has had since early colonial times both commercial and strategic importance. Consequently General Franco had stationed a significant portion of his army there. On August 7 Flores attacked, catching Franco by surprise and achieving victory in two hours. Francisco Javier Salazar, later a key general in García Moreno's second administration, bravely led a handful of soldiers into the vanguard, helping Flores carry the day. Franco, wounded twice, and some of his officers fled back to Guayaquil.[73] After the battle García Moreno wrote his wife: "To win we only had to arrive on the battlefield and do our duty: God did the rest." And he praised Flores, "the valiant general who is today the commander of the army," making a special note in his report about the timely and brilliant cavalry charge that Flores had led.[74] Clearly Flores' presence provided the provisional government with a real advantage.

Cautiously pursuing Franco's fleeing troops, Flores and García Moreno arrived at Daule, across the Guayas River from Guayaquil. Swollen by deserters from Franco's army, the provisional government enjoyed numerical superiority for the first time. García Moreno reported: "The campaign will be short and with the help of Providence we will enter Guayaquil with 4,000 men." Deserters also provided intelligence about Guayaquil's fortifications and Franco's dearth of supplies.[75] Franco was down to his last peso, and rumors that he intended to let Peru annex Guayaquil in exchange for cash and military support did nothing to enhance his popularity. Nor did his decree of September 5, conscripting every able-bodied man in the city. By all reports Franco was in a surly mood. Employing "language unbecoming a gentleman," he threatened the U.S. consul, José Canova, because he believed the latter was secretly helping the provisional government.

By now the province of Manabí had fallen and its governor, Juan José Franco, had returned to Guayaquil to help his brother. More good news for the provisional government came from Peru. Not only was President Castilla embroiled with problems in Bolivia, but a local revolt had also broken out in Peru itself—during the course of which he was wounded. Now Franco had no hope of reinforcements. Thus the provisional government stepped up efforts to take Guayaquil as quickly as possible. Not even a kick from a horse could deter García Moreno. Although the injury confined him to his bed for a couple of weeks, he directed the outfitting of the army as it prepared its final campaign. "We have a fine army, the strongest without a doubt that Ecuador has had to this time."[76]

In addition to a well-provisioned army, García Moreno held other advantages. Because of Franco's actions, García Moreno could wrap himself in the flag of nationalism (perhaps better called patriotism), as Spanish Minister Carlos de Sanquírico reported.[77] Back home in the sierra, the large landowners held steadfast in their support of the provisional government, well represented as they were in its highest councils. The church establishment also turned decisively in favor of García Moreno and the provisional government, hardly a surprise. In early January Roberto de Ascásubi appealed to Bishop Riofrío "to bless the forces of patriotism." Only one day later the Bishop agreed, writing that "the government had to use arms to preserve Ecuador." During the civil war, the church also helped the provisional government by advocating its cause to the faithful and even allowing the government to arrest "subversive" priests or remove them from the pulpit.[78]

Final operations began on the night of September 22. While one part of the provisional government's army stayed in camp and another part led by Colonel José de Veintemilla attacked from the north, the bulk of the forces waded through a mangrove swamp called the Salado. They dragged their heavy hand-forged cannon with them on balsawood rafts, attacking the city from the west. García Moreno and Flores cleverly integrated the main body of their sierran recruits with locals who had recently joined. The *montuvios* (mestizos from the coast) showed the *serranos* how to wade through the deep muddy swamp without drowning. Fortunately for Flores, Franco seems to have had neither scouts nor much imagination. He believed the force coming through the swamps to be a mere diversion, so he concentrated his army to the north, a more logical place from which to assault the city. Late the next day the bombardment began, and by the early morning hours of September 24, 1860, Guayaquil fell to the provisional government. As for Franco, he and a few of his key men again escaped by water, this time on a Peruvian vessel that took them safely into exile.[79]

Immediately, García Moreno outlawed the banner that Franco had flown, declaring that Ecuador's official new flag was to be the tricolor (yellow, blue, and red) that had graced the patriot army at the time of independence. Celebrations abounded. "Por la patria!" one might say, the first practical step in imagining the nation. The government, although later mandating temperance, even authorized the distribution of *aguardiente* for fiestas throughout the highlands.[80]

Even after Flores' and García Moreno's triumph at Guayaquil, conspirators and Castilla hoped to reverse the provisional government's triumph. Both García Moreno and Flores spent the next months in Guayaquil, awaiting an anticipated Peruvian invasion. Then it was García Moreno alone, as Flores attended the national convention in Quito: "I can't leave here until order is preserved because Flores has gone and nobody engenders respect but he and I,"[81] said García Moreno. Meanwhile he worked to crush his domestic opposition. "How can you permit the *El Segundo de Marzo (Second of March)*, a paper subsidized by the government, to be converted into an organ of opposition?" he asked his governor of Azuay.[82] There would be very limited freedom of the press in García Moreno's Ecuador, much to the disappointment of many liberals who had sided with the provisional government.

Regime change also meant an opportunity to reward, which García Moreno freely did. Not surprisingly General Flores benefited most from García Moreno's largesse, both because he had been instrumental in the victory (so much so that the British minister occasionally referred to the new government as Flores') and because in the eyes of many he had been treated unfairly when the *marcistas* reneged on the Treaty of Virginia in 1846. By decree, then, García Moreno restored Flores' property and named him the permanent commander-in-chief of the army. Again García Moreno apologized for his vehement opposition to Flores previously, saying that now "I know your merits, and appreciate them." Flores in turn recommended promotions for a list of officers.[83]

García Moreno also must have been intrigued by a letter he received from a then-unknown literary figure from Ambato, Juan Montalvo. Asserting he was neither friend nor enemy, Montalvo spoke of morality and urged temperance. He accused García Moreno of being too passionate (an apt observation) and bloody: "You seem to be excessively violent" (a comment that would prove ironic, as later events would show). Montalvo agreed with García Moreno on the importance of being resolute but warned him that excesses would be considered tyranny. Finally he encouraged García Moreno to think about Alexander Hamilton and Thomas Jefferson as role models rather than Juan Manuel de Rosas, a conservative and tyrannical caudillo who ruled Argentina from 1835 to 1852. García Moreno allegedly exclaimed after reading this letter, "This young man must think I am meek."[84]

The government recognized that it had to repay its friends who had contributed forced loans. People who claimed that the army or government had borrowed horses or money presented their documentation to government officials to receive compensation. Fortunately the government could pay these obligations because tax collections and customs-house revenues returned to normal after the conflict ended. García Moreno also tried to minimize expenses by reducing the size of the army, a delicate balancing act given the need to remain prepared in the face of possible rebellion or invasion. While many soldiers were discharged, the government simultaneously recruited men for the National Guard, probably because its members were paid only when on active duty. García Moreno hoped to establish a National Guard roster of 30,000 infantry and 1,000 cavalry, a figure he would never attain.[85]

The reward García Moreno sought for himself did not involve cash, but rather power. His enemies have always asserted that he was driven by ruthless ambition, while his friends claim that he sacrificed himself for the good of the country. Rather routinely, political leaders throughout nineteenth-century Spanish America feigned disinterest in the presidency, preferring to be courted for the job and only reluctantly accepting the office because of the need to serve their country (or so their acceptance speeches would assert). García Moreno's behavior fits this mold. For example, he told his wife, "I await the day of triumph so I can separate myself from this: My soul needs rest." To his brother-in-law he said, "Those who do not know me believe I have a heart full of ambition, soon I will convince them that I do not want any compensation."[86]

Like all victorious revolutions in Ecuador, this one ended with a call for a constitutional assembly that would rewrite the nation's charter. Until it convened, García Moreno ruled by decree and took the opportunity to reform the political system. From the moment that Ecuador had gained its independence in 1830, its presidents had been selected based on a very restricted suffrage (roughly 1 percent of the population) and an electoral-college system where each of the three political districts—Quito, Guayaquil, and Cuenca—had a single vote. Given that the sierra and the coast were always at odds, Cuenca's swing vote usually favored the liberal coastal candidate, giving *costeños* a near monopoly of the chief executive's office since independence. Rocafuerte, Roca, Noboa, Urbina, and Robles all represented the coast; only Flores had links to Quito, and then only by marriage. García Moreno believed this system unfair because the Quito region had more voters than the other two districts combined. As he said, the principle behind the electoral system was "absurd in theory, [and] subversive and ruinous in practice."

To begin, García Moreno carved Guayas into two provinces "as a safeguard against the revolutionaries of Guayaquil." He named the new more conservative interior province, which also included cantons from Chimborazo province, Los Ríos. Subregions that had demonstrated their loyalty to the provisional government, such as Paute in Azuay, were allowed to form separate cantons, giving them greater local autonomy. Adjusting provincial and canton borders and gerrymandering electoral districts guaranteed that the provisional government would win the election of 1861.[87]

García Moreno proposed a second reform, direct suffrage, for a rather different purpose. "No social regimen is beneficial or firm when it is founded upon an injustice," he wrote. Suffrage had to be broadened, and congress made more representative, he argued. At the end of October 1860, García Moreno issued a far-reaching decree that enfranchised literate male Ecuadorians, even those without property, over 21 years of age. For every 30,000 inhabitants, a province received one representative. The contest of 1860, then, would result in the election of 36 deputies: 20 from the north sierra, 9 from Cuenca/Loja, and the remainder representing the coast. As a result of the suffrage reform, the number of voters increased from 1 percent to 4 percent of the population, according to a recent estimate, and guaranteed the sierra provinces control of the government for the first time. As García Moreno put it, the new system returned power to the people's legitimate representatives and allowed for a "free expression of the popular will." Interior provinces like León, now governed by García Moreno's friend Nicolás Martínez (a writer and lawyer), liked the new electoral system and the promise of a decentralized government. Loja, too, held high hopes for regionalism and powerful municipal councils.[88] Not all provinces reacted so enthusiastically, however. Although the new system appeared both more democratic and equitable than that which had existed previously, it raised a storm of controversy with the vested interests it had displaced. French consul Joseph La Pierre noted the factionalism that seethed in areas like Azuay.

Protests surfaced quickly. Inside sources indicated that Guayaquil would elect candidates to the constitutional assembly opposed to the provisional government because of the new electoral system, the return of the Jesuits, and local issues such as García Moreno's abrupt dismissal of corrupt treasury employees. One of the city's best-known liberals, Pedro Carbo, resigned his post in anger. In Azuay, Mariano Cueva called an open meeting of Cuenca's municipal council to protest the new election law, under which Azuay would clearly lose influence. Benigno Malo—diplomat, lawyer, and newspaperman—and other local notables registered their displeasure with the new law. García Moreno responded in his all too frequently intemperate manner. He called Cueva's protest "an immoral betrayal" that "will put an end to my patience, and oblige me to take serious and decisive measures." He took a sharp tone with Azuay's governor: "I want to hear your explanations [for the open meeting and the journalistic criticism] though I fear they will be inadequate." García Moreno called him an ingrate and cut off subsidies to the newspaper. But Juan José Flores helped to smooth over the rift. Soon Cueva was back in good graces and attending the National Convention as a delegate supportive of the provisional government.[89]

Although the election might have had a broader electorate and a more

Benigno Malo, a moderate and advocate for Cuenca's regional interests (Permission of the Banco Central del Ecuador)

equitable provincial representation based on population, the provisional government employed time-honored tactics to make certain that its friends held a majority (or preferably a monopoly) of the seats. Only candidates who recognized the authority of the provisional government could get their names on the ballot, assuring that no liberals openly associated with Robles or Franco could mount an opposition campaign. Government candidates dutifully perorated about the misdeeds of the Robles years and their disastrous consequences.[90] In the north, the election seemed well in hand. One soon-to-be elected deputy told General Flores that he was working very hard on behalf of García Moreno and his friends because "only he, with his talents, judgment, and enthusiasm, can lift the Republic to its highest potential, and end the anarchy of the last 15 years." García Moreno's strategy regarding the new province, Los Ríos, also seemed to work, as at least one newly elected deputy from there firmly sided with the provisional government. When the provisional government lost in the city of Guaranda, however, García Moreno asked his governor to persuade the two elected delegates to withdraw so that they could be replaced with "patriots."[91] With the elections concluded, García Moreno and his friends expected that the swearing in to be held during the constitutional convention beginning on January 8, 1861, would result in the dawn of a new era in Ecuador.

REGIONALISM: A TEST OF LEADERSHIP AND VISION

The civil war of 1859 and 1860, while far from the final such conflict that Ecuador would endure, proved to be one of its most hard fought. In contrast to the civil war that would soon be raging in the United States, the Ecuadorian contest cost relatively few lives. Neither side ever enlisted many more than 5,000 men, and the death tolls after the bloodiest battles rarely reached 100. The low casualty figures no doubt reflect the average fighting man's uncertain commitment to either cause, yet this civil war was clearly destructive. Franco's fleeing army destroyed bridges during its retreat to Guayaquil. Agriculture, especially on the cacao plantations, languished because workers either joined the army or fled from the conflict.[92] The civil war confirmed the tradition of an unreliable and unruly officer corps, with generals who frequently switched sides (like Ayarza) or who abandoned their posts in the middle of the campaign (like Maldonado). To construct a nation, García Moreno, like other Spanish American presidents, would need to bring the military under control.

Peacetime could repair the bridges and encourage the resumption of agricultural production. Could the new government overcome the omnipresent sentiment for regionalism, though? As one of the leading officials in Loja wrote on the eve of the national convention in 1861, "This is a new era in sectional power." Such opinions ran counter to García Moreno's vision of the future: "My opinion as a member of the government, as a citizen and as a *guayaquileño* is that the Republic must be considered a single family." Ecuador must "put aside its preoccupations and interests in provincialism" in favor of the national interests, he wrote.[93]

Known initially as an intellectual and vocal opponent of the Robles government in the Senate, García Moreno had advanced from being one of a triumvirate of highland leaders in May 1859 to the undisputed political leader of the provisional government by the time of the battle of Guayaquil. During these two years, he gained experience as a diplomat (dealing with Peru and France) and as a politician (handling tricky negotiations with local leadership in Cuenca and Loja). Although the French consul in Guayaquil, like most other members of the diplomatic corps, found him to be too "proud and irascible" to be Ecuador's president,[94] García Moreno had more sense of the nation than any other member of the provisional government. Traveling through the country during the course of the war, García Moreno took advantage of his university friends (the Ordóñez family in Cuenca and the Eguiguren clan in Loja, for example) to build a larger network of allies. These regional leaders helped him create a national following. At the same time he recognized the danger of regionalism as he observed the disunity being demonstrated next door in Colombia. By this time García Moreno realized that he had to take both practical and ideological steps to overcome the centrifugal force of regionalism. Exacerbating García Moreno's difficulties would be the popular philosophy of federalism, which came to dominate the political debate in 1861 and which would cause García Moreno constant headaches during his first presidency from 1861 to 1865.

Chapter Three

A Presidency Constrained I: Federalism and Domestic Policy, 1861–1865

Having victoriously concluded the bitterly contested civil war, García Moreno faced the future with both hope and misgivings. On one hand, with General Franco and the liberal militarists exiled, García Moreno could begin to fashion his nation-building project. Years of traveling and observing the European world had provided him with ideas that he believed would transform Ecuador into a modern progressive state. On the other hand, García Moreno knew that his reforms, some of which contravened the more popular and commonplace ideas of liberal state formation, would provoke resistance and conflict. Malcontents and exiles clamored for a resumption of the civil war. Worse, bullying neighbors both to the north and south threatened to carve up what was already the second smallest country in South America, as will be explored at length in the next chapter. In fact the two wars with Colombia, along with García Moreno's brief captivity, placed tremendous strains on his domestic agenda, leaving his ideal of the Catholic nation unrealized until a successive presidential term.

Recent historians and social scientists alike have theorized about how a nation creates a sense of identity, or as the originator of the debate wondered, how an inchoate mass of humanity transforms itself into an "imagined community." Many historians agree that developing a national culture is at the heart of the matter. While most European and Asian nations define themselves based on a unique print language, clearly this distinction makes little sense when analyzing the newly independent Latin American nations (except Brazil). In fact, as the previous chapter argued, in the years immediately following independence few Ecuadorians had any sense of the nation. A small number of the upper class, such as former President Vicente Rocafuerte and Pedro Carbo (who had worked for Rocafuerte in Mexico), had even conceived of themselves expansively as Spanish Americans, equally able to serve governments abroad or in Ecuador. Most Ecuadorians thought of themselves as regional people, as the civil war of 1859 to 1861 amply demonstrated. Like Flores before him, García Moreno took a more national perspective, one he believed to be consistent with Ecuador's essentially conservative values. Yet his program was not simply a desire to impose a dictatorship by embracing popular conservative and proclerical rhetoric. Rather it was a riskier innovative program that embraced the twin doctrines of modernization and progress. First and foremost he believed in an all-pervasive Catholic culture that he thought enjoyed popular support and would unify the nation spiritually and politically.[1]

García Moreno's vision clashed with the liberal state-building formula that dominated post-independence political discussions elsewhere, ideas that had found expression among the provincial leaders of the provisional government during the civil war of 1859–1860. Nearly all the politicians who attended the post–civil war constitutional convention supported a federalistic structure of government to promote liberal goals of popular sovereignty, individual liberties, and a free citizenry. Certainly the discourse of popular sovereignty, "the will of the people," had been at the heart of the provisional government's propaganda during the civil war. Regional leaders believed that a federalist government with a weak executive lacked the power to act tyrannically and allowed individual citizens to enjoy the maximum amount of liberty possible.[2] Parenthetically it also permitted regional interests to dominate. Even though García Moreno believed that a weak national government was a mistake, initially he had no real choice but to acknowledge the pact he had made with the regional leaders of Cuenca and Loja (a bargain with the devil, he would later opine) to support the principles of federalism in the constitution.

García Moreno had more sympathy for liberal economic theory that recognized the importance of free markets, progress, and development. Like most nineteenth-century leaders, García Moreno believed that his nation's involvement in the international economy would prove beneficial. Because Europeans paid high prices for tropical agricultural exports in the 1860s and 1870s, his thinking appears sound.[3] Like his contemporaries across Latin America, he never believed that Ecuador's economy would become embroiled in a mechanistic system that would make it dependent on European purchasers and investors.[4] As a result, he pursued development strategies, usually associated with liberal state-formation theory, to expand Ecuador's economy.

Because García Moreno accepted the idea of popular sovereignty, he shared with liberals what historian-anthropologist Mark Thurner has called the "post-colonial predicament." Unlike many conservatives, García Moreno never tried to recreate the colonial system of two republics that theoretically segregated Indians and Spaniards, but rather remained committed to the idea of citizenship for all. Nevertheless his state had to wrestle with the notion of equality for subaltern people, an idea that bothered elite white republicans everywhere.[5] García Moreno's conservative vision for the Ecuadorian world, however, led to a very constrained first term, in part because of his ongoing conflicts with federalist ideals, and in part because the resources available to fund internal development never quite matched his ambitious plans, as the following anecdote illustrates.

In 1866 an angry parish priest wrote the president of Ecuador in protest. The chapel that the priest served had been leveled to make room for a new road, a project dear to the heart of President García Moreno. Being devout, García Moreno had come to the decision to destroy this chapel very reluctantly and only because his professional foreign-trained engineers had assured him that the road could not be routed elsewhere. To salve his conscience, García Moreno had promised the cleric that the government would rebuild the chapel in a better location. Four years later the priest complained that nothing had been done, to which García Moreno's successor could only respond that the government lacked the funds to comply with its promise.[6] Lack of resources, regional interests, foreign wars, and an unwieldy constitution subverted national needs all too frequently during García Moreno's first term.[7]

THE CONVENTION OF 1861

By January 1861 the provisional government legitimized its victory in the civil war in the traditional manner: by undoing all of its predecessor's "bad acts," confirming formally its own prior decrees, and beginning to write a new constitution. The convention of 1861, however, acted more cantankerously and independently than such bodies usually did, not paying much heed to García Moreno's wishes. Perhaps his youth, absence from Quito, and lack of personal military competence explain the constituent assembly's lack of deference. His colleagues often disregarded his wishes and were unwilling to forego their own regional interests. His new best friend, General Flores, presided over the convention. García Moreno had even reconciled with the meeting's vice president, Mariano Cueva of Cuenca, despite their temporary falling out in November.[8] With Flores representing the coast (his landholdings were in Los Ríos province), Cueva serving the Azuay region, and García Moreno's fellow triumvirs acting for the sierra (since he remained in Guayaquil in the event of a renewed invasion), all the major regions had powerful voices.

As the convention prepared to meet, García Moreno downplayed his presidential aspirations. "My ambition is limited to being useful to the Republic, and I prefer a more humble post [than interim president]," he wrote to Flores. Nevertheless the assembly insisted and García Moreno "reluctantly" accepted it. Within a week he appointed a cabinet and a number of governors as he was authorized to do, tried to quantify the foreign debt, and promoted officers. Yet, as he told Flores, he had no specific agenda for the interim term. "My mission is to preserve order [watching conspirators and preparing for the seemingly inevitable Peruvian invasion] while you reconstruct the country."[9]

Although U.S. commentators have uniformly described the Constitution of 1861 as centralized and authoritarian, leading Ecuadorian constitutional scholars disagree (correctly, I believe), characterizing the government created by the document as decentralized, reserving great powers to the municipalities.[10] From the moment the delegates introduced these federalist principles designed to protect the autonomy of regions, García Moreno protested. In his mind, only a powerful executive could combat domestic and external threats. Thus he advocated for a centralized regime that would enable the president to deal summarily with any "traitors" (i.e., pro-Urbina and pro-Franco supporters) who would likely abet a coup attempt. For example, he urged the convention to legalize the prosecution of individuals who even verbally conspired against the government. As he said, if the convention did not adopt stronger sedition laws, the conspirators "will never fear anything, and society will be a victim of cowardly judges and an impotent law."[11] But it was not to be. As he wrote Flores, "the worst [result] would be a government without the means to conserve order and protect the progress of the country." The idea of a centralized administration frightened many Ecuadorians in 1861, even García Moreno's friend José Eguiguren (appointed governor of Loja), who feared "that the province would become subject to the central regime."[12]

Not only did the convention refuse to consider tougher sedition laws, but it also began to undo some of García Moreno's decrees from the fall of 1860, modifying among others one that restored General Flores' rank and property. Given Flores' services to the provisional government, García Moreno believed that the former deserved this reward. Now, while Flores endured one of his sickly spells, the convention revoked portions of the decree, forcing the Flores family to litigate property claims for years. García Moreno reiterated his displeasure: "I have many reasons to resign." While past conventions had merely rubberstamped the decrees of their leader, this convention's reluctance to do so had García Moreno fuming.[13]

The regionally based opposition proposed Articles 101, 102, and 103, which would have created a federalist state by holding direct elections for all provincial offices (governor, *jefe político,* and political lieutenant), and by creating provincial legislatures.[14] According to García Moreno, this turn of events would "tie my hands." The draft constitution was "monstrous," in García Moreno's opinion, because a president could be subjected to congressional scrutiny for "political crimes." The result would be "disorder, anarchy, bloodshed, and misery; in short the contents of Pandora's Box," he wrote. So frustrated had García Moreno become that he complained to Ramón Borrero's brother Antonio that his sibling was "neither talented nor patriotic." Cuenca's delegation, including Borrero and Mariano Cueva, maintained its federalist position throughout the convention to preserve its autonomy, straining relations with García Moreno.[15]

Balking, García Moreno threatened not to promulgate the constitution if it passed (which technically he did not have the authority to do) and then he threatened to resign. The lack of a sympathetic sitting vice president, however, along with the ongoing Peruvian menace, made him reconsider his ultimatum.[16] In the end, of course, he was seeking political leverage, and he gained it almost immediately. Flores intervened on the floor and hammered out a compromise based on his previous understanding with García Moreno that essentially allowed the president to continue to appoint governors. Only the provision allowing municipal autonomy remained in effect. García Moreno accepted the middle ground, stating, "With the reforms we discussed, the monstrous draft will be converted into a reasonable and rational entity."[17] Thus in typical nineteenth-century liberal fashion, the Constitution of 1861 devolved great power onto individual citizens and local municipal government, although, because of the literacy requirement and the president's role in appointing governors, Ecuadorian politics did not evolve into the popular republicanism that made governance in southern Colombia extremely complex at roughly the same time.[18]

Still, García Moreno chafed under these constitutional limitations, which must have given him pause when the assembly chose him as president and Mariano Cueva as vice president. Evidence suggests that García Moreno agreed with the choice of Cueva to preserve his shaky coalition

Gabriel García Moreno during his first term as president (Permission of the Banco Central del Ecuador)

in Cuenca. The new president's address laid out the principles that would characterize his regime: a church-led educational program, expanded commercial opportunities, and an improved transportation network. At the core of his reform program, he argued, was the need to moralize society so that Ecuador would prevail in the struggle between good and evil. This speech launched a public celebration. Quito was lit up from 6:00 p.m. until 10:00 p.m., although the city notoriously had no night life until very recently. Flags flew and the military band played. The future looked brighter than it had in some time because, as the U.S. consul noted prophetically, "The new President is reputed to be a man of integrity and much energy, and his administration is likely to improve the finances and increase the prosperity of the country *unless* interfered with by revolution or an invasion from Peru"[19] (my emphasis).

Aside from drafting the constitution, the assembly dealt with other matters such as García Moreno's decade-old promise to invite the Jesuits to return to Ecuador. Because the delegates agreed that only the Catholic faith would be tolerated, the invitation could not have been unanticipated. Other legislation included condemning Franco's Treaty of Mapasingue with Peru and authorizing García Moreno's proposals for road and railroad construction. Finally, the delegates spelled out the details of federalism in the Law of Municipalities, which stated essentially that "communities retained their local taxes . . . for the construction, conservation, and development of public works for the community." On April 17, 1861, the completed constitution was read aloud in the cathedral, after which the archbishop celebrated another Te Deum Mass of Thanks (a Mass that also implicitly lauded the head of state). Following Mass, military parades in the cities and towns concluded the joyful celebration.[20]

Meanwhile the Peruvian crisis simmered, with Castilla verbally renewing threats of invasion. García Moreno conferred often about the dangers with the United States minister, Friedrich Hassaurek, recently arrived on the scene and ultimately well known for one of the most popular nineteenth-century travel accounts of the country. Hassaurek had a number of relationships with Ecuadorian women, which led to his wife's early departure and his subsequent divorce. As a rock-ribbed, Austrian-born anticlerical, he had little sympathy for Catholicism. Ultimately his opinion of García Moreno turned negative, although initially it had been optimistic, as noted above.[21]

During July García Moreno and the assembly began the process of defining Ecuador as a "community," with a sense of historical tradition and roots. The convention thus chose August 10, the anniversary of the abortive coup in Quito by the criollo elite in 1809, as Ecuador's official independence day (even though to the present, Guayaquil and Cuenca prefer their local independence holidays). García Moreno and the convention next organized formal elections for both houses of congress. "We have crossed the Rubicon," he told a friend, as he prepared for his inauguration in September. Nevertheless he continued in some ways to play the maverick. Rather than hold the usual inaugural dinner and invite the diplomatic corps, García Moreno decided to cancel the affair on the grounds that it cost too much in a time of need. When his wife, Rosa, insisted and gave him the money from her personal income, he stubbornly donated it instead to a hospital, saying that the infirm deserved the money more.[22]

As García Moreno readied himself to assume the presidency, he continued to have misgivings about the constitution. Allegedly he told his friends, "They have elected me president but tied my hands. I will untie them." He likened his situation to that of Samson, shorn of his powers by the biblical Delilah. He went on to say, "The constitution is a trap they put in my path, but if I have to choose between saving the nation or foregoing the constitution, I will not vacillate in choosing the country."[23] Certainly by giving Congress alone the power to declare war and raise troops in the event of internal or external emergencies, the constitution "disarmed the chief executive in times of danger," as the French minister noted.[24] Regardless, García Moreno already showed an inclination to ignore constitutional provisions when they ill suited him, as the next section will show. Perhaps had he acted more consistently with the terms of the Constitution of 1861, he would have fared better with his moderate critics, both contemporary and future. García Moreno's character would not permit him to do so, however.

THE CONCORDAT AND CHURCH POLICY

Although the convention created a government that was federalist and supportive of individual liberties, it did insist on the exclusivity of the Catholic faith. Virtually every Latin American history textbook has focused upon García Moreno's proclerical policies as the centerpiece of his first administration—and with good reason, as the role of the church was the cornerstone for his vision of a modern state. These authors err, though, when they describe his government as a theocracy, a state where the church dominates the secular government.[25] Rather García Moreno envisioned that the church and its teachings would provide unity for the Catholic state. He wanted the church to serve the state, acting as a cultural ally, rather than be its master. Because of the importance of the role of the church, García Moreno cajoled the convention of 1861 to allow him to negotiate a formal treaty, or concordat, with the pope.

Pending those negotiations, the assembly attended to church-state business as usual. After independence, political leaders in Ecuador and elsewhere in Latin America asserted that the new republics had inherited extraordinary powers of appointment of clerics (the *patronato real* or royal patronage), which Pope Julius II had granted to the Spanish monarchy in 1508. In this instance, following past practices, the delegates selected José María Riofrío to be Quito's new archbishop, even though García Moreno thought little of him. Contemporaries viewed Riofrío as an agreeable man but reclusive and certainly no leader. García Moreno believed correctly that Riofrío would not favor the reforms that García Moreno intended to propose. He would later say about Riofrío, "Integrity without firmness is like color without substance" and "Archbishop Riofrío is so poor of spirit. . . . he should not serve as the superior in a monastery." The delegates also selected Remigio Esteves y Toral to fill Cuenca's vacant episcopate. Toral was a political choice, picked because of his influential in-law, Benigno Malo. García Moreno influenced some clerical appointments, for example, by executing a veto power over bad choices, "including my brother Manuel [now a minor official in the Guayaquil cathedral], whose election [to bishop of Cuenca] would be a deplorable calamity." The reason behind this particular veto was not explained. Perhaps the president had had a falling out with his oldest brother, feared charges of nepotism, or thought Manuel would not support the reform initiative. In any event, Manuel García Moreno spent the remainder of his career as a minor church official.[26] Based on these experiences, however, García Moreno believed the selection process for high church officials to be flawed. Therefore he wanted to replace the traditional "royal patronage" system.

García Moreno also hoped that the church would rid itself of the corruption plaguing its clergy in the past. Years of lax supervision and broken vows essentially meant that the native-born clerics set poor examples for their fellow citizens, a complaint voiced over a hundred years previously by royal emissaries Jorge Juan and Antonio de Ulloa. Because of the behavior of Ecuadorian-born clerics, García Moreno preferred to bring into Ecuador the new service orders of foreign monks and nuns, who virtuously followed the rules of their orders and would teach Ecuadorians Christian values and minister to their needs when they fell ill. To summarize his thoughts, García Moreno said, "The corruption of the clergy surpasses that of all other classes of society, but I am preparing to moralize the country and I am not afraid of the difficulties." One of Ecuador's most famous clergy, José María Yerovi, had long championed such a cause and particularly favored bringing back the morally strict Jesuits to lead this reform, as did García Moreno's acquaintance, the Chilean Jesuit José Ignacio Eyzaguirre Portales.[27] A few specific examples (and the archives are full of them) should be enough to document the widespread corruption.

Seducing women in the confessional was a common occurrence, García Moreno alleged. The practice of priests having concubines and families existed from colonial times, but García Moreno wanted to end it. For example, he denounced a priest "imitating Byron's Don Juan" who had seduced three upper-class young women and gone unpunished. He upbraided priests for drinking and abusing their charges. The police reported detaining a group of drunken monks from Santo Domingo, "an event that happens all too frequently." Disorderly priests and monks beat their parishioners. Many refused to follow the rules of their orders, leaving the cloisters for long periods of time and conveniently forgetting to wear their habits. Greedy clergy took advantage of their Indian parishioners. Although long outlawed by statute, corrupt priests overcharged Indians for sacraments. For example, a priest forced his Indian parishioners to pay an excessive fee of two gold *onzas*, or alternatively two hens and thirty-five eggs, to get married in the church (which obviously did nothing to promote morality). In sum, Ecuadorian priests and monks committed more than their fair share of the seven deadly sins.[28]

Along with these personal peccadilloes, García Moreno also objected to priests who incited their parishioners against the government. A priest who openly called for rebellion was transferred to Quito, where authorities could watch him. The government also kept surveillance on a priest who stirred up trouble in Latacunga.[29] Yet Ecuador was not alone in trying to resolve the problem of scandalous behavior on the part of the clergy. Both Peru and Brazil at the same time underwent major attempts at clerical reform, although each government played a less active role than García Moreno's in directing the changes.[30]

García Moreno blamed the lax behavior partially on the aforementioned patronage system that made clerical appointments political, and partially on the abuse of clerical *fueros* or privileges that prevented legal action against wayward priests. He found fault with the new archbishop who never acted, instead responding that he was either investigating the situation, sending an inspector to make an inquiry, or preparing to hold a trial. Even after Pope Pius ordered the archbishop and bishops to become more active and clean up corruption, not much happened. Such pusillanimous behavior infuriated García Moreno. He ordered the archbishop to punish a wayward priest "for the good of the Ecuadorian clergy," and demanded a list of monks expelled from monasteries for scandalous conduct. (Undoubtedly, the list was far shorter than García Moreno hoped.) In at least one case, García Moreno took the extraordinary step on his own of forcing a priest into exile in Brazil via the infamous Napo River route "because it was necessary for the honor and morality of the Ecuadorian clergy."[31]

Therefore García Moreno proposed that the Concordat include provisions for reforming the clergy as the basis for his Catholic nation. Many historians regarded the Concordat, although not formalized until 1866 after García Moreno left office, as his most important and controversial accomplishment during the first term. Fortunately for the president, García Moreno's wish for a Concordat coincided with the desires of Pope Pius IX, who had begun to sign a whole series of such agreements with European and Latin American nations. In fact, although García Moreno's critics like to point to his Concordat as evidence of his religious fanaticism, many other countries had similar arrangements patterned after the agreement Napoleon I fashioned with the Vatican in 1801. Meanwhile, as the negotiations were under way, García Moreno continued to urge the church to reform itself, but to no avail. Rather, wranglings over *fueros* and quarrels about appointments of lesser church officials continued to dominate church-state relations.[32]

At the end of 1861, García Moreno dispatched young Ignacio Ordóñez, archdeacon of the Cathedral at Cuenca and brother of his ally Carlos Ordóñez, on a dual mission. First, Ignacio contracted with certain French religious orders to teach in Ecuador's primary schools. Then he went on to the Vatican to negotiate the Concordat with Pius IX, who had ascended to the papacy in 1846 as a moderate reformer. The liberal Italian Revolution of 1848, which captured Rome and caused the pope to flee, fundamentally altered his thinking, however. Doctrinally he became substantially more conservative, proclaiming the controversial Syllabus of Errors denouncing liberalism and promoting the even more divisive doctrine of papal infallibility in 1871. Needless to say, García Moreno would find much to admire in this conservative pope, who seemed willing to work with countries eager to settle their differences with the Holy See. In any event, García Moreno gave Ordóñez eight specific instructions to follow in his negotiations and a single guiding principle: He "wanted the Church to have all the independence it needs to comply with its divine mission. The state will guarantee that freedom." While willing to grant the clergy autonomy in ecclesiastical matters, the president made it clear he wanted reform, including the right to close the most debauched monastic establishments.[33] Apparently Ordóñez exceeded his instructions but eventually he and the pope's chief advisor, Cardinal Jacobo Antonelli, initialed an agreement, which Ordóñez returned to Ecuador for García Moreno's signature.

As part of the arrangement, Pope Pius sent a papal delegate, Monsignor Francesco Tavani, to work out details on specific issues and to protect church interests. Tavani became a controversial figure, not only because he and García Moreno disagreed about several matters, but also because the impoverished Ecuadorian government had to pay his annual salary of 6,400 pesos, a princely sum. In any event García Moreno, grievously disappointed because the pope had not included specific language in the Concordat that would require clerical reform, sent Ordóñez back to the Vatican in July 1862 to modify the document. García Moreno reiterated his desire for reform: "The Concordat is the basis for the reform of the clergy, on which depends the regeneration of the country."[34] By the fall of 1862, Ordóñez and Cardinal Antonelli had agreed upon language that would satisfy García Moreno. Ordóñez returned to Ecuador with the treaty, which the president personally ratified in April 1863. As García Moreno confided to the French minister, "the Concordat will deliver a blow to Ecuadorian clergy." Ordóñez predicted trouble from liberals in congress: "Some small number will say . . . to celebrate the Concordat is to take a step backwards." To commemorate the formal exchange of signatures, García Moreno ordered a special Mass at the cathedral, where he was compared to the Roman Emperor Constantine and the French King Louis IX, Saint Louis. Once the Mass ended, the loud ringing of bells throughout the city accompanied a military parade.[35]

The treaty's twenty-five articles profoundly altered church-state relations in the country, in that the Concordat embraced the ultramontanist philosophy of Pius IX. Ultramontanism essentially asserted the doctrine of papal supremacy in the global struggle against the liberal ideas emanating from the French Revolution. The Concordat changed the *patronato real* and permitted the president to choose from among three candidates (the *terna*) proposed by the clergy for all church offices. Roman Catholicism remained the only religion tolerated in Ecuador, and the church provided all education and determined the texts taught in school. In a practice prevented by some medieval kings, papal communications could pass unrestricted directly to the religious hierarchy, who were allowed to hold regional and national meetings. Most important, García Moreno believed that the reformed *fuero eclesiástico* would create a stricter, more moral clergy. The ancient *fuero* allowed clergy to be tried in canonical courts, which all too frequently winked at clerical immorality. In the rare case that the church court found the offender guilty, the accused could appeal to even more lenient civil courts. Now the Concordat ended domestic appeals and required the cases go directly to Rome, where stricter standards would presumably be enforced.

The pope agreed to send a letter to monastic orders informing them that they must strictly follow their rules, and Apostolic Delegate Tavani was empowered to bring new, more disciplined orders into the country to supplement the roughly 203 Ecuadorian nuns and 236 monks. Further, if a member of a religious community committed a criminal offense (such as fornication, drunkenness, or concubinage), ecclesiastical privilege did not pertain and civil authorities could try the person. Churches could no longer be used as places of asylum by political rebels. Other interesting provisions allowed the church to purchase real estate (a right being taken away in liberal states), to create new dioceses as well as retain two-thirds of the tithe income. García Moreno's celebration proved premature, though.[36]

Almost immediately, an outcry arose against the Concordat both on procedural and substantive grounds, and not just from the "few liberals" that Ignacio Ordóñez had predicted. Moderate liberal Pedro Carbo, as president of the Municipal Council in Guayaquil, drafted a document criticizing the Concordat, which focused the debate. First, Carbo argued, García Moreno had signed off on the Concordat unconstitutionally because the enabling legislation from 1861 called for congressional ratification. More important, Carbo's fellow moderate liberals, like Manuel Gómez de la Torre and Cuencan Francisco J. Aguirre (both allies from the civil war), argued that abolishing the old *patronato* was equivalent to relinquishing sovereignty over the church. One of García Moreno's short-term governors suspended the clerical appointment article as the debate swirled, while Governor Nicolás Martínez questioned the legal relationship between civil authorities and monks.[37] Ironically, opposition to the Concordat brought together an unlikely alliance of moderate liberals and the leaders of the Ecuadorian church itself, who resisted any change. Limiting the *fuero*, creating new dioceses that would reduce bishops' salaries, and enforcing monastic vows all caused the clergy to balk, and their numerous supporters in congress represented them well. As Minister of War Daniel Salvador noted, the high clergy acted "not for love of the Holy Father, but to avoid the plan to reduce their salaries to a fixed and moderate one."[38] No clearer proof exists that García Moreno was not a dictator during his first term than his inability to force the Concordat on congress in 1863.

Trying to be persuasive, he argued in his "State of the Union" message on August 10 that his ratification of the Concordat conformed completely to the law. Under no circumstances could the legislature reject the agreement, he argued. If it did so, he would resign as a point of honor. Relenting significantly in the next few days, however, García Moreno opened the door to modifications, agreeing that the Concordat could be improved and suggesting that the legislature make specific amendments. García Moreno's willingness to compromise, which surprised the papal delegate, augered well for sustaining his coalition and pleased Juan José Flores, among others. Although a few diehards like Pedro Carbo hoped to kill the Concordat altogether, most legislators worked on revisions. One proposed amendment allotted bishops and the lesser clergy fixed salaries instead of the proceeds of the tithe. Another limited the jurisdiction of church courts to matters of canon law alone. And a third allowed the government to dissolve monasteries refusing to abide by their regulations.[39] García Moreno sympathized with some of these ideas because he had grown impatient with corrupt clergy who continued to misbehave. During these debates, ongoing scandals included a public fracas between a group of monks dressed as soldiers and police, as well as another case where a monk was caught out of his habit (and most of his other clothes), drinking with his girlfriend.[40]

The debate raged for almost two months. In the end the Senate adopted the three ideas listed above, and added a fourth that allowed the bulk of tithe revenues to fall into government hands. García Moreno, by now embroiled in a foreign policy crisis with Colombia, appeared obedient to congressional wishes. Privately, however, he wondered whether a signed treaty could be revised. As he told Antonio Flores, "It is true I agreed to reforms. . . . but I accepted them because of the [Colombian] threat." In the spring of 1864, he sent Antonio Flores to the Vatican, appealing to Pope Pius to renegotiate the Concordat within the "spirit" of the congressional resolution (although he doubted success). Privately he declared: "The odious issue of the tithe, in particular, might cause the Pope to refuse further changes."[41]

Granted an audience with Pope Pius on October 3, 1864, Antonio Flores overcame the pope's initial negative impression caused by yet another request for changes in the Concordat. With the pontiff's mood improved (although he was a genuinely affable man), Flores met with Cardinal Antonelli to try to resolve outstanding issues. The cardinal yielded on the *fuero* issue and granted Ecuador the same terms (abolition of the privilege except in purely ecclesiastical cases) as in other Latin American concordats like those of El Salvador, Costa Rica, and Guatemala. Antonelli also agreed that the state could dissolve monasteries for corrupt practices. Finally the diplomats debated the tithe issue. At Antonio Flores' request, Cardinal Antonelli granted the state almost all the tithe revenue for 1863 and 1864 because of the costs of the Colombian war, but held firm on its permanent disposition. Eventually Flores and Antonelli came to an agreement similar to the one with Venezuela: to have a committee of clergy and citizens work out the precise details.[42] García Moreno was quite pessimistic that such a commission would succeed. He petulantly complained, "The tithe is the only question pending. The Holy See wants to agree with our bishops, and they will not agree to give up even a portion of their enormous incomes." The commission seemed weighted in favor of the church—comprising three clergy, with Pablo Herrera (himself a cleric) representing the government. Yet the commission and the pope concurred in 1866 that church and state should divide the tithe equally, so that the government's share in effect increased from 33 ¹/₃ percent to 50 percent.[43]

Despite such nagging issues, García Moreno moved quickly to implement a provision of the Concordat that he regarded as one of the most important. Even before the negotiations had begun, the president had suggested that the pope create three more dioceses in the country (at Ibarra, Riobamba, and Loja) to supplement the existing ones at Quito, Guayaquil, and Cuenca. Just as the lower clergy lobbied against the Concordat's proposals restricting their *fuero* appeal process, the wealthy bishops hated the idea of new dioceses, since tithe revenue would now be divided six ways instead of three. García Moreno complained about the bishop of Guayaquil earning 54,000 pesos a year—an absurd sum, in his opinion. Instead Congress proposed a salary of 8,000 pesos (still a substantial amount) for the bishop of Guayaquil, and lesser salaries of 4,000 pesos for the remaining five bishops.[44] García Moreno also believed that decentralizing the church would better meet the spiritual needs of more Ecuadorians. Of the roughly 385 priests active in Ecuador in 1860, most lived in the three principal cities. Establishing bishoprics in other regions would diffuse the clergy over the countryside and further the goal of moralizing the country.

In 1862 García Moreno conferred with General Flores and wrote the governors of the provinces where the three proposed dioceses would be erected to ascertain their opinions. The new bishops, García Moreno wrote Flores, "would be an excellent means of moralizing our depraved clergy" (presumably by closer supervision) and would result in a wider distribution of the tithes. The governor of Loja talked about the local "explosion of enthusiasm" for the idea, averring that his clergy had celebrated a Te Deum Mass to thank the government. The governor of Imbabura went further. Not only did having a local bishop for Ibarra promise better conduct on the part of the clergy, he said, but it would also bring greater wealth into the community. Chimborazo's governor, Bernardo Dávalos, enthusiastically supported the creation of new bishoprics, too.[45] These responses heightened García Moreno's enthusiasm. "I believe that the evil clergy are upset by the Concordat and the establishment of the new dioceses; this is proof that the reforms are intrinsically good." He ranted against "the greediness of the bishops opposed to the new dioceses because they don't want their incomes diminished."[46] Due to the delays associated with the ratification of the Concordat and the bishops' lobbying the pope, the three dioceses did not materialize until late in 1865. The new bishop of Riobamba, Ignacio Ordóñez, accepted his office despite gossip suggesting that he had used his earlier mission to the Vatican to promote himself, a charge the newly consecrated bishop denied at length to Antonio Flores.[47] Ibarra, likewise, opened its diocese without incident.

Loja posed two additional problems and thus took longer for its cathedral to start operating. The Concordat mandated every diocese to have a seminary to train its own priests. Struggling to find a suitable space in Loja City, officials finally decided that an unused secondary school could serve as the seminary building. Eventually Governor Manuel Eguiguren, a friend of García Moreno, completed the repairs on it. Second, the newly created diocese had to overcome the objections of the Bishop of Cuenca, who believed that Loja could not generate enough revenue to pay the salaries of the cathedral chapter (officials). Meanwhile García Moreno helped out. He ordered Ignacio Ordóñez to advance money from the tithe to pay for Loja's expenses. Some of the discord resolved itself when the commission established by the Concordat reached the final agreement about dividing the church's share of the tithe. The bishop of Guayaquil received the most total revenue (83,000 pesos for all salaries in his diocese) and the three new dioceses the least (30,000 pesos each). In addition to the stipends of church officials, the dioceses paid the costs of all existing schools and hospitals in their jurisdictions. All new social services (including education) would be funded by the government, however.[48] García Moreno had succeeded, then, in decentralizing the church, enforcing closer scrutiny of wayward priests and monks, and reducing the luxury in which the leading prelates lived. No wonder the hierarchy did its utmost to sabotage the Concordat!

As part of García Moreno's plan to create a Catholic nation, he wanted to spread the faith and sacraments to the local level. As a result the dioceses, old and new, created many additional parishes during these years. Population increases throughout the highlands in the mid-nineteenth century increased demands for new parishes. One priest reported that the laity in a remote town were performing the sacraments themselves because he could not get there frequently enough even to look after the mortally ill, and he

Clerics, the agents to reform the "Catholic Nation" (Permission of the Banco Central del Ecuador)

worried about the spiritual consequences.[49] In Ecuador's poorest province, Esmeraldas, the governor described a desperate situation. For a want of priests (the whole province had only three), "the people live like savages and die like brutes" and "if you do not attend to morality, which is at the core of progress, the criminal element will destroy society." Priests resisted going to Esmeraldas because of its deadly climate and pervading poverty, but after the Concordat the situation slowly improved. (Liberals were inclined to deny the shortage of priests, pointing out that Ecuador—with its much smaller population—now had the same number of bishops as Peru.)

All these parishes had to be economically self-sufficient because parish priests subsisted on the modest fees set by statute and generated from services like baptisms, marriages, and funerals. In addition, parish priests earned revenue from the compulsory Masses held on the village's patron saint's feast day, the Feast of the Immaculate Conception, Corpus Christi, and All Souls' Day.[50] Making the ritual available to more parishioners, then, furthered García Moreno's vision of creating a national spiritual community. Whether this vision, imposed like Bolivarian liberalism from the top down, would influence ordinary Ecuadorians over the long run remained a critical issue.

EDUCATION AND CHARITABLE WORKS

If the Concordat was the cornerstone for García Moreno's conservative state formation project, then his educational system and plan for social services constituted the foundation. Because of the difficulties described in chapter 4, García Moreno could only lay a portion of that foundation during his first term. Sound parochial education, he believed, would spread the values of Catholic civilization to the youth of Ecuador, who in turn would influence the generations to come. During García Moreno's first presidency, limited resources meant that he could only slightly expand primary and secondary educational opportunities and health care. In García Moreno's vision, religious men and women from European monastic orders could provide an inexpensive way for the country to reinvent itself.

Many Ecuadorians echoed García Moreno's cry for increased and improved education. Although it is hardly fair to pick on the nation's poorest province, Esmeraldas provided a classic case. Only three grammar schools and one secondary school existed in the whole region, condemning the residents there "to a life of ignorance and barbarism." "Civilization is far from lighting its lamp in this dark and ignorant province," the governor wrote.[51] In the highland districts, larger towns like Latacunga and Pujilí had primary schools, but few of the truly rural parishes enjoyed that luxury. Like Esmeraldas, most highland provinces had a single secondary school, although comparably better funded and staffed. On the coast an inspector found Manabí's elementary schools "in a deplorable state, only existing in the largest towns like Jipijapa."[52]

Given this bleak picture and the near universal desire of the new leadership to improve education, the convention delegates in 1861 took two remedial steps. First, they abolished the "free studies" concept that allowed university students to earn a degree by passing examinations without attending class, a reform García Moreno had urged since the time he served as rector of the University of Quito. Second, the convention authorized García Moreno to send agents abroad to contract with teaching orders. Liberals criticized him for seeking clerical educators, yet the foremost author on education in this epoch, Julio Tobar Donoso, wrote: "Who else would volunteer to come to Ecuador to serve for a paltry 30 or 40 pesos a year in salary?" To García Moreno's dismay, however, the congressional education statute of 1863, consistent with its tendency to favor regional interests, effectively federalized education, putting the creation and staffing of schools under the authority of each province's council of education.[53]

García Moreno's European envoys, Antonio Flores and Ignacio Ordóñez, negotiated contracts with the heads of appropriate religious orders for teachers and nurses. Shortly after the administration took office, García Moreno gave Ordóñez 15,000 francs to arrange a contract and sea passage for several Sisters of the Sacred Heart of Jesus who had agreed to teach girls in Cuenca and Quito. The agents also negotiated a contract with France's Christian Brothers to educate boys. Under García Moreno's ambitious plan, never realized during the first term, every parish would have a boys' school and eventually a girls' school as well. To improve secondary education, he wanted Jesuits to staff at least one secondary school in every province.[54] In short, García Moreno wanted to increase the quantity and quality of students' educational experiences because he knew from his European travels the reputation for excellence that both the Jesuits and the Christian Brothers schools enjoyed.

Specifically García Moreno believed that the Christian Brothers with their "La Salle pedagogy" would offer a high-quality education focusing on the basics (reading, writing, and mathematics) while also promoting Christian morality and spiritual awareness. Father Jean Baptiste de la Salle, who had organized this order of teaching brethren in the seventeenth century, rigorously opposed the Lancastrian method of teaching, where a "master" controlled ten or more "monitors" who in turn each instructed ten or more students. Believing that the Lancastrian system removed the teacher too far from the pupil, La Salle advocated more teachers working directly with students. In addition the Christian Brothers emphasized their duty to teach the poor and downtrodden—even prison inmates. Their mission and methodology attracted García Moreno.

Soon members of the Christian Brothers began to arrive in Ecuador, establishing boys' schools in renovated monastic buildings in Cuenca and Quito. The Brothers unveiled their modern teaching methods and added courses in French and drawing to the standard curriculum. When the official government newspaper, *El Nacional,* trumpeted the success of the Christian Brothers' experiment in Cuenca, other provinces began to clamor for the new teachers. For example, the governor of Chimborazo sent a survey to each community asking about the possibility of creating Christian Brothers schools and asking whether appropriate facilities were available. In Manabí, authorities excitedly pressed for the new schools.[55]

Because the education statute mandated local control, García Moreno could only encourage governors to establish provincial inspectors of education to ensure quality. Consequently these inspectors reported in a sporadic fashion to the secretary of the interior (*gobierno*). Like the rest of the Garcian projects discussed further in the next section, public education got off to a haphazard start because of limited finances and the decentralized system of government. Yet despite the misgivings of U.S. Minister Friedrich Hassaurek, who disliked the church-run system, ordinary Ecuadorians clearly desired the educational opportunities promised by García Moreno. As the villagers of one small parish stated in their request for a public school: "We see primary education as the foundation of public happiness and the future of families." [56]

Girls' education progressed more slowly. Once Sisters of the Sacred Heart of Jesus (the order that would staff the girls' schools) reached Ecuador, elite and middle-class daughters flocked to their institutions. The students learned not only the three R's, but also penmanship, Spanish grammar, deportment, and home economics—consistent with the mission of the new education: moral Christian doctrine. The government even provided scholarships for "poor girls to extend their education." By the end of García Moreno's first term, 57 nuns had been brought to Ecuador at government expense to staff the various girls' schools. Students paid tuition while private individuals or local governments donated funding to maintain buildings and provide scholarships where necessary.[57] While most writers have concluded that the education of females made great strides during the García Moreno epoch, U.S. Minister Friedrich Hassaurek demurred. Thus Hassaurek reported that the nuns, "being ignorant and bigoted themselves . . . will not work important educational reforms." As one governor noted, though, educating girls was essential to the Garcian project because "the fair sex prepares the way for the regeneration of Ecuadorian society."[58] Women traditionally held such positions in Latin American patriarchal culture. As the more pure and religious gender, they were viewed as the instruments for redeeming their sinful and corrupt spouses.

Secondary education remained at a standstill because the Jesuits refused to come to Ecuador from Europe until a contract had been signed. Moderate liberals objected to the Jesuits. Vicente Piedrahita, for example, wanted the secondary school curriculum to include more philosophy and humanities courses that were in "the moral and material interests of the province," while García Moreno preferred the Jesuits because they also taught math and science. García Moreno sought to overcome those concerns by saying, "We must reorganize secondary school teaching. We must have good establishments to do preparatory teaching." García Moreno would have to wait until the end of July 1863 for the Jesuit contract. Hence only a limited number of Jesuits arrived during García Moreno's first term, enough to staff one high school in Quito and another in Guayaquil. The Jesuits also agreed to undertake missionary work in the Oriente.[59]

An improved health care system began during the first term, led by the Sisters of Charity. The state of Ecuador's medical profession in the 1860s, at least in the opinion of outsiders, was deplorable. Crowded unsanitary conditions made hospitals particularly dangerous, with lepers, the insane, and even prisoners being housed near other patients. Bleeding remained a favorite cure. Because of the poor state of training of most Ecuadorian physicians, wealthy individuals preferred to be treated at home. Poor people, especially those in rural areas, resorted to folk healers, or *curanderos.*[60] As with educational facilities, the larger cities received the first grants of funds from their respective state governments (with some help from the national government and private donors) to pay for the hospitals. Guayaquil was certainly a pesthole, especially for yellow fever. The governor and bishop therefore argued a desperate need, urging García Moreno to pay the costs of bringing the Sisters of Charity from France.[61] The explosion of demands for hospitals and health care proved to be another expense that the García Moreno government could not yet afford because of the cost of disastrous relations with its neighbors and a downturn in exports.

Just as the outline of García Moreno's dreams for schools and hospitals emerged in the early 1860s, so too did a précis for his moral betterment of the Ecuadorian people. Not only did he hope to imbue Catholic values in the *gente decente,* the largely urban upper and middle classes, but he also hoped to change the lower classes. The process proved slow. He lamented that the morality laws were not sufficiently strict. He wanted to alter Indian behavior by requiring the people to attend church, something his predecessors failed to do because Sunday was also traditionally market day in the Andes. Despite García Moreno's wishes, only a few local governments voluntarily shifted market day to Saturday at this time, because the federalist Constitution of 1861 allowed municipalities alone to make the decision.[62]

The president believed he could promote the Catholic nation-building project by having his government, and himself, set an example. For example, a decree in 1861 required all members of the government to attend Mass together on specific occasions. They met first at the Government Palace and walked to the cathedral in procession. Provincial governments were required to follow the same procedure locally. The president also spent Holy Week locked in a monastery, contemplating his sins. He customarily would carry a large wooden cross throughout the streets in the Good Friday procession, a sight that provoked a great deal of commentary among foreign diplomats. Although the U.S. minister may have been oblivious to the importance of that ritual to convey the moral values of the administration, both García Moreno and modern commentators have understood it. Pedro II, the dignified Brazilian monarch, also carried religious symbols like crosses and statues of Christ in religious parades in Rio de Janeiro. In part, then, García Moreno contributed to his vision of the Catholic state by modeling devout behavior for his fellow citizens.[63]

THE DEVELOPMENT OF PUBLIC WORKS

Just as education and moral values provided the foundation for García Moreno's Catholic nation, so his economic development and public works program became the mechanical, electrical, and technological systems that made the metaphorical building modern. Those writers who would caricature the García Moreno government as a medieval or colonial-retrograde regime fail to acknowledge his Janus-like characteristics. Accepting the liberal dogma of free trade, progress, and economic development, García Moreno hoped to unite the Ecuadorian people more tangibly through his extensive public works program. He dreamed of breaking down regional barriers by constructing roads, bridges, and eventually even a railroad that would radically alter the country. Yet García Moreno did not conceive of roads and public works as ends unto themselves, but rather as means to the end of creating a growing export economy united to world markets through modified free trade.[64] During his first term, García Moreno could only lay the framework for economic development. Wars, military expenses, debt obligations, and an economic downturn in 1864 all delayed his public works program.

Building a road system required sizeable revenues, since the geography of the Andes made construction expensive. Since Ecuador had no educational institution to train engineers, foreign technocrats had to be hired to design and direct each project. Resources to fund these expenses during García Moreno's first term were nearly as scarce as the statistics that evidence them. Throughout the nineteenth century, the government's largest source of income came from taxes on exports, especially cacao, although corruption and smuggling hemorrhaged these revenues. During García Moreno's first term, 35 percent of this revenue was pledged to pay interest on the foreign debt, primarily to the aforementioned British bondholders, and much of the remainder paid civil and military salaries. Customs income in 1861 amounted to about 879,000 pesos. In 1863, the only year for which there are good statistics, the government took in 1,350,000 pesos from all sources, nearly half of which came from the export tax.[65] As already discussed, García Moreno enhanced governmental revenue from the tithe by reducing the church's share of the tax from two-thirds to one-half. Additional monies came from *aguardiente* (the fiery sugarcane alcohol consumed by the indigenous people, especially on market day) and salt, both government monopolies. Yet wars, the unpopularity of tax collectors, and wealthy Ecuadorians' historical refusal to pay their fair share of taxes made the revenue picture uncertain. Because of the unfair burden placed on the lower classes, armed guards sometimes accompanied tax collectors as they made their rounds through the countryside.[66] Many accounts of Ecuador's tax structure, however, omit another source of revenue creating discord during García Moreno's first term: the *trabajo subsidiario,* originally intended to fund local public works.

Created in 1825, this tax replaced the *mita* labor levy of pre-Hispanic origin requiring all subjects to labor for the state each year on public works. During the colonial period, the Spaniards perverted that policy and forced Indians to work on both public and private projects (like the silver mines at Potosí or the gold mines of Zaruma), a strategy that at times prevented Indians from planting or harvesting their crops. Hence the law of 1825 was intended as a reform, limiting the *mita* to four days a year of unpaid labor—or alternatively, payment of the tax in equivalent cash value. Early legislators conceived of the tax as a local one to be collected by the municipalities and used to maintain public buildings and roads within the canton.[67] García Moreno, however, wanted to nationalize these tax proceeds. He therefore decreed in 1861 that the tax must be paid in cash, from which revenue the state would pay voluntary laborers on state-organized projects. To complete his roads, he would need labor gangs for periods much longer than four days because the work stretched into remote regions. Thus García Moreno wanted to convert the *trabajo subsidiario* into a fund to buy free labor. In so doing, though, he angered regional interests.

García Moreno was incensed at the recalcitrance of local governments to contribute to national public works projects. He argued (erroneously) that the Constitutional Assembly had intended for the *trabajo subsidiario* to be dedicated to the national roads. By decree in 1862, he demanded control of these revenues, while several local governments petitioned that they be retained to subsidize more local development projects. The tax remained unpopular. The governor of Loja had problems collecting from the Saraguru (one of Ecuador's most independent-minded groups of indigenous people), so he sent soldiers "to make the Indians respect the law." Guayaquil outright defied García Moreno's mandate, when the city council, led by Pedro Carbo, claimed that said money had already been committed to local urban repairs.[68]

As historian Linda Rodríguez has demonstrated, sources of revenue available to the government essentially doubled during García Moreno's fifteen years of dominance. At the same time, however, the government became more ambitious and activist, as exemplified in its public works objectives.[69] To maximize available revenues, García Moreno wanted to cut what he regarded as the less important expenditures, at times suspending the foreign debt and reducing the military budget. He talked incessantly about the possibility of downsizing the army. "I am opposed to this mad sacrifice of the public taxes," he said, referring to military expenses. Clearly he was worried as he looked at the forecasts for 1862. "Military expenses have risen to 800,000 pesos; if we don't reduce them we cannot build roads or do any reforms." As noted previously, to cut military expenses in 1861 the government proposed to muster out significant portions of the regular army and replace them with National Guard units, who would be at the ready in times of emergency but at their normal employment (and hence off the payroll) the remainder of the time.[70] The two wars with Colombia described in chapter 4, however, made it impossible to bring military expenses under control. "We will choke for the lack of alternatives to reducing military expenses," García Moreno complained, as he increased the size of the army to meet the crises. Even after the wars the government clung to the idea of a National Guard as a means of reducing military expenses—despite the guard's unruliness, penchant for revolt, and the presence of dissidents therein. García Moreno had fewer compunctions about slashing bureaucratic salaries in times of emergency.[71]

As financial difficulties threatened to close down García Moreno's public works program, he thought he could salvage the situation by obtaining a loan abroad. As a result, Antonio Flores received instructions to negotiate a $3 million peso loan in London. With this money, García Moreno hoped to pay off internal debt, as well as purchase tools along with the services of more engineers to plan the road. By the end of 1862, Antonio Flores' efforts had proven fruitless. Generally unwilling to lend money to an unstable country like Ecuador, both British and French bankers rejected all propositions. As Antonio Flores confided to the secretary of the treasury, "There is no possibility of getting a loan without being current on the interest of the debt. . . . This is an insuperable obstacle."[72] With no possibility of a foreign loan, García Moreno, after consulting with his brother Pedro Pablo, decided to issue paper currency—which had no gold or silver behind it, only the "full faith and credit" of the government that the paper would be redeemed. In turn the bank, owned by rich cacao merchant Manuel Antonio de Luzárraga, loaned hard cash to the government for necessary transactions. García Moreno decreed that the populace must accept the paper in the regular course of business. Short-term loans quickly became the cornerstone of fiscal policy. Because of this ongoing need, Luzárraga received priority repayment.[73]

For many years Ecuador's leaders had wanted to improve the country's miserable roads. Both General Flores and Vicente Rocafuerte had unsuccessfully attempted to encourage road construction, but little had changed between then and the 1860s. During García Moreno's first term, he mapped out the skeletal framework of the road system. First he wanted to construct a wide and smooth carriage road running from Quito to Guayaquil. Almost immediately after taking office, García Moreno persuaded his old mountain-climbing friend, Sebastián Wisse, to return from Europe to serve as the supervising engineer for "the great enterprise that will change the face of the Republic." Delays occurred because Wisse took his time returning and then died after a stroke in June 1863. The first Colombian war, financial exigencies, and rainy weather also took their toll. For a while the government had to suspend work on the road.[74] As a result, when García Moreno left office in 1865, the road reached only to Riobamba.

The engineers wanted a carriage road wide and level enough to convey both people and freight to the coast. Therefore hills had to be carved away and depressions filled. Indian laborers moved the earth with simple tools, carrying the loose dirt in sacks on their backs. They lugged most of the building materials used in the project. One of the engineers pleaded with the government to smelt old cannons into tools (metaphorical swords into ploughshares), arguing that the lack of implements was significantly delaying the project. In addition, the basins along the sierra, sliced by hundreds of rivers and streams, needed expensive bridges to create a modern highway. The number and size of these projects further delayed the completion of the road. Most bridges had bases made of stone or limestone—hauled into place by Indians, of course. Bridge construction also required professional technical assistance, time, and hard work.[75] In addition to the Quito-Guayaquil road occupying so much of García Moreno's efforts, he contemplated building five other roads. They will be discussed further in chapter 7, since not much progress was made on them during the first term.

Some historians have suggested that the large highland landowners, García Moreno's allies in the civil war, opposed road construction because the work removed *peones* from their control and ended their isolation, making it easier for people to flee to the coast. Some evidence supports this hypothesis. The governor of Los Ríos reported that various proprietors from the neighboring province of Chimborazo actively impeded road construction, apparently by refusing to allow contracted workers to leave their haciendas. Landlords elsewhere for similar reasons did not want a road even near their estates.[76] Many landlords and local officials, however, saw great value in the road project. As one governor stated, "no doubt this is a great work . . . and demands great sacrifices" (of the local tax revenue). Landlords preferred that the government seize property other than theirs for the project, yet some voluntarily contributed land and labor to the great road effort.[77] Clearly landed proprietors, like people and communities in the U.S. West, understood that roads would help them get their goods to market. "The difficulties are great, but the perseverance greater," García Moreno wrote his friend Antonio Flores. When various exigencies like wars and floods caused work on the road to stop, the government assured local communities that the project would be resumed as quickly as practicable.[78]

Because of the ongoing debate over the uses of the *trabajo subsidiario* during the first term, municipalities kept some of the tax to modernize locally. In Quito, English engineers built the Tunnel of Peace, which allowed *quiteños* easier access to the valley south of the Old City. García Moreno also leveled the streets as much as possible, given the city's hilly terrain. To promote public health, he also required homeowners to clean the streets in front of their residences and banned public urination. Finally the administration fixed the aging Government Palace, repairing the portico and purchasing an expensive French clock that could be illuminated at night by kerosene.[79] Perhaps this purchase symbolized both progress and García Moreno's hope that other government officials would follow his example and work into the evening.

Because Pedro Carbo, president of Guayaquil's municipal council, refused to turn the *trabajo subsidiario* over to the national treasury, the city pressed forward with a number of public works projects on its own in these years. First, the municipality wanted to create a potable water supply. The government entertained two competing proposals from European firms, but García Moreno imposed conditions that made both unworkable. The influential Veintemilla family, whose company held an exclusive contract to bring bottled water (probably barreled) to the city, lobbied against the project as well. Because they numbered themselves among García Moreno's coastal supporters, he would not countenance offending them.[80] Despite the failure of the potable water proposals, Guayaquil's city council repaired streets and public buildings, and also contracted for and built a public library. The city spent money on public health as well, specifically by cleaning up the less than sanitary slaughterhouse.[81] Other cities made civic improvements, too, but to a much lesser degree.

Like other Andean leaders, García Moreno believed that modernization included advancing the nation's intellectual tone in the sciences and arts. Given his personal background, he particularly favored the sciences. Hence he created a National Academy of Sciences and Literature (led by Dr. Miguel Egas) and formed a school of anatomy, which published its findings "for the love of civilization and knowledge."[82] His pet project, unrealized in the first term, was the astronomical observatory that now stands in the Alameda. Again the lack of funds hampered the endeavor. "I will offer the land and the building, half of the salary and expenses, and France will pay the other half," he suggested to his representative abroad, Antonio Flores. But financial stringencies in France prevented Napoleon III, despite his intellectual curiosity, from pursuing the project. Thus construction of the observatory had to wait.[83] For the fine arts, García Moreno, at the request of painter Luis Cadena, revived the Academy of Painting and Drawing, gave it a new facility with good light, and built a museum that would showcase the masterpieces of the Quito school of colonial art.[84]

THE ELECTIONS OF 1865

To describe the political culture of nineteenth-century Spanish America as democratic would be misleading. Despite regular elections, fraud occurred frequently, as parties or individuals in power almost never lost office via the ballot box. This latter phenomenon in part explains the absence both in Ecuador and elsewhere in Spanish America of the notion of the loyal opposition, so integral to western European and United States politics, where fair elections would ultimately bring the "outs" to power. García Moreno, like so many Spanish American political leaders, justified meddling in the process by arguing that otherwise his accomplishments might be undone by a liberal successor. The Constitution of 1861 barred

García Moreno from succeeding himself. Hence during his last year in office he labored to find a candidate who would continue his work of providing stability and prosperity while developing the Catholic State. In addition he wanted to make certain that his friends won the congressional elections in 1864.[85]

Finding a suitable presidential candidate proved more onerous. Initially García Moreno favored Jerónimo Carrión over Benigno Malo because he believed Carrión possessed a "better character." In García Moreno's view, Malo had been weak and unreliable as Cuenca's governor during his recent term. García Moreno desperately wanted a popular and strong candidate. "It would almost be an act of heresy to the country to leave the electoral field abandoned to the mercy of the intriguers." Apparently, however, García Moreno's friends along the coast did not like Carrión. The president therefore proposed José María Caamaño, a conservative wealthy planter from Guayaquil who had recently moved to Quito: "a person . . . of integrity, honesty and energy." In explaining his choice, García Moreno stated that the coast would not accept another president from the interior and if such a candidate prevailed, the coast would welcome an Urbina rebellion.[86]

García Moreno's discussion about potential presidential candidates underscores two very pertinent themes. First, political parties in the modern sense did not emerge in Ecuador until the 1880s. During García Moreno's time, politics were intensely personal. Elections depended on coalitions, patronage networks, and cliques put together by a particular candidate. The nature of this informal structure made coalitions particularly fragile, especially when a person with a volatile temper, controversial policies, and an unwillingness to tolerate dissent like García Moreno was in charge. Second, a wiser and more temperate García Moreno would have accepted and encouraged a loyal opposition to emerge. Manuel Gómez de la Torre, part of the triumvirate during the 1859 civil war, for example, had remained loyal to the government and, while critical of the Concordat, could well have filled this role. Pedro Carbo had similar possibilities. Nevertheless García Moreno could not tolerate either man. Instead he labeled Pedro Carbo "the most foolish of the intriguers" and Gómez de la Torre "the greatest intriguer of the foolish ones."[87]

García Moreno felt well prepared as 1865 dawned: "In elections as in war, discipline will triumph." Counting on a majority both on the coast and in the interior, he expected Caamaño to prevail despite the "lies" of the opposition. As García Moreno confidently told Governor Nicolás Martínez: "The question will be simple: on one side Caamaño and all the venerable men, and on the other Gómez [de la Torre] and all the rogues." And of course García Moreno was not above using coercion to make certain his candidate won. He closed the Gómez de la Torre club in Quito because some of its members allegedly had affiliations with Urbina. Warning his governor of Los Ríos to prevent a similar organization from operating there, the president said, "It would return us to the time of compromises. . . . If another candidate is elected, there will surely be . . . a return of the bandits" (Urbina and his friends).[88]

Then in February, García Moreno's whole plan came unraveled because Caamaño objected to the closing of the Gómez de la Torre societies and the jailing of their members. The candidate pleaded for García Moreno to free political prisoners, to which the president privately responded that the Gómez de la Torre partisans had been implicated in a serious conspiracy occurring the previous June (see chapter 4) and that while he would free the prisoners, he would not let the club reopen its doors. Caamaño retorted that he believed in the "free suffrage of the people" and freedom of the press, withdrawing his candidacy. The rhetoric got hotter when García Moreno mailed out a manifesto in which he explained his reasons for closing the Gómez de la Torre political action committee. God would not permit a weak administration, he argued, and therefore Ecuadorians had a patriotic duty to select a candidate other than Caamaño. In García Moreno's opinion, the choice came down to the two remaining candidates, Gómez de la Torre and Carrión. "It is clear that only Carrión has the right qualities. I was Gómez's compadre in the provisional government, and I assure you on my honor that Sr. Gómez does not have the talents to be a true statesman."[89]

García Moreno continued to praise Carrión as honorable, energetic, and irreconcilably opposed to the bandits. (The word "energetic" in Spanish also infers the willingness to take strong action against enemies, a characteristic García Moreno wanted to see in his successor.) Now he urged his friends to work for Carrión's election.[90] Even though Jerónimo Carrión had once served Francisco Robles as vice-president, his credentials as a conservative and status as a leading politician from Cuenca (where García Moreno wanted to restore his linkages damaged by the fight over the Concordat) made Carrión seem like the perfect choice.

The election in May 1865 went as García Moreno hoped. Early returns showed Carrión winning in Quito and also in rural Pichincha (only one-quarter of the registered voters in the province lived in the capital). In Loja,

Carrión won by a three-to-one margin. Overall he secured 19,000 out of 25,000 votes as, in García Moreno's words, "The people showed intelligence and enthusiasm." The United States, French, and British ministers thought the balloting fair, while recognizing that Gómez de la Torre had been materially disadvantaged by the arrest of various leaders of his faction. All three diplomats seemed pleased that Carrión had won because he pledged to continue García Moreno's programs. And all three concurred (erroneously) that García Moreno would exert a very strong influence over the new president.[91] García Moreno continued to serve as president until Jerónimo Carrión's inauguration on September 5, 1865. To many observers' surprise, García Moreno had served out his full four-year term despite the incessant difficulties he faced from insurgents, Peru, and Colombia, as the next chapter will explain.

Chapter Four

A Presidency Constrained II: Foreign Entanglements, 1861–1865

As much as the federalist Constitution of 1861 and the shaky state of Ecuador's finances complicated García Moreno's desire to create a modern Catholic state, foreign policy difficulties and wars hampered progress even more. Many critical biographers have attributed Ecuador's foreign policy woes in the early 1860s to García Moreno's irascible and impetuous temperament, and rightly so. Whether slapping a minister who had insulted his brother-in-law or chiding a close friend who had not fully credited him for his mountain-climbing efforts, García Moreno had been long famous for his short temper. In addition García Moreno lacked patience, an important attribute in a good diplomat's arsenal. Although Rafael Carvajal, his former University of Quito schoolmate, formally headed foreign relations, García Moreno took such an activist role in his presidency that he constantly inserted himself into diplomatic affairs.[1] Because the Constitution of 1861 gave him more latitude in matters of foreign policy (although only congress could declare war), García Moreno may have been more assertive simply because of his frustrations with the contentious disputes over his domestic policy.

From the outset of his term, diplomatic issues plagued García Moreno. As long as Ramón Castilla held office, Peru remained a danger to Ecuador's survival. Castilla continued to send bullying diplomats, threaten naval blockades, and assist Urbina and Robles clandestinely, which kept Ecuador in a constant state of alert in the early 1860s. Likewise Colombia's caudillo, Tomás Cipriano de Mosquera, also saw Ecuador as a theater for his ambitions.[2] Not all the fault, however, lay with aggressive neighbors, as García Moreno himself on one occasion provoked conflict. Obviously no international system like the Organization of American States existed in the nineteenth century to protect smaller states from their more aggressive neighbors, so García Moreno would have to seek alternative means of self-preservation. And although Europeans regard their nineteenth century as one of peace, a remarkable number of international conflicts plagued Latin America. The constant internal and external threats had consequences beyond the survival of the García Moreno regime—they had an impact on his domestic agenda as well.

This chapter will also explore the possibility that García Moreno used his aggressive foreign policy to promote Ecuadorian state formation, much as one of Paraguay's dictators would unintentionally do later in the decade.[3] Banding together against "the other" is a natural human phenomenon. Antipathy for one's neighbor, such as the French and Germans have exhibited for centuries, certainly has played an important role in world history.[4] In the twenty-first century, Ecuadorians have often used sports as a means of national identification against outsiders. Participation in World Cup contests has greatly animated national pride, as victories against Peru bring screaming crowds to the streets at all hours. Whether such a contemporary phenomenon can be projected onto the nineteenth century, however, poses a more complex question. Recent scholarship suggests that conscription and foreign conflict can breed nationalistic sentiment, as happened in Argentina and Brazil in the 1870s.[5] Did García Moreno have the foresight to be able to manipulate xenophobia toward Colombians and Peruvians into patriotic sentiment in favor of the Catholic nation?

THE PERU QUESTION

Worried as García Moreno was about the deliberations of the constitutional assembly in 1861, he felt an even greater concern about the menacing attitude of Peru's dictator. Now that rebellions had quieted within Peru, Castilla could again make mischief to the north. García Moreno expected no less. "There is no doubt that Castilla will be more insolent now," he wrote his diplomatic representative in Lima. Castilla's ambitions prevented García Moreno from reducing the size of the army and spending more on the domestic agenda. García Moreno had his spies watching and, as mentioned previously, spent the first six months of 1861 in Guayaquil making certain that the coast remained loyal to him. Not one to remain inactive, García Moreno used that time to shore up the city's defenses by establishing cannon batteries overlooking the waterfront. When two Peruvian ships arrived in January, the interim president felt fully prepared should Castilla attempt a new blockade.[6]

To make matters worse, Peruvian diplomat Manuel Nicolás Corpancho, briefly envoy to the Franco regime, appeared in Quito in 1861 demanding that the constitutional assembly acknowledge the Treaty of Mapasingue. The convention (or perhaps García Moreno) saw a great opportunity to tweak Castilla's nose a bit over this latest effrontery, arguing that because the diplomat had been Peru's representative to Franco, he could not be received by the new "legitimate" Ecuadorian government. The more Corpancho blustered, the longer the convention rebuffed him. Finally the frustrated envoy threatened war if Ecuador did not meet Peru's demands. Corpancho launched a diatribe against García Moreno while meeting a group of people in the Spanish ministry. "I will make no arrangements with an infamous fellow like García Moreno, who would sell his country to France" (referring to the Trinité letters). Eventually the two sides compromised. Although the convention would not accept the same credentials that Corpancho had proffered to Franco, they would accept a fresh copy of them, requiring Corpancho's brief return to Peru. Apparently both Manuel Gómez de la Torre and José María Avilés, the two envoys from the provisional government in 1859, thought that the impasse had gone on long enough and supported the compromise.[7]

Meanwhile the British became concerned about the extent of Castilla's ambitions and the possibility that a renewed war with Ecuador would disrupt their commercial interests in the region. The spat over admitting Peru's representative in Quito caused hard feelings, and Castilla's ambition to conquer large portions of Ecuador did not calm matters. Not surprisingly, the convention refused Castilla's territorial demands and his claim for the repayment of the 300,000 pesos he had lent Franco. García Moreno argued that Franco lacked the authority to negotiate a loan for Ecuador and, more to the point, that Peru had greatly damaged its smaller neighbor by its bullying invasion. When the Constitutional Assembly officially rejected the Treaty of Mapasingue in April as "null, hateful, and without value or effect," Peruvian-Ecuadorian relations reached their nadir. As tensions mounted, British subjects living in Ecuador speculated that Castilla wanted to annex Ecuador's south coast and Guayaquil, for Peru had a growing navy and no place to build ships.[8]

Responding to the threat, García Moreno militarized the country while pursuing diplomatic options. Local officials recruited citizens into the National Guard, and many veterans of the civil war remained under arms. García Moreno chafed because of these expenses. "These circumstances are obliging us to spend immense amounts on the military. Reductions are impossible; in fact, we need to increase expenditures," he lamented.[9] His second strategy was to repress rather brutally conspirators who plotted against the government and in favor of Urbina, Robles, and their Peruvian friends. "Prompt, energetic, and terrible repression is the means to restraining the evildoers," he told a friend unapologetically. Suspects were exiled to Macas on the frontier of the Oriente (where a small group of settlers lived among the Shuar tribes), despite the suspect legality of this measure.[10] Faced with the possible dismantling of his country, García Moreno also took actions reminiscent of a small child picked upon by the schoolyard bully. As that child might try to make friends with an interior lineman on a football team, García Moreno sought to enlist Chile as a buffer against Peru—but a mission led by Vicente Piedrahita yielded no results.[11]

Early in September 1861, tensions escalated even further when Marshall Castilla created a pretext for war. First, he demanded that Ecuador justify the Trinité letters, asserting that the Americas could not tolerate neocolonial projects. Second, he reiterated that Ecuador must sign the Treaty of Mapasingue, a request that the assembly had already rejected. Third, he complained that Ecuador's new electoral law enfranchised people who were living in disputed territory, thereby seizing part of Peru in a de facto manner. The foreign diplomatic corps believed that Castilla was fabricating an excuse for war in the hopes of annexing territory.[12]

Meanwhile the ever-energetic García Moreno prepared for war by continuing his role as quartermaster—supplying uniforms, munitions, and cannons to the garrison at Guayaquil. By the end of 1861, he had formed four companies in the port city alone and reported to Flores that they were fit and reasonably disciplined, although they did have a proclivity for strong drink.[13] At the same time, repression worsened, as García Moreno saw the need to isolate and punish political enemies lest they serve as a "fifth column." Foreign observers like Hassaurek turned against García Moreno. Hassaurek saw "political prisoners being treated as outlaws" deprived of their liberty without charges pressed, confined in unhealthy jails, or exiled to Macas (or worse, to Brazil, through the Napo River jungle wilderness with only a footpath to follow and hostile Indians all around). García Moreno was prepared to do even more: "We will have to shoot, despite the Constitution, those who take the part of the invaders."[14]

The main deterrent to Peru's aggression, however, came from the objections of France and Great Britain. France, perhaps with larger motives in mind as the next section will explore, agreed to help protect Ecuador in 1861. The French dispatched a warship to Guayaquil and informed Castilla that they would not permit a renewed blockade, invoking a recent revision of international law that obliged the world's naval powers to intervene on behalf of a fleetless nation unjustly attacked.[15] Great Britain also expressed its willingness to help, less openly but equally effectively. London instructed its envoy to offer his "good offices to bring about an arrangement of the existing differences" between the two nations. Britain wanted peace in the region to further its commercial interests, and therefore would not countenance any unilateral exploits on the part of Peru. The actions of the great powers stalled Castilla's overt aggression, and the diplomacy concerning the border stalemated.[16]

As Friedrich Hassaurek reported, the 1861 Peruvian threat fizzled for three reasons: Castilla's inability to raise a military force, the deterrent implicit in Great Britain's "good offices," and France's strong actions.[17] García Moreno harbored no illusions about Castilla's intentions, but was feeling pretty confident now, referring disparagingly to Castilla as "the hero of guano."[18] García Moreno won this particular diplomatic battle because, to adopt another metaphor, he perceived the deterrent value of the big dog on the porch (or in this instance, two big dogs). Regardless of Castilla's designs, the Peruvian ruler recognized that his navy simply could not hope to outmuscle either the French or the British, much less the two acting in concert. Nevertheless Castilla continued to work for García Moreno's overthrow, if more cautiously. Surreptitiously he funneled money to Generals Urbina and Robles, and even offered them a vessel. Thus for the remainder of García Moreno's first term, the possibility of an exile invasion constantly existed. Dissidents within Ecuador contributed to the tension, rebelling rather regularly.[19] At least for the moment, Ecuador had temporarily gained a draw with Peru, but García Moreno knew his position was precarious. In a further attempt to ward off even more aggression, García Moreno once again turned to France.

THE FRENCH PROTECTORATE REVIVED

Gabriel García Moreno's relationship with France has raised passionate debate, both in his own time and among his biographers. Reconciling the proposed protectorate with a nationalist state-formation project clearly poses difficulties. Education and his time in Paris made García Moreno a natural Francophile, like so many of his Latin American contemporaries. Friedrich Hassaurek, the United States minister, detected French influence throughout the government. As he said, General Flores was an out-and-out monarchist. Carlos Aguirre, the treasury minister, wore the French Legion of Honor constantly on his collar. Daniel Salvador, minister of war, and other officials talked constantly of "the glories of the French empire and the greatness of the French nation." Like most Latin American nations, Ecuador and its upper class admired French culture above all others and many wealthy nationals sent their children to Paris for education.

Based on the ongoing Peruvian crisis and France's cultural importance, Hassaurek concluded that an annexation project was afoot. Interestingly, his British counterpart, while using virtually the same language and examples to describe the inner workings of the García Moreno government, was much more circumspect in his conclusion, saying that there was no real evidence behind the annexation story. The British believed that García Moreno sought a conditional protectorate whereby Ecuador would duck under the umbrella of the French if and only if Peru attacked.[20] García Moreno remained unapologetic for the Trinité letters. In the face of the renewed Peruvian threat, García Moreno boldly resumed the discussion of a protectorate. His ambassador, Antonio Flores, quietly assured Napoleon III that the "people" supported the project, while García Moreno spelled out more details to Minister Amédée Fabre.[21]

Privately García Moreno opined, "I believe now, as I did in the time of Trinité, that this beautiful and marvelous country needs to be civilized and put under the flag of France." Within days, he laid out the plan that, as the French minister said: "offers the Emperor a magnificent conquest . . . which will bring glory to his reign." According to Fabre, García Moreno's pessimistic view of Latin America's future led him to conclude that only the presence of France would prevent his country from self-destructing. Under French guidance, citizens would enjoy order and liberty. These warm words certainly enthused the minister, who now openly sympathized with García Moreno against Castilla.

As Emperor Napoleon III contemplated the offer, his agent dangled the potential riches of a South American empire in front of him and talked about the importance of France's civilizing mission. As time passed, the ever-impatient García Moreno asked Antonio Flores to inquire about the delay.[22] Unbeknownst to the Ecuadorians, the French Emperor had concocted another imperial scheme offering even more promise than empire in the Andes. Mexico, like most of the rest of Spanish America, had nearly imploded during the late 1850s as the result of an exceptionally bitter civil war between the Liberal and Conservative parties. Although defeated, the Conservatives intrigued in Europe and Napoleon III became intoxicated with their scheme offering access to precious metals and an interoceanic route to an Asian market. By early 1862, Napoleon abandoned the Ecuadorian plan for the Mexican adventure.

Faced with overwhelming evidence of the protectorate scheme, can one argue for García Moreno as a man leading a nationalistic state-building project? Obviously his critics, both at the time and recently, thought not.[23] Overall I would argue to the contrary, accepting the contemporary opinion that desperation pushed García Moreno to pursue extreme measures. In his private letters, García Moreno confirmed this view, speaking of the protectorate as a stopgap remedy. In discussing it with Antonio Flores, he wrote: "Our duty is to use *all means* to protect the country from the calamities that menace it" (my emphasis). To the much friendlier government that replaced Castilla in 1863, the Ecuadorian minister confided that the whole scheme of the French protectorate was only to shield Ecuador from a hostile invasion. In either event, García Moreno paid a price for his pro-French policy. As the only Latin American nation supportive of the French intervention in Mexico, Ecuador continued to be anathema to its neighbors for the next few years and García Moreno was saddled with the reputation of a monarchist.[24] With such a powerful ally, however, García Moreno could breathe a little easier even though the French, bogged down in Mexico after their defeat on Cinco de Mayo in 1862, could render no aid when he became embroiled in his adventures in Colombia.

THE CONFLICT WITH COLOMBIA IN 1862

Hardly had the Peruvian crisis abated when García Moreno faced the first of two threats from another aggressive neighbor, Colombia. Its aging caudillo, Tomás Cipriano de Mosquera (another of the ambitious second-tier participants from the era of independence), had by 1862 nearly defeated his Conservative Party rivals after a bitter four-year civil war. As in Ecuador, the Colombian Liberals espoused a federal system of government and free trade to open the nation to development. Most important, Mosquera and his followers gained notoriety because of their rabid anticlericalism. Given that García Moreno had already voiced his doubts about the efficacy of federalism and proclaimed his devotion to the Catholic Church, his sympathies naturally lay with Colombia's Conservatives. As Mosquera's army won victory after victory, however, eventually Conservative Julio Arboleda and his forces controlled only the extreme southwest area of the country, the region of Pasto along the Ecuadorian border. As a result of this turn of events, García Moreno felt obliged to recognize Mosquera's government.[25]

García Moreno's decision to welcome Mosquera's envoy in February 1862 created some difficulties as events unfolded. Probably he made this pragmatic decision to placate Mosquera, who was already talking about a greater Colombian union (reconnecting Colombia, Panama, Ecuador, and Venezuela)—a scheme García Moreno hoped to derail through delay, pleasantries, and the appearance of cooperation. In truth, García Moreno enjoyed few tactical options. Whereas the French and British could be persuaded to harbor a vessel at Guayaquil to prevent Peruvian aggression, no foreign nation would commit military aid to protect Ecuador's undefined border with Colombia high in the sierra. As a consequence, García Moreno had to rely on his own ingenuity in dealing with Colombia, which he did by accrediting Mosquera's diplomatic representative. To demonstrate good faith, García Moreno ordered his northernmost governor to prevent Arboleda's forces from crossing the border and acquiring weapons in Ecuador.[26]

Meanwhile García Moreno continued his cat-and-mouse game with Mosquera, feigning interest initially in the Gran Colombia scheme. Although the evidence for a deal with Mosquera (Ecuadorian assistance in the Colombian civil war in exchange for the state of Pasto) is murky at best, rumors to that effect flew around both capitals. García Moreno's correspondence makes the plan seem unlikely. Certainly such a deal was not unprecedented: In 1841 General Flores had made a similar arrangement with Mosquera, although the Colombian congress later disavowed the agreement as an "illegal private contract." García Moreno offered to mediate the ongoing civil war, probably hoping to arrange Arboleda's surrender. "Now is the time to listen to words of peace," he bombastically told the combatants. Arboleda could hardly accept the mediation of someone already publicly committed to Mosquera, though, and the peace initiative failed.[27] As the battle raged along the frontier, some of Mosquera's partisans took refuge in Ecuador and then used this safe haven to launch raids on Arboleda's territory, increasing the likelihood of international conflict.

As Mosquera pressed his Gran Colombia scheme, García Moreno thought carefully about how to formulate a noncommittal reply, forwarding a draft to General Flores. Meanwhile García Moreno hoped that the outcome of Venezuela's latest civil war would derail the plan. Another hero of independence, General José Antonio Páez, was leading a successful conservative rebellion in Venezuela, and he certainly opposed a new confederation since he had brought about the demise of the first one. What García Moreno seemed not to consider was that Páez and Venezuela were strong enough to ignore Mosquera, whereas Ecuador was not. García Moreno did, however, inform Mosquera's envoy about the constitutional impediments associated with recreating Gran Colombia, as well as noting their radically differing postures with regard to the church. As Hassaurek reported, García Moreno and his government had no intention of relinquishing power to become part of another state, especially an anticlerical one.[28]

As García Moreno tiptoed around the Gran Colombia problem, a relatively minor event precipitated a major crisis. On June 18, 1862, after a losing battle in southern Colombia, a band of pro-Mosquera guerrillas crossed the Ecuadorian border at Tulcán seeking refuge. A full troop of Arboleda's men followed in hot pursuit, hoping to finish off their enemy once and for all. As they crossed the border into the hills south of the Río Carchi, the local Ecuadorian garrison commander ordered them to halt and rode out to persuade them to desist. After a heated conversation in which the Colombians allegedly taunted the Ecuadorians as "Mosquera's pimps," the commander of the Arboleda forces unsheathed his sword and slashed the Ecuadorian officer three times across the head and once across the arms, wounding him badly, before charging off again in pursuit of the Mosquera guerrillas. Arboleda's diplomats later offered a series of excuses for the incident—it occurred in the heat of battle, the conflict actually took place on Colombian soil, the boundary in the vicinity had never been properly defined, the Ecuadorian soldiers had no uniforms identifying them as such, and the Ecuadorian commander provoked the incident because he favored Mosquera. Probably the best evidence on the score comes from the commander himself, who asserted that he carried a white flag, conversed with the Colombian, and identified himself as an Ecuadorian officer posted on the border.[29]

During the aftermath of this episode in July and August 1862, García Moreno displayed all of his worst characteristics: hot-temperedness, irascibility, rashness, bravado, and arrogance. Immediately he issued a series of demands, all of which, he stated, must be met within a twenty-four-hour period (given the difficulties of communication in the northern Andes, the requirement was ipso facto unreasonable). He insisted that the officer in command of Arboleda's southern army be dismissed and that the specific culprit who inflicted the wound be extradited for trial in Quito. At this point, Arboleda's envoy tried to interpose reason, suggesting an investigation into the incident due to the reasons (however specious) mentioned above. García Moreno demanded a quick resolution. Frustrated by inaction, García Moreno grew more and more short-tempered when Arboleda's agents shrugged off the incident. "If they don't give us satisfaction we will enter into [Colombian] territory and make reprisals against the party in control of Pasto," he raged.[30]

García Moreno, perhaps influenced by the foreign diplomatic corps urging caution, ordered forces to the border and awaited Arboleda's reply. As more time passed with no response, García Moreno decided to teach the Colombian a lesson. Ecuador's president and minister of war, Colonel Daniel Salvador, led an army of conscripts north. Three possible motives for García Moreno's bellicose behavior have emerged over time. The diplomatic corps felt that his rash and emotional personality caused him to make an imprudent decision, egged on in part by the arrogant Salvador, who needed a major military victory both to validate his promotion to general as well as to rival General Flores' prestige. García Moreno's biographical enemies later fabricated a tale that he was jealous of Arboleda's envoy to Quito, a dashing and handsome young fellow who allegedly had become intimate with Virginia Klinger. Although the story is unlikely, it is worth noting that Klinger's husband, Carlos Aguirre, did resign as minister of the treasury over the decision to go to war.[31]

The most convincing explanation for García Moreno's behavior (since it comes from private letters to friends) is that he felt obligated to defend the national honor. García Moreno himself offered this rationale to Flores: "This little campaign is indispensable for the honor and security of the country." As he told another friend: "Everything I have done was to uphold the nation's honor." García Moreno made everyone understand, including Arboleda, that this campaign would not be one of conquest but rather mere reprisal, designed to obtain satisfaction from the Pasto authorities. "You see it is impossible to close our eyes to the scandalous violation of our territory and the insult given to our border commander."[32] Nevertheless not all Ecuadorian leaders believed in the wisdom of the quixotic crusade. Treasury Secretary Carlos Aguirre stood up to García Moreno, speaking of the "maladroit ultimatum." Likewise General Flores confided to his son Antonio that the border incident was only a fleeting matter, and that "I hope he [García Moreno] will avoid external conflict." Despite his reservations, Flores told General Daniel Salvador that good soldiers like himself would support the president.[33]

Determined to act, García Moreno, Salvador, and a thousand National Guard troops joined the 300 soldiers already stationed on the border. On July 30, 1862, Arboleda crossed the frontier just east of the town of Tulcán, taking the high ground and interposing his army between García Moreno's and the road to Quito. According to Arboleda's description of the situation, one of two full accounts extant, he waited until 3:00 a.m. to secure this high ridge, only doing so after García Moreno's lone sentry lit a match, exposed his position, and fell into enemy hands. The pitched battle on the following day lasted two-and-a-half hours. The Ecuadorian cavalry broke at the first charge, and the volunteers scattered. García Moreno fought bravely and received a minor wound, but in the end he, Salvador, and a number of other officers surrendered, along with two of Mosquera's men who accompanied the Ecuadorian army.[34]

As predicted, the devastating defeat nearly destabilized the government. Many expected the pro-Urbina exiles to attack, an assumption that froze General Flores at his post in Guayaquil. Members of García Moreno's own party, such as Manuel Gómez de la Torre ("an ambitious demagogue," according to Hassaurek), plotted García Moreno's removal. Both Arboleda and García Moreno wanted peace—the former to refocus his attention on Mosquera, the latter to forestall an invasion of Ecuador. Too, they shared common principles, as one of García Moreno's officers present at the treaty-making conversation subsequently wrote.[35] Rafael Carvajal hastened to the border to negotiate the treaty, and García Moreno and Salvador were released on August 8. The published treaty, which gave Arboleda nothing, looked suspect until news leaked out about a second and secret treaty under which Ecuador would pay Arboleda and furnish 4,000 rifles, 200,000 cartridges, and 2,000 uniforms for use in the Colombian civil war. García Moreno, however, tricked Arboleda, and neither the cash nor the guns were forthcoming. Naturally García Moreno's double-dealing angered Arboleda, who threatened to invade Ecuador again. For his part, García Moreno thought he had no choice politically. "After Tulcán, honor prevents us from making common cause with Arboleda as the public would loathe me if I did."[36] The Arboleda problem soon ended, however, when some of his countrymen assassinated him in November 1862.

Disastrous as the Arboleda campaign was militarily, did the foreign crisis promote greater national sentiment? The evidence in this instance seems to support the contrary. Although the governors mobilized a fair number of soldiers, these troops had no will for battle. The indigenous conscripts had little, if any, sense of patriotism, understanding of Ecuador, or interest in García Moreno's quest for honor. Therefore he admitted after the fact: "Conscription cannot produce good results in moments of tight spots." The French minister thought that he had matured and would act less impetuously in the future, but this assumption did not prove to be the case—at least for the next few years.[37] Certainly he had behaved foolishly, demonstrating again his hot temper, rashness, exaggerated sense of honor, and arrogance. The incident reminded him he was a nation-builder and not a warrior. Ecuador would have to do more fighting as Colombia's new president, General Tomás Cipriano de Mosquera, preened his way onto the national stage in 1863, but García Moreno would ask his premier general to direct the campaign.

COLOMBIA STRIKES AGAIN: THE WAR OF 1863

Mosquera's first priority was to consolidate his control over Colombia. At the convention where the victors met to write a new constitution, he encountered considerable opposition from within his own party. Many Liberals doubted the sincerity of Mosquera's beliefs, given his antecedents as a moderate Conservative state-building president in the 1840s. Others felt the methods he used in dealing with defeated Conservatives too harsh. Eventually, however, the Colombian assembly wrote a federalist constitution that delegated additional authority to the states and elected Mosquera, after considerable debate, to a presidential term that would expire early in 1864.[38] As these events unfolded, García Moreno continued to mistrust Mosquera. He and Flores sounded out their friends' opinions about union with Colombia. Not surprisingly there was universal disdain for the idea. (To look at the matter cynically, many bureaucrats would inevitably lose their jobs to Colombians.) As a result, by the early spring of 1863 García Moreno had already concluded that "it is preferable to have a devastating and disastrous war" rather than union with Colombia. War also seemed likely to Hassaurek. Mosquera continued to arm more soldiers, even though the Colombian civil war had ended. In May 1863 he issued an invitation to García Moreno and Flores to meet with him on the border to discuss a treaty that would restore Gran Colombia, an offer that seemed to many a prelude to conflict.[39]

Some Colombian historians defend Mosquera's behavior in 1863. They claim that he properly intervened in Ecuador's affairs because García Moreno's "haughty response" to the invitation insulted Colombia and because Mosquera had a duty to spread liberty and prevent Ecuadorians from suffering the "theocratic oppression" represented by the recently promulgated Concordat. Both Mosquera and Urbina talked about the need to protect the Americas from monarchists and sell-outs (i.e., García Moreno), sizing each other up as potential allies. Some Colombians even claim that García Moreno started the war. Certainly a few Ecuadorians had designs on Pasto province, part of Cauca state. Not only did that region adhere to conservative principles, making it ideologically compatible with Ecuador, but geography also separated it from the heartland of Colombia. Although

García Moreno hemmed and hawed about his ambitions for Pasto, General Flores openly told the French consul, "If I take Pasto, I will not return it."[40] Nevertheless the argument blaming García Moreno for the onset of war seems weak.

Most in Ecuador anticipated war. Pedro Pablo wrote from Guayaquil that rumors had Urbina preparing to attack the port even as Mosquera amassed his troops near the border. Observers closer to the frontier heard from Colombian spies that Mosquera had more than three thousand battle-tested veterans ready.[41] García Moreno knew he had to prepare. Even though he had diminished the military after the battle of Tulcán in 1862 for the usual reason, now he had to reverse course. General Secundino Darquea reported that at a meeting of the Council of State, the president "in a loud voice gave support to the army" and urged recruiters to step up their efforts. Soon leading officers such as Darquea and Francisco Salazar reported that the army was on solid footing for battle. Public opinion clearly opposed the Colombian entanglement on practical grounds as well as the bad memories of the 1820s. As the French minister reported, Ecuadorians "form a compact population in the immense solitude of Spanish America [and] could not accept a central government on the other side of the insurmountable deserts."[42]

Seeing no reason to hasten the inevitable conflict, García Moreno waited nearly two months to respond to Mosquera's invitation to confer. After congratulating Mosquera on his election to the presidency, García Moreno agreed to meet with his fellow chief executive in the vicinity of Tulcán. Appended to those friendly words, he candidly wrote, "But with frankness I tell you that the joining of Ecuador in the Colombian union is entirely impossible." He also mentioned that the meeting would be delayed until the end of August because the constitution forbade the president from leaving Ecuador without congressional approval (and the session opened August 10). Although the United States minister criticized García Moreno for being undiplomatic, provocative, and hasty, García Moreno undoubtedly believed he was being forthright. García Moreno continued to muster his forces, hoping for the best. "We must prepare to fight, God help us," he told Flores. He noted that Mosquera had a sizeable army, but hoped that the Pasto region might side with Ecuador and defeat their common enemy.[43]

Preparations for war continued. General Darquea wanted to move more infantry to the border while Colonel Salazar and General Salvador requested more cavalry and more spies in Pasto (military intelligence being valued). Only General Flores believed that the war talk would soon dissipate. First, he noted that Mosquera had no legitimate grounds for invasion, he lacked congressional support, and he faced the possibility of renewed civil war should he act so rashly. He was only interested in a show of force to settle the ongoing boundary dispute, Flores opined.[44] Then came the bombshell—Mosquera's surprising proclamation of August 15.

Mosquera's "bombastic" decree fueled an already tense situation, at least in the eyes of Ecuadorians. He talked about marching to the border and urged "Colombians" in Ecuador who believed in republican ideals (Mosquera continued to label García Moreno a monarchist) to overthrow the "theocratic oppressors" governing "in the land of Atahualpa." Referring to Mosquera's proclamation as "insolent" and a provocative act, García Moreno stepped up war preparations, while at the same time sending Antonio Flores to Pasto to negotiate with Mosquera. After a heated debate on September 2, congress granted García Moreno full powers to deal with the ominous situation.[45]

Appointing Antonio Flores to undertake the diplomatic mission seemed like a brilliant stroke, resolving a rumored rift between Juan José Flores and García Moreno. The two men had disagreed in the spring of 1863 about the vice-presidential candidate, with García Moreno insisting on Antonio Borrero (who ironically would become one of García Moreno's most severe critics, succeeding him in 1875) and Flores advocating the cause of an obscure friend. García Moreno's loyal allies assured Borrero's election but he ultimately refused to serve. Flores and García Moreno made up, and Flores reconciled himself to following García Moreno's lead in politics.[46]

Antonio Flores' instructions authorized him to agree to a treaty of friendship, but to reiterate that a formal union with Colombia was impossible. He was to protest about the "hostile tone" of Mosquera's August 15 message and urge that Colombian troops be withdrawn from the border region. García Moreno chose Antonio Flores as his diplomat for a practical reason that initially worked—namely, Mosquera's close friendship with General Flores, his old comrade-in-arms. Mosquera spoke about the proposed union using soothing words that would "re-establish calm and confidence in *our* respective countries" (my emphasis). Antonio in turn refused to budge on the Concordat, though, saying that the document and García Moreno's proclerical and nation-building project "followed the national will." Furthermore Antonio argued that congress had twice rejected the idea of the Colombian union during its recent session, and noted that public opinion strongly protested against the idea. He reported that García

Moreno promised to attend the conference once General Flores, who had just begun to travel from Guayaquil, arrived. Meanwhile García Moreno told Antonio, "We will give meat and a cup of wine to the old llanero [plainsman] and nothing more."[47]

As the delays mounted, Mosquera grew impatient, "and with reason," as Antonio Flores admitted to his father. Mosquera felt García Moreno was downright rude: "He has not written me to say why he delays." Mosquera's patience ran out on October 13, when his envoy shoved a draft treaty demanding union at Antonio and gave Ecuador forty-five days to sign it. Antonio protested, the Colombian responded with a mumbled speech (or at least in tones not audible to the owner of the house where the meeting occurred) about a series of insults Colombia had experienced, and the diplomacy ended. Mosquera "comes full of fury against you," Antonio wrote to García Moreno. "He accuses you of deception by making him come to the border for no purpose." Mosquera requested a declaration of war from the Colombian congress, and asked Peru (and Urbina) to open a second front in southern Ecuador. As a result García Moreno ordered Antonio to end his mission.[48]

García Moreno now felt in command of the situation (quite wrongly as it turned out). He had resumed his familiar task of quartermaster for the army. Officers recruited troops throughout the country, "enthusiastic" to protect the country from foreign invasion. His former triumvir, estate owner Pacífico Chiriboga, contributed four thousand head of cattle. The president rounded up blankets and *ruanas* (heavy ponchos) for the coastal troops that General Flores would be bringing from Guayaquil and demanded that the governor of Guayas, Vicente Piedrahita, send him 3,000 pesos from the customs receipts biweekly to cover the wages of the soldiers and officers "in the name of the Fatherland." (The demands for cash would continue to increase throughout the crisis.) Eventually Governor Piedrahita stopped sending cash or soldiers, probably out of fear of an exile invasion. Assuming that Guayaquil would become a theater of war, he spent money setting up batteries around the city and replacing the rotted wooden reducts.[49] Nevertheless the dispute between the governor and the president in the middle of a war highlighted two problems that both Ecuador and much of Spanish America faced. First, many people continued to place their regions above their nations. Second, the Constitution of 1861 hampered a president even in times of war because of its protection of local prerogatives.

García Moreno also demanded that his governors get their troops to Quito "pronto, pronto, pronto." Even Flores did not move quickly enough to suit García Moreno. At the most defensible spot near the border, the Chota Valley just north of the city of Ibarra, García Moreno ordered General Secundino Darquea to build fortifications to protect the bridges over which invaders would have to pass. Meanwhile a coup in Peru ousted Castilla, with the new government coming out squarely in favor of preventing the Colombian union. Peru's new minister of foreign affairs, "desiring to give [Ecuador] proof of sincere friendship," sent troops to Peruvian ports to keep an eye on the exiles. The news reassured García Moreno. To the new Peruvian minister, García Moreno bragged that "Mosquera will be reduced to the alternative of asking our pardon or being humiliatingly defeated."[50]

García Moreno had another reason for his optimism. That is, in response to Mosquera's threatened invasion, Ecuadorians uniformly reacted patriotically. This time fear of the "other" did promote a greater sense of national unity. Town councils all over the country protested against Mosquera's words and his actions. Petitions from Cuenca, Riobamba, and the area where the fighting would occur all spoke to the importance of protecting the nation and religion. One town urged a struggle against "a war of conquest whose objective is to end Ecuadorian *nationhood* and the Catholic religion we all profess" (my emphasis). As the governor of Imbabura reported, never had he seen so much "patriotic spirit" as the populace, filled with enthusiasm, prepared to defend the city of Ibarra against Mosquera. Reactions against threats made by "others" did in fact stir Ecuadorian national sentiment in 1863 to "defend the fatherland."[51]

Once again García Moreno acted with great confidence when perhaps he should have been more cautious. His "volunteer" army, while enthusiastic, was untrained and consisted in part of *peones* dragooned by forcible impressments. Minister Hassaurek believed the conscripts "would fight [because of] the *spirit of nationality* aroused by Mosquera's unjust . . . pretensions"(my emphasis). But Mosquera's men were battle-hardened veterans led by a competent commander. They fought with modern rifles instead of the old flintlocks that the average Ecuadorian soldier carried. García Moreno whipped up patriotic sentiment, arguing that Ecuador would be better off should it disappear under the lava of a volcano than be captured "by a band of outlaws who do not respect religion, property, the honor of women, or the dignity of men."[52]

Now García Moreno wanted war, since he appeared to have the upper hand. A Conservative uprising in Pasto had begun, with the collusion of García Moreno (who subsidized the *pastusos* secretly). After a lengthy discussion to which General Flores contributed, congress provided a declaration of war. General Flores rode to Ibarra to take command. Impatient as ever, García Moreno never doubted the outcome. "Soon that perfidious drunk [Mosquera] will repent," García Moreno boasted. "He will pay with his life for the crimes he has committed."[53]

Initially General Flores intended to fight a defensive campaign. Expecting Mosquera to cross the frontier, Flores ordered the army to use the Río Chota in the steamy Chota Valley as its defensive perimeter. There deep waters prevented invasions, except over the few narrow bridges that Darquea had just fortified. By early November the defensive trenches overlooking the bridges were nearly completed.[54]

With the army fully assembled and equipped with a three-to-one numerical advantage, and Mosquera seemingly uncertain as to his next move, Flores decided to abandon his defensive posture. By the end of November, he had marched his forces from Ibarra to the border. Local officials continued to forward supplies and intelligence. The guerrilla campaign of the *pastusos* against Mosquera was advancing, having taken the provincial capital—although not attracting the huge following that García Moreno had anticipated. García Moreno waxed ecstatic when he heard that Mosquera was retreating. He believed that Mosquera would resort to a single battle to decide the campaign, which was about his only correct deduction. He congratulated General Flores on his decision to pursue Mosquera into Colombian territory and anticipated total victory. Up to this point, his commanders' confidence remained high. "Until now there has not been a single desertion," remarked General Darquea as the army approached the border.[55]

Within two days the Ecuadorian advance took them well into southernmost Colombia as General Flores sought a favorable battleground. He found himself a strategic location where he hoped to lure Mosquera into battle. A contingent of eight hundred soldiers hid along the road where Mosquera would have to retreat, thus creating the possibility of total victory. The wily Colombian general slipped out of the trap and marched south, however, allegedly taunting Flores as he passed by with words to the effect of "I will get to Quito long before you will reach Bogotá. Farewell." Putting aside his plan, Flores now chased Mosquera, seeking to interpose the Ecuadorian army between Mosquera and Quito. Side by side the armies raced over the gentle hills of southern Colombia, occasionally catching glimpses of each other. Finally Flores caught Mosquera at a hacienda called Cuaspud, which gave its name to the decisive battle that took place on December 6, 1863.

According to General Flores, his troops responded well to Mosquera's initial assault despite the bitter cold and a driving rain. But then the Co-

General Juan José Flores, García Moreno's premier general (Permission of the Banco Central del Ecuador)

lombians mounted a surprise flanking movement. Flores thought his only hope to save the day was a cavalry charge. Unfortunately what appeared at a distance to be a pasture turned out to be a marsh. Bogged down in the mud, the cavalry assault failed and the Colombians took the field. The dead included Major Carlos de Veintemilla and a son of the independence hero Antonio José de Sucre. The heavy fighting induced panic on the part of the soldiers, which García Moreno later referred to as "the damned fools and cowards that were with him [Flores]," and within an hour and a half the battle was over. Five thousand Ecuadorians had fled from 1,800 Colombians, hundreds were killed, and an additional 2,000 were captured. (Mosquera suffered 63 casualties.)[56] Once again the National Guard had collapsed. What had happened to the vaunted patriotism and national sentiment described by the governors and commanders who sent the units into battle? Probably the conscripted *peón* remained personally loyal to his region rather than to the larger abstract entity of Ecuador. Far from home, the average foot soldier undoubtedly thought that this was not the battle he had agreed to fight—a battle to save "the Fatherland" (however defined). Once the National Guard deserted, the victory was Mosquera's.

Slightly wounded, Flores fled the battlefield with about three hundred men, including Generals Manuel Tomás Maldonado, Secundino Darquea, Francisco Salazar, and Daniel Salvador. Because Mosquera's army stood between them and the border, Flores and his friends circled around the Colombian forces and crossed the border to the east, arriving in Ibarra days later. In Mosquera's letter to García Moreno, whom he addressed as "the President of ?" (suggesting Ecuador no longer existed), he crowed about his triumph and ridiculed the Ecuadorian army. Cuaspud was such a humiliating defeat that Flores wanted to resign his command and never fight again, once the present conflict ended. He and the surviving officer corps now planned a decisive stand at the Chota against what they assumed would be Mosquera's imminent invasion. At the same time, Flores pursued a peace initiative.[57]

Panic overtook Quito. The capital, located only a few days' easy march from Ibarra, looked to be a ripe prize, as everyone anticipated Mosquera would fulfill his dream of uniting the two countries. The French minister gloomily predicted that Ecuador would cease to exist as a nation, and stoically awaited the plundering of Quito. Desperately Flores and García Moreno rallied the resistance. The governors dispatched men to the front and General Maldonado organized volunteers. Colonel José de Veintemilla took a small squadron from Guayaquil and successfully captured a small Colombian town en route to Barbacoas, the only Ecuadorian victory in the entire war. As Flores began to sue for peace, however, Colonel Veintemilla received orders to stay put. García Moreno regained his composure and told Flores that if necessary the government would fight to the end. The U.S. minister had less confidence in Ecuador's ability to defend itself after Cuaspud, but he astutely noted that fighting on foreign soil had cost them the "patriotic" advantage. The best hope of the Ecuadorian forces remained behind the fortified locations along the Chota River.[58]

As García Moreno and Flores prepared for the worst, Mosquera expressed a surprising interest in negotiating. With the country defenseless before him, or nearly so, Mosquera appeared to have an opportunity to annex Ecuador. Although he might have hesitated because his presidential term would end in April 1864, he also recognized that a military campaign in the sierra would be difficult, and he had no navy to take Guayaquil. Also, many years previously during the wars of independence, Mosquera and Flores had been comrades-in-arms under Simón Bolívar's command—creating a lasting bond of friendship. Although Mosquera thoroughly despised García Moreno, he felt great admiration and sympathy for Flores. Three days after Cuaspud, Flores and Mosquera met, constituting "the first overture toward peace."[59]

Rumors of draconian demands circulated in the country: Mosquera allegedly would insist upon García Moreno's resignation, the expulsion of the Jesuits, the payment of a large indemnity, the cession of the northern province of Imbabura, and the creation of a conference at Panama to discuss permanent union with Colombia. None of these demands was ever actually made. While García Moreno worried and wrote many directives, Flores assumed responsibility for negotiations and conveniently ignored the president's fears.[60] Specifically Flores decided (against García Moreno's wishes) that he would grant Mosquera's request and allow the Colombian army to occupy the city of Ibarra (which had a more healthful climate than the area around the Chota River) while Flores and the Ecuadorian forces retreated to the market town of Otavalo. At the end of the month, Flores and the Colombian envoy autographed a treaty at the Pinsaquí hacienda that called for neither union nor cession of territory, but rather the mere resumption of the treaty of friendship and alliance of 1856. According to legend, Mosquera said the only clause that mattered was the unwritten one requiring Flores to give him an *abrazo* (hug). The U.S. minister rightly concluded that the treaty was far more favorable than anything Ecuador deserved under the circumstances.[61] Mosquera even forgave García Moreno, writing him a cordial note. As Mosquera and his forces returned to Bogotá, he assured García Moreno that he (Mosquera) never intended to invade Ecuador, although he still believed in Colombian unity. García Moreno responded in kind, calling Mosquera noble and distinguished (a far cry from the nickname of "the old drunk" used in the heat of battle). García Moreno also praised Flores for his good work in securing such a favorable peace: "You have carried yourself as a gentleman and I am proud to be your friend."[62]

THE ACTIVITIES OF THE URBINA EXILES AND THE MALDONADO AFFAIR

Even though relations with both Peru and Colombia normalized by early 1864, throughout the first term García Moreno also had to contend with the threat of pro-Urbina exiles who invaded the country on numerous occasions. In 1862 the exile threat heightened during García Moreno's clash with Julio Arboleda. In the aftermath of the disaster at Tulcán, García Moreno left the task of fortifying and protecting the coast to General Flores. Fortunately for the government, it received excellent intelligence about Urbina's plans from Colonel José de Veintemilla, who had been in Peru on business. Although an attempt to get the British to stop Urbina's fleet failed, the expedition of two thousand men funded by Ramón Castilla came to naught when Peru's new president preferred peace, telling his northern governor to send the disappointed exiles back to Lima.[63]

Informants in the southern province of Loja used business connections in Peru as sources of information. Rumors abounded, but the exiles posed no real threat from September 1862 until the war with Colombia in 1863, when the Peruvian government again stepped in to prevent exiles from launching an invasion.[64] From García Moreno's perspective, lack of serious consequences befalling those who plotted against the government exacerbated the problem of interminable intrigues. The solution, García Moreno told General Flores, was legislation stipulating the death penalty for conspiracies. As he told another friend, "Prompt and forceful repression is the sole means of restraining the evildoers, who become emboldened with tolerance." So the path to the Napo River became well traveled. García Moreno even requested the dismissal of the British consul in Guayaquil, Francis Mocatta, who had allegedly joined a liberal conspiracy. Ultimately, sufficient evidence convinced the British that Mocatta should be removed from the foreign service as García Moreno had requested.[65]

In the midst of all this intrigue, a new plot emerged, designed to assassinate the president and replace him with General Manuel Tomás Maldonado. Somehow García Moreno learned about the plan. When the armed conspirators, some of whom had been previously pardoned, approached the Government Palace, he sent loyal troops to capture them. (Apparently García Moreno's aide-de-camp had agreed to provide the conspirators with access to the president.) Hearing the news, Maldonado fled and the government issued a warrant for his detention. Although the aide and one or two high-ranking officers captured were sentenced to be shot, García Moreno commuted their sentences to exile.[66] But he did want to punish Maldonado, infamous for his many rebellions dating back to the 1840s.

For two months Maldonado led the government on a merry chase around the highlands. Despite García Moreno's orders, no doubt some officers felt reluctant to bring Maldonado to justice. After all, he was one of their own, and the "right of rebellion" (to rebel on principle without fear of reprisal) had been a longstanding tradition for military men in Spanish America. For much of this time, Maldonado probably hid on one of his haciendas located outside the city of Latacunga. Then he had the audacity to ride into town, confront García Moreno's governor (Felipe Serrade), and demand his military pension. After threatening García Moreno and Serrade ("one of the most disagreeable incidents of my life," said the governor), Maldonado then rode off. Soon Colonel Ignacio de Veintemilla gave pursuit, and Maldonado fled towards Peru. García Moreno anxiously followed the chase. His orders to Veintemilla were explicit: "Take him dead or alive."[67] Finally Veintemilla caught Maldonado in Guayas province. En route back to Quito, the prisoner had several opportunities to escape as part of the officers' genteel code but refused to do so, believing that García Moreno would forgive him.

Maldonado erred in his calculations. Apparently part of the confession gleaned from the co-conspirators included the revelation that Maldonado had not fought hard at the battle of Cuaspud as originally reported, but instead had helped to betray General Flores to the Colombians, nearly causing his death. Coupled with this treachery was evidence that Maldonado had been involved in other pro-Urbina conspiracies. Those with longer memories also recalled he had quit fighting for the provisional government after the Ayarza controversy in the middle of the civil war. Despite the constitutional provision prohibiting capital punishment for conspirators (Maldonado had not been among the troops trying to gain entry to the palace to kill García Moreno), the president decided on a quick execution without a trial. Influential *quiteños* pleaded for mercy but to no avail. The scene ended tragically, as a weeping Señora de Maldonado had to be torn out of her husband's arms. Reports differed as to whether this took fifteen minutes or an hour, but at the end, she was led away so that the firing squad could do its job. Nevertheless, as García Moreno reported, "Maldonado's career of betrayals ended yesterday with his death, an *example* for all the military chiefs who would imitate him"[68] (my emphasis).

By executing Maldonado, García Moreno hoped to provide a lesson for other military men considering rebellion. He expected that a firm hand would lead to stability, but his harsh punishments often caused a reaction from liberals. Although Maldonado's execution seems justifiable, García Moreno went too far in punishing others associated with the plot. Juan Borja, implicated in the Maldonado coup attempt, had been a bitter enemy of García Moreno since the 1840s, a former Urbina-Robles governor, and a member of the Quito elite. Captured after falling into a ravine and suffering serious injuries, he was fettered in jail and refused medical attention. Dragged out to witness Maldonado's execution, Borja died in prison two months later of gangrene. Another conspirator was led to his own mock execution before being returned to jail. Such mental and physical torture caused several of García Moreno's allies to repudiate him. As occurred after the Ayarza whipping, some military men reacted negatively. With both contemporaries and biographers, García Moreno's "tyrannical" behavior proved controversial.[69]

In the fall of 1864, the exiles' hopes escalated once again because of what many liberals viewed as yet another of García Moreno's diplomatic miscues. The Spanish government had sent a fleet to the Pacific under the guise of a scientific expedition, obscuring its desire to reconquer its lost colonies—especially Peru. Quickly several of the South American nations (Chile, Bolivia, Argentina, Colombia, and Venezuela) rallied behind Peru and pledged support. For several reasons discussed in the next chapter, García Moreno proclaimed Ecuador's neutrality in the impending conflict. His decision encouraged the exiles to attack what is today El Oro province, then the southern part of Guayas. Targeting southern Ecuador offered the Peruvian-based exiles the advantages of proximity and surprise. Armed with a "pro-American" slogan (as opposed to García Moreno's alleged monarchist views), the exiles—perhaps seven hundred of them—waded ashore near Machala.[70]

Meanwhile Flores had purchased a steamship, enabling him to arrive with his army at Machala in late September, in time to engage Urbina in a decisive battle. Flores directed his troops from his sickbed aboard the ship. Once again his military prowess carried the day and Urbina fled back to Peru with most of his men. The invasion was coordinated with other small revolts around the country, one of which took Azuay's Governor Carlos Ordóñez prisoner and threatened the city of Cuenca briefly before government troops prevailed.[71] Reprisals were swift. García Moreno ordered the immediate execution of the disloyal *jefe político* who had captured Ordóñez and punished other leaders of the revolt. "It is necessary to persecute them until they are corrected or exterminated," he wrote his wife.[72]

The most significant result of Urbina's invasion in the fall of 1864 was completely unforeseen. Just after the decisive battle near Machala ended, General Juan José Flores died of renal failure. His urinary tract infection had gone untreated because he preferred to fight his country's enemies. His dying words demonstrate his dedication to his adopted homeland: "Have we taken Santa Rosa? Did the troops fight well?" His doctor placed the corpse in a barrel of alcohol and shipped it to Quito, where it was buried in the cathedral. García Moreno wrote Antonio Flores about the emotional scene with Antonio's mother, saying, "I will never encounter in this world one to replace the faithful friend, and devoted, perspicacious, wise, conciliatory, intelligent, and learned counselor that I have lost." He added, "What death could be more glorious for a military man?" But García Moreno had lost his most important military asset. As he had observed at the beginning of his term, Flores, "an illustrious warrior and man of great talent, will be the principal support of my administration."[73] Now only time and additional challenges would tell if García Moreno had the abilities to become a successful extraconstitutional military leader (caudillo) on his own.

LESSONS OF THE FIRST TERM

Like most astute people, García Moreno drew certain conclusions from his experiences. By 1865 he recognized flaws in the liberal model of state formation embodied in the Constitution of 1861—an awareness most Latin American political leaders shared by the second half of the nineteenth century. Specifically federalism and municipal autonomy reinforced the problem of regionalism, making state formation difficult. Other nation-states such as Argentina and Mexico resolved this issue much as had the United States: by maintaining the liberal language but in practice allowing the central government much greater authority. García Moreno preferred another alternative. As he made clear to his friend Governor Felipe Serrade, "I will regret until the day I die that I accepted the presidency under the constitution and these laws." He urged congress to pass legislation to strengthen the executive's hand to prevent rebellions and defend against exile invasion. He felt he had no choice but to violate the constitution and exile dissidents to Macas or Brazil, or even shoot them to save the country from chaos.[74]

At the same time, García Moreno practiced some of the virtues that in the eyes of his friends would make him an ideal Catholic ruler. He was honest, austere, and hard-working. He refused his presidential salary, instead using the money for pet projects such as the expense of bringing the first Christian Brothers from France. He opposed nepotism—although two of his brothers (José and Miguel) held minor offices, as did one of his nephews. And Antonio Flores was instructed to fire the nephew if he did not work out. Meanwhile brother Fernando, still out of favor, knew better than to make a direct request for employment. Instead he asked General

Flores for help. "Nothing is advanced to me, I am estranged."[75] At the same time, García Moreno demonstrated his devotion to his faith, much to the bemusement of the anticlerical U.S. minister, who commented on the president's "monkish behavior" that "made him [García Moreno] the laughing stock of the intelligent portion of the community." On the contrary, his piety, honesty, and relative effectiveness compared to so many other Ecuadorian presidents made him attractive to conservatives. As the French minister said, "This man with all the appearances of an economic free thinker . . . . who built roads and schools [is] . . . the only man of merit in Ecuador." Beginning the state-formation project during his first term, he had created a new relationship with the papacy, outlined the structure of the modern Catholic state, adopted the national flag, established August 10 as independence day, minted the first national coins, and printed the first national postage stamps.[76]

Of course García Moreno was far from perfect. His flaws were legendary among the diplomatic corps: His mercurial personality, impetuous temperament, and penchant to apply harsh punishment sometimes led to bad decisions, as did his quest for honor and glory. During the first Colombian war, rumor had him breaking a chair over the head of one of the cabinet members in a fit of pique. As the Vatican's apostolic delegate reported, "in the period of a few hours he passes from one extreme to the other."[77] Yet the second Colombian war had furthered the nation-building project despite the persistence of regionalism and localism, even among the indigenous people. Certainly the elite and some rank-and-file soldiers felt a greater sense of national identity as they protected Ecuador against the "other." García Moreno had also taken steps, sometimes unpopular, to curb militarism. Despite his flaws, most of his civil-war coalition still held together in 1865, although some dissidents had emerged in Cuenca. Because of his disastrous foreign policy decisions and their consequences for the budget, however, much remained undone in 1865.

Chapter Five

Becoming the Indispensable Man, 1865–1869

Regionalism and state-formation projects were not the only difficult issues facing Latin Americans in the nineteenth century. Additionally they had to contend with the phenomenon of *caudillismo*, the rule of the "indispensable leader" or military boss, who alone (at least in the leader's mind) could rule a nation. During the years between 1865 and 1869, this chapter will argue, García Moreno emerged as a caudillo, although an unusual variant of the stereotype. Scholars have long debated the nature and origins of the caudillo. Some writers have viewed *caudillismo* as part of the heritage of colonial culture, which included an authoritarian tradition and a submissive lower class. Other writers focus on ambitious caudillos as tools of the wealthy, seeking control through a network of friends who became their core support. Others note that caudillos glorify local culture.[1] Caudillos often were uprooted social misfits who rebelled against their parents and other authority figures, just as García Moreno allegedly distanced himself from his father.[2] Most studies of *caudillismo* suggest that the phenomenon resulted from specific historical circumstances: the coming of independence, the slow emergence of true nation-states, and the resultant tendency towards political anarchy.[3]

Textbooks often refer to García Moreno as one of the most notable caudillos in all of Latin American history. Frequently compared to Juan Manuel de Rosas of Argentina, José Antonio Páez of Venezuela, and Rafael Carrera of Guatemala, García Moreno shared with them an aversion to the failed liberal dreams of the postindependence era.[4] Yet García Moreno differs from the other three in important ways. Each of them belonged to the earlier age of caudillos and depended on the allegiance of a local region, or *patria chica*, as a home base. Rosas and Páez owned huge ranches where they could obtain rank-and-file soldiers and sustenance. Carrera came from a region in the interior of Guatemala heavily populated with indigenous people like himself who devotedly served him. All three enjoyed access to land, resources, and jobs, which they could distribute to loyal followers.

García Moreno never owned an estate, however. He had to rely on the goodwill of elites from the north-central sierra and a lesser number of loyalists in the south and on the coast as his network of followers. In part he served as the "necessary gendarme" who protected the socioeconomic order his friends dominated. Caudillos also displayed *personalismo* (charisma), usually because as heroic military figures, they were able to raise armies and lead them to victory. Although García Moreno was not a warrior, his speeches and deeds moved people. The reliance of caudillos upon personal traits, however, came at a long-term cost to the formation of state institutions and their legitimacy.[5]

García Moreno more properly fits into the second generation of caudillos, the oligarchic leaders who dominated much of Latin America's history between 1850 and 1930. Although he would never have adopted the positivist philosophy underlying many of these regimes (mostly because positivism tended to be anti-Catholic), García Moreno endorsed the hegemonic notion of progress. He attributed much of his nation's lack of development to the instability that had characterized politics until 1861 and continued to disrupt his first administration. Proponents of progress embraced principles of liberal economic development, as did García Moreno, but he uniquely melded these ideas into a conservative state-formation project.[6]

Caudillos also fractured institutions when they attempted to extend their terms of office (*continuismo*) beyond the years constitutionally permitted, as almost all of them did. To avoid the appearance of acting illegally, many caudillos refused the sash of office until their followers begged them to make the "sacrifice" and become president, which is of course what they wanted all along. García Moreno followed this pattern—never turning down a chance to serve nor resigning an office, despite his threats to do so. The Constitution of 1861 posed a major roadblock to his remaining in power in 1865, however. Therefore he turned to the solution adopted by many other Spanish American leaders: the selection of a puppet, Jerónimo Carrión. Sometimes, however, puppets cast off their creator's strings (as Pinocchio rejected Geppetto's) and strike out on their own. Such was the situation García Moreno faced between 1865 and 1869. His growing strength, however, demonstrated he was becoming a caudillo during these years.

THE BATTLE OF JAMBELÍ

As García Moreno's first term neared its end, Generals Urbina and Franco decided to invade once again for three reasons. First, García Moreno's policies, especially the disastrous foreign wars but also the controversial Concordat, had diminished his popularity—at least according to the foreign diplomats. Second, Jerónimo Carrión had been elected president with García Moreno's blessing, and for liberals like Urbina the prospect of "four more years" of proclerical policies with conservatives holding national, provincial, and local offices meant that their friends and allies would be without jobs. Third, García Moreno, who would leave office in September 1865, looked vulnerable because of General Flores' death, which had left the conservatives without their best military leader.

Without any advance warning (the surveillance system in Peru appears to have broken down), Urbina's friends launched a surprise attack on the night of May 31, 1865. According to testimony, the U.S. civilian captain of a river-transport ship, the *Washington,* blew its horn near an island on the Guayas River (a sign he was in on the plan), at which point dozens of armed men jumped into canoes, paddling out to the *Washington* and boarding. The *Washington* then continued upriver. Three hours later, it pretended to tangle its anchor and ropes with that of the *Guayas*, Ecuador's only naval vessel. In the ensuing confusion, the armed men boarded the *Guayas*, killing its captain and many of the crew, and taking possession of the ship.[7] Shortly thereafter a third ship (the *Bernardino,* which Castilla had bought for the exiles years ago) carrying Urbina and Franco joined the fleet. The rebels offloaded the *Washington's* passengers, who quickly informed the authorities. At that juncture, the action stalled. Apparently the exiles could not land where originally planned because of the presence of government troops, and thus passively awaited an uprising in Guayaquil.

In the meantime the government responded promptly. Issuing a decree declaring the rebels "pirates," García Moreno indicated that any captured participants would be tried summarily by a council of war and shot, since pirates could be legally executed. He mounted his horse and headed for Guayaquil along with a few hundred loyal troops, some of whom he raised en route. Making remarkable time, they arrived on June 10 to find the city quiet. Miguel García Moreno, serving as governor of Guayas, had already discussed the invasion threat with the foreign consuls and asked in vain for their navies to assist. Meanwhile the rebels sat in the middle of the Guayas, waiting for their friends in Guayaquil to act despite urging from partisans on the shore that "our [joint] resolution must be violent and energetic." By delaying, they squandered a major opportunity and allowed García Moreno to prepare a counteroffensive.[8]

Brimming with confidence as always, he prepared for conflict with the rebel navy. Intelligence sources reported that they saw no more than two hundred armed men altogether on the three ships, with the *Guayas* alone having armaments. Meanwhile Urbina had received virtually no support on land. A small group of liberal *montoneros* (mestizo coastal villagers) had attacked the tiny town of Baba, but Colonel José de Veintemilla quickly dispersed the rebels. Nearby in Vinces, the National Guard led the resistance and drove out a much larger force. García Moreno remarked about the limited response among Urbina's friends. Probably many sympathizers were frozen in place, waiting for him to act.[9]

Creating a naval force became the first order of business, since the British and United States consuls had reacted unenthusiastically to the idea of having their fleets deal with Urbina. García Moreno therefore took a small squadron of soldiers and boarded the British merchant vessel *Talca*. He asserted that he was taking possession of it under the ancient maritime doctrine of Augarian Law allowing a nation without a navy to "impress" foreign ships at times of dire necessity—an admiralty legal theory apparently uncovered by his brother Miguel. The squad immediately began hammering away, tearing down the *Talca's* forecastle and mounting three guns.

At that moment a small Spanish warship sailed into Guayaquil harbor. The *Talca's* local agents, the British vice-consul among them, begged the captain's assistance. The captain, however, opined that the almost never-used Augarian Law had been misapplied because the impounded vessel could only transport supplies, not fight. The Spanish captain referred the final disposition to the consuls (including the British vice-consul, of course), who concurred with his opinion.[10] Now García Moreno had no choice but to pay the price the British demanded to buy the ship outright, some 70,000 pounds sterling that Ecuador could ill afford. He handed over the down payment and completed outfitting the ship. The United States minister held little hope for the expeditionary force. As he noted, "the chances of success are rather against García Moreno. His enemies have more vessels, and one of their steamers, the *Guayas*, is much stronger though not faster than the *Talca*."[11]

Despite Hassaurek's prediction, fortune shone on García Moreno's ships, as the *Talca* had been joined by a small river vessel. Urbina and Franco had no idea that García Moreno had armed a ship. They were thus completely surprised to see the *Talca* steam towards them as they lay at anchor in a portion of the Guayas estuary called the Canal of Jambelí. A lucky cannon shot sank the *Guayas* almost immediately, while García Moreno's men swarmed aboard the *Bernardino*. Facing impending disaster, Urbina, Franco, and other officers hastily made their way overland back to Peru, abandoning the slow *Washington* at the nearest riverbank. The battle of Jambelí could not have been a sweeter success for García Moreno. Gone overnight were the exile threats. As Hassaurek concluded, "The miserable failure of this third attempt will probably destroy General Urbina's prestige and put an end to revolutionary invasions for some time to come." García Moreno crowed, "The victory at Jambelí was a mortal blow to the pirates and traitors." His confidence increased even more after exiles who had landed near Santa Rosa were thrashed by a small segment of the regular army that sent them running for the safety of the Peruvian border.[12]

Flushed with victory, García Moreno decided to court-martial and shoot twenty-seven of the "pirates" immediately following the brief engagement. Even more controversially, he executed liberal Argentine national Santiago Viola, incriminated by the captured Urbina correspondence, as one who helped to plan the invasion. Although the U.S. minister and subsequent anti–García Moreno writers thought the evidence flimsy, García Moreno concluded that Viola had in part masterminded the planned rebellion and deserved to die. In his book, Hassaurek relates that processions of people pleaded for Viola's life, including the bishop of Guayaquil and even García Moreno's aged mother borne in a sedan chair, but he remained firm. The French charge d'affaires called him a "ferocious little despot" who was "like a tiger that licked blood." After the executions, García Moreno continued to squelch dissidents, issuing an arrest warrant for Manuel Gómez de la Torre and even placing the bishop of Manabí under house arrest for allegedly encouraging "the implacable enemies of order," since two of his nephews were involved.[13] To many observers, García Moreno had not acted unreasonably in dealing with the "pirates," given their previous records. As far as punishing Viola and other civilians, however, García Moreno had gone to extremes, and several members of his Cuenca network in particular broke with him.

Most of the country celebrated the results of Jambelí. Congratulatory petitions poured in. One small town pleaded for an exemption to the decree against bullfighting because the residents wanted to stage a *corrida* to celebrate the triumph. García Moreno feted his soldiers from the *Talca*. As was traditional, he commanded that a Te Deum Mass be held in the National Cathedral to thank God for the victory, which he attributed to the assistance of Our Lady of the Rosary. The diplomatic corps refused to attend the service, however, because of García Moreno's actions after the victory. Their objections aggravated him because he could not understand their squeamish response. The British minister diplomatically tried to convince García Moreno's assistant, Pablo Herrera, that no insult was intended.[14]

The battle of Jambelí proved extremely important. García Moreno's admirers believed his heroic actions had saved the nation from continuing turmoil and bloodshed. As García Moreno himself said, "I believe order is consolidated and it will be difficult for the 'reds' to do anything." Predictably his enemies downplayed the victory, arguing that the loss meant little because García Moreno failed to capture Urbina and Franco. Sporadic Urbina rebellions occurred over the next five years, but they were more irritants than real dangers.[15] Jambelí had great importance because García Moreno gained a reputation as a resolute commander who could inspire troops, the first step towards becoming a caudillo. For the rest of his career, the mere mention of García Moreno's name would frighten opponents. García Moreno noted the change in attitude on several occasions. "The general belief that I am commander-in-chief has contained the 'reds' and re-established tranquility as if by charm." On another occasion he stated, "It would be good fortune to clean the country of these pernicious fellows, but they are as cowardly as they are evil, and the remembrance of Jambelí still frightens them."[16] Yet many feared rather than respected him, as the diplomatic correspondence revealed. It would take an additional crisis to enhance his popularity and confirm his role as Ecuador's indispensable man.

FAMILY MATTERS

During this four-year period, García Moreno's family life changed dramatically, bringing both disquiet and peace. For many years his wife Rosa had suffered from horrible skin diseases. In the early 1860s, she began to experience intestinal disorders as well. He empathized deeply with her pain and cursed the quality of physicians: "The doctors of our country are a sad and error-prone lot." He counseled his wife to take her medicine in small doses and "to be careful with letting them bleed you; they will kill you." Out of office in 1865, he was by her side when she experienced another bad spell in November. Despite doses of the latest medicine, laudanum (now known to have serious side effects), she expired in four days. As friends and well-wishers sent condolences, García Moreno showed himself grief-stricken: "I beg God for eternal rest for my virtuous *compañera* [life companion]," whose "Christian virtues make her worthy of Heaven."[17] Life on the estate must have been quiet and lonely, perhaps explaining his brief withdrawal from politics and society and his expressed willingness to go to Guayaquil to work with Pedro Pablo in his business.[18]

Yet before he could do that, love unexpectedly intervened, and García Moreno married for a second time on April 1, 1866. The bride was his niece and adopted daughter Mariana, a rather lovely 23-year-old woman more than twenty years his junior. Apparently the union caused some tongue-wagging in Quito, not only because of the issue of consanguinity but also because of the rapidity with which García Moreno remarried after his loss. Anti–García Moreno biographies question his virtue at this moment. As Shakespeare wrote in Hamlet, "Thrift, thrift, Horatio! the funeral baked meats did coldly furnish forth the marriage tables." Despite the criticism, the newlyweds seemed very happy. At least the letters from García Moreno to Marianita, as he called her, were very loving—even more so than had been his words to Rosa. Before he left Ecuador on the state business described below, he certainly performed his husbandly duty, as in early December 1866 she would present him with their first child, a daughter. The birth was a difficult one, so Mariana stayed with the Flores family in Guaranda for several months while recuperating.[19]

In early 1867, Pedro Pablo renewed his offer to his brother to come to Guayaquil to manage the business. Gabriel worried about the risks of living in Guayaquil—especially when the baby, Mariana, and the wet nurse all came down with fevers. Eventually the rainy season ended, however, and the family regained its health. Mariana paid visits to relatives and society ladies, but García Moreno chafed to leave for the sierra. Duty compelled him to stay because Pedro Pablo and his wife, Virginia, had to remain abroad as their young son was very ill, and eventually died. By the time Pedro Pablo returned later in the year, Mariana was pregnant again. García Moreno decided that they should remain in Guayaquil until she gave birth. Unfortunately the daughter died in October 1867, shortly after her birth, leaving García Moreno grief-stricken once again.[20] His feelings for Mariana grew even stronger, as he called her "the happiness, counsel, and treasure of my life," and "the love of my soul, enchantress and happiness of my life." Right now they needed to console each other, because their first child also died of fever. García Moreno vowed never to return to his birthplace "unless God demanded it," and the saddened couple returned to the sierra.[21]

By this stage of his life, García Moreno did seem to be maturing emotionally. For the first time he displayed the ability to reconcile former friendships he had broken. Hearing that Mariano Cueva and the Borrero brothers, his former collaborators, wanted to reunite, he offered to resume friendly relations.[22] He remained a devoted family man. García Moreno and Mariana seemed happy enough. There are no letters from her, so it is more difficult to ascertain her feelings than Rosa's, but biographers have speculated about the second marriage. Those who favor García Moreno state that the union was very happy. The two had known each other since Mariana was a small child, as García Moreno had adopted her and her four sisters when she was only eight. García Moreno's critics tell a more scandalous story. They claim that he poisoned Rosa because she was old, unattractive, and well beyond childbearing years so that he could take up with the youthful and comely Mariana—even though he did not sincerely love her. Intriguing as the story is, there seems to be absolutely no evidence to support it. By the latter 1860s, García Moreno appears to have regained some familial happiness and settled down on a rented estate named Guachalá, near the town of Cayambe in Imbabura. There he raised cattle and horses, planted the first eucalyptus trees in Ecuador, sealed off the old "torture room" used in the colonial period for recalcitrant *obraje* workers, and turned the highest profits in the hacienda's history.[23] Of equal importance, his second marriage linked him to the influential Alcázar family, among the largest landowners in the north-central sierra.

DIPLOMATIC ASSIGNMENT AND INTERNATIONAL POLITICS

As García Moreno played the role of the seignorial farmer, Ecuador became deeply involved in a diplomatic controversy that had begun during his first term but now threatened to escalate into a shooting war. Hardly a battle of Ecuador's choosing, the conflict began in April 1864 when a Spanish fleet seized Peru's Chincha Islands, which supplied the guano constituting 75 percent of Peru's income. García Moreno believed that a weakened Peru could only benefit Ecuador. When called upon for assistance, he had therefore declared his nation's neutrality, meaning that the Spanish fleet could theoretically reprovision in Guayaquil. Peru requested a Pan-American conference in Lima to present a united front against Spain, and García Moreno sent Vicente Piedrahita as Ecuador's delegate. The diplomatic stalemate went on for almost a year. Finally the Chilean seizure of a Spanish ship provided the *causus belli* for renewed conflict, and in 1866 the Spanish fleet bombarded Valparaíso and later Callao, Peru.[24] As the Spanish became more bellicose, the west coast nations banded together. A special envoy convinced the Carrión government to sign an offensive and defensive alliance, despite the argument that the declaration of war made little sense in terms of Ecuador's self-interest, because Spain was Ecuador's largest consumer of cacao exports.[25]

Governor García Moreno decided to protect Guayaquil by sinking ships at the narrowest point of the channel to prevent navigation to the shore. He called it "a magnificent means of defense."[26] When news came of the Peruvian victory at Callao, ending the crisis, the nation erupted with celebrations. Despite the return of the Spanish fleet to the Old World, the Pacific nations were not convinced that they had seen the last of their aggressive parent. Therefore they resolved to meet again to coordinate strategy for response to a future threat. Thus at the beginning of June 1866, Carrión and Bustamante appointed the recently married García Moreno as Ecuador's representative to the meeting of the Pacific nations. At the end of the month, García Moreno, his trusted assistant Pablo Herrera (the well-educated son of a priest in Pujilí whom García Moreno referred to as "my library"), and his party (including his niece, Pedro Pablo's eight-year-old daughter) boarded a ship for Santiago, Chile.[27]

En route to Santiago, the group stopped briefly in Peru. García Moreno had arranged to meet the popular new president, Mariano Prado, who had organized the defense against Spain. As the party pulled into the train station near the Plaza de Armas in Lima, a man named Juan Viteri, the brother of one of the "pirates" executed at Jambelí and Urbina's nephew, rushed up to García Moreno brandishing a pistol. He squeezed off two shots, one grazing García Moreno's hand and the other passing through his hat. He and one of his companions wrestled Viteri to the ground, holding him until police arrived and took the would-be assassin away. Meanwhile President Prado sent an armed guard to protect García Moreno and escort him to the palace.[28] As usual, García Moreno saw the hand of God in his narrow escape. "This convinces me that God wants me to continue the difficult mission of consolidating our liberty on a moral basis," he wrote a friend. Almost immediately he resumed his journey to Santiago, only to hear that at trial Viteri claimed he had challenged García Moreno to a duel and that the police had arrested the wrong man. Logically, a duel would not take place in a train station with one's eight-year-old niece present. The very idea made García Moreno explode in anger. "It's not permitted anywhere in the world that the criminal eludes justice by accusing the victim."[29] Absent contradictory testimony, the tactic worked and within a short time the court freed Viteri.

García Moreno waxed enthusiastic about Chile. Because it still embraced Diego Portales' ideas for conservative modernization, García Moreno was predisposed to like the "beautiful, civilized, country that is the pride of America." "Here I have been greeted with so much enthusiasm; I never receive in my own country the public demonstrations I get here every day." He also deeply appreciated the effort Chileans made on August 10 to celebrate Ecuadorian independence.[30] Meanwhile García Moreno negotiated the alliance with Peru, Chile, and Bolivia. Ecuador had little to offer materially, since it had neither ships nor money to contribute. Yet García Moreno did promise his country's "troops, ports, resources, and whatever else is necessary to meet the terms of the alliance." Characteristically he agreed to the treaty after a private meeting with Chile's minister of foreign relations and without consulting the government in Ecuador![31]

Next García Moreno went to work on more practical matters, such as a postal treaty and a treaty of commerce and navigation. The former met with approval, but Peru blocked a regional commercial treaty. As the pace of events slowed, García Moreno demonstrated once again that he lacked the temperament of a diplomat. He told Chile's foreign minister that he wanted to get down to business and avoid "wasting time in useless and awkward formalities." Never a man of great patience, García Moreno decided to leave Pablo Herrera in charge of the stalled negotiations and return home.

García Moreno's sudden departure for Ecuador surprised both his colleagues and the Carrión government. He believed that he had family obligations to fulfill, however. As usual he provided an exact accounting of his expenses: The government owed him 246.57 pesos.[32] He arrived just in time for Mariana's first childbirth and to help Pedro Pablo, as mentioned previously.

The war with Spain had important repercussions for both Ecuador and García Moreno. His presence at the Santiago meeting enhanced his reputation. Caricatured in the liberal press, García Moreno had been portrayed as a demagogue, a fanatic lacking perspective. Spending time with the heads of state or their principal ministers softened that image. The presidents of Peru and Chile actually liked García Moreno. Most important, García Moreno saw firsthand Diego Portales' system of government in action. García Moreno brought a copy of the Portalian constitution home with him, and it would become the blueprint for Ecuador's Constitution of 1869.

THE OUSTER OF JERÓNIMO CARRIÓN

Despite frequent comments that he hoped to stay out of politics after his term ended, García Moreno clearly wanted a pliable puppet to continue his program. Initially Jerónimo Carrión seemed to fit the bill. They agreed on basic policies regarding public works, education, and the creation of the "Catholic nation." (The next section will assess what was achieved in these areas.) García Moreno also insisted, though, that Carrión remain vigilant against Urbina and his followers. Defining who was a dangerous liberal, however, became a point of contention.

From the outset of his presidency, Carrión struck an independent course, as his moderate friends in Cuenca advised. For example, he appointed his father-in-law (García Moreno's bitter enemy, Manuel Bustamante) as his prime minister, combining the portfolios of interior and foreign relations in his hands. This act led García Moreno to distrust the administration from the outset. Yet most observers thought that Carrión's moderation and his unwillingness to fawn before García Moreno gave the new president his own party and "a great majority of the [moderate liberal] opposition."[33] Winning their support, many of whom García Moreno thought to be pro-Urbina, hardly endeared Carrión to his predecessor.

Nevertheless, despite some verbal jousting with Bustamante, García Moreno remained loyal to the government until a series of events in the summer of 1867 provoked him. First, the governor of Azuay allegedly opened one of García Moreno's confidential letters and read it. Angrily García Moreno complained sarcastically to the governor by sending the next letter unsealed and asking him to deliver it after he finished reading it. The governor denied the accusation and did investigate the charge.[34] Then García Moreno lost his bid for a Senate seat in the election of 1867. Although he had fewer votes, García Moreno claimed victory because his opponent was technically ineligible. When the Senate met in August, the members voted, led by moderate liberal Pedro Carbo, to reject García Moreno's credentials and seat his opponent in accordance with "the popular will."[35] An angry García Moreno stormed out of the building.

The government's actions in the fall of 1867 continued to infuriate García Moreno, who believed that many of the newly elected congressional representatives were secretly Urbina supporters. They considered a bill to expel the Jesuits from the Colegio Nacional, the elite academies in Quito and Cuenca. Worse yet, they passed legislation granting amnesties to the rebels who had fought at Jambelí, returning their confiscated property. President Carrión did object initially to that measure, but reconciliation (or appeasement, depending on one's viewpoint) was clearly on the congressional agenda. In response, García Moreno stated, "We must defend until death the principles of religion, property, and morality."[36] His supporters began to speak out in congress.

The situation exploded when Bustamante, aggravated by this congressional opposition, sought to imprison several senators, including Manuel Gómez de la Torre and historian Pedro Fermín Cevallos. When congress declared itself in permanent session to make inquiries, Bustamante sent a military detachment to dissolve the body. Carrión compromised with congress by discharging Bustamante. Congress accepted Bustamante's resignation. On October 10, 1867, Carrión appointed three García Moreno stalwarts to the cabinet: Rafael Carvajal at Foreign Relations, Bernardo Dávalos (formerly García Moreno's key cavalry officer) at Treasury, and Manuel de Ascásubi at War. At least temporarily, García Moreno thought the crisis averted.[37]

García Moreno's optimism proved short-lived, however. At a cabinet meeting, Carrión broached the idea of proroguing congress before its session expired. García Moreno could think of but a single reason for this proposal: to bring Bustamante back into the government and thus dismiss the new ministers without raising congressional opposition. García Moreno stated: "My friends must leave their posts without exception before serving as the instruments for this unjustifiable measure." At the same time, he advised Carrión to resign because dissolving congress before its term expired was unconstitutional. Once the members of the legislature learned that Carrión intended to dismiss them, their opposition hardened and sealed the president's fate. To no one's surprise, congress leaked the not-so-secret story that Bustamante had arranged for García Moreno's exclusion from the Senate that summer. An angry García Moreno also suspected, based on hearsay, that Bustamante was behind the assassination attempt in Lima. To pressure the president, the new cabinet resigned, accusing Carrión of double-dealings with Bustamante. Making one last-ditch effort to save his presidency, Carrión named García Moreno commander-in-chief of the army, a position the latter accepted. Now the ex-president was poised to act. Once again García Moreno advised Carrión to quit. Congress censured both Bustamante and Carrión for abuse of power, threatening impeachment. Therefore, Carrión took the course of least resistance and resigned on November 6, 1867.[38]

With both the president and Bustamante eliminated, the question

LEFT: *Jerónimo Carrión, García Moreno's successor, 1865–1867;* RIGHT: *Javier Espinosa, interim president, 1867–1869 (Both courtesy of the Benson Collection)*

became who would govern the country for the remaining two years of the term. The credentials of Vice President Pedro de Arteta included a long pro-Flores service career and a brief stint as one of the triumvirs in 1859. Yet García Moreno did not feel comfortable leaving the job in the hands of this aged politician because he might die in office, resulting in his constitutional successor being the moderately liberal president of the Senate, Pedro Carbo. Thus García Moreno chose to hold an election for an interim successor who would be a reliable puppet. García Moreno vetoed the maverick Benigno Malo, then serving as envoy to Peru, because he had agreed tentatively to a treaty ceding territory to Peru as a border settlement. Ultimately a consensus emerged around the idea of nominating Javier Espinosa, a nondescript, nonpolitical, and very Catholic childhood friend of García Moreno's who served as the attorney general at the Supreme Court. Only Pedro Carbo and Ignacio de Veintemilla dissented. Espinosa's cousin, another ardent Catholic and former treasury secretary named Camilo Ponce, agreed to serve as the principal minister. "The virtues and noble precedents of the candidate, and above all his sincere and pure Catholicism, are our best guarantees," García Moreno wrote.[39]

Thus ended Jerónimo Carrión's presidency because he failed to act like a dutiful puppet on what García Moreno viewed as security issues. In addition Carrión may have been perceived by some as catering too exclusively to south sierran regional interests. Certainly the *guayaquileños* were angry that nearly half of the money Peru and Chile gave Ecuador to bolster defenses in the port ended up being used for pet projects in Azuay. García Moreno looked to the future optimistically. Following the voting, he wrote: "We have elected a most excellent president." The French minister, however, saw García Moreno's circle of friends narrowing to just the "clerical party."[40]

THE GARCIAN PROJECT CONTINUES: SCHOOLS AND ROADS

Essentially García Moreno's Catholic nation-building project continued unabated during the interim presidencies, although perhaps not as rapidly or efficiently as he would have liked. Public works projects such as schools, hospitals, and roads remained a priority from 1865 to 1869. Citizens were pleased to hear that more Christian Brothers had embarked on teaching missions, enthusiastically reiterating their belief in the relationship between expanding educational opportunities and the future prosperity of their communities. As Francisco Salazar, a prominent García Moreno supporter, phrased it: "Education is the basis of civilization, of morality, and of progress." At the same time, local officials groaned about the cost of bringing the monastics from Europe and requested financial assistance from the federal government. With the exception of some parts of the coast, where "many times it is necessary to bring the children to school by force," students flocked to the schools.[41]

Hospitals remained primitive even by contemporary standards. Generally understaffed, the facilities lacked supplies of drugs and surgical instruments. Bringing the Sisters of Charity from France helped, but raising the necessary funds took time. Advances came slowly, yet medical personnel made progress. The use of vaccine against smallpox became more widespread. The regime even took strides to improve women's health care. In 1868 Congress decreed the creation of a school of obstetrics, although it would be several years before this dream was realized.[42] In short, both Carrión and Espinosa paid attention to education and health care issues, promoting the same solutions as García Moreno. This approach attracted French brothers and nuns to provide the expertise, because Ecuadorians lacked the requisite training.

If the annual budget for 1867 is typical for the period, then the interim presidents spent twice as much on public works as on education and hospitals—which had also been true during García Moreno's term when military expenses cost eight times the education budget. As in the earlier regime, Carrión focused on road building as a means of unifying the nation. The main highway now wended its way through highly mountainous Chimborazo province on its way to the sea. In part because of the terrain and in part because of labor shortages, the work proceeded slowly when at all—often because the primitive tools used by the workers blunted themselves on the rocks and were not easily replaced.[43]

Not surprisingly, the indigenous people resented working on the project. Years of coercion under Spanish rule reduced the spirit of the *minga* (cooperative labor project) that had prevailed under the Incas and their predecessors. Workers were scarce "because of the almost unconquerable repugnance felt by the majority of the Indians of the province." When foremen mistreated the workers, as inevitably happened, the indigenous people felt vindicated in their resentment. Workers were supposed to be paid the same rate they would have earned at their agricultural labor. In Tungurahua, however, they were paid slightly less—at least until the inspector reported the abuse. Paying the same wage as on the hacienda was hardly conducive to success, though. For one reason, the workers had to travel to a designated town to collect their pay, meaning that they lost all day Sunday making the trip. For another reason, the work was harder—supervisors allowed no leaning on the shovel here.[44] No wonder Indians made excuses (such as being engaged in the harvest, festivals, or commercial activities) to avoid going to work on the road project. So desperate had the situation become that congress offered to grant land alongside the road to workers who would labor and later repair the section near their new homes. The road passed through Chimborazo province and crawled south and west, sometimes at a pace of a thousand yards a month.[45]

Progress on the main highway also may have slowed because President Carrión gave priority to another project—a road that would have connected his home city of Cuenca to a small port, Naranjal, and thereby provided a direct commercial outlet for Azuay's *cascarilla.* In January 1866 the governor of Azuay, Miguel Heredia, broached the Naranjal road project with the enthusiastic support of the Cuenca city council presided over by Benigno Malo. Soon Carrión sent Christopher Thill, one of the foreign engineers employed by the federal government, to survey the prospective route. Special legislation privileged the Naranjal road project, including language about coercing labor and requiring the city of Guayaquil to contribute one-quarter of its *trabajo subsidiario* revenue (the argument being that Naranjal was within the provincial boundaries of Guayas).[46] Funding the Naranjal road caused considerable tension between Cuenca and Guayaquil. The lukewarm feelings of Guayaquil for the project were symbolized by the gift of the "miserable" hundred pesos for the road instead of one-quarter of the *trabajo subsidiario,* as Azuay's governor had requested. Certainly Guayaquil's merchant elite had no interest in helping to create a competitive port facility in Naranjal. Without funding, the Naranjal road project languished.[47]

As previously noted, road construction was not an end unto itself but rather a means to progress and prosperity, a hegemonic goal of liberals and progressive conservatives such as García Moreno who believed in developing domestic and international trade. Paralleling the slowdown of road construction in the interim period, García Moreno's promotional scheme to participate in the Paris World's Fair of 1866 also lost momentum. Before leaving office, García Moreno had directed the governors to locate unusual minerals, agricultural products, or livestock to exhibit. As he said later, though, little happened: "Proprietors who have the most knowledge of products are the most indifferent to the idea, . . . failing to look towards the future and bettering the products that bring them riches." Even Miguel García Moreno, governor of Ecuador's most prosperous province, lamented that he had received no response to his request. "Our people are in such a state of backwardness that it is impossible for the government to remove them from it," he added. To make matters worse, those products that did arrive at the fair had wilted or suffered damage, according to Antonio Flores, who saw them in Paris.[48]

The slow growth of the export economy during these four years was not unexpected because the war between Spain and the west coast Spanish American states disrupted commercial relations with the former, and Spain was the principal consumer of cacao. Nevertheless the Ecuadorian government maintained its diversity of exports, granting concessions to miners seeking gold, while governor Miguel García Moreno encouraged a British engineer to exploit petroleum deposits on the Santa Elena peninsula, deposits utilized since pre-Hispanic times.[49] With the growing popularity of kerosene lighting, the market for petroleum had dramatically increased. Ecuador thus had a slim chance to cash in on the new boom. All in all, however, the presidential terms from 1865 to 1869 saw no marked changes in terms of García Moreno's pragmatic developmental strategy.

THE VISION OF THE STATE UNDER CARRIÓN AND ESPINOSA

The concept of a nation united by Catholic values remained central for Presidents Carrión and Espinosa. Both men were ardent Catholics, and hence each wanted to maintain close ties to the church. Espinosa's minister, Camilo Ponce, who held all the cabinet portfolios, summarized the sentiment of the government: "The Catholic religion . . . is the fundamental base of the social order, and the inexhaustible source of all human progress." During the interim years, Ecuador and the Vatican finalized the Concordat, ending the oft-stalemated negotiations.

Antonio Flores, once again in Rome, met with Cardinal Antonelli to present the recommendation of Ecuador's joint church-state commission that tithe revenues be shared equally. By the end of April 1866, Flores and the Cardinal signed off on the Concordat.[50] They discussed other issues as well. Although some high church officials had earlier complained about the expenses associated with the new dioceses, Flores reported that the bishoprics of Riobamba, Ibarra, and Loja were now functioning smoothly. Gradually the hierarchy was assigning necessary priests to remote towns, although small incomes remained an issue. Perhaps most importantly, Flores informed Antonelli that the church had cooperated with the reform program by rooting out some of the worst abusers, like a priest who forced the Colorado Indians to sell their *caucho* (rubber) to him at below market price. Thus García Moreno told Ignacio Ordóñez, bishop of the new diocese of Riobamba, that he was "very content with the means you have taken to moralize the clergy, on which depends the morality of the diocese."[51]

García Moreno's program of cultural engineering continued unabated as congress renewed its prohibition of bullfighting. To some degree, the ban on bullfighting may have been a response to the foreign community, which uniformly loathed the tradition. The new U.S. minister's daughter, Jessie Coggeshall, reported: "I have never seen a more brutal sport in my life." Ecuadorians acted foolhardily at these fights, she opined, by climbing into the ring in Santo Domingo Plaza to tease the bull and then jumping out again. A different statute banned Carnaval activities, another tradition that may have insulted foreign sensibilities of decorum. In lieu of these entertainments, congress decreed that municipalities construct theaters, presumably for more European-style entertainments, using one-tenth of their town's tax revenue for that purpose.[52] Nevertheless several governors requested exemptions to the bullfighting ban, as in the case of the Holy Family Festival sponsored by a wealthy and pious family from Loja, or the Santa Rita festival in

Babahoyo. The fact that antibullfight legislation had to be repeatedly passed suggested that the ban was not enforceable. Likewise Carnaval continued to be celebrated. Changing deeply rooted popular culture proved difficult, at least when the only choice was an outright prohibition.

No greater challenge presented itself to the Catholic state, however, than the growing number of Protestants residing in Quito and Guayaquil. Although businessmen comprised the largest portion of the Protestant community, it was the unexpected demise of British Minister Edward Neale that raised the first challenge to the all-Catholic state. Obviously heretics could not be interred in Catholic holy ground, but his family exerted pressure for a Christian burial. At first the religious establishment prevailed. Apparently he had died of a serious disease and his body needed to be disposed of quickly. As the procession arrived at the site designated for the consul's temporary deposit (a small chapel on the side of Mt. Pichincha), the Archbishop of Quito, the Papal Delegate, and some friars barred the entrance to the vault, forcing the mourners to take the body elsewhere. The city council balked at the idea of locating a cemetery within the confines of Quito. Both Neale's son and United States Minister William Coggeshall furiously protested, and received the support of the diplomatic corps save for the Papal Nuncio. Minister Coggeshall never forgave Papal Delegate Tavani's hypocrisy, pointing out that after smoking cigars and drinking brandy at the Englishman's home, he had turned around and denied him a Christian burial. Compounding the problem, the U.S. minister learned that a desperately ill United States citizen had, while in the hospital, been threatened with having his dead body thrown into a ravine to "be devoured by buzzards" if he refused to convert to Catholicism.[53]

Minister of the Interior Bustamante clearly wanted a resolution to this predicament, which the diplomats provided by pointing out that the initial treaties of friendship and commerce from the 1830s between Ecuador, Great Britain, and the United States called for the creation of a Protestant burial ground. Although the Bishop of Cuenca and others believed that such an accommodation would violate the constitution, the Carrión government pushed ahead and by June 1867 had selected a suitable site outside Quito. By the following spring, when the Protestant cemetery opened, the former British minister and Coggeshall became its first occupants.[54] Interestingly, García Moreno did not weigh in on the debate. Perhaps in reviewing Chile's constitution, he had learned about the exemption for Protestant burials and thought this practice a wise precedent for Ecuador.

If Protestants could not participate fully in the Catholic state, what role did women and Afro-Ecuadorians play? Women certainly were essential to the new state. Traditionally women were viewed as a source of morality in Latin America. Men were sinners: They drank, seduced women, gambled, and got into fights while the virtuous women held the home and family together. Women tended to be more religious and to impart these values to their children. Consequently García Moreno took very seriously the idea of educating women so that they would become an even stronger bastion of morality. Married women, however, lacked legal rights—as did minors.[55] Only widows could control their fortunes under the law, but this situation did not differ from that of women in the United States or Great Britain.

Blacks, however, remained outside the Catholic nation. García Moreno's correspondence and public speeches simply ignored them. No doubt because he had seen African slaves in his youth, he was deeply prejudiced, as was evidenced when the possibility of U.S. blacks emigrating to Ecuador was broached during his first term. Neither of the two proposed plans met official approval, and García Moreno's response reveals much about his attitude towards blacks. The first suggestion, made by Benigno Malo, was to sell the United States 50,000 acres of prime cotton land along the Suya River (part of Cañar River system) for a "mere" US$1.5 million. According to Malo, the government could resettle African Americans there, resolving the social problem of emancipated slaves in the United States and bringing needed labor to the area. The U.S. secretary of state rejected the scheme, however, calling it unconstitutional. So did García Moreno.

As the U.S. Civil War wound down and the problem of the freed slaves became more pressing, a new proposal surfaced. Hassaurek reported that the president pulled no punches: "He expressed strong antipathy against the Negro race. He regretted that there were so many of them in and around Guayaquil, and added that it would be fortunate for the white race in America if it could rid itself entirely of the Negro element, either by transporting it back to Africa or in some other way." Lest we think too harshly of García Moreno, though, we might remember that Abraham Lincoln also proposed transporting the freed slaves back to Africa. García Moreno's foreign minister, Pablo Herrera, soon told Hassaurek that the president issued orders that would prevent the freed slaves from landing at Guayaquil. Hassaurek protested García Moreno's decision, stating that not only did the Constitution of 1861 specifically encourage immigration, but as a matter of international law, all citizens from a given country (and the blacks were now U.S. citizens) had to be treated equally. García Moreno conceded the point, although he continued to hold "that the Negro element was a bad and dangerous one; that the Negroes of Guayaquil were lazy and insolent, always willing to take part in insurrections and revolutions."[56] Eventually, as Hassaurek realized, no freed slaves would come to Ecuador because of the costs and uncertainties involved. The failure of this immigration scheme, however, clearly reveals García Moreno's opinions about Afro-Ecuadorians, whom he believed were irredeemable and not part of the Catholic nation.

THE GREAT IBARRA EARTHQUAKE OF 1868

At about 1:15 on the morning of August 16, 1868, as the residents of the city of Ibarra in Imbabura soundly slept, the ground began to shake. A cataclysmic earthquake like none had ever seen before was occurring. Even in the Andes, where earthquakes and erupting volcanoes are all-too-common hazards, the earthquake of 1868 stood out as the most devastating of the nineteenth century. The quake destroyed every home, business, and public building in Ibarra, burying thousands of victims. Single walls standing here and there marked what once had been a prosperous provincial capital. To make matters worse, rain fell in torrents and many drowned in the raging floodwaters. Bodies stacked up under the rubble and wetness. Survivors lacked food, water, and shelter—and then a series of aftershocks terrorized them.[57] In the nearby Indian community of Otavalo, not a single house stood intact as an estimated six thousand people died. Because flimsier huts caused less damage to inhabitants, more rural people survived. Strewn rubble lay everywhere. Thieves began sorting through the debris, looting the remains of homes and businesses as survivors scrambled for safer environs, often with less than the clothes normally on their backs. Complicating matters further, local Indians rebelled, after seeing in the midst of chaos an opportunity to wreak vengeance on their oppressors.[58]

As people fled the towns, they discovered that the quake had destroyed roads and opened huge chasms and ravines. A clerical inspector filed reports detailing the devastation in rural Imbabura. One large abyss had swallowed most of a village, killing all of the town's inhabitants. Churches, hospitals, private residences, government buildings—nothing was spared. Although the quake struck hardest in Imbabura, ripple effects shook highland cities as far south as Latacunga and Ambato. Quito also experienced considerable destruction. As the new British minister reported, churches, public buildings, and private residences all sustained damage. While many

The ruins of Ibarra after the great earthquake of 1868 (Permission of the Banco Central del Ecuador)

of Quito's elite fled south, the majority of the population took to living in the city's plazas because the aftershocks made life inside fractured walls frightening. People were praying in the streets, while throngs awaited their turns in the confessionals. The British minister and his family pitched a tent in the Plaza de la Independencia, fearing for their safety. Despite the destruction in Quito, few lost their lives. In Imbabura, however, the death toll reached between fifteen and twenty thousand people.[59]

In the face of the emergency, the federal government decided to appoint the only person seemingly capable of directing recovery efforts, Gabriel García Moreno. Like the clerical inspector, García Moreno could not believe his eyes as he traveled to Otavalo and Ibarra. He reported that in places "it was as if the earth had boiled" and added, "My heart was destroyed like the land that surrounded me."[60] Disaster relief provided García Moreno with both a challenge and the opportunity to win the hearts and minds of the people of Ecuador, and to become a genuinely popular caudillo, the indispensable man for his country.

Sympathy for the victims of the earthquake abounded. Within days the governor of Pichincha had collected donations of money and clothing "to cover those who had been saved naked." The list of contributors showed many small donors giving a peso or two, or perhaps a couple of shirts, while a few people provided larger monetary contributions. Other governors also assisted, as did the bishop of Cuenca. Even people from the coast overcame regional biases and generously contributed cash.[61]

Imbabura's remarkable recovery resulted from the leadership, determination, and energy that García Moreno displayed in handling the crisis. His boundless enthusiasm put spirit back into the destitute. His "severe measures" regarding looters, enforced by Lieutenant Colonel José Rivadeneira and the soldiers he brought with him, quickly restored order. García Moreno requested a special judge to try these criminals, and soon reported that "there has been a return to the moral order and the administration of justice." Simultaneously he helped the victims of the disaster with emergency relief. "We'll feed those who have nothing, protect them from the violence of the perverse ones, and cure their fatigue." By the end of August, García Moreno had outlined a comprehensive strategy for Imbabura's reconstruction.[62]

With preliminary orders for relief issued, García Moreno toured the province, assessing the human tragedy for himself. As he contemplated the destruction, he reached the same scientific conclusion as the Jesuit investigator—namely, that a huge explosion of compressed gases beneath Mt. Cotocachi had caused the earthquake. His more religious side (and some clergy) saw the hand of God at work, punishing the province for its evil deeds. That spring Imbabura had elected the "fatuous" poet Julio Zaldumbide as its governor, with the support of Ibarra's bishop. "What greater sin than to have the clergy support an avowed enemy of God who doesn't even believe in His existence," García Moreno said. Some clergy also blamed the public's profanation of religious holidays with excessive drinking and dissolution.[63]

Food and clothing soon arrived from the south. Although Ibarra and Otavalo have pleasant climates, Andean nights are cold. Consequently García Moreno recognized the pressing need for clothing and blankets, as well as makeshift housing. He wrote his friend Governor Nicolás Martínez to request help from the governor's wife and the women of Ambato. He wanted them to contribute to the relief effort by making women's footwear, because many of the victims from Ibarra were "walking barefoot like Indians and suffering tremendously for it." The women of Ambato responded, and García Moreno thanked them for their assistance.[64] This episode leads to two interesting observations. First, upper-class women like Governor Martínez's wife and her circle of friends were expected as part of the *noblesse oblige* culture to participate in the charitable effort by handcrafting basic necessities. Second, García Moreno's talk of victims walking around barefoot *like Indians* demonstrates again that his was a very race-conscious society.

In the days immediately following the earthquake, the threat of disease concerned García Moreno. Rotting corpses and stagnant water led to multiple cases of fevers and dysentery. The region's largest hospital in Ibarra lay in ruins like the rest of the city. Consequently García Moreno arranged field hospitals in Esperanza and some of the smaller towns. He begged the federal government to send sheets, pillows, and mattresses. A Colombian doctor helped to set up the hospitals. Several volunteer physicians, including García Moreno's friend Miguel Egas, came from Quito to treat patients. The former president also called on the federal government to provide drugs and other medical supplies. Collapsing buildings had caused massive traumas, and the doctors needed antiseptics and other medicines to prevent infections. So well did patients respond to treatment that by the middle of November, García Moreno decided to close the field hospitals and send the few remaining patients home.[65] The humanitarian crisis had not completely ended within two months, but the worst moments had passed and most citizens could now survive on their own.

The most tangible and versatile type of disaster relief was cold hard cash. At one point García Moreno estimated that it might cost the government 500,000 pesos to succor the unfortunate victims to the point where they could regain their economic independence and return to work. Donations flowed in from all over Ecuador "to help our brothers in the north," supplemented by relief funds from the national government. Once the foreign community understood the magnitude of the disaster, additional money came from Chile and less rapidly from Peru and Colombia. As usual the British also contributed generously, as they were wont to do in the nineteenth century.[66] Meanwhile Ecuador had begun relief efforts of its own for the able-bodied widows and orphans, sending them to Quito to board with willing families who received small subsidies for their care.[67]

With the immediate needs of the unfortunate provided for by a combination of charity and government assistance, García Moreno could turn his attention to rebuilding the infrastructure of the province. In his mind relief and recovery depended on the resumption of commerce. Hence García Moreno wanted to reconstruct the roads and get the people of Imbabura back to work as rapidly as possible. Almost immediately García Moreno began to rebuild the highway through the Chota Valley and construct a new road to provide access to Salinas where salt—necessary for the preservation of meat—was extracted. His repetitious letters demanded shovels, pick-axes, and wheelbarrows so that the work could progress more rapidly.[68] By the time his tenure as civil and military commander of Imbabura ended, the roads had made considerable progress.

Reconstructing the towns and ultimately the city of Ibarra took more time. In at least two instances, García Moreno simply relocated towns to more favorable spots, despite local complaining. He widened the streets and, of course, built schools and churches. For the larger communities, he required the service of engineers, so U.S. engineer Thomas Reed and Modesto López (the only native-born Ecuadorian engineer at the time) produced plans and models. To get some additional technical assistance, García Moreno hurried seven students off to Quito for a quick course in construction so they could assist the engineers. By November 1 García Moreno moved ahead with the rebuilding of Ibarra, widening streets and bringing in a supply of pure water. In one of his last acts as the provincial administrator, he distributed cash to poor families so that they could fix their homes, although some housing needs continued thereafter. Work also began on the new cathedral.[69]

Like all good members of the elite imbued with the values of *noblesse oblige*, García Moreno himself donated cash and goods to the cause. From all over the province, town councils and individuals showered him with praise, thanking him for his "benevolent and protecting hand that rescued us from the grave," and for "rescuing us from the tombs in which we were buried by nature." Some of the grateful citizens referred to García Moreno as "our benevolent Father and Savior," and the women of Ibarra presented him with a bejeweled gold medal inscribed to "the savior of Ibarra." García Moreno, when praised by a high church official, modestly said, "I just write the checks and God pays."[70] As a result of his actions in response to this national disaster, García Moreno enjoyed the popularity necessary to become a successful caudillo. While the military victory at Jambelí made him appear invincible, he now enjoyed a reputation as a man who could accomplish the impossible, the indispensable man. As a result, García Moreno would be difficult to challenge if he decided to run for the presidency in 1869.[71]

At the same time, García Moreno wore his popularity well. He seemed much more modest and aware of his frailties and the work of others. For the first time, he gave thanks and public acknowledgment to those who had contributed to the effort in Imbabura, such as the four physicians who volunteered their services. Likewise he thanked people who had donated money or clothing, and women's groups that made shoes or shirts for the destitute. Such generosity of spirit had hitherto been absent from his character. Perhaps this newfound humility resulted from a growing awareness of his own mortality. In early October, García Moreno collapsed from unspecified causes. He refused to believe it was apoplexy (what we now would suspect as a stroke), claiming his temporary weakness was only sunstroke.[72] (Personally I suspect stress and overwork, since the attack felled him for over a month and a second attack in November caused him to resign altogether.) The Ibarra earthquake relief effort of 1868 completed the process whereby García Moreno became a caudillo, the dominant figure in Ecuadorian politics.

THE SPECTER OF URBINA: ESPINOSA'S DOWNFALL

As noted previously, from 1865 to 1869 both Jerónimo Carrión and Javier Espinosa concurred with García Moreno's ideas for conservative nation building. Both fell from power, however, because they preached moderation and did not stand up to the "reds," as García Moreno labeled the liberals. Not one to tolerate dissent, García Moreno believed that even moderates who challenged his ideas were dangerous enemies of the state. Initially García Moreno believed he and Espinosa thought alike on this issue: "That on the day of danger, which I think is near, they [Espinosa and chief minister Camilo Ponce] will display the energy that only reputable men have."[73] Disillusionment set in quickly.

In March 1868 García Moreno's good friend, Nicolás Martínez, resigned as the governor of Chimborazo after being implicated in a public quarrel between his friends and some Colombians. García Moreno recoiled when Espinosa appointed Francisco Montalvo, the brother of liberal author Juan Montalvo, to the governorship. García Moreno penned letters to Camilo Ponce, attempting to dissuade him from this appointment. Receiving no answer to his three letters, García Moreno traveled to Quito to meet with Ponce. The audience proved most unsatisfactory, for Ponce refused to explain the rationale for choosing Montalvo. García Moreno told Ponce that he was behaving like Manuel Bustamante, hardly a recommendation for longevity in office. By now García Moreno held out little hope for Espinosa either, who "seems much like the late administration of Carrión." "The administration has dropped its mask" and was acting "unjust[ly] and ungrateful[ly] like Bustamante . . . seeking out and protecting my enemies."[74] No doubt Espinosa, like Carrión, hoped to preside over an administration of reconciliation, but García Moreno refused all compromises with moderates and liberals. García Moreno swore to "defend our [conservative] principles and our country against the infamous band [liberals]."[75]

García Moreno's hackles rose again in May, when Ponce appeared to be encouraging the moderate Antonio Borrero from Cuenca to run for the presidency in the 1869 elections. García Moreno initially refused to run: "The only error I have committed in my political career was accepting the presidency in 1861 knowing the absurdities of the Constitution and the laws derived from it."[76] Given his refusal, other candidates' names came forward. Some suggested Camilo Ponce, who, García Moreno believed, had "good intentions but was weak and equivocal" and "would not be a good president." Others liked Borrero, but García Moreno vetoed him because he was too anticlerical. Nor would he support "miserable spiritual lepers like [Ignacio] de Veintemilla and all the reds [liberals]." Instead García Moreno urged the candidacy of General Secundino Darquea, who was both a fervid Catholic and strongly opposed to having Urbina or any of his friends (like Francisco Montalvo presumably) in government.[77] Darquea's candidacy failed to resonate, however. Always ambitious, García Moreno opened the door slightly for his own prospects. For example, he told friends he would accept the presidency if the people authorized him to reform the Constitution and the laws.[78] For several months, though, he laid the whole question aside because of his involvement with disaster relief in Imbabura. When approached about the presidency again in November 1868, his newfound popularity made him a much more attractive candidate.

Looking at the prospective field, García Moreno mentally disposed of all the other candidates as unacceptable. Francisco Javier Aguirre, new favorite of the Cuenca moderate liberals, was tainted not only because his wife and General Urbina's wife were sisters but also because he had spoken out against the Concordat. Pedro Carbo, the brothers José and Ignacio de Veintemilla, and Manuel Gómez de la Torre were all too liberal. Manuel Bustamante and the former governor of Azuay who had stolen García Moreno's letters were "too perfidious." Benigno Malo failed to pass muster because of his willingness to settle the boundary dispute in Peru's favor. Finally, García Moreno also rejected Vicente Piedrahita as too immature. Above all else, García Moreno wanted to prevent a rift in conservative ranks that he feared would give the liberals the chance to win an undeserved victory. Antonio Borrero urged García Moreno to accept a compromise candidate, but he felt confident of victory. "God will not permit the catastrophe of August 16 [the earthquake] to be followed up by a moral, political and religious cataclysm such as the triumph of the liberals," he said.[79]

By mid-December he had agreed to run for the presidency on the conservative ticket. Now a full-fledged candidate, García Moreno offered his platform, which reiterated the goals of his first term. Many Ecuadorians reacted enthusiastically to García Moreno's candidacy. "The moral, proven characteristics of our candidate, his knowledge of the resources of government, his belief in the education of others, his activities in improving roads that will favor commerce and foreign immigration . . . are his special characteristics that make him a necessity for our country," said one.[80]

As the year wound down, García Moreno became more and more fretful about the coming elections—not for his own sake (or so he claimed), but rather because he perceived a growing threat from Urbina. What he feared was the Espinosa government's neutral stance, which he perceived as tacit support for the liberals. Pedro Carbo and Francisco Javier Aguirre, the moderate liberal candidate, were still campaigning hard and the government did nothing to discourage them. Minister Ponce quietly told Antonio Flores, abroad on another diplomatic mission, that the race was between Aguirre and García Moreno: It "would be a hard fought and heated campaign" and the government was "entirely neutral."[81] Assuming these words got back to García Moreno in Quito, they would have raised his level of anxiety. While present-day Ecuadorians and U.S. observers would applaud a government that pledged not to interfere or rig an election, these niceties of democracy scarcely interested García Moreno. Rather he wanted assurances that the Espinosa government would control the election to prevent the victory of a candidate who might allow General Urbina and the exiles to gain a toehold in the political system (while many liberals hoped that Aguirre would win and continue Espinosa's reconciliation policy).

Of course the coming election presented the perfect opportunity for dissidents such as Urbina to change the political order. Rumors of coup attempts spread. From across the border in Peru, agents reported that the exiles were undertaking "bellicose preparations."[82] Espinosa did nothing in response, leading García Moreno to the conclusion that Espinosa sympathized with Urbina and therefore had to be eliminated. "If the President leaves his post, the country must establish an interim government, and call a new convention to reform our institutions." On the evening of January 16, 1869, García Moreno and a few soldiers entered the Government Palace and deposed Espinosa. García Moreno then marched to Guayaquil, rounding up support en route, and issued a proclamation announcing he had taken over as interim president to forestall Urbina's revolution. The coup proceeded bloodlessly, with pro–García Moreno elements taking over

Cuenca. Aside from Espinosa and Ponce, the only other political casualty of the coup was Governor Montalvo. Although one cannot easily gauge public opinion, it seems that many Ecuadorians supported the revolt.[83] The liberals did not. A brief protest arose in Guayaquil. Two months later General José de Veintemilla led a barracks revolt there with liberal support, arresting General Secundino Darquea. According to the U.S. consul, Darquea (while in custody) bribed a sharpshooter to kill Veintimilla, which the gunman did with a well-placed shot. The revolt immediately collapsed.[84]

The four-year interval between García Moreno's two terms demonstrated the continuity of the conservative nation-building project, albeit in a much more muted version. While furthering the developmental and ideological aspects of the program, both Carrión and Espinosa failed to act as puppets because they neglected the militant war against liberalism that ultramontanist Catholics like García Moreno hoped to wage. At the same time, García Moreno evolved into a caudillo, which would weaken his project in the long run because his system would depend on his presence. Nevertheless he deemed it necessary to unseat his disobedient puppets in order to continue shaping Ecuador along the lines of his vision.

Chapter Six

Forging the National Soul: The Coming of the Catholic Nation

As city after city capitulated peacefully to the coup of January 17, 1869, Gabriel García Moreno relished the opportunity to impose his vision of a modernizing Catholic state on Ecuador.[1] Not unreasonably, García Moreno interpreted the country's acquiescence as a mandate for his ideas, or at the very least a recognition of his newfound popularity in the wake of the reconstruction of Imbabura. Regardless of the reasons for his victory, García Moreno knew he could not fulfill his dream of the Catholic nation under the old constitution. As he had reiterated many times, the Constitution of 1861 had frustrated his ambitious program for Ecuador. Hence he pledged to call a convention to write a new instrument of governance and to pass legislation that would advance his agenda.

García Moreno's nation-building project emerged in what has been called the age of "adaptive nationalism." For the predominantly white leadership of the Andean nations, both the Spanish colonial and the liberal models had failed. The reconfiguration of the ancient Inca empire seemed more threatening than helpful, an ideal only for a few artists and literary figures.[2] Rejecting all three, therefore, García Moreno based his vision on a patriarchal, French, conservative, Catholic modernization plan with roots in the eighteenth century. As García Moreno contemplated the possibilities for uniting Ecuador—for finding the formula of soil, soul, and language that would carve out a unique space for his country—he harkened back to the classic words of the great liberator, Simón Bolívar, who had proclaimed: "Ecuador is a monastery." Foreign visitors in that era remarked consistently about the extreme religiosity of the highlands. For example, James Orton, who visited the country in 1871, said: "At half past nine in the morning all Quito is on its knees, as the great bell of the cathedral announces the elevation of the Host. The effect is astonishing.

Riders stop their horses; foot passengers drop down on the pavement; the cook lets go her dishes, and the writer his pen; the merchant lays aside his measure and the artisan his tool."[3] In this sense, the Catholic nation was certainly the will of the highland people.

García Moreno had also been profoundly influenced by Chile's success as a conservative republic. As noted previously, Diego Portales' Constitution of 1833 would serve as a blueprint for the new Ecuadorian charter.[4] Like adaptive nationalists elsewhere, García Moreno believed that universal public education, along with disciplined and productive European immigrants, would be agents of national transformation. Whether French or Chilean inspired, García Moreno also had his own agenda to resolve national problems. First, he wanted a strong centralized government that would prevent the incessant revolts and invasions characterizing his first term, and also allow progress. He had hopes of moralizing the nation as well. And while Catholic universal public education would imbue the proper values into the younger generation, García Moreno thought that upholding strict Catholic morality for all citizens would help the older generation conform to these ideals. Hence this chapter will explore García Moreno's attempt to employ Catholic education and values to unify all regions of Ecuador.

THE CONSTITUTION OF 1869

García Moreno's Constitution of 1869 has invited caricature among biographers. According to anti–García Moreno writers, the Constitution was flawed from the outset because the delegates, all García Moreno's close collaborators, were not chosen democratically. Calling the new constitution reactionary because of certain centralizing and pro-Catholic provisions, critics also belabored the antiquarian moral strictures that the document imposed. By ending freedom of speech, thought, and association, they argued, García Moreno's "Black Charter" created a "tomb of peace" in Ecuador.[5]

Naturally his proponents saw matters rather differently. Approving of his ideas for imposing order to end decades of civil strife, along with his project to bring the country's laws into conformity with its religious values, conservative writers have seen the Constitution of 1869 in a very positive light. Not only did the Constitution harmonize Ecuador's political structure with its devotion to Catholicism, they argued, but it also made an important statement against nineteenth-century liberalism by embracing Pope

Pius IX's teachings. By creating a strong executive branch, the Constitution "prevented abuses," kept the legislature and military in check, and allowed for the "greater glory of the entire people." An examination of both the process of writing the Constitution and the actual provisions of the document demonstrates that both these views are oversimplifications.[6]

Without a doubt, García Moreno handpicked the delegates to stand for election to the constituent assembly. Loyal names from his first presidency (Rafael Carvajal, Roberto de Ascásubi, Nicolás Martínez, Felipe Serrade, Pablo Herrera, to mention a few) abound in the roster of delegates. During the months preceding the election, García Moreno agonized over the list of candidates. He wrote his friends throughout the republic, soliciting their advice on the best possible slates. Some old allies were jettisoned. For example, the name of his promising diplomat, Vicente Piedrahita, turned up in some correspondence uncovered after José de Veintemilla's failed coup attempt in March. As a result, the governor of Guayas ordered Piedrahita confined to his hacienda during the constitutional deliberations, although ultimately he would rejoin the administration. García Moreno asked his closest advisors to meet him in Quito to help choose delegates, saying that they needed to be "all in agreement." Not surprisingly, the British minister found the elections suspect, since all the victorious candidates belonged to García Moreno's party.[7]

As the delegates deliberated about García Moreno's proposed draft constitution, a new cast of diplomatic characters entered the stage at Quito and provided a fresh appraisal of García Moreno and the constitutional assembly. The United States minister, E. Rumsey Wing of Kentucky, had been a Union supporter in a border state during the Civil War. Although not as loquacious as Hassaurek, Wing initially provided thorough reports. In addition, he bettered U.S.-Ecuadorian relations after the publication of Hassaurek's book had soured many of the elite on North Americans. In his early reports, Wing left a very favorable impression of García Moreno. Concurring with the latter's desire for strong government, Wing found the president less anti-American than Hassaurek had claimed and eager to take advantage of U.S. technological know-how in his modernization plans. If Hassaurek's vice was women, Wing's was strong drink, but he did provide capable service through early 1874. As he noted, British and French commercial interests now dominated, although he had hopes that the United States could compete in the marketplace.[8] Wing, French minister Antoine de Dulçat, and British minister Frederick Hamilton—none of whom had been in Ecuador during the early 1860s—all tended to discount stories about García Moreno's violent nature, reporting more favorably on his administration.

For about a month, the delegates considered García Moreno's draft. To avoid the appearance of undue pressure, García Moreno allowed his former brother-in-law, Manuel de Ascásubi, to preside over the assembly, retreating to Guayaquil with the title of general-in-chief of the Army. In July the assembly, which had made some minor changes to García Moreno's document, submitted the constitution to a plebiscite vote. The new instrument won overwhelmingly: Apparently only a few hundred liberals turned out to vote against it. The entire constitutional process, including the selection of García Moreno as president, was orchestrated to end on August 10, the great patriotic celebration of the nation's independence.[9]

Above all else, the new constitution embraced the Catholic Church (too closely, according to the French diplomat), and highlighted its role in Ecuador. Although most nineteenth-century constitutions, even many liberal ones, declared the exclusivity of the Roman Catholic faith (meaning no other religions were tolerated), the 1869 charter went further, declaring that one must be a literate Catholic over 21 years of age to enjoy full citizenship. Arguably Article 10 is not truly a radical departure from past practice because everyone in Ecuador, save for a tiny Jewish minority in Guayaquil and a handful of foreign Protestants, was Catholic. Article 10 did not employ the phrase "true Catholic," which García Moreno commonly used to describe his most conservative friends. Presumably, then, the article did not deny citizenship to liberals, unless they were Free Masons, a group banned by the church (Article 13). While García Moreno remained deferential to the clergy ("our obligation is to respect and obey"), these words did not alter the division of the tithe or end the process of rooting out immoral prelates. García Moreno wanted harmony between church and state. For example, after a spat between governor Carlos Ordóñez and the bishop of Cuenca, García Moreno urged the governor "to go over to the bishop's house, and tell him you had no intention of insulting him." As for himself, "My own relations with Archbishop Checa [whose appointment he opposed] are very cordial, at least on my part."[10]

Other controversial sections of the charter strengthened the hands of the executive, making him essentially a benign dictator. In addition to serving a six-year term to which he could be reelected once (Article 56), he could also decree legislation "consistent with the Constitution" through his appointed Council of State when the legislature was not in session (Article 59). Since congress met every other year for a prescribed sixty-day period (Article 19) and could not override the executive's veto of its bills until a subsequent session, the president clearly enjoyed considerable discretion. As in several earlier constitutions, the president appointed the governors, the *jefes políticos*, and the political lieutenants (Article 82). The *jefes políticos* presided over the municipal government in the provincial capitals (Article 83). Obviously the Constitution of 1869 represented a radical shift from its predecessor, which had lodged ultimate power in local government. Not surprisingly, the city council of Guayaquil, always anxious to protect its privileges, raised questions about local taxes, public lands, and woodlots! Municipalities had some prerogatives, but lost control over the *trabajo subsidiario,* which would now be administered to meet national priorities.[11] In addition to controlling the provincial government, the president could also declare martial law (state of siege), essentially allowing the president to rule as a dictator for the duration of the proclaimed emergency (Article 60 [12]).

Critics also complained that the Constitution did not provide the requisite guarantees of liberties. Articles specifically asserted that citizens would not be subjected to arrests without warrants (Article 91), and spelled out a presumption of innocence until proven guilty (Article 95), the right to free association (Article 109), and freedom of expression (Article 102)—to name a few. The latter two provisions in particular, however, were subject to important caveats. Free expression had to "respect religion, morality, and decency," as did citizens when they were "freely associating." Clearly García Moreno did not intend for the public to enjoy so much freedom that the liberals could conspire to overthrow his government. The press, hardly a vital institution, depended on government largesse to survive. Even with a pro–García Moreno editor in Guayaquil, newspapers sustained themselves for a year or two at best. As chapter 8 will describe, a critical newspaper published there was shut down.[12] In short, Ecuadorians under the Constitution of 1869 lacked the basic freedoms that most people today, and many in the nineteenth century, find vital for a civilized society. For García Moreno and his friends, however, the prospect of a few years of peace outweighed the importance of civil liberties.

Nevertheless, Ecuador's foremost constitutional commentator, Borja y Borja (admittedly a García Moreno enthusiast), identified two positive aspects of the Constitution of 1869. He noted that while voters were required to be literate (thereby eliminating most Ecuadorians) and Catholic, neither they nor members of the Chamber of Deputies needed to own property, which slightly broadened suffrage. Furthermore, the Constitution was more typical than often portrayed because it ended the failed experiment with extreme federalism and independent municipal government. Colombia, for example, would take similar steps in 1886.[13] Yet the Constitution clearly grated on many, even some of García Moreno's friends who rewrote it in very significant ways during the late 1870s. Basically the 1869 charter represented the most extreme example of centralization in Ecuador's nineteenth century and provided the superstructure for the Catholic nation.

BUREAUCRATIZING THE STATE

Historian Brooke Larson has recently argued that García Moreno's "army of bureaucrats" was one of the key elements of his state-building program.[14] This situation was certainly the case after 1869. Under García Moreno's energetic leadership, congress facilitated the growth of the bureaucracy to enforce the laws by modernizing many of the country's legal codes, which would assist in preserving order and modernizing the nation. Hence, over the next few years, congress passed new civil and criminal codes, a judicial code, a military code, and rules for civil and criminal procedure. In so doing, the Ecuadorians borrowed laws wholesale from the French, Chileans, Belgians, and Peruvians.[15] While an in-depth exploration of the codes would be tedious at best, the overarching principle remains that García Moreno wanted a legal system that would allow him to supervise bureaucrats and the military, punish criminals, and promote commerce.

Initially García Moreno tried to control the highly independent military by prescribing severe penalties for insubordination, drunkenness on duty, incompetence, and abuse of authority. The new code also set out draconian punishments for more serious matters—death for being a traitor or promoting a conspiracy, subverting the constitution, mistreating subordinates, desertion, and sentinels who fell asleep on duty during a war. Despite the rules, drunkenness and wanton behavior occurred all too frequently in and out of the barracks.[16] Like all Latin American leaders in this era, García Moreno wanted to professionalize the military, turning its members from the gangster-like tools of caudillos into national forces under the command of civilian authorities. As a result, he sent his friend General Francisco Javier Salazar to the United States and Europe looking for experts to lead the military missions. Salazar was unsuccessful, however. Thus Ecuador ended up creating a home-grown version of a military academy. García Moreno also ordered standard uniforms as well as modern foreign manufactured equipment instead of the old flintlocks.[17] Like some other Garcian reforms, though, professionalizing the military took more time and money than the regime had.

Nevertheless ample evidence exists to demonstrate that García Moreno tried to discipline the military and made some headway, beginning with the example of shooting Maldonado in 1864. Both officers and soldiers sometimes found themselves in difficulty for infractions of the military code. To maintain discipline, officers all too frequently mistreated their men, whether by striking them with a sword, whipping them until they became crippled, or punching them in the mouth—all of which violated the code and resulted in punishments. In sum, the military remained a rough-and-tumble organization in García Moreno's time. Yet many observers noticed the improvement. As Rumsey Wing stated, "President [García] Moreno is merely organizing the army to that degree of efficiency and force which it should long ago have attained, with a general view to frown down the possible plots and machinations of some of his more turbulent countrymen."[18]

García Moreno approved a revised criminal code and new procedures following the legislative session in 1871. The final version concerned the U.S. minister, who thought it harsh and "not in accordance with the enlightened and progressive tendencies of the present Ecuadorian ministry" because it criminalized vices like drinking (which would seem unreasonable to Wing), fornication, and adultery. Yet García Moreno's criminal justice system had a more progressive side. He built a state-of-the art penitentiary (the Panóptico, still in use today) and ended the practice of imprisonment for debtors.[19] As the examples of the military code and the criminal code amply demonstrate, García Moreno believed that strong measures tempered with mercy would keep Ecuadorians in line and build his ideal state.

García Moreno relied on more than fear to make his regime function, however. More importantly, he demanded a constant flow of information from his loyal subordinates so that he could track developments at the local level. As the Constitution of 1869 required, governors reported directly to the president, and they in turn received first-hand information from *jefes políticos* and political lieutenants. Traditional Indian officials in indigenous communities, in the few places where they remained, performed mostly ceremonial functions and were exempt from the reporting requirement. Hence, as García Moreno told one of his governors, "the *jefes políticos must be good agents* for the governor" (my emphasis).

By 1873 governors normally delivered their annual "state of the province" accountings to García Moreno's desk, offering all sorts of excuses (such as illness or uncooperative subordinates) when the reports came late. Typical reports covered items like public order, political matters, education, judicial affairs, and public works. Often accounts included lengthy descriptions of the particular province's geography and natural resources.[20] Given the stacks of documentation that for the first time in recent history reached the department of interior, García Moreno had an opportunity to keep abreast of all events in the country. Thus the efficiency of the administration depended on having good civil servants. García Moreno set the tone himself by picking able, or at least loyal, men to serve as governors. Unlike previous presidents, he also enforced strict office hours, from 10:00 a.m. to 3:00 p.m., for all government officials to be open to the public. Supervisors had to inform on those who were tardy or absent.[21]

Because of the close relationship between church and state, García Moreno also demanded reports from the bishops, who rendered lengthy summaries about their dioceses. These reports included details about the religious holidays, the state of the informal *cofradías* (lay brotherhoods), condition of the physical plants, church finances, and the status of seminaries. Most importantly, bishops underscored the need for more priests and improvements in the morality of both secular and regular clergy. This was particularly true on the coast, "where the majority of people are ignorant of the rudiments of the Christian faith." Like the governors, the clergy responded slowly to the government's demand for information. By 1873, though, reporting became a fairly normal phenomenon.[22]

Regular accountings mandated by the Constitution of 1869 also informed the state about the educational system. Every month inspectors detailed the number of pupils served, measured the quality of instruction, and described the adequacy of facilities—both for public and private institutions. While some inspectors initially complained about uncooperative *jefes políticos* failing to provide data, García Moreno refused to accept that excuse. Rather, he informed inspectors that he expected them to ride circuit and visit the schools, even those in rural areas. In addition he also demanded that the inspectors make specific recommendations about improvements.[23] The results of their activities will be detailed later in this chapter.

Despite greater documentation of bureaucratic activities, a few officials were tempted to stray. In one instance, townspeople denounced their political lieutenant who, they alleged, had opened a number of small taverns and eliminated the office that taxed liquor—all to enrich himself. Within two weeks he lost his post. Some treasury officials could not fight temptation and embezzled. Those who engaged in such practices lost their jobs, although by statute they could have been executed. García Moreno never sentenced an erring bureaucrat to death, preferring to dissuade rather than punish harshly.[24]

In sum García Moreno depended on an honest bureaucracy to support his efforts in creating the Catholic state. Because official corruption has been an endemic problem in Ecuador, and remains part of the political culture, some slippage from the ideal of the pure honest bureaucrat had to be expected. Despite his high standards, García Moreno knew that the problem could not be solved overnight. Hence he counseled patience over and over again: "The reform of inveterate abuses and disorder is not a day's work, but takes time" and "To govern in this country is to struggle without rest against evildoers, but the number of them decreases daily, and the good become more numerous."[25] Due to the centralized system authorized by the Constitution and García Moreno's leadership, corruption decreased on his watch and bureaucracy functioned more efficiently—all helping to strengthen the Catholic nation.

THE PRIMARY SCHOOL SYSTEM

In the twenty-first century, we take for granted the right of every child to receive a free public education. This notion actually came into existence during the latter part of the nineteenth century, especially in Latin America. Under the "Schoolmaster President," Domingo F. Sarmiento, Argentina made a name for itself as a pioneer in public education. Far less well known, however, is García Moreno's innovative educational experiment, which for a short time looked as if it would transform the nation. As a result, García Moreno's efforts to provide education merit consideration.[26]

In the main, enthusiasm for public education could not have been greater. As inspectors toured districts, they reported the need for more schools. Petitions for school construction and teachers piled up on governors' desks. These letters describe the varied motives of Ecuadorians for wanting more educational opportunities. Many believed that education would "open the door to prosperity," providing "for the material, *moral* and intellectual advancement of the people" (my emphasis). One inspector valued schools as the "sole means of perpetuating and passing from one generation to the next the nation's customs, arts, sciences and hatreds for international rivals"[27] (i.e., nation-building). Despite claims by anti–

García Moreno biographers that he wanted the lower classes to wallow in a state of ignorance, blindly following the advice of their parish priests, clearly the evidence is to the contrary. First, García Moreno wanted to modernize the country, not thrust it back into the sixteenth century, and he knew that goal required an educated workforce. "Ignorance is a fatal inheritance," he told congress. Educating the poor was also part of the Christian Brothers' mission. Second, García Moreno demanded that the morality of the poor improve, viewing education as ammunition in his war on vice. Consequently, "Schools and more schools, above all else," he told one of his friends, to whom he unveiled his broader purpose: "We must do everything possible to provide our country with morality, instruction, and roads; and God will convert it to a paradise on earth, admired and envied by all nations."[28]

Given Garcia Moreno's intense belief in education, the statute of November 1871 not surprisingly mandated education for all boys and girls between the ages of six and twelve in locations where twenty or more children could be gathered together. The statute contained an imaginative combination of plums and sticks. Education was for the first time free and mandatory, so that parents who refused to send their children to school could be fined. Gone were the Provincial Councils of Education—now inspectors reported directly to the president. Moreover the statute obliged municipalities to provide school facilities, although in many instances the federal government chipped in hundreds, even thousands, of pesos to aid their efforts.[29] García Moreno's comprehensive scheme looked positive on paper. As usual, though, many practical problems made compliance difficult, if not impossible, thus dulling the impact of the plan.

To house classes, the government needed to construct suitable schools. Initially García Moreno urged local officials to use the local government building as a schoolroom, although this measure was to be only a temporary expedient. García Moreno hoped that the municipalities would bear the burden of the cost of school construction, but their resources proved inadequate. With inspectors begging for funds, the government relented, subsidizing much of the construction effort. "We must not rest until each parish has at least one school." Schools also required chairs, benches, blackboards, paper and ink, maps, books, and a picture of the Virgin to be considered fully equipped. Provinces provided assistance. "Guilty is the governor who does not have enough money for his schools," García Moreno reminded his governors. "Make sure the treasury does not lack money for new school construction."[30] Despite high ideals, the country did not have enough resources to build all the necessary schools. For example, in 1874 the governor of Loja reported only three primary schools operating in the whole province—two in the capital.[31]

Teachers' salaries also drove up educational expenses. Low salaries resulted in some underqualified instructors. In many towns, teachers at boys' schools earned as little as six pesos a month, a salary "insufficient to meet their needs." These schools were all one-room schoolhouses, of course. Several governors suggested that the federal government should supplement these wages, which in fact happened. Eventually teachers' salaries at the primary level more than doubled to fifteen pesos a month. Schools on the coast offered even higher wages due to the greater cost of living there.[32] Better salaries and facilities improved the educational system. As one inspector proudly reported, "In the old days a schoolmaster delighted in torturing and terrorizing students." In contrast, now the inspector saw a love of learning, progress, and academic work in the schools visited. Learning and standardized curriculum also mattered to García Moreno. At a minimum he wanted students to learn the Three Rs, although with some important additions. Specifically, boys took classes in reading, writing, arithmetic, Spanish grammar (stressing the importance of a national language, even for Quichua-speaking students), geography, religion and Christian doctrine, and principles of civility and morality. Girls took domestic classes in addition to the basic curriculum to prepare themselves for what were then seen as their future roles as wives and mothers. García Moreno, as a man of science, also required schools to adopt the metric system.[33]

García Moreno's universal primary public education system tried to reach all segments of Ecuadorian society—even those previously excluded, such as indigenous children and girls. Rural schools posed the greatest hardships. Obviously opportunity did not exist for rural children who lived miles from their nearest neighbors. Those who lived on the confines of haciendas, effectively beyond the reach of the state, also represented a group difficult to assist. García Moreno certainly tried mandating a school for every estate. He held himself out as an example, noting that while residing at his rented estate of Guachalá he had created a school, paid for it, and without punishing anyone had made certain that the Indians attended twice a week. Still, rural proprietors retained a lot of latitude over their charges. In many instances, estate workers' children had no schools to attend. Thus education remained a more urban phenomenon, as it had been traditionally. Even at the end of the regime, one inspector estimated that less than one-quarter of the school-age children in his province attended classes, with girls having even fewer opportunities.[34] Even after the government built rural schools, attendance lagged there. In one town only three students appeared for class, so the inspector recommended closing the school. A governor attributed truancy to rural poverty. "Frequently fathers have to use their sons in their work in order to obtain their daily bread." On the other hand, one inspector told a moving story to demonstrate that some rural people really wanted to learn. In the course of his tour, he encountered a small boy who had traded his only rooster, presumably a source of income, to someone for an arithmetic book. Rural parents certainly posed a problem. Perhaps they could be fined, as the statute permitted, suggested one inspector. García Moreno must have chuckled upon reading this report. Patience, he counseled. "Before applying this punishment you must use milder measures, like reprimands and verbal threats."[35]

Providing indigenous communities with schools caused the García Moreno regime many difficulties. Centuries of mistreatment at the hands of governments had taught the Indians to mistrust the honeyed words of officialdom. Increased interaction with the government usually led to misery: higher taxes, increased labor demands, and forced military service, as the next chapter will explore. No wonder Indian communities reacted skeptically when García Moreno announced that his educational reforms would include them, especially when the educational policy focused on assimilation and suppression of their languages. Nevertheless the government proceeded, hoping that it could transform Spanish-Indian relations and eradicate illiteracy.

García Moreno sought to impose his standardized Spanish-language curriculum on the Indians. Initially the government tried to bring them to Quito—reminiscent of the U.S. mission policy of the late nineteenth century, which created "Indian schools" away from reservations. The natives of Ecuador's best-known Indian community, Otavalo, rioted and refused to allow their sons to attend school elsewhere. Learning from this error, the government then opted to build schools in indigenous communities like Otavalo and Saquisilí, as well as a number outside of Loja.[36] To induce attendance, the government freed parents who sent their children to the Indian schools from the *trabajo subsidiario,* fining hacendados who forced school-age children to work. Nevertheless, even with incentives, the indigenous education project often disappointed. Authorities gave up on the school in Cayapas, Esmeraldas (one of the few remaining indigenous coastal communities), "because of the semi-savage customs of these indigenous." Instead they spent the money on a girls' school for the city of Esmeraldas.[37] Ultimately García Moreno decided his rural Indian school concept would succeed only if he could train indigenous teachers who would then return to their communities, given that in the nineteenth century no one considered the possibility of bilingual education.

García Moreno also promoted education for girls, mostly so that educated women could better fulfill their traditional roles as wives and mothers. Foreign visitors before García Moreno's time commented on the woeful ignorance of upper-class women, who scarcely read anything "but a devotional" book.[38] Some inspectors displayed very enlightened attitudes, saying that neglecting girls' education was an "injustice because all persons of the society have the same right to enjoy its benefits." The 1873 statute banning coeducational primary schools temporarily slowed the progress of female education. Rather quickly, however, communities responded to the mandate, engaging in a second school-building frenzy. The new girls' schools posed problems similar to those of the boys' schools: construction costs, materials and supplies, and instructional expenses. García Moreno's federal treasury handed out money freely for girls' education, including the full salaries of some teachers. Girls' schools posed unique problems, however, as the pupils' honor had to be protected. For example, when construction on a new girls' school began in Cuenca, García Moreno became worried about its location. As a result, he agreed to pay a portion of the cost of a wall to be built around the school "to protect them."[39]

Statistically, girls' education made great progress in the García Moreno years. The number of girls' primary schools increased from 41 in 1857 to 164 at the end of his presidency. Yet much remained to be done. Of the total number of enrolled pupils in the country, only about 25 percent were girls. In addition, attention to girls' education varied regionally. Several inspectors noted that on the coast, "parents are generally indifferent to girls' education," preferring that they work instead. Where girls' schools existed on the coast, they tended to be less well equipped and funded. Coastal parents also objected to the national school calendar, September 25 to August 15, which worked well in the sierra but conflicted with their labor needs. The plight of girls living along the coast was summed up by yet another of the government's school inspectors, who noted the dearth of girls' schools in the province of Los Ríos. "As a result, the fair sex lacks the cultivation necessary to mold hearts that are moral and virtuous." Hence young women along the coast "remained subject to regrettable passion, and subject to their sensual instincts."[40]

Ideally, communities wanted Christian Brothers' schools for boys, and Sisters of the Sacred Heart schools for girls. The number of such institutions expanded rapidly during García Moreno's second term. Provincial capitals vied with each other to host a Christian Brothers' school. Most succeeded with the generous assistance of the national government, which at a minimum paid the transportation expenses of the Brothers from France to Ecuador. What a change from the 1860s! As García Moreno wrote a friend, "Ten years ago Ambato had a chance for a Christian Brothers' school when three Brothers arrived in Guayaquil. But neither Governor [Nicolás] Martínez, nor the City Council, nor a single parent wanted to help me, and I had to return the Brothers back to Europe." Now communities begged for the Brothers to help them "cultivate the vineyard Heaven has entrusted to them." No community worked harder than Loja to attract the Brothers. Inviting the Brother-Visitor to consult with them, the governor and the city council offered him several locations. Before the boys' school even opened, the municipal government promised an enrollment of 220 pupils.[41]

Likewise, larger towns could enroll sufficient numbers of girls to make the cost of bringing Sisters of the Sacred Heart feasible. For example, Juan León Mera—sometime governor and sometime school inspector, but most famously Ecuador's foremost Romantic novelist—welcomed the Sisters to Ambato, where they established a girls' school. Cities bought up suitable properties for the Sisters, as nuns continued to flow into Ecuador in the 1870s to fulfill their educational and charitable missions.[42]

Not only did the Christian Brothers' schools offer their students better-trained teachers, they also provided a broader curriculum than the statutory minimum standards. In Guayaquil the school met the more practical needs of *costeños,* providing some instruction in agricultural management and business. Solving problems and analyzing data helped prepare the next generation of *guayaquileño* businessmen, inspectors argued. As a result, everyone in the city lauded the quality of the education that the Christian Brothers provided. Most of all, the Christian Brothers proved their mettle by scoring excellent results measured by the annual tests (oral examinations) mandated by the government. Although many pupils performed well on these tests, students of the Christian Brothers and the Sisters of the Sacred Heart always did the best. For example, in Jipijapa, "in the short time [the pupils] have been under the tutelage of the Christian Brothers, they have advanced well." In Quito one student so impressed the evaluators that they said, "We could not be prouder of this student, who responded to all our questions."[43] Testing worked. Inspectors routinely identified failing schools, and the government took prompt measures to remedy defects—which included firing incompetent teachers.

Statistically, the gains for primary education were quite impressive, as the number of pupils served swelled dramatically, from 13,500 in 1867 (and that up considerably from 1859) to 32,000 in 1875. Spending on education increased from about 15,000 pesos before 1861 to over 100,000 pesos annually by the 1870s, mostly because of the significant growth of the export economy that produced greater tax revenues for public expenditures. As historian Linda Rodríguez has argued, the trajectory of expanding public education continued even after García Moreno's death, as government income also increased.[44] Of course statistics do not tell the entire story. People across the country noted the improvement in the *quality* of public education. Boasting about the advances, Minister of Foreign Affairs Francisco Javier León noted the improvements in the province of Tungurahua alone—fourteen new schools, a new science curriculum, and fully equipped laboratories for both the girls' and boys' secondary schools. Further analysis of the public education system underscores the transformation García Moreno achieved in just a few years. As one scholar of nineteenth-century Colombia noted, that country's universal public education system favored elite education. There, the largest amounts of pesos flowed to the secondary schools, where the children of the upper and middle classes studied. García Moreno took a very different approach, because he wanted *all* citizens to be schooled in the morality of the Catholic nation, as well as to acquire the basic skills necessary to prosper in a modernizing world. Hence governments on all levels helped to pay for poor children to attend school. García Moreno had this precise debate with his friend Juan León Mera, who questioned the idea of putting so much emphasis on primary schools. "To fund the *colegios* [secondary schools] without having primary schools would create an anomaly of dire consequences," García Moreno responded.[45]

SECONDARY EDUCATION

In Latin America, secondary education traditionally had been the privilege of the sons of the elite and middle classes, designed to prepare them for lives in politics and the literary arts. Secondary schools typically offered programs that culminated in the bachelor's degree (the *bachillerato*), roughly equivalent to a U.S. high-school diploma plus a year of college. By all measures, Ecuador lagged far behind most of its neighbors in the field of secondary education at the time of independence. Recall that García Moreno himself in the 1830s had to leave the third largest city in the nation because not a single secondary school operated in Guayaquil. Not surprisingly, then, García Moreno's educational program also hoped to expand the number and quality of secondary educational opportunities. Although García Moreno himself had not attended a Jesuit secondary school, his experiences in Europe convinced him that the order offered the highest quality instruction. Because the Jesuits believed in a curriculum heavily infused with natural sciences and Christian morality, ideas García Moreno endorsed, the two became natural partners in the secondary school effort. As previously mentioned, the parties signed a contract in 1863, and Jesuits began arriving in fairly sizeable numbers to staff the secondary schools.[46]

Launching new secondary schools encountered many of the same pragmatic difficulties as did the primary-school initiative—and even more. Municipalities had to construct buildings or refurbish old ones. Both students and faculty needed reasonable housing. The institutions had to earn enough income to pay their faculty and provide equipment and supplies. Indeed secondary education also became a voracious consumer of funds because the goal was to have a high school for each gender in all provincial capitals. Despite the costs, many provincial seats engaged in building projects and brought in Jesuits. Guayaquil, for example, quickly got its facility up and running. By 1873 the city had plans for a secondary school for young women. Contracting with Sisters of the Sacred Heart to staff the school, García Moreno personally urged the prompt opening of the facility "to benefit the education of the fair sex."[47]

Nevertheless, secondary education posed another challenge, that of affordability. Not only did secondary students have to pay tuition, however minimal, but they also paid for room, board, books, and supplies. Undoubtedly García Moreno remembered his own personal experiences when he relied upon a scholarship, the largesse of the Betancourt sisters, and his paid employment as a monitor to finish his degree. The government determined to provide scholarships to worthy students. The records do not reveal whether these scholarships were awarded for merit, need, or a combination of the two. Government generosity came with strings attached—specifically, students had to provide service to the state after graduation. A few committed to the military academy, but most became instructors in primary schools for a minimum of two years.[48] For young women, the issue of their honor created other encumbrances. By decree of one governor, teenaged girls had to be escorted to and from school "by a reputable person, a señora of virtue" or by their parents.[49]

Secondary education also flourished because curricular changes made it even more attractive and modern. Although previous legislation had encouraged elective courses in chemistry and physics, *colegios* had traditionally emphasized languages (Spanish, Latin, French, and English), literature, history, geography, basic mathematics, and of course religious and moral instruction. In reality, secondary schools rarely provided the science curriculum, lacking both the faculty and the laboratory facilities—a condition that García Moreno determined to change. Arriving Jesuits brought entire laboratories in their luggage, which became the soul of the science curriculum. García Moreno also reformed the old method of instruction, where a single "master" might teach ten or twelve different courses. He wanted the new faculty to be more specialized. Adding faculty obviously drove up costs, as the Jesuit inspector informed García Moreno when he examined the *colegio* at Riobamba. The demand for additional faculty encouraged García Moreno to invite more Jesuits and their scientific equipment to Riobamba and other facilities.[50]

Secondary education in the smaller cities, however, received a blow when García Moreno decided to separate seminaries from the more secular *colegios*. Loja's bishop and the governor trotted out all the arguments against the measure: two centuries of tradition, the similar curricula, the Concordat's prohibition of state interference in church matters, and the cost—all to no avail. In the end, García Moreno resolved the problem by providing Loja with more Jesuits and funds for a separate seminary facility "to satisfy the provincial youths' educational needs."[51] Likewise the separation of the two institutions triggered a debate in Cuenca. Former governor and diplomat Benigno Malo questioned the separation. Shouldn't Cuenca have a lyceum, a French-style elite academy, and teachers other than Jesuits, he asked? Enraged, García Moreno responded angrily, noting that he had tolerated Malo's "insulting letter" of 1862 but had no intention of doing so on this occasion. García Moreno asked why Malo preferred to be an obstructionist, urging him instead to raise money for the *colegio nacional*, which referred to any Jesuit-run secondary school in a provincial capital. After consulting with the Jesuit visitor, who agreed that the division made sense given high enrollments of over 470 students, García Moreno ordered it.[52]

Clearly secondary education expanded during García Moreno's second term. More students graduated with *bachilleratos* than ever before in

Ecuador's history. Most provincial capitals had at least one *colegio* for boys, and many a second one for young women. Without exception, those who observed the final examinations and regularly visited the campuses issued glowing reports about the institutions, which, one inspector said, created "good will and progress for the country." "Praise God and the zeal of our governors and our board," wrote another, "for the support they have lent to secondary education." Yet problems remained. Quito's largest *colegio*, held out as the model institution to the rest of the country, nevertheless suffered from absenteeism. The students in Guayaquil failed to work very diligently, focusing too much on business applications because "they are more interested in wealth than in morality and religion."[53] For most students, graduation meant the end of their formal education, but a select few entered the university or took other advanced training.

POSTSECONDARY AND SPECIALIZED EDUCATION

Higher education also progressed during the García Moreno years. Initially García Moreno believed he had to clean up what he perceived as the liberal nest of vipers dominating the University of Quito and warping the minds of Ecuadorian youth. Particularly noxious to García Moreno were faculty who espoused the secular utilitarian philosophy of British educator Jeremy Bentham. Other conservatives seconded García Moreno's displeasure with the liberal faculty, who had "left behind incendiary bombs . . . the most corrupt . . . heretical . . . and subversive demagoguery." As a result, García Moreno closed the university (the same institution from which he had graduated and later served as rector) shortly after the January 1869 coup. Shutting down the university allowed him to purge it of faculty except the apolitical ones in the College of Medicine, replacing them with "people of faith" (or at least so the Archbishop of Quito hoped). Ultimately García Moreno did reopen both the law school and the Philosophy and Letters school with new faculty.[54]

García Moreno's governor in Cuenca likewise closed his city's university, founded by Jerónimo Carrión in 1867 and presided over initially by Benigno Malo. Malo disagreed completely with García Moreno about higher education, believing it should be humanistic and decentralized. Before their disagreement became too strident, however, Malo died in April 1870, and one of García Moreno's friends briefly became the new rector. Nevertheless, because the faculty seemed too liberal, Governor Ordóñez fired them and brought European Jesuit faculty trained in the sciences to Cuenca.[55] As a result of these measures, higher education in Ecuador looked radically different in 1871 than it had in 1868.

Traditionally Latin American universities offered degree programs in four "professions:" law, medicine, theology, and philosophy. Students usually spent six years in medical school but less time completing degrees in law and philosophy. Most students enrolled in the latter two colleges, since these provided pathways to careers in politics and civil service and met elite requirements for a comprehension of European culture and ideas. Medicine was slowly emerging from the dark ages of bleeding. The theory that a miasma of decomposing organic materials caused disease would fall from favor and medicine would become a bona fide science based on the germ theory first explored by Louis Pasteur in the late 1850s. Giving preferential treatment to the school of medicine appealed to García Moreno for two reasons: his predilection for science and the fact that medical students tended to be less political than people in the humanities. Dr. Miguel Egas, who had attended *colegio* with García Moreno and been his vice-rector in 1857, received permission to found a medical society, which looked into virulent diseases like yellow fever. Other doctors encouraged the use of vaccine to prevent smallpox and explored a cure for the disfiguring disease of elephantiasis (caused by filaria), although success dealing with specific diseases like typhoid and malaria would come only in the 1880s.[56]

Because García Moreno wanted the school of medicine to progress, he recognized that it needed better faculty, facilities, and equipment as well as more clinical experiences for students. Not surprisingly, García Moreno decided to hire foreign experts and bring them to Ecuador. He asked his minister in Paris to find qualified faculty. Eventually, certified French surgeons and diagnosticians, who brought instruments and laboratory equipment with them, graced the halls of the medical college. García Moreno also ordered his diplomats to forward a steady supply of medical texts and equipment.[57]

Students attending medical school, however, needed a strong science background, and García Moreno determined to provide that foundation for them with his Polytechnic Institute that essentially replaced the old university in Quito. In a happy confluence of circumstances, just as García Moreno sent out the call to find Jesuit scientists to staff the Polytechnical, Germany's "Iron Chancellor," Otto von Bismarck, decided to expel the Jesuits from his country as part of his Kulturkampf program. As a result, several well-trained Jesuit scientists came to Ecuador and became the heart and soul of the Polytechnical.[58] Three of the Jesuits made lasting contribu-

The Jesuit professors at the Polytechnical Institute (Permission of the Banco Central del Ecuador)

tions to the country. Juan Menten set up the observatory, long a pet project of García Moreno. Sparing no expense, the government brought in fine wood from the sierra and hired skilled artisans for the stonework. Another of the Jesuits, Teodoro Wolf, wrote a monumental tome on Ecuador's geography and geology, still the seminal work on the subject. He also caused a stir by teaching a scientific approach to the origin of the earth. When a parent complained to García Moreno, he retorted, "I didn't bring Dr. Wolf to teach religion, but to teach geology." A third Jesuit, Josef Kolberg, after toiling in the Polytechnical, wrote a stirring memoir of his trip to the Oriente, which commented on the new Jesuit missions there.[59]

For all the good fortune associated with the founding of the Polytechnic Institute, ultimately it would fail. Rigorous high-quality education did attract some students, and the government did its best to ensure that talented students enrolled. As García Moreno said: "We don't want to close the door on qualified youth who will be of service to the country." Many students received scholarships, which included a 100-peso-a-month living stipend, on the condition that after graduation they teach for six years in a *colegio*. In addition to abstract courses like mathematics, chemistry, physics, and natural science, polytechnic students received practical training in fields that could lead to actual employment—such as engineering, surveying, metallurgy, machine design, architecture, and pharmacy. Perhaps ultimately the Polytechnical failed for the same reasons that a similar effort did not take hold in Colombia in the 1840s. Without an industrial modernizing economy, graduates found no outlets for their job skills. In Colombia disdain for manual labor, which sometimes accompanied these professions, and nearly two decades of civil war blunted the program for scientific education. García Moreno's friends attributed the ultimate failure of the Polytechnical to his own demise. Regional rivalries may also have contributed, because García Moreno refused to allow Cuenca to have a medical school or an astronomical observatory.[60]

Equally short-lived was García Moreno's attempt to create a professional school of midwifery, the College of Obstetrics, for female students. Based on his wives' personal experiences, García Moreno knew how difficult childbirth could be, especially in the highlands where the altitude allegedly complicated pregnancies for women of European descent. From all over the sierra, women flocked to the school of obstetrics, sometimes assisted financially by their communities. Once again, García Moreno sought instructors abroad. Like the medical students, the students in obstetrics followed a rigorous curriculum, studying anatomy and physiology, surgery, and children's hygiene. Candidates had to be 18, disease-free, of good character, able to read and write, and in possession of a modest trousseau. Each school day included significant hours for devotion and study, relying on the early-to-bed, early-to-rise principle (5 a.m.–9 p.m.). At the end of the academic year, teachers examined and graded the students, and they returned to their communities to practice.[61]

Other specialized training took place at the seminaries, staffed by Lazarist monks from France, and the military college, which opened with a class of forty. For primary teachers, García Moreno created normal school (teachers' college) preparation at *colegios*. In 1873 he opened a special Indian normal school in Quito, which drew students largely from the south.[62] Perhaps most unusual were García Moreno's attempts to establish a trade school. Modeled after similar United States schools called protectorates (designed to protect good Catholics from the wiles of Protestants), the trade school in Quito offered practical courses for students presumably from lower-class backgrounds. The school opened its doors in 1872, teaching masonry, cabinetmaking, carpentry, shoemaking, blacksmithing, cartmaking, agriculture, and "taxi [coach] driving." Foreign artisans from Europe, the United States, and Canada comprised the faculty.[63]

Although García Moreno's educational system at first blush seems to focus heavily on the practical, he did not ignore the fine arts. He recognized that both art and music could be molded for national purposes to create not only artistic monuments but also stirring language and sounds to promote patriotism. In 1870 García Moreno created the Conservatory of Music. For its director he chose a foreign-born but longtime Guayaquil resident. Antonio Neumane was famous for having written a beautiful song about Ecuador's first national poet, José Joaquín de Olmedo. Neumane was also known for writing the music to Ecuador's national anthem, allegedly composed in a single day when General Secundino Darquea locked him in his house and told him to produce! Under Neumane's leadership, the Conservatory began well, but the lack of interest on the part of García Moreno's successor led to its demise.[64] Nevertheless, music played a very important role in García Moreno's nation-building project. Without a national anthem for three decades, the country finally had today's patriotic "hymn" (as it was called at the time), which lauded the glories of the age of independence.

García Moreno's School of Fine Arts had even more impact than the Music Conservatory. Although painters and sculptors of the famous *quiteño* school (Miguel de Santiago, Bernardo de Legarda, and Manuel Chili—better known as Caspicara) had produced some of the most exquisite art in all of colonial Latin America, its artistic tradition had declined. Friedrich Hassaurek described the Ecuadorian artists of the early 1860s as excellent copyists, limiting themselves to reproducing works of European masters for very low prices.[65] García Moreno decided to remedy this shortcoming. During his first term, the president had given the famous portrait painter Luis Cadena the authority and some funds to open the National Museum. In 1872 Cadena became the head of the School of Fine Arts. During the second term, the government awarded scholarships for study in Italian art schools. The best known of these artists, Rafael Salas, painted one of Ecuador's national icons, *The Sacred Heart of Jesus.* After their studies in Europe concluded, the scholarship students were obligated to teach at the School of Fine Arts.[66] The school trained some of Ecuador's finest. Rafael Troya, official illustrator for two German scientists, created Ecuadorian landscapes rivaling those of American Frederick E. Church. Joaquín Pinto became known for his paintings of local folklore and the painting on the cover of this book. Although short-lived, García Moreno's School of Fine Arts created art that highlighted his nation-building project.[67]

MISSIONS, HOSPITALS, AND CHARITABLE ORGANIZATIONS

The Catholic nation also was intended to include people living beyond the pale, in this case in the jungles of the Oriente. At the constitutional assembly of 1861, delegates authorized the government to recruit Jesuits for long-abandoned missions to save those who "had fallen into savagery because of a lack of missionaries and priests."[68] In addition to spiritual motives, García Moreno wanted to integrate the Indians of the Oriente and their territory into the nation of Ecuador to secure its resources. Nor did he represent an aberrant viewpoint. As the archbishop of Quito stated, the objectives in missionizing this region were "to bring to the barbarous tribes knowledge of the true God and the practices of Christian civilization and to better the country's material enrichment." As with the education program, the government agreed to contribute monies towards the expenses the Jesuits faced implementing the plan.[69]

From the outset, however, the missionaries encountered obstacles as they tried to reestablish the frontier outposts abandoned for over a century. Isolated from the rest of the country beyond the *páramo* (the cold high plains with scrubby grasses) and raging jungle streams, missionaries wanted a road back to a highland city. Despite considerable enthusiasm on the part of the missionaries, along with efforts on the part of the converted, the task proved impossible. Downpours washed away makeshift bridges, and the verdant jungle restored itself faster than the crews could machete it down. Road-building efforts also alienated the new converts, unaccustomed as they were to regimented labor. The reawakened interest in the Oriente also brought greedy merchants to the region, who took advantage of naïve locals and abused them, forcing them to mine for gold and labor for other valuable commodities when they fell into debt (at least according to the missionaries). Faustino Rayo, a colonel in the army who will figure prominently in chapter 8, was singled out as the prime offender. García Moreno intervened on behalf of the missionaries, expelling Rayo and others from the region. Missionaries and government officials both found particularly loathsome the "perverse almost inhuman trafficking in [shrunken human] heads" and the commerce in rifles that only heightened insecurity.[70]

Nevertheless, the missionaries made some progress. All along the Napo River, they proselytized, baptized infants and adults, and performed marriages. In keeping with García Moreno's educational initiative, the religious established schools for both boys and girls in two of the larger towns, drawing upwards of 150 students in these facilities. By the

A tsantsa *(shrunken head) from the Oriente (Courtesy of the Library of Congress USZ 94524)*

end of García Moreno's presidency, the vicar-general of the mission effort estimated that the friars had saved 6,600 souls as well as built two schools and nine churches. At the same time, the missionaries failed to understand their charges' culture. Requiring the inhabitants to live in towns, dress in western clothing, and attend prayer sessions four times a week, as one missionary attempted, effectively interrupted their itinerant hunting-and-gathering lifestyle. Catholic burial rituals (many of these groups did not believe in interring bodies) also ran afoul of local custom. In the mission town of Gualaquiza, an intertribal conflict among the Shuar caught missionaries in the middle. The Jesuits and the schoolteachers wisely decided to abandon the town. Taming the frontier with Jesuits brought only modest success.[71]

The missionaries' efforts in the east had another partially intended effect: They laid the grounds for Ecuador's ongoing claim to large portions of the Amazon Basin. Hence Vicente Piedrahita, back in García Moreno's good graces and now serving as Ecuador's minister to Peru, moved quickly to defend Ecuador's interests when Peru sent an exploratory hydrographical commission into the disputed area in 1874 and 1875. When the members of the commission traveled within fifteen miles of Macas, Piedrahita protested, asserting that the scientific expedition must act "in no way contrary to the legitimate sovereignty of Ecuador." He also worried about the presence of Peruvian missionaries and soldiers in the disputed region.[72]

The orders also provided charitable social services, caring for the sick and the poor. In the 1850s, conditions in Ecuadorian hospitals were deplorable, as one female foreign visitor recounted: "The wards are merely long, narrow passages, with niches in which the poor patients lie on ox hides stretched over wooden trestles, but without pillow or covering; the filth was indescribable, the air, as I have said, poison [she doused herself with cologne before entering] and each of the wards had only one small window at each end, and even these were fast closed."[73] García Moreno also wanted to increase the quantity and quality of hospitals during his second term by increasing the numbers of the nursing order called the Sisters of Charity, along with building new facilities or remodeling older ones. During the course of García Moreno's second term, many provincial capitals dedicated a hospital facility and spent money bringing Sisters of Charity to serve (although Cuenca lagged behind). For poorer provinces such as Chimborazo, for example, the arrival of the Sisters meant a huge improvement in both the quality and quantity of health care available in Riobamba. Wards there were orderly, cleaner, and more spacious, as the federal government contributed funds to build an addition to the hospital. In the impoverished provincial capital of Babahoyo (Los Ríos), the six sisters arranged two spacious and clean wards and secured a regular supply of medications, a surgeon, and an intern.[74]

Although the Sisters of Charity played the most important role in staffing the hospitals, another order, the Lazarists, cared for patients dying from infectious diseases. Clearly the unfortunate patients so afflicted deserved the support of the federal government, as one official put it. By the end of García Moreno's term, the San Lázaro hospice in Quito had nearly 200 patients, 92 with elephantiasis, 26 with mental illnesses, and 79 so poor "that they are too weak to beg." In addition to a comfortable place to stay and square meals, the patients "also received comfort from the constant practice of Christian virtue that allowed them to overcome a life of bitterness." Guayaquil's bishop subsidized a plan, which García Moreno approved, for a similar institution for the gravely ill and the insane.[75]

Records from these facilities indicate that doctors applied a combination of European medical science and local herbal cures to treat fevers, dysentery, hepatitis, skin diseases, bronchial infections, and a host of other diseases. Hospitals also provided a place for childbirth for some poor women. Giving birth remained precarious, although obstetricians now used modern forceps to aid deliveries. A few Ecuadorian practitioners understood germ theory, but more recognized the need for cleanliness. For those diseases that seemed incurable, like elephantiasis, doctors prescribed alternative remedies, including the *cundurango* plant from Loja, an alleged miracle drug.[76]

As part of the new bureaucratic state, hospital inspectors were required to report regularly on finances as well as patients' care. Like educational institutions, hospitals proved a drain on the budget. Administrators demanded more beds and drugs, and even petitioned for better food for the patients. When the country faced a fiscal crisis in 1874, however, García Moreno made clear his priorities. After the governor of Imbabura complained of a budget shortfall, García Moreno advised him, "Do you believe it is more important to educate the girls or cure the sick? Both are works of mercy, but the *first* is more necessary" (my emphasis).[77] García Moreno clearly looked to the future and saw the youth of Ecuador as the agents of his national project—hence, they took priority.

Various orders of nuns in Quito and provincial capitals ran the orphanages, which housed mostly poor girls. Orphaned boys apparently were more likely to be taken in by relatives because they could work. Orphanages proved indispensable after the 1868 earthquake. Besides the principal public orphanage in Quito run by the French Sisters of Providence, Virginia Klinger funded a private home for foundlings (as abandoned infants were called in the nineteenth century). Whatever the source of their funding, orphanages saved "the most unfortunate members of society . . . from misery or more fatal consequences" (immorality, no doubt).[78] Girls in orphanages also received an education. In addition to the regular primary school curriculum, they learned useful skills for women in the nineteenth century: sewing, ironing, cooking, and shirt making. A few talented orphans obtained scholarships enabling them to attend secondary schools. As with the sick, however, orphanages ranked below public education on García Moreno's list of social priorities. "I do what I can for the poor," he wrote, when a friend asked him to help four orphans from Ibarra. As government shortfalls mounted and no new orphanages could be built, he advised one governor to simply send his "poor unfortunates" to the facility in the neighboring province.[79]

While orphanages and hospitals catered to law-abiding poor citizens, other institutions dealt with the wayward who strayed from the moral strictures of the Catholic state. For García Moreno, correctional facilities were designed not only to punish immoral or criminal behavior, but also to instruct inmates on ways to lead exemplary Christian lives. Starting in 1869, he contracted with the Sisters of Buen Pastor, the Good Shepherd, from France to run institutions for women convicted of crimes involving vice. Once in Quito, these nuns found a temporary home in the former Dominican convent until a new facility could be built. Their hard work started immediately. As García Moreno said, the nuns worked to "reform [the inmates'] customs and end their scandalous behavior." Interestingly, García Moreno on several occasions talked about the importance of arresting the most egregious moral offenders and sending them to Buen Pastor to set an example for the rest of society.[80] (The special relationship between these sisters and García Moreno will be further explored in chapter 8.)

The debate about reform versus punishment also influenced the government's view of criminology. The condition of Ecuadorian jails in the 1860s was horrible by all accounts. Consequently García Moreno and his government resolved to improve prisons, in part because they viewed incarceration not just as punishment, but also as an opportunity to reform inmates. To preserve morality, the government urged provinces and even small communities to build separate jails for men and women, since mixed facilities provided the opportunity for "scandalous behavior." Nevertheless the practicalities of funding shortfalls made the directive ineffectual in many instances.[81] Improving the spiritual condition of inmates also preoccupied policymakers. Governors hired prison chaplains. With rehabilitation in mind, García Moreno built the model penitentiary in Quito called the Panóptico (mentioned earlier as still in use today), which featured visiting monks and regular prayer sessions in an attempt to lead the country's most hardened criminals back to the straight and narrow. In addition to exposing convicts to Christian preaching, both men's and women's prisons attempted to rehabilitate inmates by teaching them trades. As the governor of Cuenca stated, "it is the lack of a useful occupation they can follow" that led women to a life of crime. As a solution, he recommended that the government purchase spinning wheels for the prisons. Hence García Moreno's policies for prison reform embraced both traditional and modern ideas of criminology.[82]

REFORMING A PEOPLE'S MORALS

Reforming adults has never been an easy task. Yet if they were not to have a corrosive effect on Ecuador's youth, García Moreno wanted to take measures to curb their most salacious behavior. Thus he hoped to police the actions of citizens whose lifestyle choices might corrupt those of others. García Moreno focused his morality campaign on both highland Indians and the people of the coast.[83] Laws regulating the moral conduct of citizens had long been on the books. Previous governments, however, ignored the widespread drunkenness or the private sexual activities of citizens. By statute in 1869, congress had toughened the laws, transforming misdemeanors into felonies that García Moreno enforced. For García Moreno, the battle was straightforward, nothing short of the conflict between good and evil. "I have very strong convictions and fixed rules of conduct," he told one of his governors. Empowered by the Constitution of 1869, García Moreno ordered his *jefes políticos* to enforce the new laws by collecting fines, literally a "sin tax" for peccadilloes, or by jailing the most egregious offenders.[84]

By 1870 the first step in the campaign, improving the morality of the priesthood, had been accomplished. "Scandals, common in other times, have almost completely disappeared" because many who refused to reform left the priesthood. The hierarchy itself had eliminated many of the abuses, and the presence of the dedicated Jesuits and other service orders bettered the moral environment.[85] Nevertheless, a few blemishes appeared on the church's record. In addition to occasional cases of drunkenness and general carousing, one priest fell afoul of the law for counterfeiting money, while another kidnapped a boy and ran off with him.[86] Despite these irregularities, García Moreno must have been pleased with the improved state of the clergy.

In highland rural areas, clerics joined in partnership with local officials to improve the state of morality of the indigenous people. Moments they spent away from laboring, especially on occasions of public celebrations, always raised fears among those who were not indigenous that rowdiness could lead to something worse. Hence García Moreno congratulated a governor who banned cockfights in an Indian community because they excited passions and led to immorality and drunkenness. He also statutorily banned Sunday markets in 1869. Likewise Carnaval celebrations, never one of García Moreno's favorite activities, were discontinued in some locations.[87] Religious festivals also underwent strict scrutiny. Over the years the process of syncretism had allowed many indigenous practices to creep into Catholic festivals. How else can one explain the colorful Mama Negra (Black Mother) festival in Latacunga held on September 24 on the Feast of Our Lady of Mercy? Or the Corpus Christi festivals held in communities such as Pujilí and Otavalo? Their many non-Christian elements provided "a pretext for drinking, gambling, and immorality," as Governor Felipe Serrade stated. The church and state hoped to instill more orthodoxy on these occasions. Masks, dances, and of course the accompanying drinking "occasion disorder, immorality, and disrespect of religious functions," and turn Indians away from "pure religion." From the indigenous perspective, people wanted to preserve their collective memories, demonstrate resistance to the dominant culture—and enjoy themselves. Besides banning these semi-Christian festivities, government officials reawakened the old colonial practice of encouraging *doctrinas*, or daily prayer sessions with Christian homilies, as a means to reintroduce the indigenous to the Catholic faith.[88]

García Moreno's correspondence and the government reports suggest strongly that the president concerned himself mostly with reforming two basic vices, drinking and extramarital sexual relations. Excessive drinking provoked a whole host of problems: cursing, gambling, brawling, and of course concupiscence. On the other hand, the government derived revenue from its *aguardiente* monopoly. Several of García Moreno's friends and relatives, like the Ascásubis, were in the liquor business. Nevertheless, government agents vigorously prosecuted persons who sold bootleg liquor, be it *aguardiente* or *chicha,* the corn beer of the highlands. In addition one governor imposed the extreme measure of closing taverns at 10 p.m.[89]

Personally García Moreno hated drinking. During his youth, he had loved chocolate, and later he imbibed coffee, but he never developed a taste for strong drink. Not the most tolerant person under the best of circumstances, García Moreno felt outraged by the drunkenness he saw daily in society: "I won't tolerate more drunks," he said. "[We must] make constant war against the drunks." His governors' strong measures received his complete approval. "In the holy war against drunkenness and dissolution, I will support you with all my strength."[90] The government attempted all sorts of measures to promote temperance. Besides punishments, García Moreno printed articles against the evils of demon rum in the government newspaper, threatened to cut off the pensions of government employees convicted of being publicly drunk, and authorized one governor to use military and police patrols to round up individuals seen staggering around the streets at night. Not surprisingly, the crime of public drunkenness affected mostly the poor. Wealthy Ecuadorians did not frequent taverns but instead got inebriated in their own or friends' homes. As a result, notorious drunks like U.S. Minister Rumsey Wing faced no more than García Moreno's snide comments.[91]

García Moreno had no more tolerance for people who pursued sexual relations outside of marriage than he did for drunks: "The scandal [of concubines] like gangrene affects society and . . . the infected people must be healed." Shortly after the January 1869 coup, he issued a decree criminalizing concubinage. High-ranking clerical supervisors traveled around the sierra and compiled lists of people, usually Indians, living in concubinage. With list in hand, they pressured local officials like Indian governors and *jefes políticos* to force weddings—as one said, "without me having to interpose my complaints before superior authorities." What bothered visitors the most was the traditional Indian custom of trial marriages—an unsupervised "bundling" where couples lived together before committing to marriage. Entering suspects' homes late at night, police and Indian governors arrested couples and dragged them off to separate facilities. Sometimes the couples, including one caught *in flagrante delicto,* turned out to be adulterers.[92] García Moreno reacted harshly to officials caught in such dragnets. Judges and civil servants arrested under these circumstances lost their jobs immediately and suffered maximum sentences. Neither did the handful of men convicted of sodomy fare particularly well, being sentenced to prison or exiled.[93]

Although the moral police uncovered many examples of concubinage in the highlands, the more casual society of the coast gave rise to even more cases of moral transgressions. There both sexes commonly entered into informal sexual arrangements. Because concubinage was so widely practiced on the coast (reflected in the many cases reported each month), the government faced an uphill battle in its eradication. As the governor of Guayas stated, "In the city there are more than 100 couples living in adultery or concubinage, setting a *fatal* example to the citizenry" (my emphasis). Hampered by unenthusiastic law enforcement officials, the governor asked García Moreno for his personal intervention. As in the highlands, coastal governors proceeded cautiously. For couples living in exclusive and consensual unions, the governors offered the reasonable solution of marriage.[94] Prostitutes and women who had sex with multiple partners posed more difficult problems. Those who seemed redeemable found themselves in Casas del Buen Pastor, while the more recalcitrant often fled the country.[95] Regardless of its effectiveness, the campaign to improve morality demonstrated García Moreno's commitment to change adult behavior in order to set good examples for the next generation.

GARCÍA MORENO: DEVOUT CATHOLIC OR RELIGIOUS EXTREMIST?

The question of whether Gabriel García Moreno's religiosity edged into the realm of fanaticism has been at the center of discussions about his life. Beginning with liberal opponents of his regime and foreign diplomats quoted throughout this book, García Moreno's policies in pursuing the Catholic nation have often been portrayed as excessive. On the other hand, García Moreno's defenders have rationalized his choices, arguing that they made sense for Ecuador in the 1860s and 1870s. This view fulfills Simón Bolívar's quip that the country was a "monastery," accommodating what Minister Wing called "the intense spirit of Catholicism pervading every circle in Ecuador."[96] Four policies in particular have opened García Moreno to the charge of religious extremism. First, his dogged pursuit of the Concordat with the pope aligned Ecuador with the conservative wing of the Catholic Church by openly embracing ultramontanism along with the ideas of papal infallibility and the war on liberalism expressed in the 1864 Syllabus of Errors. Second, Ecuador's Constitution of 1869 drew the wrath of liberals because it required an individual to profess the Catholic faith in order to enjoy the privileges of citizenship. As previously noted, well over 99 percent of Ecuadorians in the 1870s would have been at least nominal Catholics. Thus the requirement of a profession of faith did not in reality disenfranchise people, yet it remained a symbol for tyranny.

García Moreno also gained a reputation for extremism when he alone among the heads of state in the western world protested the Italian government's seizure of the papal domains at the end of the Franco-Prussian War in 1870. For García Moreno, the episode provided an opportunity to stake out a principled position on the world stage. Taking pen in hand, he urged King Victor Emmanuel of Italy to restore the papal territories before "the house of his illustrious ancestors is reduced to ashes by the avenging fires of bloody revolutions." The president then sent copies of this letter to the leaders of all Western Hemisphere and European nations, calling upon them to second his complaint—which none did. García Moreno made his objectives crystal clear in correspondence with his friends. "I alone complied with my duty as the Catholic head of a Catholic people. I wrote to the other republics, but I didn't expect them to follow. This was just to give more publicity to the protest." Yet García Moreno expected ardent Catholics around the world, especially in his own country, to agree with his stance, and many did.[97] Verbalizing a protest was not enough for García

Moreno. In addition he sent a single soldier to bolster the Swiss Guard (the pope's soldiers) as a symbolic gesture, and provided His Eminence with 10 percent of the tithe income, which in 1873 amounted to 10,000 pesos. In return, the pope awarded García Moreno a medal![98]

Finally, no measure did more to incur the wrath of liberals or create the image of García Moreno as a fanatic than his decision to dedicate Ecuador to the Sacred Heart of Jesus in 1873. Part of Catholic doctrine from around 1000 A.D., the Sacred Heart referred to Jesus' physical heart, the symbol of his redemptive love. Pope Pius IX encouraged families, communities, and nations to consecrate themselves to the Sacred Heart, and a number did. In the nineteenth century, the cult symbolized the rejection of liberalism because Louis XVI of France had promised to dedicate France to the advocation, had he escaped the guillotine. Hence the Sacred Heart found many followers among conservatives of late nineteenth-century France, who failed to dedicate their country to the cult but did manage to build an enormous pilgrimage church overlooking Paris at Montmartre.[99]

Initially a Jesuit from Riobamba promoted the idea of dedicating Ecuador, which the archbishop and the Third Council of Quito endorsed. Congress passed the legislation making the dedication official, asserting it was "the most efficacious mode of preserving the faith and *extending the progress and temporal welfare of the state*" (my emphasis). García Moreno believed that dedicating the country to a single cult would help promote cultural unity and national pride. Ecuador's statute ordered that a shrine to the cult be built in each cathedral in the country and that a special Mass occur at the cathedral in Quito to commemorate the dedication.[100] While dedicating Ecuador to the Sacred Heart of Jesus seemed extreme to liberals and the modern mentality, it was utterly consistent with García Moreno's belief that only the Catholic Church could bind together people as regionally, ethnically, and linguistically divided as the Ecuadorians.

Chapter Seven

Caring for Earthly Needs: The Program for Economic Development

Gabriel García Moreno was in many ways an unusual conservative politician. On one hand, he believed in conservative Catholic values as a means of unifying the country, as explained in the last chapter, while on the other hand, he strongly advocated economic and technical modernization. This chapter will focus on that second facet, the one that dwelled on the realm of the practical. Like nearly every nineteenth-century Latin American leader, he embraced the notion of progress—or in twenty-first-century nomenclature, economic development. Having lived in Paris, traveled extensively throughout Western Europe, and visited the eastern seaboard of the United States in the 1850s, he knew firsthand that Ecuador lagged behind by comparison. His diplomatic venture in 1866 further opened his eyes to Ecuador's backwardness: Both Chile and Peru had achieved greater prosperity than Ecuador in the half century since independence. Determined to reverse this course of events, García Moreno pledged to follow policies that would develop commerce, bring additional revenue into the treasury, and raise the living standards of ordinary citizens. The word "progress" emanated constantly from his pen: "We must have hope and faith in the *dogma* of progress" (my emphasis). "As you know, my principal desire for the country is to . . . bring progress and civilization."[1]

The question of why Ecuador, and for that matter Latin America, has developed only modestly has puzzled economists and historians alike, bringing forth a host of competing explanations. For decades, even going back to García Moreno's time, many thought the explanation a cultural one. The Spanish colonial authoritarian tradition, the presence of the Catholic Church, the lack of a "Protestant" work ethic, and the presence of unassimilated (in terms of values) indigenous people in the Andean nations and Mexico seemingly explained Latin American "backwardness."[2]

Of course such explanations are tainted with notions of racial or ethnic superiority, which renders them suspect. In the 1970s and 1980s, the theory of dependency came into vogue, arguing that the tentacles of capitalism generated from the metropolis (Europe and the United States) acted to impoverish the periphery (Latin America and the developing world) by controlling prices and maximizing profits for international corporations. Although this overly mechanistic and formulaic theory has generally fallen into disrepute, it contains grains of truth under some circumstances. For example, beginning in the 1890s, Ecuador became overly dependent on export earnings from the cacao trade, suffering grave consequences when the boom ended in the 1920s.[3] As critics of the dependency model have pointed out, however, Latin Americans made a rational choice to export raw materials, especially after 1850, because they earned high prices in European markets where demand outstripped supply. Real development occurred, however, only in those instances where a Latin American nation exported goods that needed processing or required foreign investment elsewhere in the economy—which in turn generated profits internally.[4] Currently no real consensus has emerged about the causes of Latin American underdevelopment. Regardless of the theoretical debate, leaders like García Moreno believed in the idea of progress and sought to implement it rapidly.

Having visualized progress on his foreign excursions, García Moreno understood the rather self-evident formula for modernization. First, a country needed to achieve political stability, for instability not only disrupted investment and trade but also diminished revenues. Instability also made a nation inhospitable to foreign immigrants, necessary in García Moreno's opinion to bring progressive work-ethic values to the country. Capital migrated to those nations demonstrating that they had a primary product or products worthy of exploitation. Although many Latin American nations have suffered from being monocultures (i.e., reliant on a single export crop), García Moreno hoped to diversify his country's economy. To improve the movement of goods to market, a nation needed the technology related to transportation and communication. Finally, a country required a positive legal environment where business could flourish.

As García Moreno's second term began, nearly all of these factors were but dreams. García Moreno could claim, however, that Ecuador had achieved stability. Ever since the 1865 battle of Jambelí, the exiles and their internal allies had been silenced. Because stability had only been achieved recently compared to other nations like Chile and Brazil, Ecuador still seemed a relatively hazardous place in which to invest. Ecuador's unrevised legal system and culture posed issues. García Moreno had generally embraced the modified doctrine of free trade sweeping Latin America in the nineteenth century. Yet foreign observers like Friedrich Hassaurek noted the presence of social customs (namely, procrastination and perfidy of merchants—at least in Quito) that worked against a sound business climate. After 1869 García Moreno had congress updating the commercial code. People in the highlands and especially on the coast soon began speaking in favor of the freedom to contract and against monopolies. In fact, one of García Moreno's former triumvirs from 1859 and reputedly the largest landowner in the north, Pacífico Chiriboga, thanked the president for breaking up a monopoly of two or three individuals seeking to control the price of beef in Quito.[5] With a stable political system in place, and a chief executive who understood the importance of business, Ecuador could now take the next steps towards modernization.

FUELING THE ENGINE: THE ACQUISITION OF CAPITAL

As a poor nation, Ecuador suffered from a lack of capital to fund enterprises that would make the economy grow. Because of unfortunate decisions made back in 1830 when Gran Colombia collapsed, as has been mentioned, the country found itself staggering under the burden of a large foreign debt. Consequently, over the ensuing decades, Ecuador had been forced to raise whatever development capital it needed internally. During García Moreno's first term, the situation improved slightly when an individually owned private bank gained the right statutorily to issue paper money. The bank then underwrote some of García Moreno's internal improvements in exchange for a guaranteed percentage of customs revenues. Yet this bank and its successor failed. By 1870 a new bank, the Bank of Ecuador based in Guayaquil, emerged. With over one million pesos in cash reserves and the authority to issue three times as much currency, the Bank of Ecuador enjoyed the capacity to open up the money supply. Its charter explicitly stated the purpose of the new institution: "to foment commerce and agriculture in the sierra and on the coast, and to exploit the mines and forests of the Republic." Rather than being owned by one person, the Bank of Ecuador had several wealthy investors, including Pedro Pablo García Moreno. The bank also lent money to the government, but as the French minister noted, there was never enough to meet all the needs.[6]

As its first step, the bank standardized all money, eliminating old paper issues as well as the Colombian, Peruvian, Chilean, and French coins in circulation. While exchanging bills did not prove problematic, people proved less willing to part with shiny foreign coins. Vendors could bite down on hard coins, but the value of paper money seemed much less tangible. The copper and silver replacement coins minted by the bank (some made in the United States) filled a vital commercial need. Because they were so trustworthy, however, people hoarded them—leading to a shortage in the marketplace.[7] Paper bills fared less well, being widely accepted in Guayaquil yet with less confidence in the sierra. Even though the law prohibited refusal of the new bills, the governor of León reported that they were regularly being turned down in the Latacunga marketplace.[8]

The Bank of Ecuador differed from its predecessor because it was a *national* bank, and not just a coastal one (although the national currency did not become the *sucre* until the 1880s). Rather soon, the president of the Bank of Ecuador decided to open branches in Quito, Cuenca, and Montecristi in Manabí. For the first time, bills and coins actually had Ecuador embossed on them. Postage stamps, issued in 1865 for the first time under García Moreno, did as well. With countrywide usage, Ecuadorian currency and stamps were part of the nation-building project.[9]

The bank also furthered this project by extending to the government lines of credit of as much as a half-million pesos for public works projects in the years from 1869 to 1874. Minimal customs duties on imports and exports provided most of the revenues in this modified free-trade system—some of which were pledged for specific purposes, including repaying the Bank of Ecuador. Ecuadorian elites imported luxury goods from Europe, and the country exported agricultural commodities.[10] Other important sources of revenue remained the same as during the first term: the tithe, the *trabajo subsidiario,* and the monopolies on salt, aguardiente, gunpowder, and legal documents.

All in all, García Moreno certainly controlled more tax revenue than his predecessors in the 1850s. According to the following tabulation, total government income increased dramatically, particularly during the 1870s. One must note that the figures for 1874 and 1875 seem high, however, given the effects of the Panic of 1873. In any event, this chart provides a reasonable understanding about the levels of governmental income during the García Moreno years.

As today, Ecuadorians of that era also believed that they were overtaxed, and resisted paying direct taxes. About 85 percent of the tax revenue came from indirect sources, which not only indicated the elite's reluctance

TABLE 1. TAX REVENUE, 1858–1875

YEAR	TAX REVENUE IN PESOS	YEAR	TAX REVENUE IN PESOS
1858	1,288,000	1867	1,610,000
1859	Unknown	1868	1,442,000
1860	Unknown	1869	1,664,000
1861	1,448,000	1870	2,248,000
1862	1,128,000	1871	2,483,000
1863	1,350,000	1872	2,909,000
1864	1,444,000	1873	3,099,000
1865	1,587,000	1874	3,092,000
1866	1,369,000	1875	2,849,000

to tax themselves, but also demonstrated the weakness of the nineteenth-century state—even under García Moreno.[11] Overall the limited revenue that the government could tap meant that dreams for modernization had to be small and often regional. To make sure that scarce money was fully gathered, García Moreno also determined to plug the traditional leaks in the collection process.

García Moreno knew that smuggling cost the treasury thousands of pesos annually. Greed and a willingness to participate in embezzlement had long been part of the job description of Ecuadorian customs officials. To make matters worse even in busy Guayaquil, customs offices stayed open only from 8:00 to 9:00 a.m. and from 11:00 a.m. to 4:00 p.m. With only four ports legally open, opportunities abounded for smugglers to land on deserted beaches and in isolated inlets. In vain the government attempted to regulate away the loopholes. Cargo ships were prohibited from docking in port at night, lest their crews unload under cover of darkness. By statute, the government banned fishing boats from leaving port before dawn, despite pleas that the calmer seas made their occupation safer at that time.[12] Of course the real problem was the malfeasance and nonfeasance of employees at the customs houses. The constant harping on the theme of smuggling and the need to stop corruption in the customs houses demonstrates García Moreno's fixation on the issue.[13] In the long run, one cannot calculate the revenues lost through contraband. García Moreno did his best to improve the system. Given his reputation for toughness, employees probably behaved better than they had at other times.

He also hoped for a loan from abroad to capitalize his ambitious public works program. Acquiring a loan and renegotiating the foreign debt downward continued to be one of García Moreno's fondest, if most illusory, dreams. The English debt had been burdensome, with millions paid in interest but not one shilling on principal. Armed with indignation over this situation, Antonio Flores left for England in 1874 faced with an impossible task. Called on not only to reduce both principal and interest owed, but also to secure a new loan to fund railroad construction, Flores could only fail. As the chair of the English bondholders and the British consul noted, "the loss of credit on the exchange of Europe which . . . placed Ecuador on the list of Insolvent States . . . . would make it [nearly impossible] to effect a loan anywhere except under very onerous terms."[14] Once the loan prospect fell through in October 1874, the government lost interest in paying the debt. García Moreno stated his position clearly: "The government wanted the loan to better its present economic situation, not to impoverish us and compromise the future under the weight of onerous conditions." Interestingly, while these negotiations went on, Ecuador did pay its much smaller debt to the United States.[15] Without prospects of a foreign loan, however, García Moreno had to continue to rely on income generated internally in Ecuador.

The coming of the Panic of 1873 further dimmed prospects for borrowing money. In the United States, the Panic began with the failure of Jay Cooke's businesses and lasted until 1879 in some places. García Moreno's letters in 1874 and 1875 are filled with talk about the economic depression. As he investigated the situation more closely, he discovered that the Bank of Ecuador was also in danger because it had issued more paper currency than allowed by law and permitted wholesale withdrawals of hard specie from its reserves. Calling in loans helped to safeguard the bank, but the reduced money supply hampered business. García Moreno outlawed the export of silver. On his own authority, he issued bills in small denominations to expedite purchases in the marketplace. Ever the optimist, García Moreno still hoped for a foreign loan: "The loan will save us from the monetary crisis, which will ruin the more developed countries of the world."[16] He did have certain insights into the situation. Because Ecuador was a rural agricultural nation, its people would not starve between 1874 and 1879. Revenues for García Moreno's cherished public works projects would seriously be curtailed, however, as imports and exports slowed.

Like any good pre-Keynesian leader, García Moreno cut expenses. Only high priority projects, like the new penitentiary and the railroad, would be completed. In the fall of 1874, García Moreno estimated he could get through the remainder of the year with just 55,000 pesos: 26,000 for an annual rent payment, 18,000 for the pope's share of the tithe revenue, and 11,000 for a contract to purchase supplies for the bureaucracy and the army. By the end of the year, García Moreno estimated "government expenses will be reduced to half what they were at the beginning of the year." Compounding the economic woes, José García Moreno uncovered a scandal in the cacao marketing system. Apparently the son of the president of the Bank of Ecuador took kickbacks and mixed high grade with poorer quality cacao, which caused the reputation and price of Ecuadorian cacao to plummet. According to José García Moreno, "that bastard who today is manager of the Bank of Ecuador" (Juan José González) also illegally charged a brokerage commission for his services.[17] So dire had the situation become in the spring of 1875 that the privately owned Bank of Ecuador decided to tighten the fiscal strings on the government, stating that the monthly line of credit would be limited to 50,000 pesos.[18]

FINDING MARKETABLE PRODUCTS

To generate tax revenue and entice potential investors, Ecuador needed something valuable to market. For many writers, especially those who adhere to the dependency theory, one of the causes of Latin America's relative poverty and underdevelopment was a given country's reliance on a single primary product for export. Obviously the export-led strategy worked well when demand remained high, but competition could ruin sales and cause wholesale economic disruption—as could the lack of a viable internal market.[19] Although the generalization about monoculture has often been applied to Ecuador (first cacao, then bananas, and now petroleum), during the age of García Moreno, as in Imperial Brazil, the country enjoyed a suitable balance of tropical agricultural products, forest items, and even artisan goods among its exports. García Moreno's letters suggest that increasing the sales volume of all products weighed more heavily on his mind than did diversification. As a former U.S. envoy stated: "The wealth of her soil and forests, and the unfathomed extent of her mineral treasures [are] yet unwrought."[20]

After the great Crystal Palace Exhibition in the 1850s (the first world fair), countries knew how to publicize the products they hoped to market. Successive world fairs offered developing nations an opportunity to display both the exotic and the practical, piquing the interest of prospective investors, merchants, and consumers. García Moreno knew the game well. He had urged Ecuadorians to participate in the Paris exposition in the 1860s but, as noted in chapter 5, had met with little success. Now he determined to try again, this time at the Philadelphia Exposition of 1876. With the aid

TABLE 2. EXPORTS VALUED IN PESOS

YEAR	CACAO	CAUCHO	CINCHONA	COFFEE	PANAMA HATS	TAGUA
1871	1,823,436	657,920	341,507	53,066	43,365	48,557
1873	3,274,455	633,502	646,666	206,753	182,180	82,506

of Antonio Flores, now minister to Washington, García Moreno suggested thirty-five natural products that could be displayed in Philadelphia. Following García Moreno's death in 1875, the project fell apart, like so many of his other initiatives. Nevertheless, customs records of the value of goods shipped provide an idea of the types of items[21] that would have been displayed in Philadelphia, as shown in Table 2.

Not surprisingly, cacao topped the list. Ecuadorians would claim that their *cacao de arriba,* raised in the low hills of Los Ríos province, ranked as the best in the world (although Venezuelans and world prices disputed this statement). As the price of cacao rose in the early 1870s, large-scale growers began appropriating adjacent communal lands and dragooning workers. Now cacao laborers had to carry identification cards certifying they did not owe debts to a planter before they could freely travel. Although some workers migrated from the highlands to earn more money in the cacao plantations, they sometimes found themselves abused, unpaid, and ill-fed. As Rumsey Wing and others noted, the coast provided a variety of tropical agricultural crops. During the U.S. Civil War, Ecuadorian planters had successfully exported cotton. Others grew coffee, rice, and bananas, and raised cattle (for hides).[22] In short, tropical agriculture offered great diversity. Some bushes, such as coffee and cacao, took a few years to mature, hence preventing an overnight transition of crops if the market weakened. In general, though, planters in this fertile region enjoyed considerable flexibility from one growing season to the next.

Next to tropical agriculture, forest products contributed the most to Ecuador's economy. Once a mere oddity, *caucho* (rubber) acquired practical applications as the bicycle craze of the nineteenth century advanced. Before the Brazilian *hevea* tree came to dominate the industry, most of the world's supply came from *caucho*. In Ecuador, *caucho* trees grow in Esmeraldas province, in the region around Santo Domingo de los Colorados, and in the Oriente—a source exploited after 1875. From the outset, *caucho* posed two problems stemming from the manner in which rubber was collected. First, because gatherers worked autonomously, regulating their activities and collecting taxes proved difficult. Second, the very idea of independence encouraged *concierto peones* on cacao haciendas in Manabí to flee their circumstances for "the imaginary advantages" of collecting *caucho.* (In modern social science discourse, *caucho* offered subalterns a little more agency.) Similar difficulties faced the government in trying to regulate another forest product, *tagua* (vegetable ivory), which in the nineteenth century could be carved into fancy buttons for expensive clothing.[23]

Forests also yielded valuable herbal medicines. By García Moreno's time, medical experts agreed that the quinine contained in *cinchona,* mislabeled Peruvian bark, could cure malaria. While perhaps the most effective variety of *cinchona* grew in Bolivia, the second best quality bark (red *cinchona*) came from the Ecuadorian provinces of Loja, "the botanical garden of America," and Azuay. As the price of *cinchona* rose, independent cutters roamed the lower mountain ranges, felling large stands of trees. The market for Ecuadorian *cinchona* remained viable until the 1890s, when South Asian production peaked.[24] Given the value of *cinchona,* the Cuenca region's most prized export, no wonder the government hoped to find other forest products that would cure loathsome diseases.

The highest hopes rested on white *cundurango,* the "vine of the condor" found roughly on the same slopes of the mountains of Loja as *cinchona.* According to rumor, an Indian woman hoped to put her husband, suffering the agonies of stomach cancer, out of his misery by poisoning him with tea made from *cundurango* leaves. Unable to find any leaves, she used a ground-up potion of the bark instead. Much to her surprise, her husband recovered from both the treatment and the cancer. News of the miraculous cure spread to the city of Loja, where Javier Eguiguren brought the discovery to the attention of the medical community in Quito and Guayaquil. A noted biologist, James Orton, who wandered through Ecuador in the 1860s, described the plant at great length and touted it as a cure for everything from snake bite to rheumatism, as did Minister Wing.

Doctors began testing it on patients with cancer and syphilis, the two major diseases it reputedly cured. According to one attending physician, the remedy resolved the cancer of not only a fifteen-year-old boy but also former president Diego Noboa. Unfortunately the latter died shortly thereafter of an unrelated illness and could not offer testimonials about the new drug. So promising did the medicine seem that García Moreno saw fit to mention it in his state-of-the-union address as a possible miracle cure.[25] Before the product could be marketed, however, international scientists wanted to test it further. García Moreno generously sent large samples to laboratories in Paris, London, New York, and Lima. When they failed to produce results, though, the *cundurango* boom came to an abrupt halt.

Since colonial times, Ecuador exported artisan goods, especially textiles made at *obrajes* (workshops usually staffed with coerced Indian labor). Yet the free-trade policies adopted first by the Bourbon monarchs and then the republicans (including García Moreno) undercut the *obrajes* that had once sold Ecuadorian textiles in markets from southern Colombia to Potosí in Bolivia. As a result, clothing and blankets continued to lose ground as export items, although they remained important for internal consumption. Now Ecuador's major artisan export was straw hats, misnamed Panama hats. Originally made in Manabí, where the *toquilla* plant grows profusely, most hats by 1850 were made in towns outside Cuenca. Even today the Panama hat business remains a cottage industry.[26]

In short, Ecuador enjoyed a varied range of export products in the 1860s and 1870s and did not suffer from the problem of monoculture, which eventually ruined a number of Latin American economies—including its own. As a nation that relied largely on indirect taxes for its income, however, Ecuador did feel the effects of the global economy despite its relative diversification. When the Panic of 1873 hit, the market for its exports shrank. Because of two structural problems, Ecuador could not recover independently. First, the huge disparity of income between the elite and middle classes compared to the very poor sector meant a limited internal consumer market. Second, economic development had proceeded regionally, with the coast far more advanced than the sierra. Many small-property owners in the highlands still engaged in subsistence agriculture, while even large-estate owners were limited to regional markets. Thus Ecuador remained in many ways a nation of distinctive regions in the García Moreno era. Yet he thought he had a solution to revive the highland economy, which was to build transportation links to markets on the coast.

THE GREAT GARCIAN HIGHWAY SYSTEM

No project, except perhaps education, aroused García Moreno's passion more than the desire to build roads, which seemed an ideal solution to rectify Ecuador's regionally unbalanced economy. With the exception of a few dissenters who feared the loss of labor, most politically aware Ecuadorians agreed that road construction would open the floodgates of prosperity for the highlands—long plagued by an inability to get products from the sierra to coastal and international markets. The clamor to build roads and end isolation led to six road construction projects. Had they been completed, these projects would also have facilitated García Moreno's second objective—to reduce the importance of Guayaquil. Although road construction proposals at times seemed haphazard, García Moreno had a broad plan in mind to create a network of highways crisscrossing the country that would improve on the pre-Hispanic system in two ways. First, because the Incas had just completed their conquest of highland Ecuador when the Spanish interrupted them, no Inca roads linked the highlands with the coast. Second, the Incas, who lacked wheeled vehicles, had in many instances simply carved steps for runners into solid rock. García Moreno envisioned modern, wide cart-paths bearing commercial traffic. As this section will demonstrate, however, both human and natural obstacles stood in the way of his dream.

At the outset, García Moreno visualized the road network to resemble the human circulatory system. Several main arteries would pump the blood of commerce to the extremities. Then smaller roads would act like capillaries, bringing life to every portion of the body. To carry out this vision, he needed both skilled engineers who could plan such a system and the technology that would allow mere mortals to undertake the hard labor. As a result, García Moreno turned to foreign engineers to lay out the roads and devise innumerable bridges over roaring streams. Such engineers commanded high salaries. They in turn struggled with a lack of technology as they begged the government to send machetes, axes, shovels, and wheelbarrows to speed progress on the road.[27]

The crown jewel of García Moreno's road system was the main highway running from Quito to Guayaquil, which had reached Riobamba during his first term. With great enthusiasm, he resumed the effort in 1869. To further commercial expansion, García Moreno had decreed that the road would be three carts wide for the entire 320-mile stretch to Guayaquil. In addition, plans called for cobblestone to combat the problem of travel during the rainy season, when muddy conditions had made the old path nearly impassible. Between 1869 and 1872, workers completed the road along the highlands and down the escarpment to the coastal plain, finally reaching the town of Sibambe. Because half of the *trabajo subsidiario* as well as some customs revenues were now dedicated to the great highway, the government could provide money for the project. Delivering the funds to workers presented the real problem, and of course the failure to do so negatively affected morale. Because this road represented García Moreno's most cherished project, both he and his governors made frequent inspections of the work to measure progress and minimize abuses.[28]

Indians walking along an uncompleted road (Courtesy of the Library of Congress USZ 62-100238)

What inevitably slowed construction and cost the most were the innumerable bridges crossing the rivers and streams between Quito and Guayaquil. Ecuador's bountiful rainfall constituted a mixed blessing. While the country was agriculturally richer than most of its neighbors because of ample water, the numerous rushing waterways hampered the road effort. Engineers spent the better part of a year constructing a new stone bridge that would bear cart traffic in the vicinity of Latacunga. The bridge over the wide and frequently flooded Babahoyo River in the lowlands proved challenging as well. After James Wilson, a U.S. engineer, completed the bridge, seasonal rains and soft soils made repairs necessary the following year. According to the U.S. minister, García Moreno built 71 bridges along the great highway as well as 55 aqueducts to capture unwanted deluges.[29] Understandably, García Moreno trumpeted the completion of the road from Quito to Sibambe as a huge triumph. Now one could travel from Quito to the coast in a matter of days rather than weeks. Although a commercially viable route from Sibambe to Guayaquil remained to be constructed, García Moreno had a radical plan for the final leg of that journey, which will be explored in the next section.

In addition to constructing the main highway, García Moreno had a second broad policy objective: to liberate the imprisoned commercial spirit of the sierra by building roads from highland cities to other ports to rival Guayaquil. To his good friend the governor of Azuay, García Moreno broached the idea of a cart road (or at least a mule path) running from Cuenca to the river port of Naranjal, which would facilitate marketing Azuay's textiles, *cinchona* bark, and Panama hats. As with all of these projects, the work began with enthusiasm. The foreign engineer, Christopher Thill, convinced Governor Carlos Ordóñez that Cuenca needed a wide cart road, even though construction would be more costly and slower than a mule path. From Cuenca, the brigades of up to 670 workers made scant progress. Nowhere did one of García Moreno's secondary road projects meet greater resistance. Benigno Malo voiced the local opposition, arguing that it would take twenty years to complete the road (it took longer) and that the drain of labor from his factory would bankrupt his family. García Moreno retorted that "the road will be done in spite of you" and pushed ahead.[30] García Moreno attributed the road's turtle-like pace in part to the lack of labor and high costs. Finally, in full retreat he suggested that if Cuencans really wanted the project to continue, they could hire private contractors to build it.[31] Thus the Naranjal road came to a whimpering halt.

Although the Naranjal route failed, García Moreno had hopes for another road that would have linked the recently reconstructed city of Ibarra to the coastal town of La Tola in Esmeraldas province. García Moreno referred to this road as "the salvation of Imbabura" because it would revitalize the economy damaged by the earthquake. Initially the work went swimmingly. A local *jefe político* noted, "There is enthusiasm by each one of [the *peones*]." Possibly the citizens of Otavalo, who comprised most of the workforce, remained grateful to García Moreno for his efforts on their behalf in 1868. Likely too, the fact that the work took place in their own neighborhood made them willing to volunteer. Despite problems with supplies and a lack of tools (many broke or were blunted on the job), the hardworking *otavaleños* and their neighbors kept the project moving forward at a rapid pace through the sierras and down the Intag River. Late in 1873, García Moreno optimistically stated, "By the end of next year we will be able to bathe in the sea in Esmeraldas." As the road descended from the familiar sierra to the tropical forests, though, volunteers became draftees. Many Indians fled to other districts or to the relative safety of the haciendas, whose laborers had been traditionally exempted from public works. So desperate did the regime become for workers that it changed the law, requiring haciendas to contribute to the workforce on a regular basis, but even this labor system failed.[32] All too quickly the tropical forest overran the hard-fought-for path, and the government abandoned the effort at a town today appropriately named García Moreno.[33]

In the 1870s, however, engineers alerted García Moreno to a third possible route to the coast—through Santo Domingo de los Colorados to Bahía de Caráquez on the Pacific. Once García Moreno heard that the new road could potentially reduce travel time from the capital to the coast to two-and-a-half days, he became excited and immediately approved initial funding for the project. Within days he sent engineer Arthur Rodgers to map out the route from Quito to Santo Domingo, while at the same time decreeing the usual inducements to workers. (Exemption from military service was a popular one.) Excited by Rodgers' report of a gentle grade of only 7 percent, García Moreno undertook several inspections of the Quito section of the new road. He stated that he expected it to reach Santo Domingo by the end of 1872 and Bahía the following year.[34] Rodgers and José Zambrano scouted the terrain from the coast to Santo Domingo, reporting that their proposed route required only four bridges. The U.S. minister shared García Moreno's enthusiasm for the commercial possibility of the new cart path that ran through the rubber-producing region, but the usual problems of funding and labor stalled the road short of Santo Domingo.[35]

The other two road projects raised enthusiasm in the far south of the country, but made little progress. Ecuador's most isolated province, Loja, hoped for a new road that would run from the state capital to the gold mining town of Zaruma, and then down to the coast at Machala. As the treasury minister stated, the plan "will better the economic situation of the province with the opening of the road to the coast that will offer the markets of the world to the products of your rich and abundant province." Engineers Thomas Rodil and Modesto López soon began mapping out the route. Despite initial enthusiasm, though, the project went badly from the beginning.[36] Finally García Moreno's ambitious road network included a sixth lesser road that would have connected Loja to the missions in the interior. Organized to further the missionary effort described in the last chapter, the road to the jungle never came close to completion.[37]

Given García Moreno's commitment to road building, what caused these projects to fail? First, although his labor policies were intended to be benevolent and fair, too often abuses prevailed. On each project a pattern emerged. Initially the government hired volunteers, paying them what they would have earned at their regular agricultural labor. The state also provided meals and health care. Supplies and wages arrived irregularly, however, leaving the men hungry after a hard day's work and feeling exploited.

Moving from high altitudes to lower ones exposed workers to fevers, and some died when the field hospitals lacked suitable drugs for treatment.[38] The farther from home the work took laborers, the more discontented they became. Because of García Moreno's strict code of morality, labor on the road did not resemble the traditional pre-Hispanic *mita,* where work was accompanied by symbolic reciprocity—including a fair amount of drinking and feasting once the project was completed. To make matters worse, overseers sometimes stole money from the *peones*, forced them to work on personal projects, beat them, or sold unwanted goods to them for profit (all legacies of the colonial period).[39] No wonder the indigenous laborers resented the road project, and the number of volunteers dwindled.

Initially, García Moreno recognized that labor abuses would ultimately be the downfall of the project. He raged, "Nobody is obligated to work for free on any public work, and to draft workers and just feed them is a joke, a crime that begs Heaven for justice, a transgression that . . . I cannot tolerate." Yet he also advocated that deserters from the road gangs should be punished and those who shirked their turns brought forcibly to the camps. Both individuals who refused to report for duty on public service projects and local officials who failed to produce their allotment of workers faced stiff fines.[40] By 1873 Indians resisted, if passively, the labor draft for the reasons outlined above.[41]

In the end, García Moreno realized that his plan for a voluntary labor draft had failed. Although he had hoped to spread the work fairly among the population, asking his political lieutenants to create lists of all *peones* "so that they can work on the road in shifts while maintaining agricultural productivity," he found that even raising the wage did not draw volunteers. When the number of laborers dwindled, Treasury Minister José Javier Eguiguren argued, "You must compel them to work by force." Hence the postconquest Andean solution prevailed once again. Other Ecuadorians, particularly the hacendados, had abetted *peones* fleeing their labor responsibilities. As mentioned previously, the labor statute had originally exempted hacienda *concierto* Indians because theoretically they worked in gainful enterprises. As a result, many free Indians placed themselves under the protection of a nearby hacienda to avoid service. Eventually, then, the government abolished this exemption. As García Moreno bitterly said, "They [the hacendados] want angels to make the roads while they have cheap labor and abundant *peones* to increase their businesses."[42]

Labor problems provided only half the reason for failure. The road projects also progressed slowly, because Ecuador (and the western world) lacked the technology to overcome the conditions that the Andean terrain imposed on engineers. Natural disasters imperiled even the best-engineered projects. Year after year, the rainy season took a terrible toll on bridges that were washed away or damaged by flooded rivers carrying heavy boulders. Wooden bridges proved vulnerable to man-made disasters, especially fire. In one instance, a careless woman cooking noodles a few feet away from a bridge managed to burn it beyond repair.[43] Floods assisted by cuts and leveling precipitated landslides, burying the roadbeds with mud many feet thick. To repair the damage, one official suggested the resumption of the traditional *minga* that would have made the local village responsible for repairs on its section of the road.[44] What García Moreno really needed was asphalt, steel, reinforced concrete, and cabled suspension bridges—none of which was available in Ecuador in his era.

In the long run, did all the time, money, and effort put into the road system really make a difference? The evidence suggests that at least for Ecuadorians it did, although some foreigners continued to decry roads not up to European standards. When a British consul arrived in 1871, he reported that "the roads through the *cordilleras* are horrible, hardly deserving the name of bridle paths, for many months of the year. In consequence of the rainy season, these roads become almost impassible." Yet two years later, other foreigners thought the main road pretty good. In 1875 García Moreno reported to his wife that his trip to Guayaquil had taken a mere four days, allowing him to stay with friends every day. Being able to take a steamship from the river port of Yaguachi to Guayaquil also sped up the process, though.[45] Given the circumstances, García Moreno did a noteworthy job constructing roads. In the process, he revealed two personality traits. Obviously he was single-minded in pursuing a goal. He drove thousands of people in this effort, with both positive and negative results. Second, the roads reinforced his pragmatic vision of a united Ecuador where all regions had an opportunity to market goods abroad and prosper. As such, many Ecuadorians have applauded his idea for a national road system, while most have decried his methods.

THE DREAM OF A RAILROAD

Kim Clark, the historical anthropologist who has written extensively about Ecuador's railroads, referred to the main line built in the twentieth century as a "redemptive work," a gift of the richer coast to uplift the impoverished sierra. A generation earlier, García Moreno perceived the railroad as an essential part of the great highway: "We are going to have, God willing, a railroad from Milagro until it *meets the road*, and it will cost less [than the road]" (my emphasis). He told his wife that a prospective passenger would take the train "from Milagro to Sibambe, from whence he will go by coach to Quito. This will reduce the time to Quito to 36 hours."[46] García Moreno viewed the tiny narrow-gauge railroad as part of an integrated transportation system that would unify Ecuador and facilitate internal trade. Such a vision contradicts, at least for the Ecuadorian case, the dependency theorists' argument that foreigners duped Latin Americans into building expensive railroad projects to bind them inextricably to foreign trade and markets, providing little or no benefit to the countries themselves.[47] While such an argument may be relevant for Bolivia and Guatemala, it hardly works in the case of Ecuador and a number of other Latin American nations.

As nineteenth-century political leaders worldwide dreamed of progress, they understood that the railroad served as a concrete metaphor for modernization. Advanced countries like Great Britain, the United States, and Germany enjoyed vast railroad networks, while lesser-developed nations did not. Not surprisingly, then, García Moreno in the 1860s and 1870s ordered his agents abroad to inquire about loans to build a railroad. Beltrán Fourquet, a continental diplomat, and Antonio Flores failed to obtain, however, either a loan or the services of U.S.-born Henry Meiggs, the railroading genius who built much of Peru's trans-Andean network. Without money or Meiggs' expertise, García Moreno compromised for a more modest project linking the coast to the national road on a narrow-gauge line, paid for internally. In the plush years, García Moreno set aside enough money to purchase two locomotives and steel tracks from the United States. With the shiny locomotives in storage at Guayaquil, all that remained was to construct the roadbed, which in typical fashion García Moreno believed would happen quickly.[48]

Approaching the railroad as he had the road network, García Moreno fought to overcome problems of labor, corruption, and expenses as the project progressed. Rather than import Chinese coolies who would work for low wages, as occurred in Peru and the United States, García Moreno turned to local *peones*. From the outset, obtaining an adequate labor supply plagued the engineers. Lowland peasants volunteered in very small numbers, although the governor of Guayas eventually scraped together a workforce of over five hundred. Other workers came from the highlands, especially after García Moreno pressed the governor of Azuay to send his volunteers to the railroad instead of fruitlessly toiling on the Naranjal road. To attract more workers, the government added an incentive bonus to cover transportation costs and set up a mobile hospital right next to the tracks. By placing the highest priority on the railroad and sparing few expenses, the crew completed the work from Yaguachi to Milagro in May 1874. Thereafter García Moreno kept on a skeleton crew to provide track maintenance in the rainy season.[49]

García Moreno's original belief that the short railroad would cost less than a road proved erroneous. In addition to very expensive equipment and the higher-than-usual wages for *peones*, he also had to pay foreign experts well. Luckily much of the project was budgeted before the worst times hit. By 1874 the government tried unsuccessfully to limit railroad expenses to 10,000 pesos a month. Because the railroad remained García Moreno's pet project, it moved forward. As he said, "we will continue the railroad . . . pay what we must." Simply stated, the railroad proved costly and required constant maintenance.[50] As usual, García Moreno pinched pesos by cracking down on corruption and immorality in the labor camp. For example, he fired an overseer illegally billing workers by "obliging them to exchange their wages for articles of commerce."[51]

Because of the railroad's high priority, officials visited the camps regularly. They ensured prompt payment of salaries, so neither skilled nor unskilled workers would walk off the job, and suggested improvements such as laying gravel across swampy portions of the land to elevate the roadbed as well as obtaining a mechanical drill to split rock. García Moreno inspected the railroad on his final visit to the lowlands in April 1875.[52] Although the record is not clear, one would like to picture García Moreno riding in the train, sitting proudly in formal attire while watching the grandeur of the Andes unfold above him. In short, García Moreno must have taken great joy in completing Ecuador's first railway—not merely a symbol of modernization but also a viable link between the coast and highlands.

THE PROSPECT OF ATTRACTING IMMIGRANTS

As the Spanish American nations emerged from the doldrums of the post-independence era, the elites generally believed that they needed to transform their people, to imbue them with some of the "characteristics" of prosperous western nations. Hence they saw immigration and the resulting "whitening" of the population as key ingredients in modernizing the nation. A combination of factors theoretically made attracting European immigration possible in the second half of the nineteenth century. A huge increase in European population, a reduction in the cost of ocean voyages, and a viable agricultural export economy in Latin America (where most immigrants knew farming first and foremost) led to a wave of immigrants. Implicit in the desire to encourage immigration was the Andean elites' contempt for their own indigenous people, often shared by outsiders like Minister Coggeshall's daughter, Jessie, who wrote that the common folk are "the dirtiest, lowest, meanest, ugliest, laziest people in the world." The French minister agreed that "the *only* solution for this evil is . . . *immigration from Europe*" (my emphasis).[53]

In Ecuador, immigration proved less successful than in Argentina, Brazil, Chile, and Uruguay. Potential immigrants no doubt feared tropical diseases in the lowlands and the isolation of the interior. Some of the blame must also fall on García Moreno and the Catholic state he had created, though. While the most successful nations (even conservative Chile) welcomed foreigners of all creeds, García Moreno insisted that all immigrants be Roman Catholic. Even though the government had grown slightly more tolerant, approving the idea of a Protestant cemetery, the policy did not work well as people pillaged Protestant burial plots and desecrated graves. Protestants also could not marry in Ecuador.[54]

García Moreno's strategy would have placed Catholic newcomers in remote regions of the republic like the Oriente and the Galápagos to make these areas economically productive. Even after the conflict with Peru and Castilla in 1859, García Moreno hoped to have English settlers in the Oriente or Esmeraldas, but free lands never enticed Europeans to the jungle.[55] Frustrated with the attempts to settle the jungle, García Moreno also hoped to encourage immigration to Ecuador's other lonely outpost, the Galápagos Islands, creating something more than a prison colony there. In García Moreno's time, the guano proved to be too inconsequential and the land too poor to exploit. Benigno Malo proposed encouraging Italian and German Catholic settlers who would pay one million pesos for farms in the Galápagos, bringing much-needed revenue to the treasury and settling the nearly vacant islands that otherwise might be taken by a hostile power.[56] None came.

Bringing immigrants to Ecuador's heartland also failed. García Moreno hoped that German Chancellor Otto von Bismarck's persecution of Catholics might result in new settlers. The government offered to sell land at reduced rates, advance some money towards the cost of the trip, and exempt the newcomers from military service for ten years. These proposals failed, however, because Ecuadorians viewed the Germans as laborers rather than as freeholders. Some Benedictine monks proposed that a group of German farmers would settle a productive area near Riobamba, where the monks would create a school of agriculture and the colonists would farm. The Benedictines arrived in the fall of 1874, but the farmers did not follow.[57] No sizeable groups of immigrants came to Ecuador, either in García Moreno's time or thereafter.

In sum, only select immigrants (monks, nuns, and foreign experts) actually arrived in Ecuador during the 1860s and 1870s, many of them directly recruited by the government to be "models for citizens to emulate." By 1875 hundreds of French monks and nuns supervised the educational system and the hospitals. German Jesuits staffed the Polytechnical. In addition, Guayaquil acquired a few less well-heralded immigrants. A Basque became the nation's largest cacao exporter in the 1860s and used his bank to subsidize the first García Moreno administration. On the whole, however, immigrants have not had a huge effect on Ecuador's development.[58] Most Ecuadorians remained pessimistic about the indigenous people, as oft-tense race relations demonstrated.

RACE RELATIONS AND INDIAN REBELLIONS

As noted in chapter 2, the colonial world theoretically bifurcated the Andean world's population into two fictional and separate republics, one Spanish and one Indian. A third group, the mixed-race mestizos, complicated the simplistic niceties of the system but as a practical matter, associated themselves culturally with one group or the other. Despite the abolition of this system of legal segregation in the 1850s, Ecuadorians in the age of García Moreno continued to think along these lines—as evidenced by the census of 1857, wherein 44 percent of the population (about 1.1 million total) perceived themselves as white, 40 percent deemed themselves to be Indians, and the category of mestizo did not even exist. According to Teodoro Wolf, Jesuit professor of geography at the Polytechnical, many observers questioned the percentage of whites reported in this census.[59] As the previous section demonstrated, being white conveyed status in this age of scientific racism. Hence the greatly exaggerated percentage of whites reported is logical. Yet García Moreno could not ignore reality. Like other Andean leaders of the nineteenth century, he had to include the indigenous peoples in his vision of the Catholic nation. Reports from his governors and foreign visitors often commented on issues of race.

Not surprisingly, of all the reports mentioning race pouring into the offices of the national government in the García Moreno era, the most perceptive (albeit still racist) came from the pen of the famous novelist Juan León Mera, governor of Tungurahua in the 1870s. Mera had overcome childhood poverty because he was adopted and tutored by his uncle, Governor Nicolás Martínez. Mera estimated more realistically than the 1857 census that in his province, slightly over 25 percent of the population descended from "the Spanish race" (although I believe that figure is probably still too high), less than 25 percent were indigenous people, and the remainder mestizo. He also understood the fluidity of the categories: "It is frequent that an Indian who has learned to read looks for a wife whiter than himself." By and large, mestizos had adopted European mores and language, although they occasionally employed *quichua* words.

Further, in Mera's view, each of the three "races" had its own characteristics. Spanish descendents were seen as honorable, hospitable, intelligent, and patriotic. Mestizos were viewed as less so because of their poorer education. The Indians were regarded as sad, servile, indolent, docile, and lacking confidence "because of the long servitude they have suffered." He bemoaned the latter's lugubrious dances and proclivity for drunkenness during fiestas. Other governors portrayed Indians less favorably, claiming they were "almost incapable of civilization." One such governor, Felipe Serrade, wrote negatively about Indian customs, including premarital cohabitation, where men could "study the characteristics of their spouses." After discussing the indigenous homes, furnishings, and diet, he described their dances, which he found often dated from pre-Hispanic days.[60] As part of the modernization program, upper-class Ecuadorians and government officials wanted to change the lifestyle of the indigenous folk, some holding an optimistic view (like García Moreno with his Indian schools) and others being more pessimistic about their prospects.

Most foreigners, fairly or unfairly, echoed these negative stereotypes of the indigenous people. For example, Minister Coggeshall thought the Indians ignorant and servile, with "no popular patriotism, none of that dear love of country that makes a people." He saw a society divided by race, with whites ruling; *cholos* (mestizos) acting as servants, agricultural supervisors, and mechanics; and Indians occupying the bottom rung of society. Rumsey Wing complained about poor Indians who did not speak Spanish but rather "an unintelligible jargon called Quichua." Looking at Ecuadorian society through North American eyes, observers found a much smaller "white" upper class than did the Ecuadorians themselves. Friedrich

Hassaurek described the upper class as a bit indolent, proud of their heritage, and racist. "Persons of doubtful color are seldom received in good society," while whites expected "doglike servility and submissiveness on the part of the Indian." Wing also found the upper class to be hospitable and courtly, adding that many had traveled widely and enjoyed solid educations. He found nothing idyllic in the lives of the lower class, however, which he described as having "an intermixture of Indian and Negro blood" reminiscent of what he had seen in the U.S. South. Like other foreigners, he saw the Indian as "filthy and shameless."[61] To a greater degree than their Ecuadorian contemporaries, the U.S. ministers recognized the sharp racial divide in nineteenth-century Ecuador.

Those like García Moreno who saw the indigenous people as redeemable in the long run did so because of their historic greatness dating back to the mythical epoch of the pre-Inca kings of Quito. For the optimists, the people who had once created sophisticated urban societies could participate in the Catholic nation once they overcame the legacies of Spanish colonialism. García Moreno saw the possibilities of molding Indians into valuable citizens, unusual for a conservative of his era—which is why he decided to create a normal school for Indians in his second term. In the meantime, they had value for him as hard workers who sometimes needed his paternalistic protection, as in the colonial world. For example, when he heard about an individual who had allegedly abused Indians, resulting in two deaths, he said, "I am going to have to judge the guilty ones; it is my duty."[62]

To incorporate Indians into the modern world, they also had to be brought out of the economic isolation in which they lived. Therefore liberal economic theory frowned upon self-sufficient, communally held, property. The assault began legislatively in 1865 and had consequences. Discontent of indigenous people in the Andes traditionally resulted from seizures of land or water, unfair taxes, abusive overseers, or demands for excessive labor and services. The coming of modernization to the sierra, slow and sporadic as it was in the 1860s, raised these very issues. Hacendados did grab land from Indians in a few instances, although no cash crop had yet emerged anywhere in the highlands to make this a widespread practice. Litigation resulted when Indians presented their claims to local authorities, asking for help "on behalf of the poor." These petitions, not exactly common in the historical record of the 1860s, seemed to be spread throughout the highlands rather than being confined to the province of Chimborazo, where trouble broke out in 1868 and 1871.[63]

Instead of conflicts over land, water, or abuse, what seems to have triggered the large-scale rebellions of 1868 and 1871 were irregular tax collection practices and the threat of conscription for the roads and the militia. Interestingly, while the 1871 Daquilema rebellion has been the subject of several books, no ink has ever been spilled about the earlier rebellion in the town of Guano. Tax collectors and military contractors, who came around on Sundays when the men were often intoxicated or hung over, precipitated both uprisings.[64] Conscription became the *cause célèbre* for social unrest in Chimborazo in 1868. Congress passed a new statute requiring service in the National Guard, apparently designed to replace the guards on a regular basis with new conscripts. People in Guano found the law unacceptable. On February 24, 1868, the *tumulto* took its usual course. The enraged Indians began by attacking the symbols of white power and breaking down the *jefe político's* door. The rioters burned the local archive, thereby eradicating any list of names of potential draftees. Then they attacked and looted the church. Next the mob freed all prisoners from the town jail. The whites wisely fled to nearby Riobamba, where they waited for reinforcements from the neighboring provinces of Azuay and Tungurahua.[65]

Getting wind of the revolt, Governor Bruno Dávalos (Bernardo's brother) took the usual steps under these circumstances. Even though the mob of Indians had grown to between six and eight thousand as a result of their pouring in from the *páramo*, Governor Dávalos and Bishop Ignacio Ordóñez of Riobamba rode to Guano to see if they could make peace. Typically the governor offered the rioters, with the exception of the leaders, immunity from prosecution if they returned home immediately, and promised an investigation into the popular grievances.[66] Governor Dávalos also took steps to defend Riobamba, the provincial capital only six miles away, to prevent the revolt from spreading. Soon a troop of National Guard under Colonel Francisco Javier Salazar occupied Riobamba. Even before the guard arrived, the elite of the city created an informal cavalry regiment. Together the volunteers and the soldiers protected private property and lives, both in the capital and in surrounding towns.[67] Even though the rioters never advanced on Riobamba, reverberations of the Guano uprising were heard nearby. Investigators found suspicious the large number of lance points that blacksmiths forged early in February. Authorities rounded up Indians who had cut off the road to Azuay, which prevented the mail carrier from making his rounds.[68]

Once the situation returned to normal, the government imposed punishments on the rioters. Draconian measures, ordinary wisdom stated, usually proved counterproductive because they could trigger another rebellion. As a result, the authorities generally treated rank-and-file rioters leniently, reserving punishment for the leaders of the *tumulto*. Eventually six principals stood trial. They were considered "a bad lot," with several having deserted from the army. This fact made them doubly troublesome, since not only were they dissidents but also privileged to know some of the strategies of the army. Ultimately the federal government pardoned them, hoping they would be grateful to the government for its leniency. After all, the rioters had killed only three people, none of whom must have been influential citizens, while the property damage had been relatively limited.[69]

To demonstrate its good faith, the government made concessions to the people of the canton. First, it removed the *jefe político* in Guano as a gesture of goodwill. Bishop Ignacio Ordóñez recommended that certain taxes he saw as the underlying cause of the revolt be reduced after he and Colonel Salazar toured the troubled region. Most importantly, the state government issued a decree suspending the Conscription Act's implementation, because "it is badly understood and poorly received by the people." Although the interior minister argued that the people of Guano were wrong, he ordered the statute shelved until congress had a chance to reform it during the regular session.[70] In effect the Indians of Guano had won a temporary respite from conscription. Such was the way of protest in the Andes.

A second better-known challenge to rural peace erupted three years later in the same province. The earliest literature on the Daquilema rebellion blamed the overzealous collection of taxes, specifically a premature attempt to collect the tithe, as the principal factor in the revolt. Although only excerpts of the original documentation still exist, contemporaneous reports hint at another underlying cause. Two recruiters for the road construction project fell into the hands of one group of Indians, who "killed them in a most cruel fashion." García Moreno's inability to provide road laborers with fair treatment and symbolic reciprocity (drinking and a fiesta) disillusioned the workers and may have contributed to the local discontent.[71] The rebellion started on December 18, 1871, when an unpopular tithe collector arrived to collect taxes early. A community leader tumbled the collector from his horse, after which a mob beat him to death and strung him up in a public place. The mob then named a locally prominent man, Fernando Daquilema, as its leader. News of the rebellion quickly spread. García Moreno responded by declaring martial law in Chimborazo and ordering National Guard units into service.[72]

Meanwhile the rebels went on the offensive. Appointing his military commanders, Daquilema directed them to attack three small towns outside Riobamba. Magically the hillsides came alive. More than ten thousand Indians were estimated crowding the slopes of the Cacha Valley, watching and waiting to see how the battle turned. Daquilema knew that quick victories could turn sympathetic bystanders into active fighters. Likewise, Governor Rafael Larrea Checa realized that strong and decisive action would quell the rebellion. Thus as Daquilema's forces attacked nearby towns and killed a number of militia, Governor Larrea Checa rounded up a force of nearly three hundred volunteers from Riobamba to combat the insurgency. As the governor admitted, however, his men owned only a few flintlocks, and his forces arrived too late to forestall the secondary attacks.

On December 22, the insurgents scored their biggest success. According to sympathetic historians, they were led by a resolute woman named Manuela León, who was unmentioned in the national documents but apparently figured importantly in local legend. The insurgents burned much of the town of Punín, causing the whites and mestizos to disperse. That night, León led the celebration as the rowdy victors broke into the *chicherías* (taverns) and danced the night away in the plaza. Unfortunately for them, Lieutenant Colonel Ignacio Paredes and his troops arrived the next morning to find most of the rebels still inebriated, resulting in the capture of many and the dispersal of the rest.[73] By the end of December, the course of the rebellion looked quite typical. Indians armed with stones and sticks proved no match for army soldiers with Winchester repeating rifles. Almost all of the former requested amnesty and left Daquilema alone on the mountainside, where he finally surrendered to Paredes.[74]

The governor rushed two of the leaders to a speedy gallows. García Moreno wanted to make certain that the remainder, including Fernando Daquilema, received justice and a regular trial under court martial as required by the state-of-siege (martial law). As a result, García Moreno lifted the state-of-siege and pardoned almost all of the several hundred jailed Indians who had requested amnesty. A few of the middling leaders received sentences assigning them to the road gangs now working in Guayas province, a punishment García Moreno had certainly used previously. García Moreno had little sympathy for Daquilema. While insisting on proper legal process, he hoped "God would not allow it [the Military Council] to fall victim to a false idea of clemency" (which it did not). So in early April, Governor Larrea Checa executed Daquilema by ordering him shot in the plaza of one of the towns he had attacked.[75]

Given the attention paid to the Daquilema uprising by twentieth-century historians, did it have any immediate consequences? Certainly work on the national road continued unabated in 1872, using labor drafts from Chimborazo province. No evidence suggests that tithe collection lessened in 1872, although perhaps the collectors behaved a bit more circumspectly. Although at the time of the revolt, officials feared that communities like Guano and Licto (another largely Indian community outside Riobamba) would support the Daquilema rebellion, these fears passed. Landlord behavior did not change. For example, a year later a local landlord had no qualms pressing for a judgment in a case where Indians claimed the disputed lands had belonged to them "since time immemorial." In short, nothing differed after the Daquilema uprising. Modern weapons, the national highway that enabled quick troop movement, and a more efficient and stronger state made the success of a localized Indian uprising unlikely. In fact, as the U.S. minister noted, in cases of serious threats García Moreno historically had taken the battlefield himself. In this instance, he sent only a few soldiers under a lieutenant colonel. "President [García] Moreno has no doubt of the immediate result of the contest between the troops, largely outnumbered as they are against the revolting Indians, or *he would have gone in person"* (my emphasis).[76]

For the rebels and modern-day Ecuadorians, however, the revolt had far more significance. On the first day of the uprising, the Indians named Daquilema "King of Cacha," the ancestral house of the Shyri people, and built him a makeshift palace. Although no mention of the royal lineage of Daquilema appears in the documents, the U.S. minister, among others, feared that the reference to ancient glories would trigger an Andean-wide response reminiscent of the massive Tupac Amaru II revolt in Peru in the 1780s. A popular idea in García Moreno's time was that the Ecuadorian highland Indians had once been united in a great confederation called the Kingdom of Quito, led by the Shyri people. According to this legend concocted by Ecuador's first great historian, Father Juan de Velasco, the Ecuadorian Indians led a great state rivaling that of the Incas in grandeur, established the boundaries for a historical Ecuadorian nation, and differentiated Ecuadorians from Peruvians even in pre-Hispanic times. Although the Daquilema revolt might appear to be only one among many Indian revolts, because of its claim to historic continuity and the rebirth of Indian greatness it has assumed greater significance in recent times.[77]

The debate over the role of the Indian continued from García Moreno's time to the early twentieth century. Race became a much less combustible issue, however, in the 1930s when Ecuadorians adopted the idea of *la raza cósmica,* the "cosmic" race, emanating from Mexico. Intellectuals there suggested that the mixture of the Spanish and Indian races through *mestizaje* had created a superior race. Not surprisingly, Ecuadorian census data in the 1930s began showing an ever-increasing percentage of people self-reporting as mestizos, a remarkable change from the 1857 census. Recently parentage mattered less than culture. Mixed-race people of whatever hue declared themselves mestizo if they spoke Spanish, wore western-style clothes, and believed in a non-Andean worldview. As Indians moved into cities and took jobs as day laborers and domestic servants, the process of *mestizaje* continued. Until the early 1990s, Ecuadorians could claim that race was no longer an issue in their country, at least in comparison to the United States. The new indigenous movement of the past two decades, however, has again changed thinking about race to the degree that Ecuadorians now acknowledge they live in a sometimes tense multicultural society.[78]

In García Moreno's time, he and other intellectuals had only begun to appreciate Ecuador's rich indigenous heritage. During the nineteenth century, many writers would extol the grandeur of past Indian civilizations while simultaneously decrying the decadence, laziness, and dirtiness of the contemporary Indian population. On one hand, García Moreno offered hope through education for the indigenous people. On the other hand, working on his road system meant more of the same for Indians—serving as drudges for very little pay. Like some of his governors and most foreign observers, García Moreno had sympathy for the native people, but clearly opined that their redemption would take time. Statistical evidence really cannot demonstrate whether the position of the average indigenous person improved or declined as Ecuador's economy grew in the 1870s. No doubt many escaped to the coast and the towns to "become" mestizos. Yet for others, like Fernando Daquilema, life remained harsh.

LESSER PUBLIC WORKS

As noted earlier, the idea of material progress fascinated García Moreno. Although the highway system and railroad were the cornerstones of his public works initiative, García Moreno also encouraged the modernization of other infrastructures. By linking Ecuador to the outside world with a modern communications system, he could advance trade. An improved internal communications system also allowed the government to respond quickly to rebellions, as had occurred in the Daquilema case. Finally, for García Moreno, modernization also meant improving the quality of life—particularly for residents of urban areas—as Ecuadorians belatedly followed the model of European cities.

Even in the 1860s, the government expressed interest in connecting Ecuador to the new underseas cable lines, the first commercially viable one having joined Europe and North America in 1866. García Moreno wrote: "The Ecuadorian people [have] demonstrated that they want to be in telegraphic contact with the world." Among others, Neptalí Bonifaz (father of a later president by the same name) offered to build a line joining the main international cable running from Central America to Chile, but diplomatic issues with Peru interfered with the project and it remained unfinished during García Moreno's era.[79] More pressing, García Moreno believed, was the internal telegraph, which would have linked Guayaquil and Quito. Congress felt this line deserved the highest priority: "The speed of communications contributes to the progress of a people and the preservation of public order." Ultimately a U.S. company won the concession and strung the lines along the cleared railroad right-of-way that reached the highlands (but not quite to Quito) by 1875.[80] Two conclusions are noteworthy. First, the telegraph served national commercial and military purposes. And second, Ecuador adopted technology very rapidly.

To increase commerce with foreign markets, García Moreno wanted to make trade safer and more efficient at Guayaquil. To help ships in and out of the estuary, the government built a series of lighthouses on treacherous rocks to "render easy and expeditious the navigation of the seas of the Republic." Once again the government needed foreign technicians. The Ecuadorian minister in France was charged with investigating the best and most economical type of lighthouses that could be purchased. By the fall of 1872, the government had installed the first of the new equipment, which proved visible from a distance of twenty-two miles. García Moreno inspected the new lighthouse himself and told the British consul in Guayaquil that he intended "to place all the lights and buoys necessary for the safety of vessels bound to *ports* in the Republic" (my emphasis). The government hired an engineer full time for the lonely job of lighthouse keeper on Santa Clara island, who unfortunately later committed suicide. A foreigner was also hired to supervise the dredging of channels in the Guayas estuary, where silting remains a problem today.[81] For the first time in the republic's history, García Moreno undertook modern methods of channel marking for oceangoing vessels.

The government also wanted to hire private contractors to modernize the port facilities at Guayaquil. In addition, the government used proceeds from the *trabajo subsidiario* to rebuild the sea wall stretching from the southern end of the city to the block where the home of García Moreno's mother stood. Although the U.S. engineer sent to evaluate the finished product criticized the quality of cement and stones employed in the construction, the new jetty protected the city from huge waves. More importantly, though, it provided a secure area where lighters could land cargo from oceangoing vessels. García Moreno's brother, Pedro Pablo, constructed a floating wharf just north of the *malecón* to transit bags of his cacao beans to market. The government allowed him to charge a fee to other businesses that wanted to use his wharf.[82] With Guayaquil's jetty greatly improved, the city could bear the increased traffic created by the commercial expansion of the early 1870s.

Like the rest of Latin America, Ecuador experienced some urbanization during the 1870s. Although highland cities managed only slight population increases, Guayaquil attracted significant numbers from the interior. Whether in the sierra or on the coast, cities wanted to embrace changes similar to those that had transformed Dickens' London to a clean, healthy, urban environment (relatively speaking). For *guayaquileños,* their hopes for modernization centered on two projects. As Governor Vicente de Santisteban stated: "Public lighting is not a luxury in the civilized world, it is a necessity . . . , [a] noble conquest of progress." After about a decade with city lights powered by kerosene and whale oil, Guayaquil installed a modern gaslight system in 1873 to illuminate portions of the city—thereby reducing crime, which otherwise flourished in darkened alleys.[83] The other project, bringing potable water into the city, proved beyond the technical capacity of engineers in the 1870s. Neither a system of pipes bringing water from the Daule River nor a series of deep-drilled wells (nearly 1,200-feet deep) panned out. Only in the 1880s would some city residents enjoy fresh water. To solve a couple of the city's other endemic problems, the governor established a fire department (which could not contain the devastating blaze of 1896) and a system for waste collection (particularly of "night soil") under a new Department of Health.[84] Despite García Moreno's efforts, Guayaquil remained "the pesthole of the Pacific" until U.S. engineers in the twentieth century helped civic leaders conquer yellow fever.

Quito also improved its infrastructure. Not only did García Moreno flatten and pave some of the hilliest streets, but he also transformed the centrally located Plaza de la Independencia from an open pasture where impromptu bullfights took place to a garden where strollers could enjoy the springlike highland weather (although for awhile he had to post troops

The astronomical observatory in Quito's Alameda Park (Courtesy of the Benson Collection)

there to prevent the populace from cutting the trees and trampling the flowers). García Moreno's hallmark projects—the ultramodern penitentiary called the Panóptico and the Astronomical Observatory in Alameda Park—were but two of the city's modern features. The city council repaved downtown streets with stone and arranged for a water supply to be brought from a nearby hacienda. Like Guayaquil, Quito hoped for modern gas lights. Instead, the Jesuit professors at the Polytechnical brought electric lights, although to a limited part of the city.[85] Not quite as modern as Guayaquil, Quito preserved much of its colonial charm in the 1870s, a trait that still entices visitors to "Old Town" today.

Other cities and towns embraced the mantra of progress as well. The reconstruction of Ibarra set the standard. Hiring U.S. engineers to oversee the final stages of the reconstruction effort, the project that García Moreno began in 1868, neared completion by 1874. Wide streets, squares planted with trees and gardens, and an irrigation system that watered public lands—all led to a renaissance in Ibarra. Although not without its failures, Ibarra became a modern city with plenty of fresh potable water. Inspectors praised García Moreno and his governor, Juan España, who had "reestablished the city and almost all of the province in . . . a little more than two years."[86] Other cities updated their public buildings. Cuenca reconstructed its city hall, and Latacunga undertook projects to fix streets and repair the holy water font in San Francisco Church.[87] In short, in addition to the schools and hospitals previously mentioned, public works projects flourished throughout the country in the 1870s. Given the traditional regional and local outlook of Ecuadorians, these projects undoubtedly enjoyed more popular support than did some of his national programs.

MATERIAL PROGRESS AS OF 1875

Like other Latin Americans in the mid-to-late nineteenth century, García Moreno sought to emulate the European and U.S. march to progress. Few nations have been able to self-capitalize their transformation. Most have needed funding from abroad. While several nations in Latin America attracted huge amounts of foreign capital, Ecuador found very few willing foreign investors. Hence, García Moreno had to fund his development program through internal borrowing from Ecuador's bank, secured by pledging tax revenues. Despite the lack of resources and technology, in addition to the negative impact of modernization on the indigenous people,

Joaquín Pinto's Allegory of Don Quixote *(Permission of the Banco Central del Ecuador)*

the project must rank among García Moreno's greatest achievements. Just as his ideas for the Catholic state furthered national unity ideologically, so his program for economic development led to greater unity among Ecuadorians in a practical way.

Does García Moreno deserve credit for being the first great nation-builder in his country's history, as many Ecuadorians would assert, or did his administration merely continue previous policies agreed upon by regional elites?[88] Two factors make a strong case in favor of the traditional view of García Moreno. First, in terms of sheer numbers of public works, García Moreno initiated 178 projects during his second term—a number not surpassed until after the Liberal Revolution of 1895, when national revenues dramatically increased.[89] Second, the qualitative evidence suggests that the modernization was observable. Foreign consuls, old Ecuador hands, and government officials all leave the impression that the scope of García Moreno's public works projects was both innovative and visionary. Although earlier presidents may well have favored constructing a national highway, none actually *accomplished* this objective. García Moreno deserves credit for trying to modernize Ecuador, even though his dream remained largely unrealized at the end of his second term. Perhaps the best visualization of his failure was depicted in Joaquín Pinto's famous painting entitled *Allegory of Don Quixote* (the cover of this book), in which García Moreno plays the idealistic knight bearing a Jesuit on a broken-down steed passing over a rough dirt road while a drunken farmer observes. His successes were modest indeed.

Chapter Eight

Death and the Hereafter

The previous chapters have examined García Moreno's life and times chronologically while exploring themes of nineteenth-century Andean history, especially state formation. In contrast, this final chapter will focus on the events of a single day—August 6—during the remarkable year of 1875, in which Alexander Graham Bell made the first telephone call, Georges Bizet's opera *Carmen* opened to rave reviews, and the initial Kentucky Derby was run. A drama of Shakespearean proportions was about to be played out on the grand stage of this country straddling the equator. The upcoming play brilliantly juxtaposed characters straight from Stratford-on-Avon. We will find Iago, the most villainous villain in all of literature from *Othello*, in the same story as *Julius Caesar*'s Brutus. Even the Bard himself could not have penned such a script. The shots and machete blows that rang out across the Plaza de la Independencia not only resonated for years in Ecuadorian discourse, but also influenced the European conservative Catholic world, underscoring Gabriel García Moreno's long-term legacy for both.

Often in the study of biography, a dramatic death lends heightened grandeur to the subject's life, and so it would be in the case of García Moreno. Both he and Ecuador's most famous Liberal Party leader, Eloy Alfaro, suffered similarly gruesome deaths—rather remarkably, because despite its many coups, the nation's political culture has frowned on assassinations and violence in general. Not only is the story of García Moreno's death fascinating, replete with all the features of a fictional whodunit, but it also raises important questions about his legacy.

Right up to the present, García Moreno's supporters have argued that his brutal murder in the square, in part motivated by his religious policies, qualified him to be a martyr and might place him on the path to sainthood. His enemies, on the other hand, have characterized him as a tyrant who deserved death in order to liberate Ecuador's people. Both images have been useful in constructing discourses about the Ecuadorian state. Martyrdom, a violent death for the sake of conviction, comes from a Greek word meaning "firsthand witness" and was initially invoked to describe the death of Socrates. Christian martyrs, of course, "bear witness" to Jesus' ultimate sacrifice, his crucifixion at Golgotha. The term "tyrant" likewise first saw light in ancient Greece, and was used to describe a ruler who exercised absolute authority without the legal right to do so. Death and the political afterlife of Latin American leaders has recently become a subject of considerable interest. Like the cases of Eva Perón, Che Guevara, and other key figures, the usages of García Moreno's memory and even his physical remains have contributed to his enduring political legacy.[1]

THE ELECTIONS OF 1875

The election of 1875 posed an interesting question about the degree to which the political system was open and democratic or whether it had degenerated into tyrannical dictatorship. Predictably García Moreno's adherents find the elections fair, contested, and popular—while his detractors claim they were no more than a farce and the onset of a "perpetual dictatorship."[2] Certainly his contemporary supporters hoped he would seek reelection as the Constitution of 1869 permitted, despite the economic downturn in 1874. At first, García Moreno played the role of a demure but calculating maiden, expressing no real interest but at heart wanting it to happen. To his loyalists, he responded that he "would accept the command of the people and God's will," despite his desire to retire. He demanded only a single condition: that the elections take place "without my intervention, direct or indirect, or frauds and intrigues of any kind." Free elections would, in his opinion, stop his enemies' personal attacks.[3] Probably García Moreno believed that his recent policy of granting pardons and encouraging most exiles to come home had lessened his reputation for being vengeful and repressive. At the same time, now that his most extreme enemies had been expelled, he no doubt felt that he had cleansed the body politic of the toxins that had infected it in the past. The latest incursion, for example—that of Eloy Alfaro in Esmeraldas in 1871—fizzled before it caused problems.[4] Yet García Moreno's hopes for a peace and perhaps an uncontested election ended in the fall of 1874.

At the end of October, Ecuador's brilliant liberal essayist, Juan Montalvo (then living in Colombia), responded to an editorial in a Panamanian newspaper endorsing García Moreno's reelection. Unleashing a vitriolic attack, Montalvo opined in his essay, *La dictadura perpetua* (The Perpetual Dictatorship), that García Moreno had no sincere interest in democracy and was a "little tyrant." In the pamphlet, Montalvo blasted all of García Moreno's achievements: The roads had cost thousands of lives and remained unfinished, education was in the hands of "pestilent floods of scum from the convents of Italy and Spain," and the morality program was a joke. He trotted out old saws—the Trinité letters, Ayarza's whipping and death, the pro-Spanish stance in 1864, and General Maldonado's execution—to paint García Moreno in dark hues.[5] Hyperbolic in the extreme, Montalvo's diatribe almost makes the reader lose sight of his valid point, that human dignity and many civil liberties had been suppressed in Ecuador (although not to the extreme Montalvo claimed—that the Ecuadorian people are divided "into three equal parts": the dead, the exiled, and the enslaved).

Almost immediately, García Moreno's friends published a rejoinder, which circulated widely in Ecuador. After engaging in the typical ad hominem attack (Montalvo borrowed money prodigiously and never repaid it, fathered at least one child out of wedlock, and abandoned his wife in Ambato), the pamphleteers responded point by point to Montalvo's critique by defending the educational system and highlighting recent pragmatic advances, especially the roads and the telegraph. Most importantly, they argued, García Moreno's religious program and his personal relationship with the pope concurred with the sentiment of the vast majority of the population: Montalvo was the one who was out of touch with the people of his own country.[6] After the exchange of these pamphlets, keeping rancor and contention out of the elections of 1875 proved impossible.

Soon a number of candidates volunteered to run against García Moreno. Antonio Borrero seemed to have the greatest likelihood of success. He was a former friend who took a moderately liberal turn in the 1870s, becoming a close associate of the bishop of Cuenca, who disliked García Moreno. Borrero actually would win the election of 1876, although he lasted less than a year in office. To advance his candidacy, two young men in Guayaquil began publishing a newspaper, *La Nueva Era,* containing articles critical of García Moreno and favorable to Borrero. Soon the two youths were jailed in Quito and their paper closed. Accusing the two of sedition, García Moreno told a friend: "We will make them respect morality and the laws." When a court found the two guilty as charged, guards escorted them on the long and dangerous march to the jungle. Clearly García Moreno had forgotten his promise to hold an election without his personal interference. As had been his habit, he asked his governors to help him. In the opinion of the U.S. minister, "the present excellent president" would win another term.[7]

Despite some manipulation, then, the presidential election of 1875 was reasonably honest. With popular support for the theoretical and pragmatic aspects of the Catholic nation-building project, García Moreno swept to an easy victory, gaining 22,726 votes against scattered opposition. He thanked his friends for their assistance in "holding free elections in every province." Yet even one of his friendliest biographers noted that ten thousand fewer people voted in 1875 than in 1868, the last contested election. Undoubtedly some voters felt intimidated. Others, especially in Cuenca and Guayaquil, had abandoned García Moreno's original coalition. Nevertheless, even if one assumes that all those who abstained would have voted for Borrero or another candidate, García Moreno easily won the election. Voters knew well what he offered: peace, stability, Christian education, public works, and (one hoped) renewed economic progress once the depression ended. As he told his friends: "We must trust in God that the Republic will advance more rapidly in 1875 on the path of prosperity."[8] Still, even supporters like his former brother-in-law, Roberto de Ascásubi (who had been relegated to the Senate and other inconsequential posts since 1861), painted a grim picture, acknowledging that the third term broke with tradition. Don Roberto remarked: "Up to a certain point the re-election of García was necessary," but he suffered from "much self-love and in addition to not finishing any public works, he has done much wrong."[9] The letter was not exactly a sterling endorsement from a former best friend.

If the presidential election of 1875 mirrored public sentiment, the congressional contests may not have. As usual, the governors submitted slates of candidates for García Moreno's approval. All looked acceptable except for the roster from Imbabura, where Juan Montalvo's name appeared on the ballot as a congressional candidate from Tulcán. (In García Moreno's time, Tulcán was part of Imbabura province.) García Moreno advised his governor to use all his wiles to exclude Montalvo: "I would not like the scandal of a single vote for Montalvo." Conduct such as this suggests that only true believers in the *garciano* (as García Moreno's dictatorship is sometimes called) won seats in congress in 1875. Following the events of August 6, demands for new congressional elections thus reached a fever pitch because many Ecuadorians felt that congress consisted only of García Moreno's sycophants.[10]

Given the claims of electoral fraud, coercion, and obvious muzzling of the press, did García Moreno qualify in 1875 as a tyrant who warranted assassination? Clearly Ecuadorian political culture has frowned on consecutive presidential terms since independence. (Only three men have tried: Flores was expelled, and García Moreno and Eloy Alfaro were brutally murdered.) Technically speaking, however, García Moreno had acted legally because the Constitution of 1869 barred a third consecutive term, but not a second one.

Although speculative, some evidence suggests that García Moreno would have died of natural causes before 1881. In 1874, he began to experience recurring health problems, attacks much like the one he endured in 1868 while under the stress of reconstructing Imbabura. In August 1872, he did not respond to his correspondence for two weeks—most unlike him—because of an unspecified illness. In August 1874 and March 1875, he suffered relapses temporarily affecting his vision. During these episodes, he took up to thirty doses a day of his prescription medicine, suggesting a serious problem. In a telling letter, he also stated, "If God will give me life to conclude the second term, I will carry out my program."[11] While some writers have taken this statement as a premonition of his impending fate, a more likely reading is that he understood his health was declining. Certainly an examination of photographs from 1875 shows García Moreno as a worn-out and tired man. Nevertheless, whether through the elections of 1881 or through García Moreno's natural death, the evidence implies that the liberals could have been patient and awaited their turn at a state-formation project rather than stooping to murder in 1875.

GARCÍA MORENO'S CHANGING PERSONALITY

García Moreno's assassins and their sympathizers also claim that he had the personality of a tyrant. They paint García Moreno as a cruel, bloodthirsty, and murderous villain. Further, these writers suggest accurately that García Moreno executed more people than any other nineteenth-century Ecuadorian president save one—Vicente Rocafuerte. They conveniently neglect to mention that Rocafuerte was a liberal of whom they uniformly approved, however.[12] While García Moreno clearly acted harshly, methodically, forcefully, and at times excessively against his opponents in the period from 1861 to 1865, after that date the evidence suggests that age and maturing political judgment tempered his extremism. In fact, during the second term no political executions occurred at all and only a very few individuals were exiled.

Some personal characteristics remained consistent. After all, rarely do people totally remake their personalities. In the 1860s, García Moreno's seeming paranoia had a rational basis. He had reason to see plots everywhere. Thus, he ordered the governor of Guayas to maintain a list of riverboat captains plying the estuary, demanding that the governor restrict the licenses to those without connections to Urbina (to avoid a repetition of the events leading up to the battle of Jambelí). Now García Moreno seemed more secure.

Second, when a revolt occurred, he still responded vindictively, as in the aftermath of the José de Veintemilla episode in March 1869, where he ordered the widows and children of the rebels to forfeit their pensions.[13] The flash of temper quickly passed, though, and ultimately he rescinded the order. As time passed, García Moreno seemed more confident. Perhaps he correctly perceived that his position was unassailable, since the military and bureaucracy strongly endorsed him and he seemed to have considerable popular support among the elite of the north-central highlands, the extreme south, and the commercial leadership of the coast.

Third, García Moreno continued to hold his friends to impossibly high standards of conduct. A retired general who did not do his part in the election of 1869 lost a chance to become an interim governor. Governor Carlos Ordóñez, who precipitated a political crisis in Cuenca by declaring martial law unconstitutionally, lost his job and received such a stern rebuke from García Moreno that they did not communicate for years.[14]

He could hold a grudge passionately. Previous chapters have recounted the bitter exchange he had with Benigno Malo in 1869 over policy differences. That letter began, "I remember the insulting letter I received from you in 1862," before attacking Malo once again. García Moreno sent an equally hostile letter to his old Colombian nemesis, Tomás Cipriano de Mosquera, who had defeated the Ecuadorian army (as described in chapter 4). Not forgetting Mosquera's humiliating letter directed to "Sr. ?, President of Ecuador," García Moreno responded in kind. Now in 1870, he addressed his letter to *José* C. de Mosquera. Noting that Mosquera intended to change ships in Guayaquil, García Moreno issued a stern warning: "If you come within the jurisdiction of our laws you will be arrested, judged, and will suffer the consequences."[15] Admittedly Mosquera's ambition had caused a costly war—but after all, he had signed the generous Treaty of Pinsaquí, which left Ecuador territorially intact. García Moreno certainly knew how to stoke a fire! Both of the incidents were indicative of the old temper.

Apart from these two lapses, García Moreno seemed much more forgiving than he had been in the past. He awarded Benigno Malo's daughter a scholarship and renewed relationships with other members of the old Cuenca network. Rather than continuing his quarrel with Bishop Toral of Cuenca, García Moreno elected to talk with him about banalities, thus lessening tension. When Camilo Ponce, turned out of office by García Moreno's coup in 1869, stood up in the Senate to oppose a bill that would have conferred the title Head of Ecuador on García Moreno—a designation that Ponce argued would violate the Constitution—García Moreno congratulated the senator, saying, "Give me your hand. Men like you are very rare." Later, García Moreno allegedly said that Ponce might qualify as a successor (unlikely, given Ponce's role in the Espinosa government) "because you have a calm demeanor, not like mine." Finally, García Moreno pardoned a man caught up in a liberal intrigue when his wife provided proof that as a young child she had helped hide García Moreno in 1853 from General Franco's soldiers.[16]

Another example of García Moreno's more forgiving nature during the second term occurred in 1873, when he offered a general amnesty to his political opponents living abroad. His diplomats congratulated him on the decision. Vicente Piedrahita pointed out that the exiles constituted "a national richness," otherwise condemned to live out sterile lives on foreign shores. While the French minister agreed that the amnesty represented an important step, he was less optimistic about its success. The procedure was simple enough—exiles only had to request permission in writing from the secretary of the interior—but few of the three thousand exiles estimated by his enemies to be living abroad responded.[17] A similar offer for safe-conduct passes in 1871 had elicited a sparse result. Yet García Moreno clearly did want to welcome moderate dissenters home if they behaved themselves. He commuted death sentences handed down to liberal rebels in Manabí. Nevertheless, García Moreno drew a line between acceptable criticism and seditious language that was sometimes difficult to discern, which the editors of *La Nueva Era* discovered in 1874. As García Moreno himself stated at the outset of his term, he welcomed criticism from his old friends "as long as they don't enter into conspiracies."[18] On the whole, however, García Moreno seemed more willing to forgive than he had ever been previously.

He retained all of his good qualities, ones that even his detractors grudgingly admired. Rumsey Wing noted his high level of energy. Although to a lesser degree than in the first term García Moreno traveled throughout the republic, inspecting roads and schools as well as visiting friends and family in Guayaquil. Modern observers would probably label him a workaholic, as he spent long days in the Government Palace studying myriad reports that crossed his desk. He remained scrupulously honest. For example, when he asked a local official to do a favor for his friends, the Aguirres (namely, to procure some muleteers so they could transport their cotton to market), he went on to add, "If you can't help my friends in an equitable way that is fine."[19] Likewise, as the next section will detail, he proceeded aboveboard while building his new home, taking out a bank loan like any other elite or middle-class citizen and making certain that he paid for both materials and his workers' wages.

His mellowing personality probably resulted from two changes in his life. First, his religious zeal heightened, becoming almost mystical in nature. García Moreno's hagiographers have interpreted his increased religiosity as an anticipation of his martyrdom, reading much into his words. Although he had always been a religious man, his letters in the 1870s reflected a deepening faith. Even in the 1860s, he had been confident that God favored Ecuador and would protect it from belligerent neighbors. Early in the second term, he reiterated these sentiments: "We all serve the Republic, but its fate depends on Providence which will continue to favor us whether I am president or not" and "God will protect us, I am sure, and will frustrate the hopes of our perverse enemies."[20]

By the end of his term, García Moreno's letters expressed a different sentiment. In them, he suggests that he has delivered *his* life into God's hands and will accept whatever end God has in mind for him. This sense of fatalism, perhaps triggered by declining health, echoes throughout the later correspondence: "We deserve the merciful punishments God sends us during life; we are so ungrateful for his blessings" and "I am resigned to the will of God, whom I adore and who blesses me." Perhaps the most touching evidence of his personal faith comes in his final letter to Pope Pius IX. After asking the pope's blessing, he assured Pius that he would be faithful to the church and begged for "the heavenly strength and light that I need."[21] In addition, García Moreno continued his outward professions of faith, praying daily and playing his usual active role in Quito's famous Good Friday celebration in 1875.

In addition to García Moreno's intensifying religious fervor, his family life became blissful. His letters, filled with honeyed phrases, reveal that he adored his young and attractive wife. Because he traveled less frequently than he had in the 1850s and 1860s, he wrote her less often than he had Rosa, so that details about his domestic life are sparse. Nevertheless, he showered Marianita with words of love during his absences, recalling his youthful attempts at romantic poetry: "I think of you every minute" and "My everything, I want you, my love, with such urgency that after God and the Virgin, you are first in my thoughts, and the only one in my heart." In all his letters, he kept Marianita informed not only about family business but also matters of state, indicating they had a true partnership and confided in each other. Little bits of gossip and family news (Pedro Pablo's son got engaged in 1875; José Sucre's new wife was nice, but ugly) and promises of little extravagances (a gift of pretty clothes, fresh fruit, or perhaps perfume) accompanied many of these letters—along with his promise "to gallop right home" to her as soon as possible.[22] In short, García Moreno was a devoted, loving, and aging husband who relished his domestic felicity.

With Marianita his relationship seemed particularly tender, perhaps because, unlike Rosa, she gave him a child who lived and upon whom he doted. In January 1870, she gave birth to Gabriel, Jr. Despite some bouts of illness, the son survived to adulthood. Openly adoring, García Moreno never forgot to bring the boy presents from his trips. Late in 1870, he decided his son was old and healthy enough to travel to Guayaquil and meet his paternal relatives (Uncles Pepe and Pedro Pablo, Aunt Rosario, and perhaps others). In addition to three daughters, who died shortly after birth, the couple had another daughter who lived several years. The death of his last daughter in July 1875 weighed heavily on García Moreno. As she struggled for breath, he neglected his correspondence and even state business. Afterwards he fondly prayed that a better life would await her in Heaven. Days after the little girl's death, he learned that his last living sister, Rosario, had passed away as well. The confluence of the two events left him inconsolable. "I have been sick physically and morally," he wrote at the end of July.[23]

Despite these personal tragedies, García Moreno tried to provide his family with a normal upbringing. To symbolize his new domestic happiness, García Moreno built his growing family a home in Quito facing the Santo Domingo plaza. During his entire life, he and his wives had lived with relatives—first with Rosa's family at the Ascásubi mansion and then with Marianita's family, the del Alcázars, at their home at what is now the Banco Central's Numismatic Museum, or at the rented hacienda at Guachalá.

In 1871 he took the plunge into home ownership, obtaining a 9,000-peso loan from the bank and paying back 800 pesos a month from his presidential salary. The work proceeded slowly and cost more than he had estimated. Cash poor but ever honest, García Moreno had to forego a trip to Cuenca to see his friend Rafael Borja because of the cost. His finances never got better. Just before his death, he noted: "I don't have a centavo, only debt."[24] Eventually the family moved into the spacious home where they were living in August 1875. Domestic tranquility and growing religiosity seemed to have moderated García Moreno's personality by 1875. In short, he hardly acted despotically during his second term.

THE PLOT COMMENCES: THE YOUNG IDEALISTS AND "IAGO"

García Moreno's biographers report six intrigues against his life after he became a major public figure during the civil war of 1859–1860, one of which resulted in a bona fide assassination attempt (as narrated in chapter 5). All others, including the fifth plot in December 1869, had been foiled.[25] As the excitement over the 1869 intrigue waned, García Moreno lamented, as he would on other occasions: "What is our youth coming to?" and "The liberals corrupt them and send them to the scaffold."[26] Not one was actually executed, though.

The presence of youth in the 1875 plot would underscore a typical Latin American tradition manifested in these earlier conspiracies. Young men, especially those trained at a university, often espoused liberal politics, much as García Moreno himself had in the 1840s. Nevertheless, García Moreno no doubt felt disappointed that his educational system had failed to convert these students to devotees of the Catholic nation. At the same time, even though assassinations of chief executives around the world became almost commonplace in these decades, governments provided little in the way of security. Certainly that was the case in Ecuador, where García Moreno walked around Quito with a single aide-de-camp.

According to one of the conspirators, Roberto Andrade, the planning commenced in May 1875 when he obtained a copy of Juan Montalvo's pamphlet, *La dictadura perpetua,* and spent an evening reading it aloud to two of his friends—one of whom became a participant. As Andrade gave voice to Montalvo's harsh words cataloguing all of García Moreno's errors, he and Manuel Cornejo resolved to topple the regime and kill the tyrant.[27] One might note that their many years as university students had not honed their critical thinking skills, as they glossed over the many exaggerations contained in Montalvo's screed. For example, as residents of Quito, they had to have known that a third of the population was not behind bars nor did the streets run red with blood. Perhaps they willingly suspended disbelief, or granted Montalvo poetic license. In any event, these two young men were well connected, well educated, and idealistic. Second, they wanted to do more than simply eliminate García Moreno. Rather, they dreamed of a new Ecuador with more civil liberties and a liberal state.

Andrade, who would write prolifically about the events of August 6, came from a family of fourteen siblings raised in quiet rustic comfort in Imbabura. Although Jesuit educated, he came to despise many of García Moreno's proclerical policies, especially the sharing of tithe money with the pope, the Catholic school system, and the president's protest (which many liberals saw as embarrassing) against the Italian invasion of the Papal States. By 1875, Andrade had entered his fifth and final year of law school. Like most students, he lived in modest quarters in a rooming house. (The pro–García Moreno sources describe these rooms as a veritable cesspool of sexual activity, with various lower-class women dallying with the conspirators, but there is no way of verifying these ad hominem attacks. If true, however, they do not speak well for the effectiveness of García Moreno's morality campaign.) Seemingly happy and loquacious, Andrade was often the life of the party. Montalvo's pamphlet became his passion. By the summer of 1875, he forgot all other activities except the conspiracy.

As Andrade read that evening in May, Manuel Cornejo likewise found his imagination ablaze.[28] Cornejo was the eldest son of a wealthy elite family. At age 26, he was the oldest of the three idealists. A formal fellow, he had a winning smile, readily making friends. His stepfather's early death made him head of the household. He had literary ambitions, and history fascinated him. At his father's death, he had inherited documents about Ecuador's independence, which he hoped would become the subject of his muse. Cornejo prided himself on clean living. He did not drink or gamble. According to his siblings, he had no vices—although of course the pro–García Moreno sources cite sexual promiscuity. Those same sources dubbed Cornejo the Brutus of the ensuing theatrics. Back in 1869, Cornejo and his brother had both loudly advocated for García Moreno's coup against Javier Espinosa while being frequent guests in the president's home. Even in August 1875, Cornejo maintained an apparent friendly relationship with García Moreno, exchanging pleasantries as they passed on the street.[29] Like Brutus, Cornejo must have believed that his duty to the republic took priority over his friendship with García Moreno, who had to be overthrown in the name of liberty.

The third idealist, Abelardo Moncayo, joined the conspiracy considerably later. Like the other two, he had received an excellent education. As a teenager, he decided to enter the Jesuit order, where he became good friends with Federico González Suárez, the future famed historian, author, and later archbishop of Quito. The two worked together in Quito's National Library in 1868, restoring order to the books jumbled together on the floor following the massive earthquake. Completing that assignment, Moncayo became a teacher and was posted to a number of locations, ending up in Cuenca in 1869. Moncayo knew García Moreno and had also voiced support for the 1869 coup. In Cuenca, however, he slowly turned away from the Jesuit order, allegedly because of the pervasive influence of liberals in the city who helped to educate him in the Enlightenment classics. As a frustrated provincial official noted, trying to prevent the introduction of forbidden books and pamphlets accomplished little. The ready access to these materials "nourishes [the liberal youth] with the venom that obscures their brilliant intelligence and perverts the noble sentiments of their heart." In any event, Moncayo left the Jesuits to become a teacher, and by 1875 had also turned against the García Moreno government. When he and Andrade met at a literary society gathering, the latter quickly convinced Moncayo to join the conspiracy.[30]

During June and July, the three friends and probably a few of their acquaintances continued to scheme. The group divided over which of two plans to follow. The first (Cornejo's) called for the conspirators to capture García Moreno alive, convince the garrison to rebel, and then hold a summary trial of the president. The remainder believed that they had to kill García Moreno first, because only his visible corpse would inspire the army to rebel. The debate continued through the beginning of August. Had one additional person not been involved, the conspiracy might well have ended as an engaging tale one tells in dotage to assembled grandchildren sitting at one's knees. After all, until the morning of the actual deed, neither Andrade nor Moncayo owned weapons, and neither had actually ever discharged a gun.[31] Someone else was deeply involved, though—a man who aptly has been described as the Iago of the plot.

In Shakespeare's play *Othello,* Iago demonstrates a particularly evil form of villainous behavior. Almost without fail, he incites others to do his malevolent bidding while remaining in the background as "honest Iago." Whether using a spurned lover or even his own wife in these machinations, Iago hides behind the scenes while his words advance the plot. Even when exposed in Act V, Iago is the only one of Shakespeare's villains who escapes death on stage.

In many ways, Manuel Polanco's behavior in July and August is reminiscent of that of Iago. After dissolute teenage years, Polanco entered the Jesuit order in 1862 on the strength of García Moreno's letter of recommendation. His time in the order met with mixed reviews. Eventually he turned instead to the study of law, securing his degree in 1872. His client base in Quito included prominent people, such as Juan José Flores' widow, Mercedes Jijón. Ironically, Manuel Polanco also had been an advocate of García Moreno's 1869 coup. His brother, Colonel José Antonio Polanco, served the García Moreno government faithfully, most notably at Cuaspud. Yet by 1875, Manuel Polanco publically supported Antonio Borrero's presidential candidacy. After that disappointing defeat, Polanco decided that García Moreno had to be eliminated at all costs. Under the pretext of inspecting a mine in Ipiales, Colombia, he crossed the border to meet with Juan Montalvo. García Moreno suspected he was up to something and asked that he be watched.[32] Upon his return, Polanco became a full-fledged member of the conspiracy.

Polanco's presence offered the three younger men some real advantages. In the first place, through his brother Polanco knew a number of high-ranking officers including Francisco Sánchez, second-in-command of the artillery regiment garrisoned just a half-block from the Government Palace. To achieve their liberal revolution, the conspirators knew they needed military support. Otherwise the idealistic rationale for the assassination would disappear. As a result, the group agreed that Polanco and Juana Terrazas, a 20-year-old beauty whose looks had bedazzled Sánchez, would attempt to enlist General Sánchez in the plot. Sánchez and Polanco met three times, but the content of their discussions remains unknown. According to Roberto Andrade, Polanco told the conspirators that Sánchez insisted García Moreno must be assassinated at the outset, as his dead body would rally troops otherwise fearing retribution.

Polanco also allegedly encouraged Captain Faustino Lemos Rayo, a retired military officer with a grudge against García Moreno, and enlisted him in the plot.[33] Because neither Sánchez nor Rayo ever testified on the record, however, the precise role of the officers stationed in Quito remains murky. Consequently, a conspiracy theory emerged.

THE CONSPIRACY: WHO ELSE WAS (OR WAS NOT) INVOLVED

Because of their notoriety and shock value, assassinations often lend themselves to conspiracy theories. Most U.S. readers are familiar with the

Faustino Lemos Rayo, who wielded the fatal blade (Courtesy of the Benson Collection)

speculation emerging after the murder of President John F. Kennedy. Although many people continue to believe in such tales, the stories do require a complex twisting of simple facts to make them plausible. Likewise, the evidence for a conspiracy in the death of Gabriel García Moreno seems farfetched.

Without a doubt, one military man did participate, for it was a former army captain who struck the fatal blows. García Moreno and Captain Faustino Rayo had crossed paths for well over a decade, almost always on friendly terms. Born a Colombian, Rayo left his native soil after ending up on the losing side of a civil war. In 1859, Rafael Carvajal enlisted him in the provisional government's army. He fought valiantly for García Moreno's cause, as he did at the battle of Cuaspud against Mosquera a few years later. So loyal had Rayo become that he renounced his Colombian citizenship, preferring to be Ecuadorian.[34]

The cozy relationship eventually soured, though. Appointed by García Moreno to a military post in the Oriente, where he also held a license to trade with the Indians, Rayo soon clashed with the Jesuits. They accused Rayo of forcing Indians to purchase unwanted goods at exorbitant prices and then compelling the native people to collect vanilla beans and pan gold to pay off the debts. Rayo denied all charges. He claimed that the missionaries—with their incessant demands for labor to build churches, schools, and roads—were the ones who abused and angered the Indians. The dispute raged through the usual bureaucratic channels, with Rayo petitioning in the 1870s to be posted again to the Oriente. Absent his employment, he argued, he would be reduced to begging. The Jesuit fathers remained equally adamant in their opposition to Rayo. By the end of 1873, García Moreno arrived at what he believed to be a statesmanlike solution. The government paid Rayo all the money he claimed the Indians owed him, but forbade him from ever returning to the Oriente.[35]

Although payment of the debt should have lessened Rayo's ire with García Moreno, liberal writers in the twentieth century have suggested the assassin had even more personal reasons to despise the chief executive. According to these stories, while Rayo served in the Oriente, García Moreno attempted to seduce his attractive wife. But Sra. Rayo remained faithful and was "sentenced to prison for her virtue." This rumor has the double advantage of not tarnishing Rayo's spouse, while sullying García Moreno's reputation.[36] Although everyone enjoys a good tale of lust and revenge, this one seems to have been fabricated out of whole cloth. None of the participants in the assassination, all very anxious to blacken García Moreno's name, ever mentioned the incident until forty years later. In fact, the claim first emerges in the 1920s, apparently as Roberto Andrade continued to embellish the rationale for the assassination. Even if the seduction story is false, which I would argue it is, the economic motive seems sufficient. Rayo must have felt embittered, deprived of his chance to make money in the Oriente and cashiered from the military. He tried to regain his Colombian citizenship and move back home, to no avail. The life of a retired lower-ranking officer was difficult.

With small pensions and nothing productive to occupy their time, retired officers sometimes fell into the trap of scheming and conspiring. Such was the case of one of Rayo's closest friends, a veteran named Gregorio Campuzano, who in addition to his poverty suffered from a debilitating case of rheumatism. After attempting to foment an 1874 army rebellion in Guayaquil, he was placed under house arrest in Quito and forbidden to travel outside the province. Disgruntled and without prospects, he frequently complained to Rayo about the unfortunate hand life had dealt him.[37]

As noted previously, a third military man, Comandante Francisco Sánchez, appears to have been at least aware of the plot. He met with Polanco on three occasions, but did not testify at the trials of any of the accused. This prosecutorial omission (or commission) led liberal writers to conclude that a conspiracy existed, including Minister of War Francisco Javier Salazar. Allegedly, Salazar wanted to use the assassination as a means to vault himself into the presidency. Thus he subsequently engaged in a coverup, ordering a soldier to shoot the assassin to silence him before he could relate details of the conspiracy (as Jack Ruby allegedly did to Lee Harvey Oswald). General Salazar denied these charges, both when they first emerged in 1875 and later when Andrade revived them in the 1880s.

Salazar cited several reasons why the conspirators' assertions were unfounded. First of all, he and García Moreno had been close friends for more than ten years, despite a brief fallout in 1870. To plan his murder would be a most despicable betrayal. Second, he stated he had no desire to establish a military dictatorship. And third, he was in the garrison when someone else shouted the order to shoot Rayo. Letters and testimony verify all three of these protestations.[38]

Logic also suggests that the military conspiracy stopped short of Salazar for three additional reasons. First, the Constitution of 1869 stated that in the event of a president's death, the office devolved upon the secretary of the interior (Francisco Javier León) and not the secretary of war. Hence Salazar could not have constitutionally succeeded to the job he allegedly coveted.

Second, no military coup occurred after the assassination, largely because of Salazar's actions. According to the conspirators themselves, the time was ideal. García Moreno's body lay in the cathedral as the plaza filled with milling citizens. Instead of taking over the government, however, Salazar ordered his soldiers back to the barracks and harangued them about proper presidential succession.

Third, the timing of the accusations remains suspicious. Manuel Polanco first claimed Salazar's involvement during his trial in 1875. The talk died down when Salazar lost his job as secretary of war, only to resurface in 1887—just as he launched his candidacy for the presidential election of 1888. That Roberto Andrade would want to derail a strong conservative candidate is hardly a surprise.[39] Both logic and the absence of direct evidence exonerate General Salazar from being a participant in the plot. Clearly, however, he did use his influence to cover up the guilt of his close friend and *compadre,* Francisco Sánchez.

While the complicity of the military in García Moreno's assassination seems farfetched, another conspiracy theory has surfaced in the writings of clerical pro–García Moreno authors—one that has direct relevance to conservative state-building theory. Allegedly orders to "do something about

Ecuador" emanated from Masonic Grand Master Otto von Bismarck, the anti-Catholic chancellor of Germany, to the Masonic lodge in Lima. In addition to providing moral support, the Masons supposedly sent money to the conspirators—especially Rayo, whose pockets allegedly contained large amounts of Peruvian currency at the time of his death.

García Moreno certainly believed that the Masons constituted a danger. In his last letter to Pope Pius IX in July 1875, he stated that the "lodges of Germany and neighboring countries are vomiting injurious and horrible lies about me," and he implored the pope for protection. Vicente Piedrahita sent warnings about the Masons from Peru. According to Council of State member Pablo Herrera, García Moreno discussed the fact that "the secret societies of Germany have decreed my death" on the very eve of the event.

After the assassination, however, Bismarck's consul wrote a very flattering description of García Moreno: "This nation prefers Christian conservative government to that of egotistical and inept adventurers," suggesting a lack of German involvement.[40] The conspirators adamantly denied any Masonic participation in their enterprise. First, they pointed out that all of them were practicing Catholics. They also asserted that they had never received any money from the lodges, that they lived in relative poverty, and that one of them even bought the revolver used on August 6 on his father's credit—not with money from the Masons.[41] As was the case with the military conspiracy, a worldwide Masonic plot to kill García Moreno seems highly unlikely. Yet the suspicion of a Masonic conspiracy has furthered the claims of Catholic writers who assert that García Moreno deserves to be recognized as a martyr, and therefore serve as the symbol for the ideal Catholic nation.

THE PLOT UNFOLDS: THE DEATH OF GARCÍA MORENO

August 6 dawned bright and sunny, but Gabriel García Moreno and the conspirators would spend their time in rather different ways. The president awoke early, as was his custom, and by 6:00 a.m. had walked to the cathedral for early Mass. As he and Marianita left the cathedral, Faustino Rayo greeted them and the two men began to chat. Allegedly García Moreno invited Rayo to walk them home to see a turtle, a gift that had recently arrived from England. Once there, the two continued to talk briefly. By 9:30, García Moreno and Mariana sat down to the morning meal. In the nineteenth century, South Americans ate but two meals a day, the other at 3:00 p.m., and then retired early within a couple of hours after darkness fell. After breakfast, García Moreno closeted himself in his study. He had a deadline: The speech he would deliver to congress on August 10, Independence Day, needed to get to the printer. Usually García Moreno finished his speeches early, but he had been waiting for some financial data from the Treasury Department so he could detail how much progress the country had made in the past six years.

By noon he finished the task, and decided that he and Mariana should go to her family home on what is now García Moreno Street, two long blocks from the Government Palace. Because he had been ill and the weather was a little cool, García Moreno buttoned up his coat. When they got to the Alcázar house, he spent a little time playing with his son, who was visiting there, and drank a glass of chicha (unusual for him).[42]

Meanwhile the conspirators had also risen early, knowing that they needed to strike because Comandante Sánchez had allegedly insisted that the coup go forward on the sixth. The conspirators had met late into the evening of the fifth to review plans. At some point after 10:00 a.m., they gathered near García Moreno's house on Santo Domingo plaza to await their victim. On Fridays García Moreno normally walked to the office after his midmorning meal, but on this occasion, as noted above, he sought the solitude of his study. As the conspirators continued to stalk him, they worried about the change in the president's routine. Around 11:30, a conspirator asked one of García Moreno's aides about the delay and learned that the president would not be leaving his home until the afternoon. Disappointed, the young men sauntered away, maintaining their vigilance farther up the street in the lobby of the Hotel Bolívar. Suddenly they saw García Moreno stride by, heading for the Alcázar mansion. Elsewhere Rayo had been drinking and conversing with his old army companion, Gregorio Campuzano. Around 1:00 in the afternoon, García Moreno left his in-laws' home.[43]

García Moreno walked down the street now bearing his name in the company of his aide-de-camp, Manuel Pallares. He passed a scribe's office, the barracks of the artillery brigade, and the Polytechnic Institute. Then he climbed the steps of the Government Palace. Andrade, Cornejo, and Moncayo (who had been lounging along the street) fell in silently behind the president, as did Rayo. Neither the president nor his aide heard them coming. Climbing up the stairs beside García Moreno, Pallares saw García Moreno's hat fly off as Rayo landed a glancing blow with his machete. Pallares turned to face the assailants just as Rayo landed a second blow. By now, both the victim and his assailants stood in front of the Treasury Department's entrance into the palace. The youthful conspirators fired their guns at García Moreno, but apparently the bullets barely grazed him.[44] Firing the

The Government Palace, where the assassination occurred (Courtesy of Library of Congress LC USZ62-100236)

weapons alerted the attention of many people doing business in the plaza to the events taking place on the porch of the Government Palace. Naturally the presence of these witnesses, many of whom testified in the ensuing trials, led to many different versions of what happened next. Despite these inconsistencies, the general pattern of events seems clear enough.

Many people saw a struggle ensue. Witnesses variously gave the number of participants from four to eight. Apparently the figure did vary even during the brief fight. Years after the struggle, Roberto Andrade exaggerated his role, claiming that he and Moncayo grabbed Pallares to prevent him from aiding García Moreno—and this account may be accurate. Then, however, Andrade asserts that after hearing García Moreno cursing and making a dash for the palace door, Andrade raced to the entrance. There he says he smashed García Moreno across the chest with his pistol so that the latter reeled back against a column on the porch. This scenario clearly did not happen. Not a single witness saw García Moreno move towards the palace doors. They uniformly saw him stagger backwards against the column, shielding his head with his left hand from the impact of Rayo's second blow.[45]

The most reliable testimony came from a fellow who tried to stay Rayo's hand. Coming out of the Treasury Office door to post a letter, he saw the altercation begin. Thinking quickly and acting bravely, he ran up behind Rayo and grabbed his right arm. After a short struggle, the powerful Rayo tossed the would-be rescuer off before resuming the attack on García Moreno. Simultaneously Pallares, wounded in an attempt to stop Rayo's furious attack, opened the Treasury door and yelled for help.

While Andrade claims that these events took a long time to develop, the rest of the witnesses agree that this initial struggle took no more than two minutes. People in dramatic situations often later exaggerate the length of time it took for events to unfold. Already three soldiers (the guards outside the Artillery barracks and their lieutenant) were running to the plaza to investigate.[46]

As Rayo hit García Moreno for the second time, breaking his left arm, the president probably tried to unbutton his coat to get at his pistol. The wound, though, interfered with his ability to move his fingers, rendering him helpless. As Rayo advanced to strike a third blow, the parties exchanged words. Allegedly Rayo said something like, "Die, tyrant, die." García Moreno responded that "God never dies," shorthand for one of his oft-used phrases, "there is no irreplaceable man; God never dies." In the face of the onslaught, García Moreno slipped over the edge of the porch, where in 1875 no railing existed as it does today. He next plunged about ten or twelve feet to the plaza below, landing in front of a tavern. Meanwhile, the bleeding Pallares asked Andrade, "Roberto, what have you done?" to which the young man asserted, "Long live the Republic. We have brought you freedom."[47]

As García Moreno landed on the ground, he apparently cried out "God help me." Women from the nearby shops—including the tavern owner, Margarita Carrera—rushed out to render assistance. Other people milling in the plaza also came over, one of whom cradled García Moreno's head in his arms. At the same time, Rayo and the young men rushed down the palace steps towards the fallen president. Pushing aside the crowd of women, Rayo delivered the two fatal blows to García Moreno's head, while the youths fired several more shots with their accustomed accuracy—only grazing the body. As the three military men ran up, the young men shouted slogans to the effect of "Down with tyranny, we are free," and ran away. Rayo also tried to run, but before he could get out of the plaza the three soldiers caught him.[48]

Even before Rayo struck the fatal blows, a couple of people in the crowd had run off to find a priest for García Moreno. One wonders at his

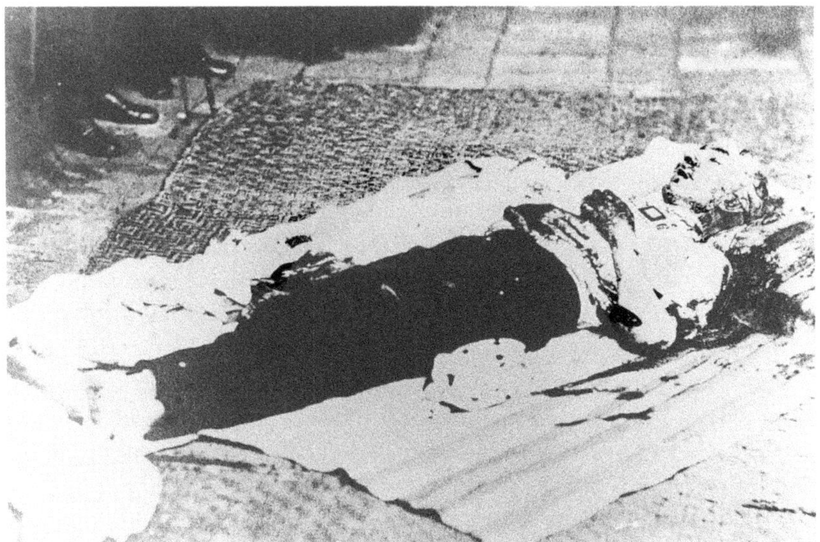

García Moreno's corpse (Permission of the Banco Central del Ecuador)

final thoughts. Did he remember his childhood boast after being locked outside in a thunderstorm: "Now I no longer need to fear a bolt of lightning"—*un rayo*? Or more likely, did his thoughts turn to the future disposition of his soul? In any event, several of his friends carried him into the cathedral, laying him down gently in a chapel behind the main altar. The hastily summoned priest administered the last rites. According to García Moreno's friends, when the priest asked the president whether he forgave his enemies, he opened his eyes, which the priest interpreted as an affirmative sign.[49] With his mind at ease, García Moreno expired. His death in a church and in a state of grace would bolster the claim for martyrdom.

Shortly thereafter, surgeons from the medical college performed an autopsy, which left the question of time of death somewhat open. Even modern forensics could not make this close a determination. According to the medical examiners, García Moreno could have survived the initial assault. The gunshot wounds barely grazed him. Rayo's first two machete blows, even the near amputation of the left arm, were not life threatening. As several witnesses testified, he survived the fall, because he was still talking. Death resulted from Rayo's repeated machete chops to the head when García Moreno lay on the ground. Remarkably, despite all the blood and cuts, the assassins had not hit any vital organs. Whether García Moreno died at the moment Rayo inflicted the last blows, as the assassins would have it, or later in the cathedral as his friends asserted, cannot be definitively decided.[50]

News of the president's demise spread rapidly, aided by the modernized transportation and communications systems he had built. The caretaker government asserted control quickly, preparing an impressive funeral to demonstrate the strength and durability of the regime. After the autopsy was finished, the doctors stitched García Moreno's wounds and dressed him in a military uniform with white gloves and a hat with a feathered plume. Then they sat him in a regal chair in a chapel in the cathedral, surrounded by five presidential guards for the public viewing. Indeed, outpourings of grief and funeral Masses offered for García Moreno's soul went on for the better part of the month, certainly not the sort of reaction the liberal conspirators had anticipated. According to a pro–García Moreno source, thousands of people traveled thirty or forty miles to view the remains.

The next day, the cathedral was packed for the service presided over by Bishop Ignacio Ordóñez of Riobamba, who happened to be in Quito and thus could officiate. The archbishop had undertaken a visitation to a distant part of Tungurahua province and could not return in time. At the funeral Mass, García Moreno's corpse faced the audience in the same unusual way, sitting in a chair. Apparently this rarely used funerary practice dated back to the French medieval monarchy, symbolizing the continuity of the government.[51] The funeral was brief, which the French minister attributed to the fact that the government feared a liberal revolt. The brevity may also have been because García Moreno's body had putrefied and "presented a horrible spectacle." Mariana took the death hard. Two months passed before she found the strength to respond to the well-wishers who grieved for her and her son. She asked for their prayers and forgiveness for the assassins, speaking of her husband as a "martyr for his faith."[52]

THE FATES OF THE ASSASSINS

Under almost all circumstances, the assassination of a nation's president leaves the country stunned. Most Americans of a suitable age can tell questioners exactly where they were when they heard that Lee Harvey Oswald shot President Kennedy in 1963. When Rayo's machete cut down García Moreno, many people shared feelings of horror. According to trial testimony, average citizens bewailed the loss of their leader, enhancing his image as a national symbol and vowing retribution on the assassins—which explains why they fled and hid. Furthermore, despite a national history filled with political turmoil, García Moreno remains the sole proven

The funeral of Gabriel García Moreno (Permission of the Banco Central del Ecuador)

example of an Ecuadorian president assassinated while in office. (Rumors do suggest, however, that the 1979 plane crash in which left-wing reformer Jaime Roldós was killed may not have been accidental.)

Horror at the bloody deed spread with the news. People in Cotacachi—in Imbabura, a town García Moreno had helped rebuild in 1868—erupted in grief at the news. The governor of Loja reported seeing "the population inconsolably weeping over the loss of the Father of the nation." Loyal officials, both at home and abroad, mourned "the death of our friend Gabriel," as interim President Francisco Javier León stated.[53] Consequently, the government pursued the assassins forcefully.

Faustino Rayo fell into official hands first. As he stood over García Moreno, slashing him with the machete, a lieutenant and two noncommissioned officers approached with rifles at the ready. They grabbed Rayo, who was bespattered with García Moreno's blood and still holding the machete, and ordered him to drop his weapon. With their bayonets at Rayo's back, the soldiers marched him across the plaza in the direction of their battalion headquarters.

In the meantime, two generals, fearing a possible rebellion, had rallied their soldiers. General Julio Sáenz, the battalion commander who outranked Comandante Sánchez, was a man loyal to García Moreno. Sáenz saw his subordinates approaching with Rayo in tow. Someone shouted, "Kill the assassin!" A soldier stepped out of the ranks and shot Rayo in the head, spilling his brains on the sidewalk.[54] Apparently after that, the mob took Rayo's body to a cemetery and desecrated it, leaving it out in the open air for vultures to feed upon. Rayo's death raised many subsequent questions and encouraged conspiracy theorists, who believe that someone (usually General Salazar) had purposely silenced him.

The evidence about who gave the order to fire is contradictory. Roberto Andrade alleged that back in the barracks, General Salazar told a soldier to shoot Rayo. Andrade was in no position to know this, since he claimed to have heard it from someone who interviewed the soldier years later. This account presumes that Salazar knew Rayo was the killer and that he would be captured alive. In fact, Salazar remained in the barracks, calming the soldiers. Several witnesses claimed to have heard a single voice (maybe the lieutenant's, maybe Captain Pallares') call out the order. Other sources, including the British minister, claimed that the enraged crowd demanded Rayo's execution.[55] Given the hubbub that must have ensued after the assassination, the identity of the person or persons who shouted the fatal words will never be known. Absent the presence of a military conspiracy, for which little evidence exists (as previously argued), the officers would have had no motive to kill Rayo. Passion and the desire for revenge seem like good reasons to explain the shooting, as the British minister indicated. With Rayo's death occurring before he gave any testimony, however, those who believe in the larger conspiracy can never be totally disproved.

With the deed committed and no coup ensuing, the young idealists fled from the Plaza de la Independencia, looking for places to hide until the furor died down. Given the relatively small size of Quito and the notoriety of its even tinier elite, witnesses identified Cornejo and Andrade immediately as the two men who had stood near García Moreno and fired their weapons. Orders went out for their arrest, as the interim president declared martial law and convened a military court to hold trials. Fewer witnesses claimed to have seen Abelardo Moncayo, perhaps because he stood farther back.[56] The fourth major conspirator, Manuel Polanco (true to his Iago-like nature), had remained aloof from the action and was in a shop more than a block away during the whole episode. He never tried to flee, but officials soon linked his name with the bloody deed. Witnesses had seen him talking to one or more of the conspirators both before and after the assassination. When the police finally captured Cornejo, he betrayed Polanco, blaming him for the failure of the coup. Because no one saw him brandishing a weapon near the president, Polanco received a lighter sentence—ten years in the Panóptico. After the frenzy died down, his lawyer published a lengthy defense, arguing that the military tribunal lacked jurisdiction. When the government changed hands in 1876, Polanco served his sentence more in the breach than the observance, being let out every evening to spend the night with his girlfriend. He offered to take up weapons in defense of the new government against an unsuccessful conservative rebellion in 1877, and was killed in the streets of Quito.[57]

As the investigation progressed, authorities arrested and tried several suspects. An individual who happened to be carrying a revolver in the Plaza de la Independencia that day, some people who hailed from Rayo's region in western Colombia, and others who had talked to military officers in Guayaquil were tried and exonerated.[58]

One fellow seemed particularly suspicious, however—retired officer Gregorio Campuzano. As Rayo's drinking companion, Campuzano had held a longstanding grudge against the government. Swooping down on Campuzano, the government promptly tried him. Although he swore that he had only conversed with Rayo a couple of times and that he had been at home on August 6, other witnesses had seen them drinking together that morning at Margarita Carrera's tavern. The court initially found the evidence too circumstantial. Interim President Francisco Javier León, however, asked them to reconsider when new witnesses came forward, proving Campuzano knew Rayo much better than the retired officer had admitted. Upon rehearing, the court found Campuzano guilty and had him executed on August 11. Given the hysteria following the assassination, some officials declared this to be a "just result" that would help to preserve the peace.[59] Upon reflection, however, the evidence in its totality suggests Campuzano's innocence and that he was only a cantankerous old man who made friends with the wrong drinking companion.

While Campuzano was a scapegoat, the government case was much stronger against the three visible participants: Manuel Cornejo, Roberto Andrade, and Abelardo Moncayo. Unfortunately they had all successfully escaped. For several days (and in one instance the better part of a month), the assassins laid low in Quito, hiding in friends' homes before fleeing to the countryside. Manuel Cornejo left his sisters' house and traveled under cover of darkness through Papallacta and then southeast to a small village. He wrote his mother telling her he was safe, but entrusted the letter to a man who fell into government hands. Within days, two squads of soldiers hurried to find him. Warned of their approach, Cornejo fled to the high *páramo* of Antisana volcano, where he nearly froze to death. Captured in dire condition, he was brought back to Quito to face court-martial. He argued that the plot had been to overthrow the government and take García Moreno prisoner, but as previously noted, many witnesses had seen him fire his revolver several times. Although his mother pleaded for mercy, the government had Cornejo executed on August 27.[60]

The other two young assassins were more fortunate. Both headed north, where they had relatives who could protect them. Moncayo made for Imbabura. Whenever police came looking, friends would hide him. Local officials promised to capture Moncayo but never could locate him. Unlike the garrulous Roberto Andrade, Moncayo's later writings reveal nothing about either his role in García Moreno's assassination or his years in hiding. Instead they focus on broader social and cultural themes. Because Moncayo lived quietly, caused no trouble, and did not flaunt his role in the assassination, the Conservative government in the 1890s agreed not to impose any sentence on him when he finally surfaced. Years later, he worked closely with Liberal President Eloy Alfaro, serving for awhile as minister of the interior, before being forcibly exiled following Alfaro's death.[61]

Andrade, who wound up in Peru, reacted rather differently to his status as fugitive. Well aware that the government had issued warrants for his arrest, Andrade broke his silence in the 1880s. He wrote a series of books about García Moreno and his assassination—more than enough to constitute a confession. Because Andrade revisited the old conspiracy theory about General Salazar's involvement, the Ecuadorian government worked hard to extradite him from Peru and bring him to justice. Finally caught and tried, Andrade toned down his bragging considerably, claiming that he served the country as a dissident—an argument so convincing that he was spared the death penalty. After the Liberal Revolution of 1895, Andrade worked briefly in Alfaro's government and kept writing. His constant political intriguing, however, resulted in his exile to Cuba in the 1920s, where he heavily influenced two anti–García Moreno writers.[62]

And what of the famous essayist, Juan Montalvo, whose words had inspired the young men? When he heard of García Moreno's murder, Montalvo allegedly stated, "No doubt my ideas took root; it is not Rayo's steel; it is my pen that killed him." This boast was certainly an exaggeration, because Rayo had not read his essay and the assassins who had did not strike the mortal blows. Montalvo spent much of the remainder of his life in exile, carping cynically against his enemies and whichever Ecuadorian government was in office.[63]

Yet Rayo's machete blows, the young men's shots, and even Montalvo's words resonated far beyond the confines of the Plaza de la Independencia that August afternoon. Contemporaries feared that García Moreno's work, especially the hard-earned stability, would be gone. "The Republic is on a volcano," wrote one of his associates. Foreign representatives feared that the era of revolutions had returned, noting that a number of Jesuits had quietly packed up and left Ecuador. García Moreno's former in-laws, Manuel and Roberto de Ascásubi, were concerned about the future. Perhaps repenting his critical letter of early August, Roberto de Ascásubi took the first ship home and volunteered to help the struggling government in any way possible. His brother Manuel, now an aged 75, played an instrumental role in pursuing the assassins, demanding full vengeance for García Moreno's death.[64] Yet the pundits' worst fears were not realized. Elections in October came and went peacefully, resulting in the selection of Antonio Borrero, the moderate liberal who had criticized García Moreno at times but whose views on issues were actually very similiar. Many of García Moreno's policies would prevail until 1895. Hence the assassins did not succeed in bringing a liberal regime to Ecuador.

MARTYR OR SAINT?

Recent scholarship has demonstrated the importance of the veneration of dead heroes and their remains as bodies transmitting political values.[65] So it is with García Moreno, who remains a powerful political symbol for conservatives even today. The titanic debate over his historical memory began even as his friends prepared his burial. Because ardent Catholics feared that liberals would attempt to desecrate his remains, he was buried in secret. Those who believed that García Moreno might be canonized and become the symbol of a Catholic nation hastened to gather relics of his death.

Conservative clergy eulogized García Moreno both in Europe and Ecuador. Pope Pius IX, for example, heaped praise on García Moreno and commissioned a statue to commemorate the memory of the fallen Catholic leader to be placed in the yard of the Colegio Pío Latino Americano, an exclusive Vatican school that trained Latin Americans for the priesthood. French Catholics received permission to create a García Moreno monument (funded at least in part by Ecuadorians), to be housed in the Basilica of Paray-le-Monial (where the original Sacred Heart Basilica was located).[66] Ecuadorians likewise lauded his memory. In September, the legislature named García Moreno "the Illustrious Regenerator of the Fatherland and Martyr to Catholic civilization." In addition, the government commissioned both a statue and a portrait, and decreed that the National Road would henceforth be designated as the García Moreno Highway.[67] This label remained in place for years, whereas the title "García Moreno railroad" quickly slipped into oblivion.

García Moreno's friends also pushed for his recognition as a martyr and saint, mostly because the European Catholic right viewed his Catholic-nation concept as a viable alternative to the liberalism of the French Revolution, and sought to inspire European Catholic leaders to follow his example. Being declared a martyr or saint would make García Moreno in effect a symbol, much as Joan of Arc had come to embody the French nation in many of her fellow citizens' eyes.

Ultimately, though, martyrdom is a status conveyed by religious, not secular, authorities. Such standing is granted by the pope once the victim has met specific tests—which, in García Moreno's case, are questionable. Hence those mounting the campaign paid particular attention to the words that Pius IX and subsequent popes used to describe García Moreno's assassination. Although both Pope Pius IX and his successor, Leo XIII, admired García Moreno, their ambiguous language fell short of conveying the status of martyrdom. Nevertheless, European Catholics, led by the popular nineteenth-century writer Louis Veuillot, have continued to make the case right up to the present.[68]

The road to martyrdom and sainthood has always been a slow one in the Catholic Church, at least until the twenty-first century. For those believing in this process, the preservation of mementos, officially called relics, associated with the victim and his or her martyrdom was essential. Consequently, fragments of García Moreno's skull hacked off by Rayo's machete, his blood-stained shirt, and a handkerchief with which a believer sopped up some of his still-moist blood are currently located in the Jesuit museum in Cotocallao (near Quito) and in private collections. The blood-soaked pages of the inaugural address had an even more intriguing destination. Gathered up by the editor of *El Nacional*, the document and some blood in a container ended up in the Vatican Museum, a gift of envoy Antonio Flores.

García Moreno's physical remains, however, constituted the most important relic. The corpse was concealed, as was the jar containing his heart, in separate locations. Only in 1975 did amateur historian Francisco Salazar Alvarado (a descendant of General Salazar), with the cooperation of Quito's archbishop and several elderly nuns, unearth the mystery—García Moreno's heart had ended up in the Convent of Buen Pastor and his bones in the Convent of Santa Catalina (both in Quito)—just in time to commemorate the centennial of the murder in August of that year. On the appropriate day, church officials and two former presidents watched as García Moreno's remains were reburied in a niche in the cathedral.[69]

García Moreno's designation as a saint seems unlikely. Because García Moreno's political legacy rests on his reputation as the advocate of the Catholic nation, liberal governments after 1895 discouraged the idea. The campaign gained occasional traction, as for example in 1921 on the centennial of García Moreno's birth. To bolster the case for García Moreno's sainthood, conservative Ecuadorians collected a list of miracles attributed to their hero. Some seemed eminently pragmatic—as Latin American miracles often are. For example, a woman from Guayaquil received a sewing machine for which she had been praying for months. Another woman tending a finicky oven in Cuenca found her burnt rolls had turned a beautiful brown, saving her from getting sacked by her employer. And a shepherd girl did not lose her cattle to rustlers. All of these events were ascribed to García Moreno's intervention. García Moreno healed the sick—whether suffering from an ulcerated foot, tuberculosis, or typhoid fever. The more spiritual miracles were equally impressive. A man prayed for his dying son to return to the faith, which he did. A libertine finally saw the light and repented. As one would expect, liberal authors poked fun at the alleged miracles, denying their authenticity.[70] Despite the miracles, as of this writing, all efforts to convince a pope to declare García Moreno a saint have fallen short.

Since 1875, Ecuadorians have scrapped over García Moreno's historical memory as part of a broader political division between liberals and conservatives. Annually on the anniversary of his death on August 6, adherents march in front of the Government Palace paying homage to their hero. As noted in the preface, even contemporary citizens hold strong opinions about García Moreno and his death. Unlike the many assassinations of political leaders occurring in the United States and Europe in the late-nineteenth century, the events of August 6 were not the anonymous actions of a crazed malcontent but rather a highly personal attack on a familiar figure. Consequently, the analogy to Julius Caesar's murder at the hands of friends like Brutus informs us about both the tale of the deed and the closed nature of nineteenth-century Ecuadorian politics.

In the long run, the campaign to sanctify or vilify García Moreno symbolized the great national divide of the nineteenth century. That discussion of the liberal-conservative debate about state formation will provide a fitting conclusion to the tale of the life and times of Gabriel García Moreno.

Conclusion

The heated debate between liberals and conservatives about García Moreno and his role in the formation of the Ecuadorian state continues to the present. Perhaps the best evidence of the bitterness of this quarrel can be encapsulated in the controversies over whether statues of García Moreno ought to be placed in public spaces in Quito and Guayaquil. Given his troubled relationship with many influential *guayaquileños,* a frosty reception to the idea of a monument there should have been anticipated. Nevertheless, during the 1950s friends of the fallen dictator hired a sculptor to carve a bust of García Moreno for display in the Americas Park, where the forces of the provisional government had defeated General Franco in 1860 to end the civil war. The mayor of Guayaquil blasted the project, however, refusing to grant the necessary permission to display the sculpture. A compromise to locate the statue at the corner of Junín Street and the Malecón, where García Moreno's house once stood, also met steadfast opposition despite advocacy by two past presidents of the country.[1] To this day, Guayaquil has no monument to García Moreno, one of its most famous sons.

That liberal *guayaquileños* might oppose a García Moreno statue in their city makes sense, but the hostility towards such a figure in more conservative Quito seems surprising. The location of the first controversial García Moreno statue, in the little plaza at the intersection of Calles Amazonas and Jorge Washington, sees thousands of people pass on a daily basis. In the 1970s, the government decided to place busts of Ecuador's most famous politicians (Vicente Rocafuerte, Eloy Alfaro, José María Velasco Ibarra, and García Moreno) at the street corners for passers-by to admire.

Immediately the "scandal" hit the newspapers. One editorial thundered: Why are we erecting statues to two traitors (García Moreno and

Velasco Ibarra)? After condemning García Moreno's treacherous relationship with France and Peru (in the 1860 civil war), the paper catalogued the many tyrannical deeds "of the darkest figure in our history." Most importantly, the paper argued, unveiling the statue would lead to a didactic disaster, where youths would be confused about who were the real founders of modern-day Ecuador.[2]

Despite the clamor, the city government eventually placed the carved images at the intersection. In 2005, a second García Moreno statue, long hidden in an obscure corner of the great basilica dedicated to the Sacred Heart of Jesus, became prominently relocated in the newly named Plaza García Moreno—a small grassy park in front of the basilica—with much less disputation. García Moreno still remains Ecuador's most controversial figure, however, in part because the liberal-conservative debate over who laid the foundations of the modern state remains unresolved even in the twenty-first century.

Certainly the struggle between liberal and conservative ideology dominated a good deal of the political rhetoric in García Moreno's time. Although as a young student he participated in this debate, even taking arms against conservative dictator Juan José Flores, by the 1850s his thinking had changed substantially. Influenced both by a reawakening of his personal faith and the progress he witnessed while residing in Napoleon III's authoritarian France, García Moreno's ideas gravitated in the direction of a modern conservative vision of state formation. His chance to explore these possibilities arose after the horrendous civil war of 1859 and 1860, when the nation was nearly torn asunder by competing regional factions and an invading Peruvian caudillo. The civil war, however, exacerbated two issues related to the liberal-conservative debate. First, the praetorian army left over from the days of independence and often led by foreigners was neither patriotic nor trustworthy—prone to frequent rebellion. Second, strong feelings of regionalism forced García Moreno to strike deals with would-be autonomous elites, arrangements that proved inconsistent with his vision of state formation.

The close relationship between regional interests and doctrinaire nineteenth-century liberalism dominated the debates surrounding the Constitution of 1861. Much to García Moreno's displeasure, the delegates endorsed the states-rights version of federalism that found favor in many Latin American countries in the 1850s and 1860s. Despite García Moreno's warnings that the system's weak chief executive and strong local autonomy would prove unworkable, the moderate liberal coalition at the constituent assembly created a system of municipal autonomy that deprived the central government of revenues needed to fund García Moreno's pragmatic policies to build national unity. The Concordat stood almost alone as García Moreno's most concrete achievement during his first term. The fragile state wobbled also because of the two Colombian wars and countless exile invasions, reinforcing García Moreno's belief in the importance of a centralized government.

To make matters worse, these wars, instead of inspiring patriotism, hindered the weak federalist state and encouraged military coups. Acting with questionable legal authority, García Moreno responded harshly to these attempted disruptions of order. Because of his military victory at Jambelí and his successful disaster relief efforts in Imbabura, by 1869 he had become a caudillo—able to recapture the presidency on his own terms. In so doing, he prematurely pronounced the death of political liberalism, finding it antithetical to the spirit and essential beliefs of most Ecuadorians.

Not surprisingly, then, García Moreno's brand of modernizing conservatism dominated his final term. The Constitution of 1869 represented the most extreme nineteenth-century version of a centralized state, since it banished federalism and municipal autonomy permanently from the Ecuadorian scene. With its six-year presidency and the intrusion of the executive branch down to the local level, the centralist constitution provided a mechanism for enforcing order and quashing even hints of political disturbances. In this sense, Ecuador foretold what would happen all over Latin America: Classical liberalism would be abandoned during the final quarter of the century.

The resolution of the fracas about the nature of government did not silence the debate over state formation because no issue divided liberals and conservatives more than the role that the Catholic Church should play in society.[3] Here García Moreno provided an alternative to the anticlericalism sweeping the remainder of Latin America. Arguing that a reformed church could best educate and provide social services to the faithful of Ecuador, just as it had done in the colonial era, he wrought a new state-dominated relationship with the church and attempted to banish liberal anticlerical ideas. Some of the specifics of this policy, such as the protest against the Italian invasion of Rome and the dedication of Ecuador to the Sacred Heart of Jesus, isolated García Moreno from other Latin American conservatives, however. In sum, much of the story of García Moreno can be understood in light of the liberal-conservative divide that splintered the

Latin American elite in the nineteenth century. Specifically his career informs us about the less well understood conservative side of that debate.

To conclude merely that García Moreno's career illuminates conservative thinking would, however, do great injustice to his significance for Ecuador and Latin America as a whole. He did not think of himself as an ideologue but rather as a nation-builder, and as such most of his compatriots have perceived him.[4] If nationalism is in reality a "cultural artifact" or an "imagined community," as some commentators have declared,[5] then García Moreno envisioned a unique nation that captured the spirit of the Ecuadorian people. For him, the nation-building project consisted of both theoretical and practical aspects. Noting that language, regional origins, and ethnic identities divided Ecuadorians, he thought he could build upon the one thing all Ecuadorians had in common—their Catholic faith.

As a result, he believed that a state-managed Catholic education designed to eliminate illiteracy, with instruction provided by the best-qualified monastic teaching orders, would instill common Catholic values among young people. To make certain that adults shared these core values, he embarked on a moralizing campaign, criminalizing social behaviors he deemed destructive. Ultimately, use of the Catholic faith as the center of the nation-building project failed for two principal reasons. First, the plan ran afoul of regional and cultural variations. While many Ecuadorians shared García Moreno's vision of state formation, others did not. Second, García Moreno simply did not have enough time. To make the program successful would have required at least a generation of consistent enforcement.

The pragmatic program for the unification of Ecuador also fell short for similar reasons. García Moreno intended to link sierra and coast with a series of highways and a railroad built to accommodate the passage of both people and goods. Although through sheer force of will García Moreno completed one highway, other road projects halted because of regional conflicts, limited resources, and differing opinions about the nation's future direction. Had the García Moreno era lasted a generation, then perhaps his concrete plans for roads and a railroad would have been realized. Yet some specific symbols of Ecuadorian nationalism do date from the Garcian period: the flag, national anthem, Independence Day holiday, and idea of a national museum, among many others.

Regional forces often undercut his efforts. Although García Moreno had created an extensive patronage network through family, university friends, and fellow legislators, ultimately many of these elite (notably those from Cuenca) placed a higher priority on local rather than national interests. Regional sensibilities also threatened the coalition García Moreno created between the coastal business community and the highland elite. This alliance was a result of the structural changes Ecuador underwent in the 1860s and 1870s, as noted by the most recent generation of historians.

In the end, García Moreno's state rested on a compromise that would prove unsustainable. The central and northern highland elite monopolized political power while the south highland elite tried to preserve some autonomy—and the coastal elite pursued economic wealth unrestrained by the national government. García Moreno made this accommodation in order to balance regional interests threatening to divide the nation. As a result, he was able to consolidate, at least for the moment, an oligarchic state.[6] The tension between the regions would re-emerge later in the century and remains an ongoing issue today.

In looking at the broad sweep of Ecuadorian and Andean history, did García Moreno's career make a difference? From this writer's perspective, the early historians had it right. People like García Moreno do count, because as leaders they leave distinctive marks on their societies. Like many caudillos, García Moreno possessed physical characteristics that captured observers' attention. In addition, his deep powerful voice and ability to reason persuasively allowed him to convince the uncertain. More importantly, the innovative story he told, that the Catholic faith could serve as a unifying force in a nation hitherto lacking cohesion, was a compelling one. To dramatize the narrative, he believed and lived it, behaving in a way no other contemporary Catholic politician did.[7] In García Moreno's absence, the vision began to disintegrate.

Although the fundamental precepts of his beliefs dominated the country in modified form until 1895 and have some resonance today, his contemporaries noticed that some things came undone rather quickly after 1875. Within a few years, the Polytechnical, the School of Fine Arts, and the Conservatory of Music closed their doors. Work on the astronomical observatory halted. Congress repudiated his Concordat, and a number of the French monastics returned home. In the words of one old Ecuadorian hand in 1880, "The country has gone backwards in the past five years." Equally obviously, the civilian-dominated stability García Moreno desperately wanted dissipated, and the military reasserted itself in politics.[8] García Moreno's hidden bones must have wept when his old enemy, General José María Urbina, made a triumphant return—though he played a minimal role in the military government that ruled from 1876 to 1883.

Yet in many ways, Ecuador remained faithful to García Moreno's vision. Progressive presidents, moderate liberals, and not surprisingly military dictators after 1875 all agreed that a centralized form of government best met Ecuador's needs in the modern world. No one challenged the system of democratic capitalism that he nourished, as private banks continued to fund national enterprises for generations to come, relying on export income to repay borrowed money. Compared to the other Andean nations today, with the exception of Colombia, Ecuador enjoys the best roads and the most efficient transportation system—certainly a Garcian dream. Only his vision of Catholicism as the unifying force of Ecuadorian nationalism has truly failed, replaced by more secular notions. In short, García Moreno deserves credit for his innovative leadership and unique ideas of nation-building that put Ecuador on the map for late-nineteenth-century Europeans.

Biographers also have to wrestle with the quirks of their protagonists' personalities. Years ago, my dissertation advisor concluded his book on one of Mexico's antiheroes by saying that, all things considered, he would have chosen to share a meal with Mexico's first "Revolutionary" president rather than the general about whom he wrote.[9] For myself, after spending a number of years and all these pages getting to know Gabriel García Moreno vicariously, I believe that it would be a shame not to take the opportunity to break bread with him—although I would be inclined to keep a cautious tongue in my head. No doubt many Ecuadorians today would share these feelings about a man who remains lodged in the national consciousness more than 125 years after his death.

Notes

ABBREVIATIONS

AARZO – Archivo Arzobispal
AF – Archivo Juan José Flores
AGMD – Archivo General de Ministerio de Defensa
AMAE – Archives du Ministère des Affaires Étrangères (France)
AMRE – Archivo de Ministerio de Relaciones Exteriores
ANHC – Archivo Nacional de Historia, Criminales
ANHF – Archivo Nacional de Historia, Fondo Especial
ANHG – Archivo Nacional de Historia, Ministerio del Gobierno
ANHH – Archivo Nacional de Historia, Ministerio del Hacienda
BAEP – Biblioteca Aurelio Espinosa Pólit
BCH – Banco Central/Hacienda
BC/JJC – Banco Central, Fondo Jacinto Jijón y Caamaño
BPL – Biblioteca del Poder Legislativo
FHP – Friedrich Hassaurek Papers
FO – Foreign Office Reports (Great Britain)
GGM – Gabriel García Moreno
HAHR – Hispanic American Historical Review
JJF – Juan José Flores
LC – Loor, Cartas de García Moreno
RdA – Roberto de Ascásubi
RDS – Records of the Department of State
USDG – Dispatches from U.S. Consuls in Guayaquil
VSA – Vatican Secret Archive
WCP – William Coggeshall Papers

INTRODUCTION

1. Ayala Mora, "García Moreno," 143.

2. Anderson, *Imagined Communities;* Corrigan and Sayer, *Great Arch;* and Castro-Klarén and Chasteen, *Beyond.*

3. Hook, *Hero in History*. For patronage, see Graham, *Patronage and Politics;* and Rock, *State Building*.

4. Backscheider, *Biography;* and Nicholson, *English Biography*.

5. Berthe, *Vengador;* George-Kaufmann, *Gabriel García Moreno; and* Gálvez, *Vida*.

6. Andrade, *Montalvo y García Moreno;* Borrero Cortázar, *Refutación;* and Moncayo, *Ecuador.* See also: Agramonte, *Psicopatológico;* and Carrión, *Patíbulo*.

7. Xavier, *García Moreno*; and Ordóñez Zamora, *García Moreno*.

8. Robalino Dávila, *García Moreno;* and Pattee, *García Moreno*.

1. PREPARING FOR NATIONAL LEADERSHIP, 1821–1859

1. Berthe, *Vengador*, I, 78; and Gomezjurado, *García Moreno*, I, 23–46.

2. Gomezjurado, *García Moreno*, I, 9–24; Agramonte, *Psicopatológico*, 15–20; and Carrión, *Patíbulo*, 19–21.

3. Destruge, *Revolución de Octubre;* and *Recopilación*, 206–8. The best overview is Rodríguez O, *Independence*. Pérez Moscoso, *Campeón*, 17–18.

4. Berthe, *Vengador*, I, 78. Mercedes Moreno's will is in BAEP, reel 34. She left her home and half of her income to the three unmarried daughters (because they had no other income and one was blind) and the other half equally to her sons. Gabriel served as the executor: GGM to Rosa Ascásubi de García Moreno, March 19, 1847, BAEP, reel 33.

5. GGM to JJF, July 17, 1844, and November 1841, BAEP, reel 34. Manuel joined the Cathedral chapter in 1860; J. A. Gómez to RdA, October 31, 1860, BAEP, reel 26. Loor, *Jesuitas*, 86–87, 117.

6. Gálvez, *Vida*, 17. Gomezjurado, *García Moreno*, I, 20–21.

7. Clayton, *Caulkers and Carpenters;* Pineo, *Life and Work;* and Orton, *Andes*, 25–33.

8. Hall, *Extracts*, II, 108–10; and Pfeiffer, *Lady's Second Journey*, 362, 395–96.

9. Hamerly, *Historia*, 65–67.

10. Carrión, *Patíbulo*, 21; and Gomezjurado, *García Moreno*, I, 19–20. Pérez Moscoso, *Campeón*, 8–9, argues that the family was not impoverished.

11. Carrión, *Patíbulo*, 30–40.

12. Berthe, *Vengador*, I, 79; and Gálvez, *Vida*, 18. Mera, *García Moreno*, 212–13; and Andrade, *Montalvo y García Moreno*, I, 61–62. Three individuals left personal memoirs from García Moreno's lifetime: his friend Juan León Mera, Antonio Borrero Cortázar, *Refutación*, and Pablo Herrera. Unfortunately, Mera only finished chapters on García Moreno's early life and Borrero had little contact after 1864. Herrera knew García Moreno after 1858.

13. Agramonte, *Psicopatológico*, 25–27, 59.

14. Gomezjurado, *García Moreno*, I, 70–77; and Pérez Moscoso, *Campeón*, 26–27.

15. Pfeiffer, *Lady's Second Journey*, 362–78; Hassaurek, *Four Years*, 16–45; and Fitzell, "Cultural Colonialism," 127–63.

16. Gomezjurado, *García Moreno*, I, 118–19; Gálvez, *Vida*, 27; Carrión, *Patíbulo*, 64; Hassaurek, *Four Years*, 48–51; and Whitaker, *United States*, 37.

17. Gomezjurado, *García Moreno*, I, 128–30; and Mera, *García Moreno*, 222–32.

18. Berthe, *Vengador*, I, 89–93; Carrión, *Patíbulo*, 97–103; Mera, *García Moreno*, 218; and Tobar Donoso, "Wisse," 178.

19. Berthe, *Vengador*, I, 91. University records dated September 12, 1839, show "distinguished" scholarship in Latin, BAEP, reel 34.

20. Carrión, *Patíbulo*, 67–69. Rafael Carvajal hailed from Ibarra and became a very important collaborator, serving as a diplomat, cabinet member, vice president, and Supreme Court member.

21. Carrión, *Patíbulo*, 110–11; Gomezjurado, *García Moreno*, I, 153–54; and Mera, *García Moreno*, 223.

22. GGM, "Letrilla," in Pólit Laso, *Escritos y Discursos*, I, 333–35; Gomezjurado, *García Moreno*, I, 164–65; and Carrión, *Patíbulo*, 161–73.

23. Berthe, *Vengador*, I, 101–6; and Gálvez, *Vida*, 48.

24. Rodríguez O, *Revolución política.*

25. Bushnell, *Santander Regime;* and Van Aken, *King*, 35–37.

26. Rodríguez O, *Vicente Rocafuerte.*

27. Van Aken, *King;* Spindler, *Nineteenth Century Ecuador;* Gomezjurado, *García Moreno*, I, 218–20; and Benigno Malo to Governor, April 24, 1845, BAEP, reel 34. García Moreno's political activity resulted in his suspension from the university: See GGM to Ministerio de Gobierno (hereafter Gobierno), March 11, 1844, BAEP, reel 34. Liberal enemies claim that García Moreno tried to assassinate Flores. Mera, *García Moreno*, 228–31, and Pattee, *Tiempo*, 213, adamantly deny it.

28. Berthe, *Vengador*, I, 99–107; Gomezjurado, *García Moreno, I*, 205–10, 222–38; GGM to William Jameson, January 13, 1858, in "Cartas sobre exploraciones"; and GGM to RdA, December 29, 1849, LC, I, 147–51. See also: Sebastián Wisse to GGM, March 21, 1849, BAEP, reel 35, and his letters of August 11, 1847, and May 24, 1847, BAEP, reel 35. García Moreno's friend, Governor Felipe Serrade, climbed Mt. Cotopaxi: See his letter to Gobierno, September 15, 1869, ANHG, León, #96.

29. Berthe, *Vengador*, I, 105–6; Gomezjurado, *García Moreno*, I, 202–3, 243; Agramonte, *Psicopatológico*, 83–84; Carrión, *Patíbulo*, 222–36; and Romero and Andrade Andrade, *Estructura agraria*, IV, 55–63, 166–67.

30. GGM to Rosa, March 7, 1849, BAEP, reel 33, LC, I, 84; and GGM to Rosa, July 31, 1850, LC, I, 173–80. For suggestions of other pregnancies, see GGM to RdA, January 5, 1848, BAEP, reel 33, LC, I, 24; and GGM to Rosa, December 21, 1849, LC, I, 146–47. See also: Gangotena y Jijón, "Los Ascásubi," 241–47.

31. GGM to Rosa, May 2, 1849, BAEP, reel 33, LC, I, 110–12; and GGM to Rosa, June 13, 1849, BAEP, reel 33, LC, I, 125–26.

32. Gomezjurado, *García Moreno*, III, 439; Jurado Noboa, *Quiteñas*, 200–11; Agramonte, *Psicopatológico* 89; and Carrión, *Patíbulo*, 527–30.

33. Namier, *Structure of Politics.*

34. GGM to RdA, September 16, 1846, BAEP, reel 33, LC, I, 7–8; and GGM to RdA, October 7, 1846, BAEP, reel 33, LC, I, 11–12.

35. Berthe, *Vengador*, I, 125–37; and Gomezjurado, *García Moreno, I*, 244–69. Issues of *The Whip* (*El Zurriago*), *The Avenger (El Vengador)*, and *The Devil (El Diablo)* are in Pólit Laso, *Discursos*, I. Van Aken, *King*, 209–48.

36. *El Nacional*, December 8, 1847. Roca invited García Moreno to the Government Palace in 1848: See GGM to RdA, August 2, 1848, BAEP, reel 33, LC, I, 41–42.

37. The transcript is found in ANHC, Caja 268, #25, esp. 28, and in Caja 277, 4–xi, 1848. See also: GGM to Rosa, January 16, 1849, BAEP, reel 33, LC, I, 59–61.

38. José García Moreno to RdA, January 3, 1849, BAEP, reel 33, LC, I, 51–52; and GGM to RdA, February 21, 1849, BAEP, reel 33, LC, I, 72–75.

39. GGM to Rosa, July 11, 1849, BAEP, reel 33, LC, I, 38–140; GGM to RdA, July 13, 1849, BAEP, reel 33, LC, I, 141; and Gomezjurado, *García Moreno*, I, 432–45.

40. GGM to Rosa, July 13, 1849, BAEP, reel 33, LC, I, 140–41; and GGM to RdA, December 29, 1849, BAEP, reel 33, LC, I, 147–50.

41. GGM to Rosa, March 12, 1850, BAEP, reel 33, LC, I, 166–68; GGM to RdA, March 12, 1850, LC, I, 168–69; and to Rosa, April 16, 1850, BAEP, reel 33, LC, I, 169–71.

42. GGM to RdA, May 14, 1850, LC, I, 173–80; and GGM to RdA, April 16, 1850, LC, I, 171–72.

43. GGM to Rosa, April 16, 1850, LC, I, 169–71; Gomezjurado, *García Moreno*, I, 494–98; and Loor, *Jesuitas*, 16–17.

44. Delpar, *Red Against Blue*. Many supported the recall: Benigno Malo to RdA, LC, I, 208–9; Pedro Moncayo to RdA, March 6, 1851, LC, I, 210; and Rafael Carvajal to RdA, July 26, 1851, LC, I, 211–12.

45. The text of *Defensa de los Jesuitas* is in Pólit, *Discursos*, I, 3–98.

46. GGM to RdA, February 4, 1852, LC, I, 217–19; GGM to RdA on February 18, 1852, LC, I, 221–22; and GGM to RdA, April 7, 1852, BAEP, reel 33, LC, I, 225–27.

47. GGM to and from his family, May 1852 in LC, I, 229–41; and Loor, *Jesuitas*, 117, 154–55.

48. GGM to RdA, June 30, 1852, LC, I, 245–50.

49. GGM correspondence with family, August 1852, BAEP, reel 33, LC, I, 259–62; and José García Moreno to GGM, November 17, 1852, BAEP, reel 33, LC, I, 293.

50. See family letters from September to December 8, 1852, BAEP, reel 33, and LC, I, 262–309.

51. GGM to RdA, October 6, 1852, BAEP, reel 33, LC, I, 275–80; Mercedes Moreno to GGM, October 13, 1852, LC, I, 281–82; and Loor, *Jesuitas*, 211–14. One of those Jesuits, Manuel José Proaño, persuaded him to dedicate the nation to the Sacred Heart of Jesus in 1873.

52. "Adiós a los Jesuitas," *Discursos*, I, 99–101.

53. José García Moreno to GGM, February 16, 1853, LC, I, 339–40; his letter of March 2, 1853, to GGM, LC, I, 344; and Manuel García Moreno (hereinafter Manuel) to GGM, LC, I, 340.

54. José García Moreno to GGM, January 26, 1853, LC, I, 343.

55. Pólit, *Discursos*, I, 191–206. Carlos Aguirre to GGM, February 12, 1853, LC, I, 344.

56. GGM to RdA, March 27, 1853, BAEP, reel 33, LC, I, 353–54, 348–49.

57. Walter Cope to Lord Earl of Clendenon, July 30, 1853, FO, Box 26, 48; Courtland Cushing to Philo White, October 30, 1853, RDS, reel 2; and Gomezjurado, *García Moreno*, II, 143–49.

58. Borrero, *Refutación*, 76–77, correctly points out that although García Moreno complained that Urbina rejected claims for legislative immunity, García Moreno would act similarly in the 1860s. Guillermo Franco to Miguel García Moreno (hereinafter Miguel), September 9, 1853, BC/JJC, Libro 00449, no #; and Francisco Robles to Miguel, September 16, 1853, BC/JJC, Libro 00449, no #.

59. GGM to Ascásubi sisters, June 29, 1854, BAEP, reel 33, LC, I, 472–73; GGM to RdA, January 12, 1854, BAEP, reel 33, LC, I, 439–40; and Murray, *For Glory.*

60. GGM to Ascásubi sisters, December 13, 1853, BAEP, reel 33, LC, I, 430–31; and GGM to RdA, February 15, 1854, LC, I, 451–55.

61. GGM to RdA, February 27, 1854, BAEP, reel 33, LC, I, 455–56.

62. GGM to RdA, June 15, 1855, LC, II, 23–24.

63. GGM to RdA, October 30, 1855, and November 14, 1855, LC, II, 32–33.

64. GGM to RdA, January 14, 1856, and April 15, 1856, LC, II, 35–36.

65. GGM to RdA, June 29, 1855, LC, II, 24; GGM to RdA, February 14, 1856, LC, II, 37–38; March 14, 1856, LC, II, 39–40; June 14, 1856, LC, II, 45–46; and August 14, 1856, LC, II, 48. GGM to RdA, September 15, 1856, LC, II, 50–51.

66. Berthe, *Vengador*, I, 222–30. See Rohrbacher, *Histoire Universale*; and Armijos Suárez, *Gabriel García Moreno,* 4–5, 10–11.

67. de Groot, *Brazilian Catholicism,* 82–83.

68. GGM to RdA, February 29, 1856, LC, II, 38–39; and GGM to RdA, June 14, 1856, and March 31, 1856, LC, II, 41, 45–46.

69. Williams, "Popular Liberalism," 697–730; O'Connor, *Gender, Indian, Nation;* Sattar, in Clark and Becker, *Indigenous Peoples;* and Van Aken, "Lingering Death."

70. GGM to Gobierno, February 7, 1857, LC, II, 54–55. In the García Moreno years, Education and Public Works reported to the Ministry of the Interior (Gobierno).

71. GGM to Gobierno, December 19, 1857, LC, II, 74; GGM to Gobierno, March 31, 1857, LC, II, 55–56, and his letter to Gobierno, May 2, 1857, LC, II, 58; Berthe, *Vengador*, I, 244; and GGM to William Jameson, January 13, 1858, LC, II, 75–78, and to Joaquín Tamaríz, May 6, 1857, LC, II, 58–59.

72. GGM to Gobierno, June 30, 1858, LC, II, 84–85. GGM's report as Rector, 1857–1858, in Pólit Laso, *Discursos*, II, 127–28.

73. GGM to RdA, September 17, 1857, BAEP, reel 34, LC, II, 69–71.

74. Manuel to GGM, May 6, 1857, LC, II, 61; and Gomezjurado, *García Moreno*, II, 363–66, 384–93. García Moreno's speeches on education are in Pólit Laso, *Discursos*, II, 56–70.

75. GGM to Rosa, August 19, 1857, BAEP, reel 34, LC, II, 67.

76. GGM to RdA, December 29, 1858, BAEP, reel 34, LC, II, 92, and to RdA, January 5, 1859, LC, II, 96–97; and Gomezjurado, *García Moreno,* II, 376–77.

77. GGM to RdA, January 29, 1854, BAEP, reel 33, LC, I, 444–47.

78. Manuel to GGM, May 6, 1857, LC, II, 61; and GGM to RdA, April 14, 1856, LC, II, 42–43.

79. GGM to Rosa, January 5, 1859, BAEP, reel 34, LC, II, 95–96; and GGM to RdA, January 26, 1859, BAEP, reel 34, LC, II, 100–1.

80. Ayala Mora, *Lucha política*, 167.

2. Regionalism and Civil War, 1859–1860

1. Carlos Aguirre to GGM, August 5, 1846, in LC, I, 4; and GGM to Joaquín Tamaríz, June 10, 1857, LC, II, 63–64, spoke of "your Cuenca."

2. Loor, *Victoria*, 64–65.

3. Karnes, *Failure of Union;* Pineo, *Life and Work*, 39; and Applebaum, *Race, Region*, 32–33.

4. Mörner, *Region and State*, 9–18; Véliz, *Centralist Tradition;* Anderson, *Imagined Communities;* and Castro-Klarén and Chasteen, *Beyond.*

5. Maiguashca, *Región.* Benigno Malo, an important figure in this story, completely ignored the Galápagos: See *Exposición*, 16–17.

6. Pineo, *Life and Work*; and Chiriboga, *Jornaleros.*

7. Saint-Geours, "Sierra centro y norte," in Maiguashca, *Región*, 158–59. Palomeque, *Cuenca.* Marxists would see the tension between the bourgeoisie coastal elite and the feudal highland landlords as the cause of the civil war of 1859: See Cordero Aguilar, in Ayala Mora (ed.), *Nueva Historia*, VII: 202–4.

8. Costales Samaniego and Costales Peñaherrera, *Macas.*

9. Darwin, *Beagle.*

10. Spruce, *Botanist;* and Bollaert, *Antiquarian Researches*, 101–4.

11. Philo White to William Marcy, March 12, 1856, RDS, T-50, reel 3.

12. Herz and Pontes Nogeira, *Ecuador vs. Peru*; Zook, Jr., *Zarumilla-Marañón;* and Denegri Luna, *Peru and Ecuador*, 155–70.

13. Juan Celestino Cavero to Antonio Mata, November 17, 1857, AMRE, Reservado, G3.1, 30.2, Vol. 93, 53–55; and his letter to Mata, March 8, 1858, AMRE, G3.1, 30.2, 93, 67–77.

14. Walter Cope to Earl of Malmesbury (hereinafter London), September 22, 1858, FO, 25/32, 118–23; October 3, 1858, FO 25/32, 138–41; and November 23, 1858, FO, 25/32, 142–45. The Ecuadorian correspondence is in AMRE, Comunicaciones, 40, G3.1, 30.1, 25, #152–57; and Arendaño, *Imagen*, 217–18. See Villacrés Moscoso, *Ambiciones internacionales*, 82–86; and Gruss, "Mission," 162–69.

15. Charles Buckalew to Lewis Cass, November 24, 1858, RDS, T-50, reel 5. García Moreno's impassioned speech of October 27, 1858, is in Pólit Laso, *Discursos*, II, 72–84. See Moncayo, *Ecuador*, 232–34; and BPL, Actas (1858).

16. Loor, *Victoria*, 29; and GGM to Rosa, January 12, 1859, LC, II, 97–99. The blockade is described in Arendaño, *Imagen*, 234–36.

17. GGM to RdA, February 23, 1859, LC, II, 107–8; and Benigno Malo to Antonio Mata, April 12, 1859, AMRE, C.35.5, 5, no #.

18. GGM to Antonio Borrero, January 14, 1859, LC, II, 99–100, and his letters to RdA, February 9 and 29, 1859, BAEP, reel 35, LC, II, 104–8; and GGM to Rosa, February 2, 1859, BAEP, reel 35, LC, II, 101–2.

19. GGM to Rosa, March 4, 1859, BAEP, reel 35, LC, II, 109–10; Pedro Pablo García Moreno (hereinafter Pedro Pablo) to Rosa, March 9, 1859, LC, II, 110–11; Gomezjurado, *García Moreno*, II, 442–43; and Vice-Consul Letelier to Relaciones, April 26, 1859, AMRE, Series F, 14, #50.

20. Loor, *Victoria*, 47–48; José María Borrero to Gobierno, April 13, 1859, ANHG, Chimborazo, 1859, #18; and Governor Manuel Tobar to Gobierno, April 24, 1859, ANHG, Pichincha, 1859, #73.

21. Gomezjurado, *García Moreno*, II, 442–47; Loor, *Victoria*, 50–51. Agramonte, *Psicopatológico*, 109–10; and Carrión, *Patíbulo*, 357–60.

22. Declaration of May 1, 1859, AMAE, 4, #317.

23. Lázaro E. de los Montes to Provisional Government, May 5, 1859, ANHG (León, now Cotopaxi), 1859; Manuel Sáenz to Provisional Government, May 5, 1859, ANHG, Imbabura, 1859; Manuel Tomás Maldonado to RdA, May 5, 1861, ANHG,

León, 1859; Andrés Villamús to Quai d'Orsay, May 10, 1859, AMAE, 4, #309–12; and Jerónimo Carrión to RdA, May 19, 1859, ANHG, Chimborazo, no #.

24. Valentín Espinosa to RdA, May 8, 1859, ANHG, Imbabura, 1859; RdA to Governor of León, May 11, 1859, and June 1, 1859, ANHG, Comunicaciones, León, #7 and #26; and RdA to Bernardo Dávalos (hereinafter Dávalos), May 8, 1859, ANHG, Comunicaciones, Chimborazo, #1, and BAEP, reel 25. See the proclamation of the triumvirate, Pacífico Chiriboga, Manuel Gómez de la Torre, and José María Avilés, May 5, 1859, AMAE, 4, #315.

25. Gomezjurado, *García Moreno*, II, 456–60; Berthe, *Vengador*, I, 289–90; and Dávalos to General in Chief at Guaranda, May 21, 1859, ANHG, Chimborazo, 1859, #42.

26. Dávalos to RdA, May 11, 1859, ANHG, Chimborazo, 1859, #12; RdA to the Governor of León, May 18 and 20, 1859, ANHG, León, Comunicaciones, #11 and #14.

27. General Antonio Franco to the commander of forces in Chimborazo, May 21, 1859, ANHG, Chimborazo, 1859, no #.

28. GGM to Rosa, June 2, 1859, LC, II, 123–24; GGM to War, June 2, 1859, LC, II, 124; Loor, *Victoria*, 57–58; Gomezjurado, *García Moreno*, II, 466–69; Dávalos to War, June 4, 1859, ANHG, Chimborazo, 1859, no #; Andrés Villamús to Quai d'Orsay, May 25, 1859, and June 16, 1859, AMAE, 4, #319–23; Destruge Illingworth, *Urvina*, 207–11; and Veintemilla, *Páginas*, 28, Guzmán Polanco, *Entretelones*, 11–13.

29. Pedro José Cevallos to RdA, June 8, 1859, BAEP, reel 25; Manuel Gómez de la Torre to Governor of Ibarra, June 26, 1859, BAEP, reel 25; and Aparicio Rivadeneira to Gobierno, July 4, 1859 and July 7, 1859, BAEP, reel 25. See also F. Valverde to the General of the Division (surrendering), June 24, 1859, BC/JJC, Caja 00464, no #.

30. Decree of Provisional Government, June 7, 1859, ANHG, Pichincha, no #; and Loor, *Victoria*, 61–64.

31. Proclamation of García Moreno, July 2, 1859, LC, II, 125–27; Moncayo, *Ecuador*, 243–44; unsigned to Benigno Malo, June 15, 1859, ANHG, Los Ríos, 1859, 16–V, 1859; and Avelino Rivadeneira to Gobierno, July 8, 1859, BAEP, reel 25.

32. Walter Cope to London, July 20, 1859, FO, 25/34, 48–50; Loor, *Victoria*, 71–72; Benigno Malo to Governor of Guayas, June 12, 1859, and July 2, 1859, AMRE, C.35.5, 5, #000124 and 000130; Emile Trinité to Quai d'Orsay, July 21, 1859, AMAE, 4, #326–29; and Avelino Rivadeneira to Hacienda (Treasury), July 28, 1859, ANHH, Imbabura, 1859, Box 331, #67.

33. Francisco Icaza to the Consul from New Granada, July 24, 1859, AMRE, C.35.5, 5, no #; Francisco Icaza to the Governor of Guayas, August 5, 1859, BC/JJC, Libro 00464, #75; Avelino Rivadeneira to Gobierno, August 25, 1859, BAEP, reel 25; Carlos Auz to Alcalde of Tulcán, August 5, 1859, BAEP, reel 25; and Rivadeneira to Governor of Guayas, August 11, 1859, AMRE, Series F, 14, 124–27.

34. Dávalos to RdA, September 8, 1859, ANHG, Chimborazo, 1859, no #; RdA to Governor of León, September 14, 1859, ANH, León, Comunicaciones, #5; Lorenzo Espinosa de los Monteros to Gobierno, August 21, 1859, BAEP, reel 35; and Cevallos Salvador, *Moncayo*, 211–14. See the service record of Manuel Yépez, AGMD, Carpeta 4.

35. GGM to Guillermo Franco, July 12, 1859, LC, II, 127–28; Loor, *Victoria*, 77–78;

and GGM to Rosa, August 24, 1859, LC, II, 128–29. The meeting is confirmed by Herrera, *García Moreno,* 11. See GGM to Dávalos, September 5, 1859, LC, II, 130–32; and GGM to Rosa, September 7, 1859, LC, II, 132.

36. A. Baquero Sr. (a pro-Robles civilian) to his son, Antonio Baquero, September 7, 1859, intercepted by Dávalos to RdA, September 12, 1859, ANHG, Chimborazo, 1859, #10; Trinité to Quai d'Orsay, September 28, 1859, AMAE, 4, #364; and Decree of October 8, 1859, ANHG, Pichincha, 2-V–1859, and García Moreno's proclamation, October 3, 1859, LC, II, 133–34.

37. P. Urquilla to Dávalos, September 16, 1859, ANHG, Chimborazo, 1859, #15; Ramón Borrero to RdA, October 3, 1859, ANHG, Azuay, 1859, #4; and RdA to Ignacio Mariátequi, September 19, 1859, BAEP, reel 25.

38. Ramón Borrero to RdA, September 28, 1859, ANHG, Azuay, 1859, #2; Manuel de Ascásubi and Francisco Carrión to RdA, September 26, 1859, ANHG, Azuay, 1859, no #; RdA to Governor Borrero, October 5 and 18, 1859, ANHG, Azuay, Gobernación de Cuenca, 1859, #2 and #12; and Williams, "Anti-landlord State," 707–10, 726.

39. Dávalos to RdA, September 27, 1859, ANHG, Chimborazo, 1859, #21.

40. Manuel Carrión Pinzano (hereinafter Carrión Pinzano) to the Provisional Government, October 2, 1859, ANHG, Loja, 1859, #6; Jaramillo Alvarado, *Loja,* 337–49; Carrión Pinzano to Guillermo Franco, September 21, 1859, AMRE, Series F, 14, 1859–1861, #165; and Eguiguren Valdivieso, *Crisis de 1858,* 79–82.

41. Berthe, *Vengador,* I, 306–11; Gomezjurado, *García Moreno,* III, 62–76; and GGM to RdA, November 11, 1859, LC, II, 142–43.

42. Loor, *Victoria,* 133–34; José León to RdA, November 16, 1859, ANHG, Chimborazo, 1859, #30; Francisco Iglesias to Gobierno, December 19, 1860, BAEP, reel 26; Angel Ubillús to Franco, January 21, 1860, ANHG, Esmeraldas, #1; and Juan José Franco to Gobierno, ANHG, Manabí, 1859, #55.

43. Perú, *Boletín,* #1 and #2, October 12, 1859, and October 27, 1859, in *Dos.*, Ramón Castilla to Provisional Government, October 9, 1859, AMRE, Series F, Vol. 1859–1861, no #.

44. Perú, *Boletín,* #3, November 13, 1859, *Dos.* Velarde, *Expedición de Castilla,* 12; Loor, *Victoria,* 127–29; and Villacrés Moscoso, *Historia diplomática,* III, 16–18.

45. José García Moreno to GGM, November 16, 1859, LC, II, 143–44, and also his letter of November 30, 1859, LC, II, 145–46; Castilla's decrees, November 12 and 23, 1859, BAEP, reel 25; José María Caamaño to RdA, November 16, 1859, AMRE, C. 35.5, Vol. 5, #000140–142; and Loor, *Victoria,* 133–44. The agreement signed by Franco, Caamaño, and Guillermo Bodero representing Cuenca is in BAEP, reel 25. See also AMRE, C.35.5, 5, #000143–144; and Castilla to RdA, November 30, 1859, AMRE, Series F, 14, no #.

46. RdA to Castilla, December 10, 1859, BAEP, reel 25; and GGM to Trinité, December 14, 1859, LC, II, 153.

47. Carrión Pinzano to RdA, December 27, 1859, and January 1, 1860, ANHG, Loja, no #; RdA to Governor of Cuenca, December 7, 1859, ANHG, Gobernación, Cuenca, #23; and Manuel Gómez de la Torre and José María Avilés to Guillermo Franco, January 3, 1860, BAEP, reel 25.

48. Unsigned letter (probably Guillermo Bodero) to RdA, January 6, 1860, ANHG, Guayas, 1860, no #; and José N. Canova to Washington, December 31, 1859, USDG, reel 3.

49. *Boletín*, January 28, 1860, #14, *Dos.*, translated in FO, 25/35, 45–59; and Cope to Russell, February 3, 1860, FO, 25/35, 40–41.

50. Antonio Gómez de la Torre to Governors of Provinces, February 14, 1860, ANHF, Caja 365, Libro 982, #55; José Nieto Maldonado to RdA, February 25, 1860, ANHG, Chimborazo, 1860, #13; Herrera, *Observaciones sobre el tratado*, 1–3; and GGM to Manuel Gómez de la Torre, José María Avilés, and Rafael Carvajal (hereinafter Carvajal), January 22, 1860, LC, II, 166–67.

51. Howe, "García Moreno's Efforts," *HAHR*, XVI, 257–62; Robertson, "Sueño," *Boletín de Historia*, 25, 67–80; Gómez de la Torre and Avilés, *Refutación del impreso*; and Amédée Fabre to Quai d'Orsay, February 1, 1862, AMAE, 5, #236-54.

52. GGM to Trinité, December 7, 1859, LC, II, 150–51, December 14, 1859, LC, II, 153, and December 21, 1859, LC, II, 155–57; and Friedrich Hassaurek to William Seward, August 28, 1861, RDS, T-50, reel 5. Gómez de la Torre and Avilés admitted they knew about the plan: See Tobar Donoso, *Urvina*, 23 and Herrera, *García Moreno*, 13.

53. Forwarded translations are in FO, 25/37, 125–29, FO, 25/37, 131–39, and FO, 25/37, 133–35. See Carrión, *Patíbulo*, 398–410; and Loor, *Victoria*, 163–68.

54. See service records of Pedro Jaramilla, AGMD, Carpeta 2; Francisco Javier Martínez, AGMD, Carpeta 3; José Illescas, AGMD, Carpeta 2; and Francisco Marchán, AGMD, Carpeta 3.

55. GGM to RdA, January 20, 1860, LC, II, 165–66; GGM to RdA, January 22, 1860, and January 26, 1860, LC, II, 166–67 and 168–69. See also Cope to London, February 29, 1860, FO, 25/35, 61–63; Maldonado to RdA, January 29, 1860, BAEP, reel 25; and Guzmán Polanco, *Entretelones*, 14–21.

56. Manuel Vega (hereinafter Vega) to RdA, November 23, 1859, BAEP, reel 25; General Raimundo Ríos to Guillermo Franco, February 8, 1860, BAEP, reel 25; and Ríos' letter of February 17, 1860, to Franco, BAEP, reel 25.

57. Manuel T. Maldonado (hereinafter Maldonado) to Fernando Ayarza, February 17, 1860, BAEP, reel 25, and his letter dated February 24, 1860, BAEP, reel 35; and Secundino Darquea to GGM, March 3, 1860, LC, II, 190. See also Maldonado to GGM, March 2, 1860, and March 6, 1860, BAEP, reel 35; and Albornoz, *Paute*, 49–57, *El Nacional*, March 16, 1860.

58. Secundino Darquea to GGM, March 3, 1860, LC, II, 190; and Ramón Borrero to GGM, March 3, 1860, BAEP, reel 35.

59. Carrión Pinzano to RdA, March 9 and March 17, 1860, ANHG, Loja, 1860, no #s; GGM to Gobierno, Loja, March 18, 1860, LC, II, 193–94; Gomezjurado, *García Moreno*, III, 130; Carrión Pinzano to RdA (protesting the troops in Santa Rosa), March 13, 1860, BAEP, reel 25. LC, II, 195; Eguiguren Valdivieso, *Crisis de 1858*, 113–14; and Carrión Pinzano to GGM, March 24, 1860, ANHG, Loja, 1860, no #.

60. José Vicente Maldonado to GGM, April 14, 1860, BAEP, reel 35; Ramón Borrero to GGM, April 18, 1860, BAEP, reel 35; Agramonte, *Psicopatológico*, 141–42; Carrión, *Patíbulo*, 373, 380–82; and Loor, *Victoria*, 259–61, 276–78.

61. Affidavit of José Salvador and Nicolás Espinosa, April 17, 1860, ANHG, Pichincha, 1850, no #; Manuel Gómez de la Torre to Maldonado, May 2, 1860, LC, III, 413–14; Carrión, *Patíbulo*, 429–31; Gálvez, *Vida*, 169–70; Loor, *Victoria*, 283–85; and Avelino Ribadeneira to GGM, April 28, 1860, LC, II, 204.

62. Secundino Darquea to GGM, April 24, 1860, LC, II, 203; Maldonado to GGM, LC, II, 205–6. See also: García Moreno's responses to Maldonado, April 25, 1860, and May 2, 1860, LC, III, 413–14.

63. Dávalos to RdA, January 10, 1860, BAEP, reel 25; GGM to Dávalos, December 10, 1859, LC, II, 151; and GGM to Rosa, November 8, 1859, LC, II, 141.

64. GGM to JJF, May 16, 1860, LC, II, 212–13; Luciano Solano de la Sala to GGM, May 20, 1860, LC, II, 214; Dávalos to RdA, May 26, 1860, ANHG, Chimborazo, 1860, #44; and José Antonio Eguiguren to Flores, June 2, 1860, BC/JJC, Libro 00153, #62.

65. José Nieto Maldonado to RdA, March 18 and 24, 1860, AHNG, Chimborazo, 1860, #26, no #; Daniel Salvador to JJF, July 3, 1860, BC/JJC, Libro 00153, #174; Mariano Cueva to RdA, August 15, 1860, ANHG, Azuay, 1860, #89; and Miguel Heredia to GGM, August 19, 1860, BAEP, reel 26.

66. GGM to JJF, May 26, 1860, LC, II, 217; JJF to Tomás Cipriano de Mosquera (hereinafter Mosquera), June 18, 1860, BL/JJC, Libro 00153, #84; Lorenzo Solano de la Sala to RdA, July 21, 1860, ANHG, Imbabura, 1860, #63; and JJF to Mosquera, May 21, 1860, AF, #00810.

67. GGM to JJF, June 1, 1860, LC, II, 218–19 and BC/JJC, Libro 00153, #34. See also: GGM to RdA, June 13, 1860, LC, II, 220.

68. Berthe, *Vengador*, I, 303–4; José Nieto Maldonado to Hacienda, March 17, 1860, ANHG, Chimborazo, 1860, #28; RdA to the Governor, December 14, 1859, BAEP, reel 25; Loor, *Victoria*, 369–70; and GGM to JJF, July 13, 1860, LC, II, 225–27.

69. Raymundo Ríos to Guillermo Franco, February 17, 1860, ANHG, Guayas, 1860, no #; and Loor, *Victoria*, 350–51.

70. RdA to the Governors, February 27, 1860, ANHF, Caja 365, Libro 982, #109; Ramón Borrero to RdA, November 4, 1859, ANHG, Azuay, 1859, #16; And GGM's "tax" decrees, March 5, 1860, AHNF, Caja 366, Libro 983, #10, and July 1, 1860, ANHG, Pichincha, 1860, #38. List of contributors, n.d., BC/JJC, Libro 01453, #3: Pichincha contributed 202,000, Azuay 180,000, Chimborazo 50,000, Tungurahua 30,000, Los Ríos 30,000, Imbabura 28,000, Loja 15,000, and León 10,000 pesos.

71. Dávalos to Hacienda, December 24, 1859, ANHH, Pichincha, Libro 170/509, #30; and Antonio Yerovi to the Governor of Pichincha, December 4, 1859, ANHF, Caja 365, Libro 979, #15.

72. GGM to JJF, July 17 and 30, 1860, LC, II, 230–31, 241.

73. Francis Mocatta to Lord John Russell, September 14, 1860, FO, 25/35, 194–96. The British and French referred to this battle as Bodegas, the old name for Babahoyo. See Carlos Sanquírico (the Spanish minister) to Quai d'Orsay, August 22, 1860, AMAE, 5, #28–29; Guzmán Polanco, *Entretelones*, 19; César Guades, AGMD, Carpeta 2; and Julián Palacios, AGMD, Carpeta 3.

74. GGM to Rosa, August 1, 1860, LC, II, 243; and GGM to RdA, August 6, 1860, LC, II, 244.

75. GGM to Guerra (War Department), August 11, 1860, LC, II, 246–47, and his letter of August 15, 1860, to RdA, LC, II, 247–48; Julián Moreno to JJF, August 17, 1860, BC/JJC, 007452; and Antonio Flores (hereinafter Antonio), diary, I, entry of October 13, 1860, AF.

76. Decree of Guillermo Franco, September 5, 1860, BAEP, reel 26; José N. Cano-

va to Washington, August 28, 1860, USDG, reel 3; Loor, *Victoria*, 334–43; and GGM to Rosa, August 23, 1860, LC, II, 250–251, his letter to RdA, August 30, 1860, LC, II, 253–55, and his letter to Rosa, September 6, 1860, LC, II, 256–57.

77. Carlos de Sanquírico to Quai d'Orsay, July 20, 1860, AMAE, V, #26.

78. RdA to Bishop José María Riofrío, January 12, 1860, AARZO, Caja 55, File G-E, and Riofrío's reply, January 13, 1860, BAEP, reel 25; and RdA to Riofrío, February 9, 1860, AARZO, Caja 55, File G-E, and his letter of March 31 to the Bishop, same source.

79. The campaign is described in Army Bulletin #60, "Toma de Guayaquil," in RDS, T-50, reel 5; Julio Castro's account, LC, II, 263–69; Loor, *Victoria*, 387–98; García Moreno's account to RdA, September 24, 1860, BAEP, reel 24; and General Antonio Martínez Pallares to RdA, September 26, 1860, and October 3, 1860, BAEP, reel 26.

80. The decree is in BC/JJC, Libro 01521, #1, September 26, 1860, translated in RDS, T-50, reel 5; and RdA to the Governor of Pichincha, October 15 and October 17, 1860, ANHF, Caja 367, Libro 990, #44 and #48.

81. Mariano Cueva to RdA, October 24, 1860, ANHG, Azuay, 1860, #135; and GGM to RdA, December 5, 1860, LC, II, 312, and his letter to JJF, December 22, 1860, LC, II, 325–27.

82. GGM to Mariano Cueva, November 24, 1860, LC, II, 306, and his letter to JJF, December 22, 1860, LC, II, 325–27.

83. GGM to JJF, October 5, 1860, BC/JJC, Libro 00154, #13, #18. LC, II, 282. See also GGM to JJF, October 4, 1860, BC/JJC, Libro 00155, #6 and #13.

84. Juan Montalvo to GGM, September 26, 1860, LC, II, 271–75; Gálvez, *Vida*, 176; and Lynch, *Argentine Dictator*.

85. Proclamation of the Provisional Government, October 27, 1860, ANHF, Caja 367, Libro 990, #86; GGM to JJF, December 15, 1860, LC, II, 320; *El Nacional*, September 2, 1861; GGM to RdA, December 15, 1860, LC, II, 319–20; and García Moreno's decree, undated, BAEP, reel 26.

86. Agramonte, *Psicopatológico*, 116; Carrión, *Patíbulo, passim;* Gálvez, *Vida*, 179; GGM to RdA, August 30, 1860, LC, II, 253–55; Luciano Solano de la Sala to JJF, November 16, 1860, BC/JJC, Libro 00155, #146; and GGM to Rosa, November 28, 1860, LC, II, 308.

87. GGM to Pedro Carbo, October 6, 1860, LC, II, 283–84; GGM to RdA, August 30, 1860, LC, II, 253–55; Muñoz, *Geopolítica*, 24–25; and Albornoz, *Paute*, 74–75.

88. GGM to Pedro Carbo, October 6, 1860, LC, II, 283–84; Maiguashca, "Electoral Reforms of 1861," 101–2; and Decree of October 26, 1860, in ANHG, Pichincha, 1859, Decretos. The breakdown of the provincial seats were: Imbabura 4, Pichincha 6, León 3, Tungurahua (another newly created province) 3, Chimborazo 4, Los Ríos 3, Guayaquil 5, Manabí 2, Cuenca 6, Loja 3, and Esmeraldas 1. See Quintero and Silva, *Nación*, I, 100, 123–24; Joseph La Pierre to Quai d'Orsay, October 4, 1860, AMAE, 5; and the Informe (León), December 16, 1860, BAEP, reel 26, and the Informe (Loja), December 15, 1860, BAEP, reel 26.

89. Herrera, *García Moreno*, 22–24; GGM to Antonio Borrero, November 24, 1860, LC, II, 304–5, and his letter to Mariano Cueva on the same day, LC, II, 306. JJF to GGM, January 12, 1861, BAEP, reel 35, tries to smooth over the quarrel. Malo, *Recuerdos*, 2–5, and his *Escritos*, I, 142–43 both note his discontent with the new system. See GGM to Mariano Cueva, December 22, 1860, LC, 328.

90. Pablo Herrera to the Governor of Pichincha, November 6, 1860, ANHF, Caja 367, Libro 991, #12; and his letter to the governors, November 13, 1860, same source, #23.

91. Luciano Solano de la Sala to JJF, November 17, 1860, BC/JJC, Libro 00154, #228; Francisco Javier Piedrahita to JJF, November 21, 1860, BC/JJC, Libro 00154, #258; and GGM to Agustín Barreiro, December 12, 1860, LC, II, 318.

92. Antonio Borrero to RdA, May 9, 1860, ANHG, Azuay, 1860, #51; and Mocatta to London, June 14, 1860, FO, 25/35, 74–76.

93. Benjamín Pereira to RdA, December 15, 1860, ANHG, Loja, 1860, no #; and GGM to Pedro Carbo, October 6, 1860, LC, II, 283–84, and December 8, 1860, to Antonio Borrero, LC, II, 314–15.

94. Joseph La Pierre to Quai d'Orsay, December 18, 1860, AMAE, 5, #33.

3. A PRESIDENCY CONSTRAINED I: FEDERALISM AND DOMESTIC POLICY, 1861–1865

1. Anderson, *Imagined Communities*; Castro-Klarén and Chasteen, *Beyond*—especially Chambers, "Letters and Salons," 57; and Ayala Mora, *Nueva Historia*, VIII, 24–32.

2. Peloso and Tenenbaum, *Liberals and State Formation*, provides a good overview, 1–29. The classic: Jane, *Liberty and Despotism*, passim.

3. Bushnell and Macauley, *Nineteenth Century*.

4. Burns, *Poverty of Progress*; and Stein and Stein, *Colonial Heritage*.

5. Mecham, *Church and State;* Pike, *Andean Republics;* and Thurner, *From Two Republics*.

6. Nicolás Tovar to Hacienda, December 1, 1866, BCH, Caja 15-3-1.

7. Rodríguez, *Public Policy*.

8. GGM to Mariano Cueva, December 22, 1860, in LC, II, 328.

9. GGM to JJF, January 2, 1861, LC, II, 331–33; GGM to RdA, January 17, 1861, LC, II, 341, BAEP, reel 34; and GGM to JJF, January 17, 1861, LC, II, 348–49.

10. Spindler, *Nineteenth Century Ecuador*, 57–59, errs regarding the constitution. See Borja y Borja, *Constituciones*, cxix, 293–326; Maiguashca, "Electoral Reforms of 1861"; and Williams, "Negotiating the State."

11. GGM to JJF, January 5, 1861, LC, II, 336–38; GGM to JJF, January 2, 1861, BC/JJC, Libro 00157, #7; and La Pierre to Minister of Foreign Affairs, January 15, 1861, AMAE, 5, #35–36.

12. GGM to JJF, January 5, 1861, BC/JJC, Libro 00157, #24; and José Eguiguren to Gobierno, January 29, 1861, ANHG, Loja, 1861, #5. Much to García Moreno's dismay, some *Lojanos* were still using the term "Republic of Loja" late in 1861: See GGM to Daniel Salvador, October 1, 1861, LC, II, 448.

13. García Moreno's decree BC/JJC, Libro 01459, #5; GGM to JJF, February 6, 1861, BC/JJC, Libro 00157, #220; and JJF to GGM, January 16, 1861, BAEP, reel 35.

14. Miguel Heredia to JJF, January 16, 1861, BC/JJC, Libro 00157, #80; and José María Vázquez to JJF, BC/JJC, Libro 01461, #5.

15. GGM to Antonio Borrero, February 23, 1861, LC, II, 374–75; GGM to Felipe Sarrade, February 15, 1861, LC, II, 370, BAEP, reel 34; and Ayala Mora, *Nueva Historia,* VII, 88–89.

16. GGM to JJF, February 20, 1861, LC, II, 372–73; or BC/JJC, Libro 00157, #301.

17. Pablo Herrera and Julián Castro to GGM, February 27, 1861, ANHG, Pichincha, no #. Most of the convention's decrees are in this source. The debates are in *Diario de la convención.* See GGM to JJF, February 27, 1861, LC, II, 377–78.

18. Sanders, *Contentious Republicans.* The municipal law statute is in *Colección de Leyes,* 45–57.

19. Pablo Herrera and Julián Castro to Governor of Pichincha, March 10, 1861, ANHF, Caja 368, Libro 996, #24. See Charles Buckalew to Seward, April 10, 1861, RDS, T-50, reel 5; and GGM to Antonio Borrero, April 10, 1861, "Borrero Cartas," 156.

20. GGM to Head of Jesuits in Rome, February 13, 1861, LC, II, 369–70, BAEP, reel 34; Decree of April 8, 1861, ANHG, Pichincha, 1861, #15; Julián Castro's note, April 22, 1861, same source, no #; Decree of the Constitutional Convention, June 4, 1861, n.d., ANHG, Pichincha, 1861, #40; and Decree of GGM, ANHG, Caja 90, File 9, 2.

21. Hassaurek, *Four Years;* and Theodore de Sabla to Hassaurek, June 24, 1863, FHP, Box 3, Folder 4.

22. Decree of the Convention, May 1, 1861, ANHG, Pichincha, 1861, no #; Carvajal to Gobierno, July 2, 1861, BAEP, reel 26; Mariano Cueva to Gobierno, July 2, 1861, BAEP, reel 26; GGM to Carlos Ordóñez (hereinafter Ordóñez), August 21, 1861, LC, II, 432; and Gomezjurado, *García Moreno,* III, 351–52.

23. GGM to Antonio Borrero, September 21, 1861, "Borrero Cartas," 159–60.

24. Moreuil to Quai d'Orsay, October 7, 1864, AMAE, VI, #253.

25. Mecham, *Church and State,* 142; and Crow, *Epic,* 624–31.

26. GGM to JJF, January 12, 1861, LC, II, 341–42; GGM to Antonio Borrero, January 12, 1861, LC, II, 343–44; GGM to Antonio Borrero, June 19, 1861, LC, II, 408–9; GGM to Ignacio Ordóñez, April 10, 1862, LC, III, 59–60; and Benigno Malo to JJF, n.d., BC/JJC, Libro 00156, #91.

27. GGM to Nicolás Martínez, March 8, 1862, LC, III, 45; José María Yerovi to Gobierno, May 25, 1853, BAEP, reel 25; Armijos Suárez, *Gabriel García Moreno,* 8, 15; and Tepaske (ed.), Juan and Ulloa, *Discourse,* 280–316.

28. GGM to JJF, August 29, 1863, LC, III, 152–53; Hassaurek, *Four Years,* 173–74; Report of Provincial Enrique Neira, July 14, 1863, BAEP, reel 27; GGM to Ignacio Ordóñez, April 10, 1862, LC, III, 59–60; Bruno Estupiñán to Gobierno, December 6, 1864, BAEP, reel 27; Pablo Bustamante (hereinafter Bustamante) to Gobierno, September 5, 1863, BAEP, reel 27; Vicente Espinosa to Riofrío, November 21, 1863, AARZO, Caja 61, G-E; S.M. Maldonado to Gobierno, June 12, 1863, BAEP, reel 27; and Carvajal to Riofrío, July 17, 1862, AARZO, Caja 56.

29. Pedro Cruz to Governor of León, January 26, 1861, BAEP, reel 26; Carvajal to Riofrío, November 23, 1861, AARZO, Caja 56; and J. F. Noriera to Governor of the Province, January 20, 1864, BAEP, reel 27.

30. De Groot, *Brazilian Catholicism;* and Klaiber, *Church in Peru,* 105.

31. Riofrío to Gobierno, December 18, 1862, BAEP, reel 27, and his letter of January 14, 1863, BAEP, reel 27; José Checa to GGM, April 26, 1862, BAEP, reel 26; two

papal decrees, September 25, 1861, BAEP, reel 26; Carvajal to the Vicar General, March 17, 1864, AARZO, Caja 56 GE; Carvajal to Riofrío, March 29, 1862, AARZO, Caja 56; and José María Espinosa to Gobierno, February 8, 1862, BAEP, reel 26.

32. King, "Ecuadorian Church"; Bustos-Videla, "Church and State"; Demélas and Saint-Geours, *Jerusalén,* 129–202; Coppa, *Pius IX,* 115–16; and Julián Aureliano Alvarez to Gobierno, March 2, 1861, ANHG, Azuay, no #.

33. Carvajal's instructions to Ignacio Ordóñez, n.d., AMRE, Instruciones, C. 39.1., 1 (1839–1867); Ignacio Ordóñez to Relaciones, January 11, 1862, AMRE, C. 39.1., #000319; and King, "Ecuadorian Church," 120–21.

34. Berthe, *Vengador,* 375–90; King, "Ecuadorian Church," 120–58 and 263–329. See also Ignacio Ordóñez to Antonio, September 6, 1862, BC/JJC, Libro 01532, #15, and Carvajal to Antonio, July 9, 1862, same source, #4; and GGM to JJF, June 21, 1862, LC, III, 83.

35. A translation in English dated April 17, 1863, is in FO, 25/42, 108–27; Hassaurek to Seward, April 20, 1863, RDS, T-50, reel 6; Fabre to Quai d'Orsay, November 4, 1862, AMAE, 5, #411; and Ignacio Ordóñez to Relaciones, October 14, 1862, AMRE, C. 39. 1, #000321-322.

36. King, "Ecuadorian Church," 47, 122–65.

37. Letter from the Cantonal Civic Body of Guayaquil, May 14, 1863, FO, 25/42, 93–103. Pedro Carbo was recommended for a job as a minor prebendary in the Guayaquil cathedral, so he was not anticlerical: See Bishop José Tomás to Gobierno, September 30, 1863, BAEP, reel 27. See also Pattee, *Tiempo,* 282–87; Carbo, *Obras,* 21–28; Luciano Solano de la Sala to Gobierno, May 2, 1863, ANHG, Imbabura, 1863, #40; Nicolás Martínez (hereinafter Martínez) to Gobierno, April 29, 1863, ANHG, Tungurahua, #14; and Fabre to Quai d'Orsay, May 9, 1863, AMAE, 6, #26.

38. José Tomás, Bishop of Guayaquil, to Apostolic Delegate Francisco Tavani, November 17, 1863, VSA, reel 4. See also Antonio Martínez Pallares to JJF, August 22, 1863, BC/JJC, Libro 00167, #82; Daniel Salvador to Flores, August 22, 1863, BC/JJC, Libro 000167, #80; and GGM to Pedro Pablo, May 30, 1863, Villalba, *Epistolario,* xlix–l.

39. GGM to Antonio Borrero, August 5, 1863, LC, III, 148; State of the Union message, August 10, 1863, FO, 25/42, 141–53; and Hassaurek to Seward, August 19, 1863, RDS, T-50, reel 6. For Gómez de la Torre's role, see Tobar Donoso, "Concordato," in *Monografías,* 288–89.

40. Hassaurek to Seward, September 9, 1863, RDS, T-50, reel 6. García Moreno's willingness to accept reforms "because public opinion has pronounced in a loud and clear voice" is mentioned in BPL (1863), *Actas,* 1, 17–25. See also Antonio Martínez Pallares to JJF, August 22, 1863, BC/JJC, Libro 000167, #82; and *Congreso constitucional de 1863,* 131–35.

41. BPL (1863), 1, 152–55. See also Senate Resolution, September 26, 1863, BAEP, reel 27; GGM to Antonio, February 10, 1864, in Pólit Laso (ed.), *Doce Cartas,* #9, 21–22, or LC, III, 200; and *El Nacional,* February 8, 1864, and April 20, 1864. Excerpts from Antonio's diary are reproduced in Villalba, *Epistolario,* 67–83. See Diary of Antonio, AF, 2. GGM to Francisco J. Hernáez, January 14, 1865, LC, III, 279.

42. Diary of Antonio, AF, II; Antonio to Quai d'Orsay, October 25, 1864, AMRE, C. 39. 1, 1 (1839–1867), #000331-351; and Pablo Herrera to Antonio, December 7, 1864, AMRE, Comunicaciones, 42, 52–66. García Moreno's instructions to Antonio stated that if the pope refused to change the Concordat, it must stand as written.

43. GGM to Antonio, February 22, 1865, LC, III, 286, BAEP, reel 34; King, "Ecuadorian Church," 381; Antonio to Relaciones, October 25, 1864, and November 12, 1864, AMRE, C. 39. 1, #000348-349, and 000360-362. García Moreno's successor briefly suspended the Concordat to pressure for the modifications. See Bishop Ignacio Ordóñez to Apostolic Delegate, December 23, 1865, VSA, Reel 2.

44. GGM to Antonio, February 22, 1865, LC, III, 286, BAEP, reel 34; and Antonio to the pope, November 3, 1864, AMRE, C. 39.1, #000350-357.

45. GGM to JJF, March 12, 1862, LC, III, 46–47; Manuel Eguiguren (hereinafter Eguiguren) to Gobierno, March 24, 1862, ANHG, Loja, 1862, #26; Luciano Solano de la Sala to Gobierno, March 15, 1862, ANHG, Imbabura, 1862, #31; and Dávalos to Gobierno, March 1865, ANHG, Chimborazo, 1865, #65.

46. GGM to JJF, May 31, 1862, LC, III, 80, and his letter to Vicente Piedrahita (hereinafter Piedrahita), January 31, 1863, LC, III, 125–26.

47. Archbishop of Quito to Governor of Chimborazo, July 7, 1865, AARZO, Caja 55 G-E; Ignacio Ordóñez to Riofrío, October 8, 1865, AARZO, Caja 57 G-E; and Ignacio Ordóñez to Antonio, May 20, 1864, AF, #01014.

48. Eguiguren to Gobierno, June 1, 1865, ANHG, Loja, 1865, #34; Eguiguren to Gobierno, May 30, 1863, BAEP, reel 27; Bishop Remigio to Gobierno, June 19, 1863, ANHG, Azuay, 1863, no #; Ignacio Ordóñez to Antonio, December 30, 1862, BC/JJC, Libro 01532, #38; and Agreement of Commission, April 3, 1865, ANHG, Pichincha, 1865, no #.

49. Manuel to Gobierno, February 8, 1865, ANHG, Guayas, 1865, #15; Eguiguren to Gobierno, August 8, 1863, ANHG, Loja, 1863, #82; and Manuel Orejuelas to the Governor of Pichincha, September 27, 1864, ANHG, Pichincha, 1864, no #.

50. Bruno Estupiñán to Gobierno, June 9, 1861, ANHG, Esmeraldas, 1861, #25; Riofrío to Gobierno, May 17, 1862, BAEP, reel 26; Borrero, *Refutación*, 633; and Hassaurek, *Four Years*, 85–87, 188–89.

51. Bruno Estupiñán to Gobierno, April 16, 1862, AHNG, Esmeraldas, #29; and Luis Pólit, Informe of the Governor, July 11, 1865, same source, no #.

52. Rafael N. Vázquez, Informe of Inspector of Education for León, December 31, 1860, BAEP, reel 26; and Francisco J. Salazar to Gobierno, October 14, 1864, ANHG, Manabí, no #.

53. Tobar Donoso, *Instrucción pública*, 114–28; BPL, *Actas* (1863), I, 144–52; and *Lei orgánica de instrucción pública.*

54. GGM to Antonio, February 19, 1862, LC, III, 37–38, BAEP, reel 34; Vega to Gobierno, December 26, 1862, ANHG, Azuay, 1862, #14; and Tobar Donoso, *Instrucción pública*, 140, 171. For a copy of the Christian Brothers contract, see Frére Philippe to GGM, no date (but 1863), BAEP, reel 27.

55. Benigno Malo to Gobierno, July 13, 1864, ANHG, Azuay, 1864, #7. Benjamín Chiriboga to Gobierno, November 4, 1865, ANHG, Chimborazo, 1865, #96; Francisco J. Salazar to Gobierno, April 20, 1864, ANHG, Manabí, no #; and Malo, *Escritos*, I, 465–73.

56. Hassaurek, *Four Years*, 122; and Petition from Parents and Inhabitants of Parish of Atuntaqui to Gobierno, May 10, 1862, ANHG, Imbabura, 1862, #47.

57. Benigno Malo to Gobierno, July 13, 1864, AHNG, Azuay, #7; Luis Malo to Gobierno, December 7, 1864, ANHG, Azuay, 1864, #391; and Contract with Sisters of the Sacred Heart, February 25, 1865, BAEP, reel 27.

58. Piedrahita to Gobierno, February 9, 1864, ANHG, Guayas, 14; and Hassaurek, *Four Years*, 92.

59. GGM to Hernáez, S.J., January 24, 1861, LC, II, 355–57; GGM to Piedrahita, March 25, 1862, Villalba, *Epistolario*, xlii–xliii; Piedrahita to Gobierno, March 28, 1863, ANHG, Guayas, 1863, #42; and Jouanen, *Historia*, 108–9. The Jesuit agreement is dated July 28, 1863, FO, 25/44, 244–49.

60. Hassaurek, *Four Years*, 118–21; and Sowell, *Miguel Perdomo Neira*.

61. Juan Antonio Gómez to Secretary of Gobierno, March 22, 1862, ANHG, Guayas, 1862, #61; and José Tomás de Aguirre, Bishop of Guayaquil to Gobierno, July 2, 1862, BAEP, reel 26. García Moreno donated. *El Nacional*, August 17, 1864.

62. Bromley and Bromley, "Sunday Markets," 85–108; and Williams, "'Empire of Morality'," 149–74.

63. Decree of Vice President Mariano Cueva, n.d., ANHG, Pichincha, 1861, no #; and Hassaurek to Seward, February 18, 1864, RDS, T-50, reel 6. The term "pueblo católico," which historian Derek Williams uses to describe the morality project, appears in García Moreno's address to congress in 1864: See Pólit Laso, *Discursos*, II, 273–81; and De Groot, *Brazilian Catholicism*, 12, 44.

64. For example, statutes allowed the export of *paja toquilla*, the straw from which Panama hats were woven. *Cascarilla* seeds, however, were protected. See *El Nacional*, May 7, 1861.

65. Rodríguez, *Public Policy*, 184, 216; GGM to RdA, January 30, 1861, LC, II, 358–59, BAEP, reel 34; and Vicente Márquez to Hacienda, April 26, 1861 AHNH, Manabí, #3. See also *Informe, Hacienda*, 1863.

66. Rodríguez, *Public Policy*, 59–72; Vicente Espinosa to Hacienda, August 19, 1865, ANHH, Chimborazo, #200; JJF to Hacienda, November 8, 1863, ANHH, Los Ríos, Caja 416, #303; and Vicente Espinosa to Hacienda, November 8, 1862, ANHH, Chimborazo, #243.

67. Ackerman, "Trabajo Subsidiario," 155–67.

68. GGM to JJF, January 11, 1862, LC, III, 20–21. See also GGM to Agustín Barreiro, May 31, 1862, LC, III, 80; GGM to Martínez, January 12, 1862, LC, III, 22, BAEP, reel 34; Martínez to Gobierno, March 15, 1867, ANHG, Tunguragua, 1866, #10; Eguiguren to Hacienda, November 3, 1862, ANHH, Loja, Caja 388, #202; and Ackerman, "Trabajo Subsidiario," 49, 155–57.

69. Rodríguez, *Public Policy*, 53–87, 187, 210.

70. GGM to JJF, May 4, 1861, LC, II, 400–1, and GGM to JJF, January 1, 1862, LC, III, 17; and *El Nacional*, April 20, 1861.

71. GGM to JJF, May 2, 1863, BC/JJC, Libro 00165, #191; Secundino Darquea to JJF, May 20, 1863, BC/JJC, Libro 00165, #194; Hassaurek to Seward, May 23, 1863, RDS, T-50, reel 6; and Martínez to Hacienda, April 21, 1861, ANHH, Tungurahua, Caja 541, #51.

72. GGM to Antonio, April 10, 1862, LC, III, 60–61, BAEP, reel 34; Antonio to JJF, July 1, 1862, BC/JJC, Libro 01532, #1; and Antonio to Hacienda, December 15, 1862, BC/JJC, Libro 01529, #30.

73. Fagan to Russell, January 10, 1863, FO, 25/42, 49–51; GGM to Pedro Pablo, May 20, 1863, Villalba, *Epistolario*, xlvii–xlviii; and Piedrahita to Hacienda, March 14, 1863, ANHH, Guayas, Caja 206, #121.

74. Van Aken, *King;* Hassaurek, *Four Years,* 63, 108; GGM to Martínez, January 18, 1861, LC, II, 349–50; GGM to Martínez, December 14, 1861, LC, II, 487, BAEP, reel 34; and *El Nacional,* October 21, 1862.

75. Vicente Espinosa to Gobierno, March 8, 1862, BCH, 476-9-11-11; and Felipe Sarrade to Gobierno, September 18, 1865, BCH, 515-13-10-2.

76. Demélas and Saint-Geours, *Jerusalén,* 170–71, 182–83; Ayala Mora, *Nueva Historia,* VIII, 14–15; Agustín Barreiro to Gobierno, February 2, 1861, ANHG, Los Ríos, 1861, no #; and Gomezjurado, *García Moreno,* III, 466–68.

77. Felipe Barriga to Governor of Pichincha, June 3, 1862, BCH, Caja 9-14-3; Carlos Pólit to Governor of Pichincha, June 3, 1862, BCH, Caja 9-14-2; and Martínez to Gobierno, January 15, 1867, ANHG, Tungurahua, #9.

78. GGM to Antonio, February 19, 1862, *Doce Cartas,* #5, 15–16.

79. Gomezjurado, *García Moreno,* III, 382–83; GGM to Martínez, October 25, 1864, LC, III, 253–54, BAEP, reel 34; Lara, *Quito,* 207–13; RdA to Governor of Pichincha, July 5, 1860, ANHF, Caja 366, Libro 987, #13; and GGM to Antonio, July 20, 1864, Villalba, *Epistolario,* cxxxvii–cxxxviii. A complete list of García Moreno's public works projects for the first term is in Rolando, *Obras públicas,* 24–27.

80. Juan Antonio Gómez to Gobierno, February 5, 1862, ANHG, Guayas, 1862, #30; J. A. Gómez to Gobierno, June 8, 1861, ANHG, Guayas, 1861, #39; and Juan Antonio Gómez to Gobierno, March 1, 1862, ANHG, Guayas, 1862, #41.

81. Guayaquil City Council Decree, April 11, 1862, same source, no #; Miguel García Moreno to JJF, August 22, 1863, BC/JJC, Libro 001476, #15; and Piedrahita to Gobierno, December 10, 1862, AHNG, Guayas, #265.

82. Miguel Egas to Secretary of Gobierno, August 6, 1861, ANHG, Pichincha, 1861, #240; Safford, *Ideal;* and Benjamín Ayara to Gobierno, January 24, 1863, ANHG, Pichincha, 1863, no #.

83. GGM to Antonio, June 22, 1861, *Doce Cartas,* 1, 9–11; Larrea, *Antonio,* 28–30.

84. Luis Cadena to GGM, March 31, 1862, ANHG, Pichincha, 1862, no #; his letter of April 7, 1862, to GGM, same source, no #; and his letter to GGM, August 23, 1862, BAEP, reel 26.

85. GGM to Vega, February 24, 1864, LC, III, 202, BAEP, reel 34; and GGM to JJF, May 25, 1864, LC, III, 218. See Borja y Borja, *Constituciones,* 273. The French minister noted fraud in Guayas, Moreuil to Quai d'Orsay, January 10, 1865, AMAE, 7, #4.

86. GGM to Antonio Borrero, March 16, 1864, LC, III, 204–5; and GGM to Borrero, April 23, 1864, LC, III, 211–12. García Moreno and Flores agreed on Caamaño, GGM to JJF, April 9, 1864, BC/JJC, Libro 000171, #53.

87. GGM to Felipe Sarrade, November 26, 1864, LC, III, 263.

88. GGM to Martínez, December 4, 1864, LC, III, 267–68, and his letter to Martínez, February 1, 1865, LC, III, 282, BAEP, reel 34; and GGM to Agustín Barreiro, February 1, 1865, LC, III, 283.

89. José María Caamaño to GGM, February 8, 1865, LC, III, 288; García Moreno's response, February 18, 1865, LC, III, 288–89; and Caamaño's rejoinder, March 8, 1865, 291–92. Circular of GGM, February 28, 1865, LC, III, 287–88; and Hassaurek to Seward, April 27, 1865, RDS, T-50, reel 7.

90. GGM to Agustín Barreiro, March 1, 1865, LC, III, 290; Borrero, *Refutación,* 280–81; and GGM to Felipe Sarrade, March 10, 1865, LC, III, 293–94, BAEP, reel 34.

91. GGM to Martínez, May 3, 1865, LC, III, 299, BAEP, reel 34; Report from Governor of Loja to García Moreno and Carvajal, May 18, 1865, ANHG, Loja, 1865, no #; GGM to Martínez, May 10, 1865, LC, III, 301, BAEP, reel 34; Hassaurek to Seward, May 11, 1865, RDS, T-50, reel 7; Fagan to London, May 7, 1865, FO, 25/46, 93–94; and Saint-Robert to Quai d'Orsay May 3, 1865, AMAE, 7, #22-25.

4. A PRESIDENCY CONSTRAINED II: FOREIGN ENTANGLEMENTS, 1861–1865

1. Moreuil to Quai d'Orsay, April 1, 1864, AMAE, 6, #205-10.

2. Burr, *Reason or Force.*

3. Whigham, *Paraguayan War.*

4. Eric J. Hobsbawm, *Nations and Nationalism,* 20, 37–38, 79; and Shafer, *Nationalism,* 45–47.

5. Miller, "Historiography of Nationalism," 201–21; Deas, "Man on Foot" in Dunkerley, ed., *Studies,* 77–93; and Beattie, *Tribute of Blood,* 10–14.

6. GGM to Piedrahita, February 13, 1861, Villalba, *Epistolario,* v–vi; GGM to JJF, January 9, 1861, LC, II, 339; GGM to JJF, January 19, 1861, BC/JJC, Libro 00157, #106; and J.A. Gómez to Hacienda, January 22, 1862, AHNH, Caja 205, Guayas, #29.

7. Manuel N. Corpancho to RdA, January 5, 1861, AMRE, G.3.1.30.2, 93, 127–28, and RdA's response, January 9, 1861, same source, 126; GGM to Antonio, January 24, 1861, AF, #00817; Pablo Herrera and Julián Castro to GGM, February 13, 1861, BAEP, reel 26; GGM to Antonio, February 28, 1861, AF, #000822.

8. James Wilson to Lord Palmerston, June 24, 1861, FO, 25/39, 4–5; and H. Villamar to Ecuadorian representative in Lima, March 25, 1860, AMRE, G 3.1.30.1, 25, #280, and Decree of National Convention, April 2, 1861, AMRE G.3.1.30.2, 93, #156.

9. GGM to RdA, February 2, 1861, LC, II, 364; and GGM to Vega, September 4, 1861, LC, II, 437.

10. GGM to Vega, n.d. [but April 1861], LC, II, 396; and Dávalos to Gobierno, April 13, 1861, ANHG, Chimborazo, 1861, #24.

11. The Piedrahita mission to Chile from November 1860 to August 17, 1861, can be found in AMRE, G.2.1.4, #1-16. See GGM to Piedrahita, October 28, 1861, AF, #00843.

12. Hassaurek to Seward, September 20, 1861, RDS, T-50, reel 5; Carvajal to Fagan, October 5, 1861, FO, 25/37, 139–41; and GGM to Piedrahita, September 28, 1861, Villalba, *Epistolario,* xxii–xxiii.

13. GGM to JJF, December 22, 1861, LC, II, 488–89; and GGM to Vega, November 2, 1861 "Vega Cartas," #3, 259.

14. Hassaurek to Seward, December 19, 1861, RDS, T-50, reel 5; and GGM to Antonio Borrero, September 21, 1861, LC, II, 444–45.

15. GGM to Vega, September 28, 1861, LC, II, 447; and Fabre to Quai d'Orsay, November 16, 1861, AMAE, 5, #180-84.

16. Fagan to Russell, December 20, 1861, FO, 25/37, 169–71; and Fagan to Carvajal, February 17, 1862, FO, 25/40, 72–73.

17. Hassaurek to Seward, February 1, 1862, RDS, T-50, reel 5.

18. GGM to JJF, February 1, 1862, LC, III, 30.

19. For example, see J. A. Gómez to Gobierno, January 10, 1862, ANHG, Guayas, 1862, #7; and Vega to Gobierno, February 19, 1862, ANHG, Azuay, 1862, #25.

20. Hassaurek to Seward, December 19, 1861, RDS, T-50, reel 5; and Fagan to Russell, December 20, 1861, FO, 25/37, 164–67.

21. Howe, "García Moreno's Efforts," *HAHR*, 36, 257–62; GGM to Fabre, June 22, 1861, LC, II, 409–13; GGM to Antonio, July 6, 1861, LC, II, 417–19; and AF, I, #00797, 21–129 (1860–1863).

22. Fabre to Quai d'Orsay, June 22 and 27, 1861, AMAE, 5, 46–57, and BAEP, reel 34; Fabre to Quai d'Orsay, October 17, 1861, AMAE, 5, #166-72; and GGM to Antonio, October 29, 1861, AF, #00846.

23. Carrión, *Patíbulo*, 398–410.

24. GGM to Antonio, September 12, 1861, AF, #00840; Minister José Urrea to Relaciones, January 13, 1863, AMRE, C 35.6, 6, #000030; and Fabre to Quai d'Orsay, August 14, 1863, AMAE, 6, 54–55.

25. Robalino Dávila, "Conflicto," 93–107; and Pattee, "García Moreno," 185–208.

26. Fagan to Russell, March 20, 1862, FO, 25/40, 105–6; and Luciano Solano de la Sala to Gobierno, February 1, 1862, ANHG, Imbabura, 1862, #13.

27. Vicente Cárdenas to Julio Arboleda, March 27, 1862, in Gonzalo Arboleda, *Arboleda*, 25–26; Robalino Dávila, "Conflicto," 27–32, 102–3; and Vicente Cárdenas to GGM, April 11, 1862, AMRE, Series F, #102-3.

28. GGM to JJF, March 8 and 12, 1862, LC, III, 45–47; and Hassaurek to Seward, March 18, 1862, RDS, T-50, reel 5.

29. For Colombian excuses, see Vicente Cárdenas to Friendly Governments on the War with Ecuador, July 27, 1862, in Gonzalo Arboleda, *Arboleda*, 19–25, and Zarama, *Arboleda*, 111–16. Commander Vicente Fierro's report is in P.H. (probably Pablo Herrera), "Verdad," in *Homenajes*, II, 5–8. See Hassaurek to Seward, July 15, 1862, RDS, T-50, reel 5; and *El Nacional*, July 11, 1862.

30. GGM to JJF, June 25, 1862, LC, III, 83–84; and Carvajal to Fagan, June 24, 1862, FO, 25/40, 168–69.

31. Hassaurek to Seward, July 18, 1862, RDS, T-50, reel 5; Fagan to Russell, July 18, 1862, FO, 25/40, 156–61; Fabre to Quai d'Orsay, June 29, 1862, AMAE, 5, #306-16; Jurado Noboa, *Quiteñas*, 202–11; and Fabre to Quai d'Orsay, June 29, 1862, AMAE, 5, #306-16.

32. GGM to JJF, July 5, 1862, LC, III, 85; and GGM to Vega, August 13, 1862, "Vega Cartas," #4, 338–39.

33. JJF to Antonio, July 17, 1862, BC/JJC, Libro 00161, #198; and JJF to Daniel Salvador, July 2, 1862, BC/JJC, Libro 00187, #17.

34. Julio Arboleda's report on the battle of Tulcán, August 2, 1862, in Arboleda, *Julio Arboleda*, 50–55; P.H., "Verdad," 7–10; Guzmán Polanco, *Entretelones*, 24–28; and Zarama, *Arboleda*, 237–39. César Guades, Manuel Yépez, and Modesto Torres Burbano all fell prisoner at Tulcán, AHDN, Carpeta 2, Carpeta 4, and Carpeta 1.

35. Fagan to Russell, August 8, 1862, FO, 25/40, 172–78; Hassaurek to Seward, August 9, 1862, RDS, T-50, reel 6; and Guzmán Polanco, *Entretelones*, 30–31.

36. Fagan to Russell, August 20, 1862, FO, 25/40, 182–84; and Fabre to Quai d'Orsay, September 22, 1862, AMAE, 5, #389-90. The secret treaty is in LC, III, 91–92. See Julio Arboleda to Daniel Salazar, September 14, 1862, BC/JJC, Libro 00187, #214,

379; Manuel de Ascásubi to Daniel Salvador, November 8, 1862, BC/JJC, Libro 00187, #137, 235; and GGM to JJF, November 15, 1862, LC, III, 118.

37. GGM to Nicolás Martínez, November 5, 1862, LC, III, 114; and Fabre to Quai d'Orsay, September 19, 1862, AMAE, V, #367-68.

38. Delpar, *Red Against Blue*, 1–13; and Helguera, "First Mosquera Administration."

39. A. Martínez Pallares to JJF, April 1, 1863, BC/JJC, Libro 00165, #7; GGM to Martínez, March 25, 1863, LC, III, 129–30; Hassaurek to Seward, February 7, 1863, RDS, T-50, reel 6; and Mosquera to JJF, May 26, 1863, BC/JJC, Libro 0165, #232.

40. López Alvarez, *Cuaspud*, 6–17; Destruge Illingworth, *Urvina*, 222–39; Fabre to Quai d'Orsay, October 21, 1863, AMAE, 6, #88-91; and GGM to Piedrahita, October 14, 1863, LC, III, 164, or BAEP, reel 35.

41. Pedro Pablo to JJF, March 21 and March 25, 1863, BC/JJC, Libro 00164, #205 and 216. See also Lorenzo Solano de la Sala to JJF, June 20 and July 11, 1863, BC/JJC, Libro 00166, #71 and 137.

42. Secundino Darquea to JJF, May 16 and 20, 1863, BC/JJC, Libro 00165, #137 and 150; and Fabre to Quai d'Orsay, March 3, 1863, AMAE, 5, #274-76.

43. GGM to Mosquera, July 15, 1863, LC, III, 145, or BC/JJC, Libro 00166, #147; and Hassaurek to Seward, August 8, 1863, RDS, T-50, reel 6. See also Fabre to Quai d'Orsay, July 22, 1863, AMAE, 6, #40-43; and GGM to JJF, August 5, 1863, LC, III, 147.

44. Secundino Darquea to JJF, July 29, 1863, BC/JJC, Libro 00166, #96; Francisco J. Salazar to JJF, August 8, 1863, BC/JJC, Libro 00167, #27; Daniel Salvador to JJF, August 5, 1863, BC/JJC, Libro 00167, #17; and JJF to Antonio, August 5, 1863, BC/JJC, Libro 00167, #18.

45. Hassaurek to Seward, September 9, 1863, RDS, T-50, reel 6; and GGM to JJF, September 2, 1863, LC, III, 153–54. Mosquera's August 15 proclamation is in BC/JJC, Libro 00167, #59. Congress's declaration is in ANHG, Pichincha, 1864, no #.

46. Fabre to Quai d'Orsay, May 9, 1863, AMAE, 6, #29-36; GGM to Vega, May 12, 1863, BAEP, reel 34; Hassaurek to Seward, May 9, 1863, RDS, T-50, reel 6; and Borrero, *Refutación*, 193–98.

47. Carvajal to Antonio, September 3, 1863, AMRE, G.2.1.4, 114–15; Mosquera to Antonio, September 17, 1863, BC/JJC, Libro 01536, #1; Antonio's diary, AF, I, 153–88; Antonio to Carvajal, September 23, 1863, AMRE, C.8.4, #0000002; conference notes between Antonio and Manuel de Jesús Quijano, September 24, 1863, AMRE, C.8.4, #000019-21; Antonio to Quijano, September 29, 1863, same source, #000049; GGM to Mosquera, October 1, 1863, BC/JJC, Libro 01536, #4; and GGM to Antonio, October 2, 1863, Villalba, *Epistolario*, lixiii.

48. Antonio to JJF, October 12, 1863, BC/JJC, Libro 01536, #6; Mosquera to Antonio, October 14, 1863, AMRE, C.8.4, #000028; Statement of Manuel Dávila (and other witnesses), October 18, 1863, AMRE, C.8.4, #10-25; and Antonio to GGM, October 16, 1863, BC/JJC, Libro 01536, #10.

49. GGM to JJF, September 13 and 16, 1863, LC, III, 157–59; and GGM to Piedrahita, October 17, 1863, Villalba, *Epistolario*, p. lxviii, and Piedrahita to Gobierno, March 29, 1864, BC/JJC, Libro 00476, no #.

50. José Celedonio Urrea to Relaciones, September 24, 1863, AMRE, C.35.6, 6, #000085; GGM to JJF, September 18, 1863, LC, III, 158–59; and GGM to José Celedonio Urrea, October 7, 1863, LC, III, 163–64.

51. Citizens of Tulcán to GGM, July 31, 1863, BAEP, reel 27; Petition from Municipal Council of Riobamba, September 11, 1863, BAEP, reel 27; Petition from Cuenca, undated, BAEP, reel 27; Petition from Paute, Azuay, September 13, 1863, BAEP, reel 27; Agustín Barreiro to JJF, October 29, 1863, BC/JJC, Libro 00171, #127; and Luciano Solano de la Sala to JJF, September 19, 1863, BC/JJC, Libro 00167, #193.

52. Hassaurek to Seward, October 4, 1863, RDS, T-50, reel 6; GGM to Martínez, September 9, 1863, LC, III, 156; and De Sabla to Hassaurek, September 9, 1863, FHP, Box 3, Folder 4.

53. GGM to Piedrahita, LC, III, 167; GGM to JJF, November 9, 1863, Villalba, *Epistolario*, lxxxv; and Herrera, *Apuntes*, 36–39.

54. Daniel Salvador to JJF, September 5, 1863, BC/JJC, Libro 00167, #135; and Hassaurek, *Four Years*, 192–94.

55. Luciano Solano de la Sala to JJF, November 28, 1863, BC/JJC, Libro 00169, #87; and GGM to JJF, November 16, 1863, Villalba, *Epistolario*, xc–xci. Some Ecuadorians joined the *pastusos*, AGMD, Carpeta 1. See Secundino Darquea to JJF, November 10, 1863, BC/JJC, Libro 00171, #217.

56. López Alvarez, *Cuaspud*, 52–57; and Quijano Wallis, *Memorias*, 110–17. For General Flores' account to GGM, December 7, 1863, see BAEP, reel 35, and Records of Julio Sáenz, AGMD, Carpeta 4 [taken prisoner], Manuel T. Campuzano [wounded, taken prisoner, awarded medal], Carpeta 1. Veintimilla, *Páginas*, 27. See Guzmán Polanco, *Entretelones*, 38–45; and de Sabla to Hassaurek, December 24, 1863, FHP, Box 3, Folder 4.

57. Mosquera to the President of the Sovereign State of ?, December 8, 1863, BC/JJC, Libro 00169, #140.

58. Piedrahita to Gobierno, December 15, 1863, ANHG, Guayas, 1863, #189; Manuel Eguiguren to Gobierno, December 24, 1863, ANHG, Loja, 1863, no #; Aparicio Cornejo to Gobierno, December 13, 1863, ANHG, Esmeraldas, no #; Manuel Yépez, AGMD, Carpeta 4; Fabre to Quai d'Orsay, December 9, 1863, AMAE, 6, #164-65; Hassaurek to Seward, December 17, 1863, RDS, T-50, reel 6; and GGM to JJF, December 16, 1863, LC, III, 178.

59. Mosquera to JJF, December 9, 1863, Villalba, *Epistolario*, cxiii.

60. Mocatta to London, undated, FO, 25/42, 201–3; and Mosquera to JJF, December 22, 1863, Villalba, *Epistolario*, cxix–cxx.

61. JJF to Mosquera, December 25, 1863, BC/JJC, Libro 00169, #280; Hassaurek to Seward, January 8, 1864, RDS, T-50, reel 7.

62. Mosquera to GGM, January 4, 1864, LC, III, 192; GGM to Mosquera, January 5, 1864, LC, III, 192–93; and his letter to JJF on the same day, LC, 193.

63. Piedrahita to Gobierno, October 8, 1862, ANHG, Guayas, 1862, #210; *El Nacional*, October 12, 1862; GGM to RdA, October 11, 1862, LC, III, 105; Fagan to Russell, October 16, 1862, FO, and Russell's response, December 24, 1862, FO, 25/40, 51–52; Eguiguren to Piedrahita, October 13, 1862, AHNG, Loja, no #; Eguiguren to Gobierno, October 24, 1862, ANHG, Loja, 1862, #108; and GGM to JJF, October 25, 1862, LC, III, 109–10.

64. Eguiguren to Gobierno, December 1, 1862, ANHG, Loja, 1862, #126.

65. GGM to JJF, April 6, 1864, LC, III, 206; GGM to Manuel Vega, April 17, 1861, "Vega Cartas," # 2, 134; and Pablo Herrera to Russell, April 23, 1864, FO, 25/44, 390–92.

See also de Sabla to Hassaurek, May 16, 1863, FHP, Box 3, Folder 4; and Fagan to Russell, August 15, 1864, FO, 25/45, 58–64.

66. Pablo Herrera to Governor of Guayas, June 24, 1864, BC/JJC, Libro 00476, #34; Bustamante to JJF, June 26, 1864, same source, no #; and Hassaurek to Seward, July 1, 1864, RDS, T-50, reel 7.

67. Felipe Serrade to Gobierno, July 16, 1864, ANHG, León, 1864, no #; A. Martínez Pallares to JJF, July 20, 1864, BC/JJC, Libro 00173, #109; and GGM to Felipe Serrade, July 17, 1864, LC, III, 229–30.

68. Conservadores de Pichincha, *Liberales*, 24–26; GGM to Felipe Serrade, August 31, 1864, LC, III, 243–44; Gomezjurado, *García Moreno, IV*, 343–64; and GGM to Antonio, October 6, 1864, LC, III, 252; and Rafael Villamar to JJF, August 3, 1864, BC/JJC, Libro 00174, #240.

69. Gálvez, *Vida*, 261–65; and Carrión, *Patíbulo*, 483–87.

70. Moreuil to Quai d'Orsay, October 29, 1864, AMAE, VI, #274-76; Eguiguren to JJF, September 14, 1864, BC/JJC, Libro 00175, #46; and L. E. Provost to Washington, August 11, 1864, USDG, reel 3.

71. Eguiguren to Gobierno, October 8, 1864, ANHG, Loja, 1864, #97; GGM to JJF, August 24, 1864, LC, III, 242–43; José León to Gobierno, November 21, 1864, AHNG, Chimborazo, #92; and Iglesias, *Cañar*.

72. GGM to Rosa, November 21, 1864, LC, III, 260–61; and Manuel de Ascásubi to JJF, September 17, 1864, BC/JJC, File 01490.

73. GGM to Antonio, October 29, 1864, LC, III, 256–57; Herrera, *García Moreno*, 53; and L.E. Provost to Washington, October 13, 1864, USDG, reel 3.

74. GGM to Felipe Serrade, May 15, 1865, LC, III, 302; and Fagan to Russell, September 20, 1865, FO, 25/46, 166–68.

75. Hassaurek to Seward, January 4, 1862, RDS, T-50, reel 5; Saint-Robert to Quai d'Orsay, November 30, 1865, AMAE, VII, #78-89; GGM to Antonio, February 19, 1862, LC, III, 37–38, BAEP, reel 34; and Fernando García Moreno to JJF, May 22, 1861, BC/JJC, Libro 00159, #63.

76. Hassaurek to Seward, January 10, 1863, RDS, T-50, reel 6; and Saint-Robert to Quai d'Orsay, April 2, 1865, AMAE, VII, #16.

77. De Sabla to Hassaurek, April 29, 1863, FHP, Box 3, Folder 4; King, "Ecuadorian Church," 295; and Saint Robert to Quai d'Orsay, January 5, 1865, AMAE, VII, #61-63.

5. BECOMING THE INDISPENSABLE MAN, 1865–1869

1. Dealy, "Public Man," in Hamill, *Caudillos*, 42–61; Safford, "Politics, Ideology," in *Cambridge History*, III, 372–75; Haigh, *Güemes*; Wolf and Hansen, "Caudillo Politics," 168–79; and de la Fuente, *Children of Caudillos*.

2. Goldwert, *Psychic Conflict*, 27–30.

3. Lynch, *Caudillos*, 409–10.

4. Lynch, *Rosas;* Woodward, *Rafael Carrera;* Lynch, *Caudillos*, 275–315; and Cunninghame-Graham, *Páez*.

5. Mörner, *Region and State*, 1–8; and Lynch, *Caudillos*, 3–7.

6. Lynch, *Caudillos*, 426–29.

7. "The Case of the Washington," ANHC, Caja 297, #15.

8. Decree of GGM, June 6, 1865, ANHG, Caja 92, File 43, 6; and Hassaurek to Seward, June 13, 1865, RDS, T-50, reel 7. The Urbina battle plan fell into government hands: See José María Erigoyen to José María Urbina, June 4, 1865, AMRE, Section F, 18–19, #14-15.

9. Agustín Barreiro to Gobierno, June 21, 1865, ANHG, Los Ríos, 1865, #42; and Agustín Barreiro to GGM, June 21 and 30, 1865, BAEP, reel 28.

10. Hassaurek to Seward, June 24, 1865, RDS, T-50, reel 7; and Fagan to Russell, July 4, 1865, FO, 25/46, 114–17.

11. Hassaurek to Seward, June 27, 1865, RDS, T-50, reel 7.

12. Miguel to Gobierno, June 26, 1865, ANHG, Guayas, 1865, #75; GGM to Antonio, June 30, 1865, LC, III, 312; Hassaurek to Seward, June 28, 1865, RDS, T-50, reel 7; and GGM to Guerra, June 27, 1865, LC, III, 308–9.

13. GGM to Miguel, June 28, 1865, LC, III, 310; Gomezjurado, *García Moreno,* V, 50–60; Carrión, *Patíbulo,* 505–6; Hassaurek, *Four Years,* 133–35; Saint-Robert to Quai d'Orsay, July 20, 1865, and August 1, 1865, AMAE, 7, #40-49; GGM to Bishop of Guayaquil, July 11, 1865, VSA, Reel 3, Fasc. 39 (1a); and the Bishop to García Moreno, July 12, 1865, same source.

14. José Peñaherrera to Gobierno, July 15, 1865, ANHG, Imbabura, 1865, #56; Fagan to Russell, August 2, 1865, FO, 25/46, 133–36; and service records of Juan Manuel Uraga, commander of Talca, AGMD, Carpeta 4.

15. Berthe, *Vengador,* II, 54; Gálvez, *Vida,* 270; Carrión, *Patíbulo,* 496–97; and GGM to Pablo Herrera, November 15, 1866, LC, III, 343.

16. GGM to Juan León Mera (hereinafter Mera), October 26, 1867, LC, III, 379–80; and his letter to Nicolás Martínez, May 21, 1868, LC, IV, 17–18.

17. GGM to RdA and Rosa, November 16, 1861, LC, II, 472; GGM to Ordóñez, November 9, 1865, LC, III, 322; and his letter to Petronila Egüez, November 28, 1865, LC, III, 323.

18. GGM to Martínez, February 7, 1866, LC, III, 325; and Saint-Robert to Quai d'Orsay, November 18, 1865, AMAE, 7, #74-76.

19. GGM to Mercedes Moreno, December 15, 1866, LC, III, 345; and his letters to Martínez, December 18, 1866, LC, III, 345–46.

20. GGM to Martínez, February 2, 1867, and March 30, 1867, LC, III, 349; 352–53; GGM to an unspecified person, May 18, 1867, LC, III, 355–56; GGM to José María Lasso, July 17, 1868, LC, III, 362; and his letter to Vicente Lucio Salazar, October 9, 1867, LC, III, 371–72.

21. GGM to José María Lasso, October 9, 1867, LC, III, 373–74; and GGM letter to Ignacio Paredes, January 29, 1868, LC, IV, 2.

22. GGM to Mariano Cueva, November 27, 1867, LC, III, 388.

23. Gomezjurado, García Moreno, V, 159–70; Agramonte, *Psicopatológico,* 85–88; and Carrión, *Patíbulo,* 533–39. See Bonifaz, *Guachalá.*

24. Davis, *Last Conquistadores.* Piedrahita's mission is documented in AMRE, C. 35.7, 7. See Guzmán Polanco, *Piedrahita,* 49–55.

25. L.V. Prevost to Seward, March 21, 1866, RDS, T-50, reel 7.

26. Bartolomé Huerta to Gobierno, May 30, 1866, ANHG, Guayas, 1866, #65.

27. Sir Edward Neale to London, June 2, 1866, FO, 25/48, 136–39; and Barrera, "Pablo Herrera," *Boletín,* 84–87.

28. Gomezjurado, *García Moreno,* V, 221–24; Berthe, *Vengador,* II, 72–76; and Herrera, *García Moreno,* 58–59.

29. GGM to Mera, September 2, 1866, LC, III, 335; and GGM to Rafael Borja, August 16, 1866, LC, III, 329–30. Manuel Bustamante protested officially on August 3, 1866, AMRE, Comunicaciones, 44. The liberal argument that García Moreno stopped in Lima only to assassinate Viteri makes no sense: Moncayo, *Ecuador,* 301.

30. GGM to Rafael Borja, August 16, 1866, LC, III, 329–30.

31. Treaty of Ecuador and Chile, August 10, 1866, BC/JJC, Libro 01560, #2.

32. GGM to Relaciones, September 16, 1866, LC, III, 336–77; GGM to Relaciones, August 1, 1866, AMRE, C. 14.1, #000267-301, and BAEP, reel 35; Manuel Bustamante to GGM, October 12, 1866, AMRE, Comunicaciones, 44; and Neale to Stanley, December 5, 1866, FO, 25/48, 266–73.

33. Hassaurek to Seward, September 30, 1865, RDS, T-50, reel 7; Saint-Robert to Quai d'Orsay, January 18, 1866, AMAE, 7, 98–104; GGM to Martínez, October 11, 1865, LC, III, 321; and Hassaurek to Seward, November 7, 1865, RDS, T-50, reel 7.

34. GGM to Rafael Borja, June 29, 1867, LC, III, 358–59; Miguel Heredia to Gobierno, July 17, 1867, ANHG, Azuay, 1867, #64; and to Gobierno, August 7, 1867, same source, #69.

35. BPL, Actas, 1867.

36. Tomás Noboa to Antonio, September 28, 1867, BC/JJC, Libro 01555, #7; Pedro Antonio Sánchez to Gobierno, October 3, 1867, ANHG, Pichincha, 1867, #24; and GGM to Vicente Lucio Salazar, October 5, 1867, LC, III, 369–70.

37. Vaillard to Quai d'Orsay, October 19, 1867, AMAE, 7, 252–55, and BPL, Actas (1867); Javier Endara to Gobierno, October 4, 1867, ANHG, Pichincha, 1864, no #; and Decree of Jerónimo Carrión, October 10, 1867, ANHG, Caja 92, File 43, 375.

38. GGM to Vicente L. Salazar, October 16, 1867, LC, III, 375–76, and his letter of October 26, 1867, to Rafael Borja, LC, III, 381–82; GGM to Jerónimo Carrión, October 30, 1867, LC, III, 383–84; P. Vaillard to Quai d'Orsay, November 1, 1867, AMAE, 7, #256-61; and Herrera, *García Moreno,* 62–63.

39. GGM to José María Lasso, October 26, 1867, LC, III, 383, and his letter to Bishop Remigio, November 12, 1867, LC, III, 385–86; and GGM to Martínez, November 13, 1867, LC, III, 386.

40. GGM to José Félix Luque, December 25, 1867, LC, III, 390; and Vaillard to Quai d'Orsay, February 15, 1868, AMAE, 7, #262-65.

41. Rafael Paz to Gobierno, January 6, 1866, ANHG, Los Ríos, no #; Francisco J. Salazar to Secretary of Public Education (Gobierno), May 20, 1867, BAEP, reel 28; and Carlos Pereira to Gobierno, May 16, 1867, BAEP, reel 28.

42. Ignacio Andrade to Gobierno, March 8, 1866, ANHG, Los Ríos, 1866, #20; Miguel to Gobierno, February 21, 1866, ANHG, Guayas, 1866, #21; and Decree of Congress, February 15, 1868, ANHG, Pichincha, 1868, no #.

43. Abdon Ricaurte to Governor of Chimborazo, July 14, 1866, ANHH, Tungarahua, Caja 542, 1866, no #; Francisco Montalvo to Gobierno, October 29, 1868, BCH, Caja 16-6-12; Manuel Escandera to Gobierno, September 12, 1866, BCH, Caja 15-3-2; and budget report for 1867, n.d., BCH, Caja 16-3-6.

44. Francisco Montalvo to Gobierno, July 26, 1868, BCH, Caja 16-5-4, and his

report of August 23, 1868, BCH, 16-5-18; Francisco Moscoso to Gobierno, June 7, 1868, BCH, Caja 16-3-17; and Francisco Montalvo to Gobierno, August 12, 1868, BCH, Caja 16-5-13.

45. Francisco Montalvo to Gobierno, August 19, 1868, BCH, Caja 16-5-16, and his report of May 31, 1868, BCH, Caja 16-3-15; *Leyes* (1867), 26–27; and Francisco Moscoso to Gobierno, December 2, 1868, BCH, Caja 16-7-1.

46. Miguel Heredia to Gobierno, January 10, 17, and June 13, 1866, ANHG, Azuay, #7, #13, and #83.

47. Miguel Heredia to Gobierno, October 17, 1866, ANHG, Azuay, 1866, #12, #139; and Miguel to Gobierno, October 24, 1866, ANH, Guayas, #156.

48. Carlos Pereira to Gobierno, August 2, 1866, ANHG, Los Ríos, 1866, #56; Miguel to Gobierno, September 29, 1866, ANHG, Guayas, 1866, #141; and Diary of Antonio, II, AF.

49. Hamilton to Stanley, May 20, 1868, FO, 25/53, 49; Neale to Clarendon, April 18, 1866, FO, 25/48, 97–98; Bartolomé Huerta to Gobierno, June 20, 1866, BCH, Caja 15-2-3; Benjamín Chiriboga to Gobierno, January 19, 1867, ANHG, Chimborazo, 1867, #7; and Miguel to Gobierno, April 18, 1866, ANHG, Guayas, 1866, #47.

50. Camilo Ponce to the Vicar-General of Quito, January 29, 1868, AARZO, Caja 57, G-E; and Antonio to Manuel Bustamante, April 1, 1866, ANHG, Pichincha, 1866, no #, and his letter of April 24, 1866 AMRE, C.39.1, #000372.

51. Antonio's correspondence, AMRE, C.39.1; Ignacio Ordóñez (now bishop of Riobamba) to Gobierno, September 9, 1865, ANHG, Chimborazo, 1865, no #; José Ignacio Checa, Archbishop of Quito (hereinafter Checa) to Gobierno, July 9, 1868, BAEP, reel 29; Manuel Tobar to Gobierno, March 13, 1867, ANHG, Pichincha, 1867, #23; and GGM to Ignacio Ordóñez, August 23, 1865, LC, III, 319.

52. Fidel Egas to Gobierno, February 8, 1868, ANHG, Pichincha, 1868, no #; Decree of Camilo Ponce, February 11, 1868, same source; Carlos Pereira to Gobierno, October 11, 1866, ANHG, Los Ríos, 1866, #73; Jesse Coggeshall to her mother, October 3, 1866, WCP, Box 1, Folder 7; and Ramón Samaniego to Gobierno, April 4, 1868, ANHG, Loja, 1868, #38.

53. Neale to Stanley, June 12, 1867, FO, 25/50, 98–101; Coggeshall to Seward, July 16, 1867 and December 20, 1867, RDS, T-50, reel 8; and Manuel Bustamante to Fernando de Lorenzana, January 19, 1867, AMRE, Comunicaciones, 44.

54. Coggeshall to Seward, June 18, 1867, RDS, T-50, reel 8; narrative report of Coggeshall, December 1866, WCP, Box 1, Folder 7; Coggeshall to Hassaurek, January 27, 1867, FHP, Box 2, Folder 8; and Koch, *Coggeshall,* 141–51.

55. O'Connor, *Gender,* 56–58.

56. Benigno Malo to Hassaurek , July 30, 1861, RDS, T-50, reel 6; Seward to Hassaurek, November 6, 1862, RDS, M-77, reel 7; Hassaurek to Seward, January 16, 1863, RDS, T-50, reel 6; Pablo Herrera's note to Hassaurek, July 22, 1863, RDS, T-50, reel 7; Hassaurek to Seward, February 3, 1864, RDS, T-50, reel 7; and Gold, "Negro Colonization Schemes," 306–16.

57. Germán Pascal, *Terremoto,* 9–11; and Miguel Egas to Gobierno, August 22 and 24, 1868, BAEP, reel 29.

58. Miguel Dávila to Gobierno, August 18, 1868, ANHG, Imbabura, 1868, no #; and Federico C. Aguilar to Gobierno, August 21, 1868, same source, no #.

59. Federico C. Aguilar to Gobierno, September 4, 1868, ANHG, Imbabura, 1868, no #; and Hamilton to London, August 19, 1868, FO, 25/53, 61–62.

60. GGM to Gobierno, August 24, 1868, LC, IV, 32–33; and his letter to Martínez, August 28, 1868, LC, IV, 36–37.

61. Manuel Tobar to Gobierno, August 21, 1868, ANHG, Pichincha, 1868, #47; Rafael Villamón (director of charitable giving in Quito) to Gobierno, September 7, 1868, BAEP, reel 29; Bishop Remigio to Gobierno, September, 1868, BAEP, reel 29; and José María Avilés to Gobierno, October 22, 1868, ANHG, Manabí, #98.

62. GGM to Gobierno [Camilo Ponce], August 25 and 26, 1868, LC, IV, 33–34; and GGM to Gobierno, August 28, 1868, LC, IV, 37–38.

63. GGM to Gobierno, September 3, 1868, LC, IV, 42–44; and to Rafael Borja, September 5, 1868, LC, IV, 45–47; and Kolberg, *Hacia*, 343.

64. GGM to Martínez, September 12, 1868, LC, IV, 58–59; to Martínez, October 10, 1868, LC, IV, 68–69; and to Gobierno, September 5, 1868, ANHG, Imbabura, 1868, no #.

65. GGM to Gobierno, August 30, 1868, and September 5, 1868, LC, IV, 40–41, 49–50; and Francisco Antonio Vélez to GGM, September 7, 1868, BAEP, reel 35.

66. GGM to Gobierno, September 5, 1868, LC, IV, 51; Miguel Fernández de Córdoba to Gobierno, September 2, 1868, ANHG, Azuay, 1868, #115; Luis Salazar to Relaciones, November 25, 1868, AMRE, C. 8.4, 000136-139; Antonio to Relaciones, September 10, 1868, AMRE, C.35.8, #000242-244; and Hamilton to Lord Stanley, December 19, 1868, FO, 25/53, 68–75.

67. GGM to Gobierno, September 10, 1868, ANHG, Imbabura, 1868, no #; and Miguel Dávila to Gobierno, September 17, 1868, same source, no #.

68. GGM to Gobierno, September 10, 12, and 17, 1868, LC, IV, 52–54, 57–58, 59–60; GGM to Gobierno, November 14, 1868, AHNG, Imbabura, no #.

69. GGM to Gobierno, September 10, 1868, LC, IV, 52–54; GGM to Gobierno, September 30, 1868, LC, IV, 65, November 1, 1868, LC, IV, 73–74, and November 14, 1868, LC, IV, 83–84; and Fernando Pérez to Gobierno, December 12, 1868, ANHG, Imbabura, 1868, no #.

70. Berthe, *Vengador*, II, 109–12; Manifesto from Cotacachi canton, September 25, 1868, ANHG, Imbabura, 1868, no #; Cuatro palabras de gratitud, n.d., same source, no #; Villegas Domínguez, *Imbabura*, 192–93; and Germán Pascual, *Terremoto*, 21.

71. Martínez to president of the Patriotic Society of Quito, November 6, 1868, BAEP, reel 29. Kolberg, *Hacia*, 333, noted the resemblance to the great Lisbon earthquake, which catapulted the Marquis de Pombal to power.

72. GGM to Gobierno, November 14, 1868, ANHG, Imbabura, 1868, no #; and GGM to Ignacio del Alcázar, October 25, 1868, LC, IV, 71–72.

73. GGM to Rafael Borja, February 19, 1868, LC, IV, 5.

74. GGM to Martínez, March 12, 1868, BAEP, reel 34, LC, IV, 8; and GGM to Vicente Lucio Salazar, May 4, 1868, LC, IV, 14–15.

75. GGM to Ignacio Paredes, May 24, 1868, LC, IV, 18.

76. GGM to Vicente Lucio Salazar, June 14, 1868, LC, IV, 19–20; and GGM to Mera, July 12, 1868, LC, IV, 23–24.

77. GGM to Bishop Remigio, June 22, 1868, LC, IV, 21–22; and GGM to Mera, July 12, 1868, LC, IV, 23–24.

78. GGM to Ignacio Paredes, August 12, 1868, LC, IV, 30–31; and Martínez, August 19, 1868, LC, IV, 31.

79. GGM to Rafael Borja, November 8 and 28, 1868, LC, IV, 75–77, 85–86; and Antonio Borrero to GGM, October 28, 1868, LC, IV, 86–87.

80. GGM to the president of the Conservative Society of Azuay, December 16, 1868, LC, IV, 88–90; and Rafael Jaramillo to Antonio, December 2, 1868, BC/JJC, Libro 00481, no #.

81. GGM to Bishop Remigio, December 23, 1868, LC, IV, 93–94; Camilo Ponce to Antonio, December 5, 1868, BC/JJC, Libro 01560, #20; and his letters to Antonio, October 17, 1868, and December 18, 1868, AF, #01071 and 01073.

82. Miguel to Gobierno, January 9, 1869, ANHG, Guayas, 1868, #7; and Governor of Loja to Gobierno, enclosing intercepted letter authored by Pedro Franco, January 16, 1869, BAEP, reel 45.

83. GGM to *Guayaquileños,* January 21, 1869, LC, IV, 98–99; GGM to Gobierno, January 23, 1869, BAEP, reel 35; A. de Dulçat to Quai d'Orsay, February 6, 1869, AMAE, 7, #283-89; and Hamilton to Stanley, January 30, 1869, FO, 25/55, 49–55.

84. Luis Salazar to Relaciones, August 28, 1869, AMRE, C.8.4, #000239-240; Miguel García Moreno to Gobierno, March 7, 1869, BAEP, reel 29; and George Bragdon to Seward, March 26, 1869, RDSG, reel 4.

6. FORGING THE NATIONAL SOUL: THE COMING OF THE CATHOLIC NATION

1. GGM to José María Lasso, February, 1869, LC, IV, 113–14; GGM to Luis Salazar, February 23, 1869, LC, IV, 108–9; and Bragdon to Seward, January 20, 1869, USDG, reel 4.

2. Flores Galindo, *Buscando un Inca,* 219–23; Vélez, *Centralist Tradition,* 143–53; and Safford, "Politics and Ideology," 397–401.

3. Masur, *Bolívar,* 422; and Orton, *Andes,* 90.

4. Collier, *Chile;* and Armijos Suárez, *García Moreno,* 3–8.

5. Carrión, *Patíbulo,* 667–83; and Agramonte, *Psicopatológico,* 152–53. Terán-Guerrero, *Dictadura neroniana,* states that "swords, gallows, and whips were the principal methods of procuring peace," 16.

6. Gomezjurado, *García Moreno,* VI, 86–103; Berthe, *Vengador,* II, 158–73; and Castillo D'Imperio, *Piedad intolerante,* 64–73.

7. GGM to Rafael Borja, February 6, 1869, LC, IV, 104–5; GGM to Mera, February 20, 1869, LC, IV, 107–8; Hamilton to London, May 19, 1869, FO, 25/55, 76–78; GGM to Mera, March 6, 1869, LC, IV, 117; unsigned letter (probably Governor Vicente de Santisteban, hereinafter Santisteban) to Gobierno, April 18, 1869, ANHG, Guayas, #53; GGM to Rafael Borja, March 3, 1869, LC, IV, 114–15; and GGM to Antonio Zambrano, February 11, 1869, LC, IV, 105–6.

8. Wing to Fish, June 24, 1870, RDS, T-50, reel 8, #1; Wing to Fish, August 11, 1870, same source, no #; Wing to Fish, November 10, 1870, RDS, T-50, reel 8, #40; Francisco Javier León to Fish, August 19, 1874, RDS, T-810, reel 1, and October 17, 1874; and Charles Weile to Fish, January 20, 1873, USDG, reel 4.

9. Antoine de Dulçat to Quai d'Orsay, August 14, 1869, AMAE, 7, #314-17;

and GGM to the president of the Constitutional Assembly, August 9, 1869, LC, IV, 149–51.

10. GGM to Mera, April 7, 1869, LC, IV, 120–21; GGM to Ordóñez, May 19, 1869, LC, IV, 132; and GGM to Rafael Borja, February 24, 1869, LC, IV, 109–10.

11. Santisteban to Gobierno, December 25, 1869, ANHG, Guayas, no #.

12. Destruge, *Prensa de Guayaquil*, 135–46, 173–83.

13. Borja y Borja, *Constituciones*, cxxiv and cxxvii–cxxviii, 327–54.

14. Larson, *Trials*, 112–14.

15. Many of these codes can be found at Indiana University. Francisco J. Salazar to Antonio, September 18, 1869, BC/JJC, Libro 01572, #62.

16. Ley de la Guardia Nacional, September 15, 1869, in *Leyes, Decretos*, 231–41; Ayala Mora, *Lucha Política*, 136–38; and *Código Militar*, 225–48.

17. Lieuwen, *Arms and Politics*; Loveman, *For la Patria*; Wing to Fish, August 17, 1870, and October 27, 1872, RDS, T-50, reel 8 and reel 11; Walter Grinnell to Guerra, December 17, 1871, AMRE, Series F, 18–19, 60–64; Bustamante to Hacienda, May 18, 1872, ANHH, Pichincha, Caja 512, #218.

18. See files in ANH, Milicias: cases of Luis Torres, June 27, 1872; Antonio Gómez, July 16, 1872, and many others, Caja 25, File 1-1-1872; and Wing to Fish, August 17, 1870, RDS, T-50, reel 8, #23.

19. Wing to Fish, September 6, 1871, RDS, T-50, reel 10; and *Leyes, Decretos*, 126–27, 168–69.

20. Santisteban to Gobierno, July 15, 1871, ANHG, Guayas, 1871, #187; GGM to Ordóñez, February 23, 1873, *Ordóñez Cartas*, 216; Guerrero, *Curagas*, 54–55; and M. Rodríguez Parra to Governor of Azuay, March 28, 1873, BAEP, reel 47.

21. Alfonso Velasco to Gobierno, November 30, 1873, ANHG, Esmeraldas, 1873, #71; GGM to Manuel Andrade Marín, August 24, 1869, LC, IV, 151–52; and Francisco Javier León to Chief Justice of the Supreme Court, June 21, 1870, ANHG, Caja 94, File 1, #54.

22. Archbishop Checa to Gobierno, April 22, 1873, BAEP, reel 47; Bishop Luis of Manabí, March 18, 1875, ANHG, Manabí, 1875, no #; Bustamante to vicar-general, August 25, 1869, AARZO, Caja 58, G-E.

23. Manuel Andrade Marín to governor of Imbabura, January 25, 1873, ANHG, Imbabura, 1873, no #; and Santisteban to Gobierno, May 3, 1873, ANHG, Guayas, 1873, #5.

24. Juan España (hereinafter España) to Gobierno, February 3, 1872, ANHG, Imbabura, #18, and a dismissal, #19, dated February 17, 1872; JJF (Jr.) to Hacienda, July 31, 1870, ANHH, Los Ríos, Caja 419, #445; and case against Joaquín Febres Cordero, July 18, 1874, ANHC, Caja 321, Case 31.

25. GGM to Antonio Rivera, February 4, 1873, LC, IV, 317; and GGM to Ordóñez, January 5, 1870, *Ordóñez*, 109–11.

26. Carrión, *Patíbulo*, 678–381; and Herrera, *García Moreno*, 75.

27. Mera to Gobierno, May 21, 1873, ANHG, Tungurahua, 1873, #18; Miguel Morán to of Gobierno, ANHG, Pichincha, 1874, #50; and L.V. de la Torre to Gobierno, May 20, 1875, ANHG, Manabí, no #.

28. GGM to Juan Villavicencio, February 18 and 25, 1873, LC, IV, 318, 321–22; and GGM to Congress, *Mensaje*, in Pólit Laso, *Escritos*, I, 321–34.

29. Tobar Donoso, *Instrucción püblica*, 196–201; and Kingman Garcés, "Escuela moderna."

30. JJF (Jr.) to Gobierno, January 21, 1872, ANHG, Los Ríos, #15; GGM to Juan Villavicencio, March 18, 1873, LC, IV, 327; and Santisteban to Gobierno, October 15, 1873, ANHG, Guayas, #26.

31. Eguiguren's report for 1874, November 24, 1874, ANHG, Loja, no #; and GGM to Juan Villavicencio, June 24, 1873, LC, IV, 352.

32. Mera to Gobierno, July 6, 1873, ANHG, Tungurahua, 1873, #23; Carlos Andrade to Gobierno, December 20, 1872, ANHG, Esmeraldas, #69; and Bustamante to Víctor José de la Guerra, ANH, Copiadores, Pichincha, Caja 85, no #.

33. Manuel Andrade Marín to Gobierno, March 27, 1875, BAEP, reel 29; curriculum is in *Lei Orgánica*; and Santiago Tobar to Gobierno, December 4, 1869, ANHG, Imbabura, 1869, #1.

34. Mera to Gobierno, November 9, 1873, ANHG, Tungurahua, #38.

35. Carlos Pereira to Gobierno, May 15, 1870, ANHG, Los Ríos, 1870, #115; Mera to Gobierno, February 7, 1875, ANHG, Tungurahua, 1875, #2; Francisco Moscoso to Gobierno, December 31, 1874, Gobierno, Chimborazo, 1874, no #; and GGM to Mera, May 24, 1873, LC, IV, 347.

36. España to Gobierno, November 29, 1871, and December 19, 1871, ANHG, Imbabura, no #; España to Gobierno, February 22, 1873, ANHG, Imbabura, #11; Camilo Proaño to Gobierno, March 31, 1874, ANHG, León, 1874, no #; and Eguiguren to Gobierno, September 23, 1871, ANHG, Loja, #91.

37. Yáñez Cossío, *Educación indígena*, 27–23; and José María Pallares to Gobierno, November 18, 1869, ANHG, Esmeraldas, #58, and December 23, 1869, same source, #75.

38. Pfeiffer, *Lady's Second Journey*, 381; *El Nacional*, May 1, 1875, and May 5, 1875; and Williams, "Negotiating the State," 155–59.

39. Francisco Moscoso to the governor of Chimborazo, December 31, 1874, ANHG, Chimborazo, 1874, no #; Mera to Gobierno, August 3, 1873, ANHG, Tungurahua, #28; Eguiguren to Gobierno, May 6, 1871, ANHG, Loja, #3; GGM to Ordóñez, October 29, 1869, and November 13, 1869, LC, IV, 165–9; and *Ordóñez Cartas*, 64–66, 69–71.

40. Tobar Donoso, *Instrucción pública*, 208–38; José P. Zambrano to Gobierno, April 26, 1871, ANHG, Manabí, #67, and his report to Gobierno, June 25, 1874, ANHG, Manabí, #93; and Teodoro García's report for 1873 to Gobierno, May 25, 1873, ANHG, Los Ríos, no #.

41. GGM to Mera, April 23, 1873, LC, IV, 335–36; Manuel Ortíz to Gobierno, October 6, 1872, BAEP, reel 46; and Eguiguren to Gobierno, December 24, 1870, ANHG, Loja, #29, and his letter of October 28, 1871, ANHG, Loja, #10.

42. Mera to Gobierno, August 26, 1873, ANHG, Tungurahua, 1873, no #; and Ordóñez to the Hacienda, August 23, 1870, ANHH, Azuay, #248.

43. Report of Francisco Campos to Gobierno, July 9, 1873, ANHG, Guayas, no #; *Reglamento de escuelas primarias*; José Zambrano to Gobierno, August 22, 1872, ANHG, Manabí, #110; and F. Arboleda to Gobierno, December 10, 1873, ANHG, Pichincha, #11.

44. Uzcátegui, *Desarrollo de la educación*, 18; and Rodríguez, *Public Policy*, 82–84.

45. Francisco Javier León to James Gall (in Kingston, Jamaica), May 18, 1872, AMRE, Comunicaciones, 47; Bustamante to Gobierno, February 25, 1874, AHNG, Pichincha, #6; Safford, *Ideal*, 49–52; and GGM to Mera, June 1, 1870, LC, IV, 201.

46. Tobar Donoso, *Instrucción pública*, 252–62; and Miranda Ribadeneira, *García Moreno y la Compañía*, 4–7, 32–45.

47. Ignacio del Alcázar's report to Governor of León, n.d., 1873, ANHG, León, no #; Rafael Larrea Checa (hereinafter Larrea Checa) to Gobierno, August 30, 1873, ANHG, Chimborazo, #26; *El Nacional*, February 20, 1864; and Francisco Javier León to Francisco J. Salazar, August 21, 1873, AMRE, Comunicaciones, 47.

48. Larrea Checa to Gobierno, April 11, 1874, ANHG, Chimborazo, #9; JJF (Jr.) to Gobierno, September 9, 1869, ANHG, Los Ríos, #161; Hernáez to Gobierno, September 23, 1870, ANHG, Pichincha, 1870, no #; and Francisco A. Arboleda and Octavio Vega to Gobierno, January 20, 1872, same source, 1872, no #.

49. JJF (Jr.) to Gobierno, September 30, 1869, ANHG, Los Ríos, #193.

50. *Lei orgánica, 1865*, 7–9; Tobar Donoso, *Instrucción pública*, 254–257; and Hernáez to Gobierno, February 18, 1870, BAEP, reel 46.

51. Bishop José María of Loja to the apostolic delegate, Maya 19, 1870, VSA, reel 4, Fasc. 50(5); Eguiguren to Gobierno, November 6, 1869, ANHG, Loja, #105; and Eguiguren to Gobierno, October 19, 1872, ANHG, Loja, #17.

52. Benigno Malo to GGM, November 10, 1869, LC, IV, 170–71, and GGM's response, November 17, 1869, LC, IV, 171–73; and GGM to Visitador Agustín Delgado, S.J., August 30, 1871, LC, IV, 256.

53. Víctor Antonio Sanmiguel to Gobierno, October 18, 1874, ANHG, León, #78; Francisco Hernáez to Council General of Education, September 26, 1870, BAEP, reel 46; Clemente Faller to Gobierno, March 6, 1875, BAEP, reel 29; and unsigned letter to Gobierno, n.d., BAEP, reel 46.

54. Tobar Donoso, *Instrucción pública*, 286–309; Ramón Aguirre to Gobierno, January 19, 1869, ANHG, León, no #; Decree of GGM, February 13, 1869, ANHG, Caja 92, File 43, #37; and Archbishop Checa to Gobierno, March 6, 1869, BAEP, reel 45.

55. Manuel Dávila to Gobierno, August 23, 1871, ANHG, Azuay, #25; Miguel Franco to Gobierno, September 21, 1870, ANHG, Azuay, no #; Cárdenas et al., *Universidad de Cuenca*, 43–47, 66–74; and Borrero, *Refutación*, 472–73.

56. Bustamante to Gobierno, May 21, 1870, ANHG, Pichincha, #33; Antonio J. Sucre (Jr.) to Gobierno, November 20, 1871, ANHG, Guayas, #276; Rafael Borja to Gobierno, December 31, 1873, ANHG, Azuay, #356; and Bustamante to Director of the Police, April 14, 1874, ANH, Copiadores, Pichincha, Caja 85, no #.

57. Paredes Borja, *Historia de la medicina*, 238–56; Carvajal to Beltrán Fourquet, February 17, 1869, AMRE, Comunicaciones, 44; Francisco Javier León to Fourquet, August 13, 1872, AMRE, Comunicaciones, 47; Francisco Arboleda to Antonio, November 30, 1870, same source; and Francisco Javier León to Beltrán Fourquet, November 4, 1871, same source.

58. GGM address to congress, August 10, 1871, RDS, T-50, reel 10; Miranda Ribadeneira, *Escuela politécnica;* and GGM to Francisco J. Salazar Cartas, September 17, 1873, *Salazar*, 41–42.

59. Brother Conald to governor of Pichincha, March 7, 1873, ANHH, Pichincha, Caja 513, no #; and Bustamente to Hacienda, January 22, 1873, same source, #19. See also Brother Juan Menten (the Jesuit in charge) to Gobierno, January 5, 1871, BAEP, reel 46. For their books, see Wolf, *Geography and Geology*; Kolberg, *Hacia*; and Destruge, *Prensa*, 184–85.

60. GGM to Ordóñez, November 9, 1871, *Ordóñez Cartas*, 183; Safford, *Ideal*, 117–23; *El Nacional*, October 16, 1873; Clemente Faller's report on the Polytechnical, March 20, 1875, BAEP, reel 29; Ordóñez to Gobierno, May 11, 1872, ANHG, Azuay, #29; and GGM to Ordóñez, October 31, 1872, LC, IV, 294–95.

61. España to Gobierno, June 13, 1874, ANHG, Imbabura, #14; and Francisco Javier León to Beltrán Fourquet, September 17, 1876, AMRE, Comunicaciones, 47. The rules and regulations "Statuts de l'ecole d' Obstetrique" can be found in BAEP, reel 46. Final grades for the cited year are in Escuela de Obstetricia, 1872 á 1873, n.d., ANHG, Pichincha, 1872, no #.

62. GGM to Francisco J. Salazar Cartas, August 25, 1871, *Salazar*, 16–17; Tobar Donoso, *Instrucción pública*, 408–11; and Bishop Luis to Gobierno, January 13, 1873, ANHG, Manabí, no #.

63. Tobar Donoso, *Instrucción pública*, 403–8; Francisco Javier León to Antonio, February 1, 1871, AMRE, Comunicaciones, 47; contract of George Cooke, carpenter, signed by Antonio, November 21, 1871, BAEP, reel 46; and Lara, *Quito*, 220, 228–29. The graduates revitalized *gremios* and maintained *cofradías*.

64. J. Agustín Guerrero, *Música ecuatoriana*, 5–6, 28–46; and Tobar Donoso, *Instrucción pública*, 388–90. Neumane's contract dated March 18, 1870, is in ANHG, Pichincha, 1870, no #. Darquea allegedly gave Neumane chocolate to help inspire his muse.

65. Hassaurek, *Four Years*, 113–16.

66. Cheryl Hartup, "Artists," 41–49. For one scholarship, see Francisco Javier León to Victor Gabriac in Rome, April 16, 1873, AMRE, Comunicaciones, 47.

67. Vargas, *Maestros del arte ecuatoriano*, III, 155–60; Hartup, "Artists," 9, 71–75; and Kennedy Troya, *Rafael Troya*, 79–83.

68. Jouanen, *Jesuitas y el oriente*, 12–23; and Antonio Rodríguez to Gobierno, October 21, 1865, ANHG, Chimborazo, #92.

69. Miranda Ribadeneira, *García Moreno y la compañía*, 99–103; Archbishop Checa to Gobierno, January 6, 1872, AARZO, Caja 60, G-E, #4; and Archbishop Checa to Gobierno, March 19, 1870, BAEP, reel 46.

70. Costales Samaniego and Costales Peñaherrera, *Macas*, 84–87; Archbishop Checa to Gobierno, June 11, 1870, BAEP, reel 46; report of Andrés Justo Pérez to Gobierno, June 8, 1873, BAEP, reel 47; Carlos Zambrano to Gobierno, with enclosed letter from Mariano Maldonado, May 23, 1864, ANHG, Chimborazo, #83; and Wing to Washington, February 27, 1872, RDS, T-50, reel 11, #201.

71. Jouanen, *Jesuitas y el oriente*, 88–100; Ambrosio Fonseca to Gobierno, April 24, 1870, BAEP, reel 46; Manuel Dávila to Gobierno, December 2, 1871, ANHG, Azuay, #257; and Simson, *Travels*, 87–95.

72. Piedrahita to Relaciones, January 4, 1875, AMRE, G 3.1.30.1, 25, 272–73; his letter to Relaciones, August 19, 1874, AMRE, C. 35.10, #000148; and Antonio to Relaciones, May 13, 1869, AMRE, G. 3.1.30.1, 25, #191.

73. Pfeiffer, *Lady's Second Journey*, 382.

74. Francisco Javier León to Beltrán Fourquet, August 17, 1870, AMRE, Comunicaciones, 47; list of schools and hospitals, *Exposición Hacienda* (1871); Larrea Checa to Gobierno, May 12, 1873, ANHG, Chimborazo, no #; and Teodoro García to Gobierno, May 25, 1873, ANHG, Los Ríos, no #.

75. Juan Bustamante to Gobierno, May 31, 1875, BAEP, reel 29; Rafael Salvador to Gobierno, February 17, 1870, ANHG, Pichincha, #14; and Santisteban to Gobierno, September 7, 1872, ANHG, Guayas, #219.

76. Statistics for the House of Maternity, November 1872, ANHG, Pichincha, no #; and Report of Hospital of San Juan de Dios, December 1873, same source, no #. The Sister in charge of the Caridad Hospital wanted a baptismal font for her hospital, suggesting a high infant mortality rate: See Sister María to Archbishop Checa, January 5, 1872, AARZO, Caja 61, G-E. See also: Bustamante to Gobierno, July 5, 1870, ANHG, Pichincha, #91.

77. Bustamante to Gobierno, February 19, 1870, ANHG, Chimborazo, #35; hospital inspector to governor of Los Ríos, July 1, 1874, ANHG, Los Ríos, no #; and GGM to Juan Villavicencio, September 8, 1874, LC, IV, 472–73.

78. Larrea Checa to Gobierno, December 5, 1874, ANHG, Chimborazo, #93; Sister Honoria to Governor of Pichincha, February 28, 1875, ANHG, Pichincha, #8; and the report of the governor of Pichincha, 1869, BAEP, reel 45.

79. Sister Honoria's program for teaching, August 6, 1872, BAEP, reel 46. For the orphanage see report of April 1, 1873, ANH, Hijos y Naturales, Caja 7, #20. See also: GGM to Juan Villavicencio, June 12, 1871, LC, IV, 250–51; and his letter to Mera, May 13, 1874, LC, 443.

80. Secundino Darquea to José Ignacio Checa, February 16, 1870, AMRE, Comunicaciones, 44; Juan Jaramillo to Gobierno, March 14, 1874, ANHG, Azuay, #40; GGM to Mera, March 12, 1873, LC, IV, 325; and GGM to Juan Villavicencio, December 9, 1873, LC, IV, 398.

81. Juan José Peñaherrera to Gobierno, December 19, 1874, ANHG, Chimborazo, #97; and Mariano Barona to Gobierno, June 18, 1874, ANHG, Los Ríos, #231.

82. Víctor Antonio de Sanmiguel to Gobierno, June 24, 1874, ANHG, León, #115; Gomezjurado, *García Moreno,* VIII, 412–15; Rafael Borja to Gobierno, April 27, 1874, ANHG, Azuay, #66.

83. Williams, "Negotiating the State," 166–80.

84. GGM to Felipe Serrade, March 25, 1871, LC, IV, 243–44; and Ordóñez to Gobierno, April 19, 1873, ANHG, Azuay, #122.

85. Archbishop Checa to Gobierno, March 29, 1873, ANHG, Chimborazo, no #; and Benedicto López to Gobierno, January 30, 1873, ANHG, León, #26.

86. Bustamante to Gobierno, April 18, 1871, ANHG, Pichincha, #49; Ignacio Holguín to the Archbishop, November 1, 1871, AARZO, Igl. Caja 18; and Bishop José Antonio of Guayaquil to Gobierno, November 13, 1872, BAEP, reel 47.

87. GGM to Ordóñez, November 2, 1872, *Ordóñez Cartas,* 203; and GGM to Rafael Borja, February 25, 1874, LC, IV, 424–25. Hassaurek, *Four Years,* 104–5, describes these customs, as does Fermín Cevallos, *Resumen,* VI, 128–31.

88. Archbishop Checa to the Hacienda of Tolontag, September 24, 1874, AARZO, Caja 61, G-E; Felipe Serrade to the vicar general, November 16, 1869, AARZO, Caja 58, G-E, and his letter of June 19, 1871, to Gobierno, ANHG, León, #89; and Williams, "Negotiating the State," 170–74.

89. Vicente de Santisteban to Gobierno, February 25, 1874, ANHG, Guayas, #37, discussing a case where a man got a 14-year-old girl and her mother drunk, with foreseeable consequences. See also: Mariano Barona to Gobierno, October 18, 1874,

ANHG, Los Ríos, #354; José Zambrano to Gobierno, June 5, 1873, ANHG, Manabí, #82; and JJF (Jr.) to Gobierno, April 7, 1873, ANHG, Los Ríos, #61, noting fines and jail time.

90. GGM to Marianita Lasso de García Moreno (Marianita), July 14, 1872, LC, IV, 279–80; his letter to Rafael Borja, July 23, 1873, LC, IV, 358–59; and GGM to Rafael Borja, March 14, 1874, LC, IV, 428.

91. *El Nacional,* February 13, 1875, and February 17, 1875; José María Pallares to Gobierno, December 15, 1869, ANHG, Esmeraldas, #68; España to Gobierno, February 10, 1872, ANH, Imbabura, #15; GGM to Juan Villavicencio, October 6, 1874, LC, IV, 479.

92. GGM to Mera, February 21, 1874, LC, IV, 423; Francisco Javier Cevallos, Provincial Judge for Pichincha, November 1, 1869, ANHG, Pichincha, no #; and Visitador to *jefe político* of Machachi, August 28, 1869, AARZO, Caja 58, G-E. For complaints about "public concubinage," see Ciro Peñaherrera's report, March 1, 1872, ANHG, Tungurahua, 1872, no #. For *amenanza,* see Fermín Cevallos, *Resumen,* 6, 112–14. See also: P. del Alcázar to Gobierno, April 16, 1873, ANHG, León, no #.

93. Francisco Javier León to governor of Chimborazo, September 27, 1871, ANH, Copiadores, Caja 80, Libro 297, #75; and the case versus Marino Sandoval, Camilo Mantilla, and Nicolás Fermín, ANHC, Caja 325, Case #18.

94. Santisteban to Gobierno, February 21 and September 5, 1872, ANHG, Guayas, #55 and 217; José Zambrano to Gobierno, May 2, 1872 and February 20, 1873, ANHG, Manabí, #62 and #35; Benavides, *Ecuadorian Histories,* 131–33; and GGM to Mariano Barona, August 26, 1874, LC, IV, 470–71.

95. Rafael Borja to Gobierno, February 7, 1874, ANHG, Azuay, #25; Ramón Cevallos' summary on Sra. Teresa Orellano, September 20, 1874, ANHG, Azuay, no #; and GGM to Juan Villavicencio, April 7, 1874, LC, IV, 433–34.

96. Borrero, *Refutación,* III, 141–44; Carrión, *Patíbulo,* 432–35; Pattee, *García Moreno,* 343–50; and Wing to Washington, January 23, 1871, RDS, T-50, reel 9.

97. Francisco Javier León to the King of Italy, January 18, 1871, AMAE, 8; GGM to Rafael Borja, June 3, 1871, LC, IV, 249; and Hales, *Pio Nono,* 316–17.

98. Gomezjurado, García Moreno, VII, 327–29; Act of Congress, October 3, 1873, ANHG, Pichincha, no #; Ligne Boulard to Quai d'Orsay, March 19, 1874, AMAE, 8, #80-83; and GGM to Pope Pius IX, n.d., BAEP, reel 35.

99. De Groot, *Brazilian Catholicism,* 104–6; Gomezjurado, *García Moreno,* IX, 160; Klaiber, *Peru,* 92; and Jonas, *France and the Sacred Heart.*

100. *Leyes,* 1873, 354–55; RdA, president of senate's report, October 8, 1873, RDS, T-50, reel 13; José Antonio, bishop of Guayaquil, May 23, 1874, BAEP, reel 29; Gomezjurado, *García Moreno,* IX, 150–63; and Heredia, *Consagración.*

7. CARING FOR EARTHLY NEEDS: THE PROGRAM FOR ECONOMIC DEVELOPMENT

1. GGM to Ordóñez, June 19, 1869, *Ordóñez Cartas,* 46–48; and GGM to Larrea Checa, July 27, 1870, LC, IV, 210.

2. Jane, *Liberty and Despotism,* 4–15; and Barrett, *Impulse,* 179–87.

3. Cardoso and Faletto, *Dependency;* and Burns, *Poverty of Progress.* For criticism

of dependency, see Packenham, *Dependency Movement.* See also: Pineo, *Life and Work,* 159–60.

4. Bushnell and Macauley, *Nineteenth Century;* and Bulmer-Thomas, *Economic History,* 53–57.

5. Hassaurek, *Four Years,* 52–53; Case of Manuel Julián Peña, January 13, 1866, ANHG, Caja 92, File 45; Pacífico Chiriboga et al., memorandum to secretary of Gobierno, April 11, 1875, ANHG, Pichincha, 1875, no #; and Ayala Mora, *Lucha,* 114–25.

6. Estrada Ycaza, *Los bancos,* 23–49; Nicolás Morán of the Banco del Ecuador to governor of Guayas, September 5, 1868, ANHH, Guayas, Caja 211, no #; *Ley de Bancos (1867);* and Miguel to Hacienda, November 7, 1868, ANHH, Guayas, Caja 211, #639.

7. *Exposición de hacienda (1871),* 35–37; Santisteban to Hacienda, April 29, 1871, ANHH, Guayas, Caja 213, #338; Wing Papers, 98 SC 282, 65, 79; Santisteban to Hacienda, April 26, 1873, ANHH, Guayas, Caja 219, no #; and Bustamante to Hacienda, October 15, 1869, ANHH, Pichincha, Caja 511, #370.

8. Santisteban to Hacienda, February 1, 1871, ANHH, Guayas, Caja 213, 1869, #76; Juan José González and Francisco Febres Cordero to Hacienda, January 31, 1874, BCH, 22-1-14; and Ignacio del Alcázar to Hacienda, July 2, 1873, ANHH, León, Caja 366, #222.

9. Estrada Ycaza, *Bancos,* 65–70; Ayora A., *Primera emisión,* 11–30; and Wing to Washington, December 23, 1871, RDS, T-50, reel 10, #174.

10. Juan José González to Hacienda, April 12, 1875, BCH, 23-2-17; *Ley de Aduanas, (1873)*; Rodríguez, *Public Policy,* 187 (Appendix C); and Charles Weile to Wing, December 9, 1872, USDG, reel 4.

11. Rodríguez, *Public Policy,* 59, 223–24 (Appendix L). *El Nacional,* November 14, 1873.

12. "*Ley de Aduanas,*" Article 32; *El Nacional,* September 1, 1873; and Simon A. Zavallos to Governor of Manabí, June 29, 1868, ANHH, Manabí, Caja 463, #123.

13. José Eguiguren to governor of Guayas, April 11, 1874, ANHH, Guayas, Caja 220, no #; and Francisco R. Muñoz to Gobierno, April 10, 1872, ANHG, Guayas, no #.

14. Antonio Flores Jijón, *Conversión de la deuda,* 48–49, 154–60; instructions from GGM to Antonio, n.d. [but early 1874], BAEP, reel 34; José M. Eguiguren to Antonio, January 2, 1874, BC/JJC, Libro 01589, #1; GGM to Antonio, July 4, 1874, AF, #01147; and John Field to GGM, January, 1874, FO, 25/64, 247–48.

15. José Eguiguren to Flores, October 17, 1874, BC/JJC, Libro 01589, #14.

16. Fels, *American Business Cycles,* 83–112; GGM to Rafael Borja, December 31, 1873, LC, IV, 405–6; and Estrada Ycaza, *Bancos,* 68–78. Limiting spendthrift bank president J. J. González's authority also restored confidence. See: Hamilton to London, January 17, 1874, FO, 25/61, 13; and GGM to Rafael Borja, January 10, 1874, LC, IV, 412–13.

17. GGM to J. J. González, July 4, 1874, LC, IV, 456–57; GGM to J. J. González, n.d. [but September 1874], LC, IV, 475; GGM to González, October 6, 1874, LC, IV, 479; and José García Moreno to Hacienda, January 30, 1875, BCH, 23-1-14.

18. José Eguiguren to Governor of Guayas, April 1, 1875, ANH, Copiadores, Guayas, Caja 85, #235.

19. Hunter and Foley, *Economic Problems,* 157–60; and Stein and Stein, *Colonial Heritage,* 134–35, 147–49.

20. Philo White to Antonio, January 12, 1872, BC/JJC, Libro 001580, #1.

21. Tenorio-Trillo, *World's Fair*; and Wing to Fish, April 29, 1872, RDS, T-50, reel 11.

22. Chiriboga, *Jornaleros*, 34–40; Maiguashca, "Ecuadorian Cocoa," 65–83; and Santisteban to Gobierno, September 11, 1872, ANHG, Guayas, #222.

23. *El Nacional*, April 29, 1872; Mariano Barona to Gobierno, December 18, 1874, ANHG, Los Ríos, #429; and Pérez Estupiñán, *Esmeraldas*, 92–95.

24. Eguiguren to Gobierno, April 17, 1865, BAEP, reel 27; Ordóñez to Gobierno, February 18, 1871, ANHG, Azuay, #55; Honigsbaum, *Fever Trail*, 44–140.

25. Wing to Fish, January 4, 1870, January 5, 1871, March 5, 1872, and RDS, T-50, reel 9-11; Bustamante to Gobierno, September 13, 1869, ANHG, Pichincha, #63; Antonio to Fish, April 28, 1870, RDS, T-810, reel 1; George Barrows to president of the Royal College of Physicians, December 20, 1872, FO, 25/28, #201-2; José Félix Luque to director of Medical Faculty, July 1, AMRE, C.35.9, 9, no #; and Francisco Javier León to Antonio, March 2, 1872, AMAE, Comunicaciones, 47.

26. Andrien, *Quito*; and Miller, *Panama Hat Trail*.

27. Contract with Arthur Rogers (1870), BC/JJC, Libro 01573, #24. Modesto López, born in San Antonio de Ibarra, was the only Ecuadorian engineer: Madera, "Modesto López," 105–14. See also: Wiles, "Land Transportation"; Bustamante to Hacienda, August 26, 1869, ANHH, Pichincha, Caja 511, #299; and *El Nacional*, November 3, 1869. García Moreno employed road inspectors as part of the bureaucratic state.

28. Wing to Fish, January 31, 1871, RDS, T-50, reel 9, #65; José Zambrano to Hacienda, April 3, 1869, ANHH, March 12, 1870, Chimborazo, Caja 111, no #; Gabriel Luque to Hacienda, October 21, 1871, ANHH, Guayas, Caja 215, #854; and Ignacio Holguín to Hacienda, August 3, 1870, ANHH, Tungurahua, Caja 543, #315.

29. Ignacio del Alcázar to Hacienda, April 19, 1874, ANHH, León, Caja 367, #25; James Wilson to Hacienda, March 11, 1870, ANHH, Los Ríos, Caja 418, no #; and Wing to Fish, October 4, 1870, RDS, T-50, reel 8, #33.

30. Ordóñez to Gobierno, March 13, 1869, BCH, 17-1-16; Ordóñez to Gobierno, April 3, 1869, BCH, 17-1-27; Benigno Malo to GGM, November 10, 1869, LC, IV, 170–71; and GGM's reply, November 17, 1869, LC, IV, 171–73. Palomeque, *Cuenca*, 54.

31. GGM to Ordóñez, March 12, 1873, *Ordóñez Cartas*, 218; and GGM to Rafael Borja, July 30, 1873, LC, IV, 361–62.

32. GGM to Juan Villavicencio, July 12, 1870, LC, IV, 207; and España to Hacienda, November 19, 1870, ANHH, Imbabura, Caja 336, #55. Williams, "Negotiating the State," 221–79, describes the Esmeraldas road project. See: España to Hacienda, November 5, 1870, ANHH, Imbabura, Caja 336, #45; and GGM to Juan Villavicencio, December 15, 1873, LC, IV, 400–1.

33. GGM to Juan Villavicencio, June 22, 1875, LC, IV, 531.

34. José J. Eguiguren to GGM, January 11, 1871, ANH, Copiadores, Caja 78, Libro 290, #2; José J. Eguiguren to governor of Manabí, March 1, 1871, same source, #6; and GGM to Francisco Javier Salazar Cartas, March 6, 1872, *Salazar*, 28–29.

35. José P. Zambrano to Hacienda, October 10, 1872, ANHH, Manabí, Caja 465, #319, and his letters to Hacienda dated December 5, 1872, #417; and Wing to Fish, December 28, 1873, RDS, T-50, reel 13, #356.

36. José Eguiguren to the governor of Loja (his brother), July 30, 1875, and October 1, 1875, ANH, Copiadores, Caja 78, Libro 290, #1, #4.

37. Wiles, "Land Transportation," 122–24, 145–47, 166–67, 183–85, 211–12; Rolando, *Obras públicas*, 33–39; and Wolf, *Geography and Geology*, 225–33.

38. España to Hacienda, April 22, 1871, ANHH, Imbabura, Caja 337, #56; Dr. Federico Jaramillo to the governor of Imbabura, November, 1873, ANHH, Imbabura, Caja 339, no #; and Dr. Gabriel Córdova to the governor of Imbabura, December 4, 1873, same source.

39. Larrea Checa to Hacienda, November 8, 1871, ANHG, Chimborazo, Caja 113, no #; his letter of November 19, 1872, to Gobierno, same source, #97; Ignacio Holguín to Hacienda, April 24, 1870, ANHH, Tungurahua, Caja 543, #183; and GGM to Juan Villavicencio, April 29, 1873, BC/JJC, ADQ 46, Caja 16, Carpeta 153, 4.

40. GGM to Juan Villavicencio, April 23, 1873, LC, IV, 336–37; Bustamante to parish lieutenant of Sangolquí, August 28, 1871, ANH, Pichincha, Copiadores, Caja 77, Libro 287, #109, and his letter to Villavicencio, November 4, 1873, LC, IV, 389–90; and Bustamante to parish lieutenant of Uyumbicho, December 22, 1873, ANH, Pichincha, Copiadores, Caja 85, no #, and his letter to the Parish Lieutenant of Tumbuco, July 2, 1874, same source.

41. Antonio Zambrano to Gobierno, August 10, 1869, BCH, Caja 17-3-3; and Felipe Serrade to Hacienda, April 29, 1872, ANHH, León, Caja 365, #404.

42. GGM to Antonio Zambrano, March 6, 1869, LC, IV, 116; GGM to Mariano Barona, August 4, 1875, LC, IV, 542–43; José Eguiguren to governor of Manabí, December 11, 1872, ANH, Copiadores, Caja 78, Libro 290, #39; Mariano Barona to Gobierno, February 22, 1874, ANHG, Los Ríos, #73, and his letter of July 19, 1874 to Gobierno, ANHG, Los Ríos, #238; and España to Hacienda, July 26, 1873, ANHH, Imbabura, Caja 339, #101.

43. Mera to Gobierno, April 26, 1873, ANHG, Tungurahua, no #; and JJF (Jr.) to Gobierno, November 9, 1871, ANHG, Los Ríos, #237.

44. José Zambrano to Gobierno, March 14, 1872, BCH, 20-5-15; and Pedro del Alcázar to Hacienda, October 5, 1873, ANHH, León, Caja 366, #180.

45. Hamilton to London, January 12, 1871, FO, 25/57, 39–41; GGM to Mariana, April 15, 1875, LC, IV, 518–19; Kolberg, *Hacia*, 349; and Simson, *Travels*, 4–5.

46. Clark, *Redemptive Work*, 1–2; GGM to Marianita, August 28 and 31, 1872, LC, IV, 283–85; and Wolf, *Geography and Geology*, 225.

47. Burns, *Poverty of Progress*, 135–37.

48. Diary of Antonio Flores, May 10, 1870, AF, 3; Francisco León to Beltrán Fourquet, June 1, 1870, AMRE, Comunicaciones, 44; and unsigned letter to Henry Meiggs, May 25, 1870, AMRE, C.35.9, #000091-92. For the contract with the Bank of Ecuador's guarantee, see BC/JJC, Libro 01587, #10, and BC/JJC, Libro 01736, #4. See also: GGM to Antonio, December 18, 1872, BCH, 20-6-28; and Francisco Javier León to Antonio, June 18, 1873, AMRE, Comunicaciones, 47.

49. Santisteban to Hacienda, July 11, 1874, ANHH, Guayas, Caja 220, #60; GGM to Ordóñez, March 12, 1873, *Ordóñez Cartas*, 218; and Decree of GGM, July 23, 1873, ANH, Copiadores, Caja 79, Libro 90, #4.

50. Santisteban to Hacienda, June 5, 1875, ANHH, Guayas, Caja 221, #24; *El Nacional*, February 6, 1874; and GGM to Juan Aguirre Montúfar, June 16, 1875, LC, IV, 529–31.

51. José Eguiguren to governor of Chimborazo, August 20, 1873, BCH, 21-6-115; and José Eguiguren to governor of Guayas, September 2, 1874, BCH, 21-6-121.

52. José Eguiguren to governor of Guayas, August 9, 1874, BCH, 21-6-48; and José Eguiguren to governor of Guayas, June 17, 1874, BCH, 21-6-72. See also: Antonio Sucre to Hacienda, November 11, 1874, ANHH, Guayas, Caja 220, #111; Clark, *Redemptive Work*, 17–25; and GGM to Marianita, April 20, 1875, LC, IV, 518–19.

53. Mörner, *Adventurers and Proletarians*, 4, 26, 56; Jessie Coggeshall to brother Willie, September 14, 1866, WCP, Box 1, Folder 6; and Saint-Robert to Quai d'Orsay, October 10, 1866, AMAE, VII, #180-82.

54. Harry Cartwright to Consul C. L. Smith, February 3, 1874, FO, 25/61, #79-80; Wing to Fish, August 28, 1872, RDS, T-50, reel 12, #326; and Malo, *Exposición*, 52–56.

55. Statement of Pablo Bustamante, July 30, 1864, AMRE, Series F, 20, 187–92; and Contract with Victor Bazerque, in *El Nacional*, August 28, 1870.

56. Benigno Malo to Relaciones, August 11, 1865, AMRE, G.3.1.30.1, 25, #189-90; and Malo, *Exposición*, 52–53.

57. Miranda Ribadeneira, *García Moreno y la compañía*, 72–73; Francisco Javier León to Antonio, November 9, 1872, AMRE, Comunicaciones, 47; and GGM to Mera, September 26, 1874, LC, IV, 476.

58. Clarence-Smith, *Cocoa and Chocolate*, 108–9; and Heiman Guzmán, *Inmigrantes*, 56–57.

59. *Journal of the American Geographical and Statistical Society*, I, No. 1, 24–26 (January 1859); Cevallos, *Resumen*, VI, 148–51; Sattar, "Indigena," in Clark and Becker, *Highland Indians*, 22–36; and Wolf, *Geography and Geology*, 540–41.

60. Mera to Gobierno, April 26, 1873, ANHG, Tungurahua, no #; Victor Antonio de Sanmiguel to Gobierno, April 1, 1875, BAEP, reel 29; and Felipe Serrade to Gobierno, 1871, ANHG, León, 1871, no #; and Wolf, *Geography and Geology*, 540–41.

61. Pratt, *Imperial Eyes*; Hassaurek, *Four Years*, 61, 171; Wing to Fish, August 11, 1870, RDS, T-50, reel 8, no #; Frizell, "Travelers in Nineteenth Century Ecuador," 251–57; William Coggeshall to Governor Cox, January 15, 1864, WCP, Box 3, Folder 1; and Jessie Coggeshall to Willie, September 14, 1866, WCP, Box 1, Folder 6.

62. GGM to Juan Villavicencio, April 23, 1873, LC, IV, 336–37.

63. Chiriboga, *Jornaleros*, 88–90, 111; Francisco Javier León to governor of León, May 6, 1871, ANH, Copiadores, Caja 79, Libro 296, #41, and his letter to governor of Tungurahua, August 26, 1871, ANH, Copiadores, same source, #73, 1870; Juan José Lazo to Gobierno, March 13, 1867, ANHG, Pichincha, 1867, no #; Antonio Ribadeneira to Gobierno, February 2, 1867, ANHG, Imbabura, 1867, #12; and Lyons, *Hacienda*, 48–54.

64. Ramón Samaniego to Gobierno, September 12, 1868, ANHG, Loja, 1868, #74; and Miguel Fernández de Córdoba to Gobierno, September 1, 1868, ANHG, Azuay, 1868, #112.

65. Bruno Dávalos to Gobierno, enclosing *jefe político* Antonio Rodríguez's account, February 26, 1868, ANHG, Chimborazo, 1868, #28; and his report of Feburary 29, 1868, to Gobierno, same source, #30.

66. Bruno Dávalos to Gobierno, February 28, 1868, ANHG, Chimborazo, 1868, #23; Francisco Javier Piedrahita to Dr. Carbo, February 29, 1868, VSA, Reel 1 (Fasc. 14-5A); and Francisco J. Montalvo to Gobierno, February 29, 1868, ANHG, Tungurahua, 1868, #28.

67. Bruno Dávalos to Gobierno, March 1, 1868, ANHG, Chimborazo, 1868, #36; and his letter to Gobierno, March 4, 1868, same source, #33.

68. Benjamín Chiriboga to Gobierno, April 2, 1868, ANHG, Chimborazo, 1868, #31; and Miguel Fernández de Córdoba to Gobierno, March 3, 1868, ANHG, Azuay, 1868, no #.

69. Carlos Zambrano to Gobierno, April 25, 1868, ANHG, Chimborazo, 1868, #43; and his letter of June 28, 1868, same source, #95.

70. Bruno Dávalos to Gobierno, March 13, 1868, ANHG, Chimborazo, #39; Bishop Ignacio Ordóñez to Gobierno, March 7, 1868, ANHG, Chimborazo, 1868, no #; Miguel Fernández de Córdoba to Gobierno, March 11, 1868, ANHG, Azuay, 1868, #41; and Camilo Ponce to president of the Council of Government, March 17, 1868, ANHG, Pichincha, 1868, #2.

71. Costales Samaniego, *Daquilema*, 148–50; Garcés, *Rex*, 95–97; Costales Samaniego, *Último guaminga*, 35–37, 65–67; Ibarra, *Nos encontramos amenazados*; Juan José Valencia to Gobierno, December 19, 1871, ANHG, Chimborazo, #115; Wing to Fish, December 23, 1871, RDS, T-50, reel 10, #175; and Larrea Checa to Hacienda, December 23, 1871, ANHG, Chimborazo, Caja 113, no #.

72. Costales Samaniego, *Daquilema*, 150–53; Darío Latorre to Larrea Checa, December 19, 1871, ANHG, Chimborazo, no #; Ministerio del Gobierno, *Informe, 1872–1873*, 4–5; and Francisco Javier León to governor of Chimborazo, December 21, 1871, ANH, Copiadores, Caja 80, Libro 297, #98.

73. Larrea Checa to Gobierno, December 19, 1871, ANHG, Chimborazo, #116, and Juan José Valencia to Gobierno, December 20, 1871, same source #117; Larrea Checa to governor of Tungurahua, December 22, 23, 26, 1871, ANHG, Chimborazo, no #; #119 and #121; and Ignacio Paredes to Larrea Checa, December 23, 1871, ANHG, Chimborazo, no #.

74. Larrea Checa to Gobierno, January 3, 1872, ANHG, Chimborazo, #1; and Francisco Javier León to Larrea Checa, January 6, 1872, ANH, Copiadores, Caja 80, Libro 297, #2.

75. Larrea Checa to Gobierno, January 10, 1872, ANHG, #5; *El Nacional*, May 13, 1872; GGM to Ordóñez, March 27, 1872, LC, IV, 268; and Costales Samaniego, *Daquilema*, 194–203.

76. Larrea Checa to Gobierno, October 29, 1872, ANHG, Chimborazo, #90; and Wing to Fish, December 23, 1871, RDS, T-50, reel 10, #175.

77. Wing to Fish, December 23, 1871, RDS, T-30, reel 10, #175; Velasco, *Historia*; and Costales Samaniego, *Daquilema*, 138–40.

78. Guerrero, "Ventriloquist's Image"; and Espinosa Apolo, *Mestizos ecuatorianos.*

79. Francisco Luque to Relaciones, November 10, 1871, AMRE, C.35.9, no #; *El Nacional*, June 21, 1865, and the proposal of Neptalí Bonifaz, August 25, 1869, BAEP, reel 45; and Ahvenainen, *Cable Companies*, 96–106.

80. *Leyes, Decretos Legislativos*, 250–51; Proposals from Neptalí Bonifaz, September 4, 1868, BAEP, reel 45, and José Eguiguren to Governor of Guayas, October 22, 1873, BCH, 21-6-216; and Vacas Galindo, *Telégrafo nacional*, 8–9.

81. Hamilton to Earl of Derby, May 23, 1874, FO, 25/61, #63-64; Francisco Javier Salazar to Beltrán Fourquet, October 6, 1869, AMRE, Comunicaciones, 44; C. Y. Smith to Derby, September 10, 1872, FO, 25/58, #143-143; and Medina and Smith Company to Hacienda, February 28, 1872, BCH, 20-5-8.

82. José Eguiguren to governor of Guayas, September 24, 1870, ANH, Copia-

dores, Caja 77, Libro 286, #847; Enrique McClellan to governor of Guayas, November 4, 1874, ANHH, Guayas, Caja 220, no #; Santisteban to Gobierno, January 17, 1872, ANHG, Guayas, #19; and Francisco Arboleda to Council of State, February 8, 1872, ANHH, Consejo de Estado, Caja 4, no #.

83. Pineo, *Life and Work*; Gómez Iturralde, *Guayaquil,* II, 50–52; and Santisteban to Gobierno, July 2, 1870, ANHG, Guayas, #319.

84. Santisteban to Gobierno, July 23, 1870, ANHG, Guayas, #343; Gómez Iturralde, *Guayaquil,* II, 42–46, 125–26; Santisteban to Gobierno, September 20, 1873, ANHG, Guayas, #207; and Juan José Eguiguren to governor of Guayas, February 25, 1874, ANH, Copiadores, Guayas, Caja 85, #123.

85. Hassaurek, *Four Years*, 48–49; *El Nacional,* August 30, 1872, and December 4, 1874; Kolberg, *Hacia*, 191; Lara, *Quito*, 208–11; and Bustamante to parish lieutenant of Tabacundo, June 19, 1874, AHN, Copiadores, Caja 85, no #.

86. Wing to Fish, October 16, 1870, RDS, T-50, reel 8, #34; España to Gobierno, April 9, 1875, BAEP, reel 29; and España to Gobierno, March 4, 1871, ANHG, Imbabura, #26, and his letter of May 23, 1874, ANHH, Imbabura, Caja 340, #58.

87. Ordóñez to Gobierno, February 21, 1871, ANHG, Azuay, #46; Nicolás Rendón to Governor of León, January 12, 1871, ANHH, León, Caja 364, no #; and Rolando, *Obras públicas.*

88. Efrén Reyes, *Breve historia*, III, 609–10; and Rodríguez, *Public Policy*, 84–85.

89. Rolando, *Obras públicas*, 33–41.

8. DEATH AND THE HEREAFTER

1. Johnson (ed.), *Death, Dismemberment.*

2. Berthe, *Vengador*, II, 340–51; Gomezjurado, *García Moreno*, IX, 241–55; and Carrión, *Patíbulo*, 691–93. Borrero, *Refutación*, 83–91.

3. GGM to Ignacio del Alcázar, July 22, 1874, BAEP, reel 35; GGM to Juan Borja, June 8, 1874, LC, IV, 449; and García Moreno to Borja, October 21, 1874, LC, IV, 481–82.

4. José P. Zambrano to Gobierno, July 13, 1871, ANHG, Manabí, #123; José Navarrete to Gobierno, July 12, 1871, ANHG, Manabí, no #; Carlos María Baldas to Gobierno, August 31, 1871, same source, #150; and GGM to Francisco J. Salazar Cartas, July 26, 1871, *Salazar*, 11–12.

5. Montalvo, *Dictadura perpetua;* Spindler and Brooks, *Selections*, 93–107; and Barrera, *De nuestra América*, 35–63.

6. Anon., *D. Juan Montalvo.*

7. Destruge, *Guayaquil*, 186–95; GGM to Rafael Borja, November 18, 1874, LC, IV, 489–90, and his letter to Borja, December 9, 1874, LC, IV, 495–96; and Wing to Fish, August 12, 1874, RDS, T-50, reel 13, #409.

8. "Candidato para la presidencia de la república," October 8, 1874, ANHG, Imbabura, no #; and Gomezjurado, *García Moreno*, IX, 252–54. The consul at Guayaquil reported that the polling places were empty: See Charles Weile to William Hunter, June 24, 1875, USDG, reel 4. See also: GGM to Juan León Mera, December 30, 1874, LC, IV, 498; and GGM to Juan Villavicencio, May 25, 1875, LC, IV, 525–26.

9. RdA to Lucio Salazar, August 5, 1875, BC/JJC, File 01781, no #.

10. GGM to Juan Villavicencio, April 6, 1875, LC, IV, 515, and April 13, 1875, LC, IV, 516–17; and L. Boulard to Quai d'Orsay, September 3, 1875, AMAE, 8, 474–80.

11. GGM to J. J. González, August 19, 1874, LC, IV, 469; GGM to Juan Villavicencio, August 23, 1874, LC, IV, 470, and his letter to Marianita, August 31, 1872, LC, IV, 284–85; and GGM to Juan Villavicencio, May 25, 1875, LC, IV, 525–26.

12. Carrión, *Patíbulo*, 429–31, 473–506; and Montalvo, *Dictadura perpetua*.

13. GGM to governor of Guayas, December 9, 1870, LC, IV, 228; and GGM's decree, March 24, 1869, LC, IV, 118.

14. GGM to Manuel Andrade Marín, October 12, 1869, LC, IV, 162; and GGM to Ordóñez, April 30, 1873, LC, IV, 339–40.

15. GGM to Benigno Malo, November 17, 1869, LC, IV, 171–73; and GGM to José C. de Mosquera, November 26, 1870, LC, IV, 225.

16. GGM to Rafael Borja, December 9, 1874, LC, IV, 495–96; GGM to Antonio Mancilla, June 5, 1869, LC, IV, 138–39; GGM to Rafael Borja, November 25, 1874, LC, IV, 490–91; and GGM to Mercedes Rives de Robinson, May 22, 1869, LC, IV, 133–36.

17. José Félix Luque to Relaciones, October 11, 1873, AMRE, C.35.10, #000060-61; Piedrahita to Relaciones, December 11, 1873, AMRE, C.35.10, #0000117; St. Robert to Quai d'Orsay, October 4, 1873, AMAE, 8, no #; Francisco Javier León's decree, February 14, 1871, in RDS, T-50, reel 9; and GGM to Francisco Javier Salazar, August 16, 1871, *Salazar Cartas*, 14.

18. GGM to Ordóñez, July 3, 1869, LC, IV, 144.

19. Wing to Fish, December 21, 1871, RDS, T-50, reel 10; and GGM to Juan Villavicencio, September 2, 1873, LC, IV, 370.

20. GGM to Francisco Javier Salazar, April 6, 1872, *Salazar Cartas*, 31; and GGM to Salazar, October 5, 1872, *Salazar Cartas*, 37.

21. GGM to Mera, February 14, 1874, LC, IV, 418; GGM to José García Moreno (Pepe), July 28, 1875, BAEP, reel 35; and GGM to Pope Pius IX, July 17, 1875, *Salazar Cartas*, 47–48.

22. GGM to Marianita, June 12, 1872, LC, IV, 276; GGM to Marianita, August 31, 1872, LC, IV, 284–85; and GGM to Marianita, September 14, 1872, LC, IV, 290–91, and his letter to Marianita, April 24, 1875, LC, IV, 519–20. The family destroyed her letters to Gabriel.

23. GGM to Marianita, September 7, 1872, LC, IV, 287–89; and GGM to Rafael Borja, October 6, 1874, LC, IV, 480. See also his letters to J. J. González, July 3, 1875, LC, IV, 532–33; and Mariano Barona, July 28, 1875, LC, IV, 539.

24. GGM to Francisco J. Salazar, September 20, 1871, *Salazar Cartas*, 19; GGM to Rafael Borja, November 19, 1873, LC, IV, 394; GGM to Rafael Borja, June 24, 1874, LC, IV, 453; and GGM to Juan Villavicencio, February 2, 1875, LC, IV, 503–4.

25. Gomezjurado, *García Moreno*, X, 33–37; Berthe, *Vengador*, II, 174–82; Ayala Mora, *Lucha política*, 168–69; and Charles Weile to Washington, December 24, 1869, USDG, reel 4. The 1869 conspiracy broke out in several cities, and García Moreno's good friend, Governor Carlos Ordóñez, was nearly killed.

26. GGM to Mera, December 22, 1869, LC, IV, 180.

27. Andrade, *Seis de Agosto*, 66–67; and Andrade, *Montalvo y García Moreno*, II, 294–96. The best-researched volume on the assassination is Loor, *Asesinos*.

28. Andrade, *Seis de Agosto*, 65–66; and Loor, *Asesinos*, 92–98. See also: Rafael and Federico Cornejo, *Conspiración*, 9.

29. Loor, *Asesinos*, 112–13, 118–19; Andrade, *Seis de Agosto*, 62–63; and Cornejo and Cornejo, *Conspiración*, 2–9.

30. Loor, *Asesinos*, 74–82; Andrade, *Seis de Agosto*, 63–64; Cornejo and Cornejo, *Conspiración*, 8; and Villegas Dominguez, *Abelardo Moncayo*, 65–100. Daniel Gómez [Jesuit] to Gobierno, May 19, 1875, ANHG, Azuay, #29; and Loor, *Asesinos*, 81–83, suggest that Moncayo had a sexual relationship with Juana Terrazas.

31. Andrade, *Seis de Agosto*, 68–77, 108–9; and Cornejo, "Juicio Criminal," August 10, 1875, ANHC, Caja 324, 44–45.

32. Loor, *Asesinos*, 57–68; GGM to Padre Pablo de Blas, April 21, 1858, LC, II, 82–83; GGM to Juan Villavicencio, June 25, 1875, LC, IV, 528–29; and Guzmán Polanco, *Entretelones*, 21–53.

33. Andrade, *Seis de Agosto*, 77–87; and Loor, *Asesinos*, 65–71, 143–44. Andrade suggests that Rayo acted on his own, but the idea of two plots coming to fruition simultaneously seems far-fetched.

34. Loor, *Asesinos*, 158–61; and Manuel Echevarri to Gobierno, October 30, 1863, ANHG, Pichincha, #84.

35. Apostolic Vicar Vicente Daniel Pastor to Gobierno, December 3, 1867, BAEP, reel 35, and Faustino Rayo to Gobierno, November 23, 1867, same source; Faustino Rayo to Gobierno, March 8, 1872, BAEP, reel 35; Father Andrés Pérez to Francisco Javier León, August 26, 1873, BAEP, reel 35; and Jouanen, *Jesuitas y el oriente*, 35, 42–43.

36. López, *Muerte de García Moreno*, 25; and Agramonte, *Psicopatológico*, 251–52. Loor, *Asesinos*, 107. Rayo's son stated that the only cause of his father's hatred was the business motive: Pérez Moscoso, *Habla el hijo.*

37. Loor, *Asesinos*, 174–77, 128–31.

38. Andrade, *Seis de agosto*, 125, 130–32; López, *Muerte de García Moreno*, 24–25; and FIS (Francisco Ignacio Salazar—a brother), *Defensa*, 15–31.

39. Francisco Javier Salazar, *Verdad*, 1–2. Andrade, *Montalvo y García Moreno*, II, spends many pages talking about Salazar's role, as does his *Seis de agosto*, 259–79.

40. Gomezjurado, *Mártir García Moreno?*, 72–92; Loor, *Asesinos*, 206–23; Herrera, *García Moreno*, 85–92; GGM to Pope Pius IX, July 17, 1875, *Salazar Cartas*, 47–48; GGM to Juan Aguirre Montúfar, June 16, 1875, LC, IV, 529–31; and Proaño y Vega, *Seis de agosto*, 20.

41. Andrade, *Seis de agosto*, 73–75, 96–98; Borrero, *Refutación*, 692–94; and Weile to William Hunter, August 24, 1875, USDG, reel 4.

42. Loor, *Asesinos*, 226–28, 235–39.

43. Andrade, *Seis de agosto*, 107–13; and Loor, *Asesinos*, 224–26, 233–36. See also testimony of Manuel Pallares, García Moreno's aide-de-camp, about the drinking: ANHC, Caja 324, 28–29.

44. Testimony of Antonio Martínez, ANHC, Caja 324, 14, and Rafael Morillo, same source, 19, and Vicente Monteros, same source, 29; testimony of Manuel Pallares, ANHC, Caja 324, 28; and Herrera, *García Moreno*, 93. Herrera was working in the palace that day, although not a witness to any of the events.

45. Testimony of: Roberto Andrade, ANHC, Caja 324, 143–44, and Andrade, *Seis de agosto*, 118–19; Ulpiano Coronel, ANHC, Caja 324, 22–23; and Emilio Vaca, same source, 25–26.

46. Testimony of: Daniel Cortés, ANHC, Caja 324, 23–24, and Manuel Vaca, same source, 39–40; Andrade, *Seis de agosto*, 128–30; and Rafael Bedoya, ANHC, Caja

324, 20, Lieutenant Darío Buitrón, same source, 40–41, and Mariano Carrión, same source, 41–42.

47. Andrade, *Seis de agosto,* 120–22; and testimony of: Antonio Montiel, ANHC, Caja 324, 18, and Rafael Murillo, same source, 19.

48. Testimony of: Margarita Carrera, ANHC, Caja 324, 21–22, Angela Sagú, same source, 27, and Antonio Martínez, same source, 14–15; and Daniel Cortés, ANHC, Caja 324, 23–24, Rafael Puerta, same source, 29–30, and José Mosquera, same source, 36–37.

49. Testimony of: Emilio Vaca, ANHC, Caja 324, 25–26, Vicente Monteros, same source, 29, and Ignacio Sánchez, same source, 37–38. See also: Francisco Javier León's memoirs, August 11, 1875, printed in *El Derecho,* November 4, 1921; and Proaño y Vega, *Seis de agosto,* 11–13.

50. See the autopsy report: ANHC, Caja 324, 10–13, in Herrera, *García Moreno,* 93–94. See also: Andrade, *Seis de agosto,* 121–22; and Francisco Javier León's memoirs, *El Derecho,* November 4, 1921. Many eyewitnesses, such as Antonio Martínez, thought García Moreno was dead as he lay in the plaza (see Martínez testimony, ANHC, Caja 324, 14–15), while Daniel Cortés said GGM was still asking for help (see Cortés testimony, same source, 23–24). See also: L. Boulard to Quai d'Orsay, August 17, 1875, AMAE, 8, no #. Eloy Proaño y Vega, the editor of *El Nacional* who helped carry García Moreno into the cathedral, also asserted he was alive, as did Francisco Javier León (see Proaño y Vega, *Seis de agosto,* 11).

51. Miguel Cevallos et al., petition memorializing García Moreno from the town of Carapungo, August 22, 1875, BAEP, reel 29; Santisteban to Gobierno, August 12, 1875, ANHG, Guayas, #175; Demélas and Saint-Geours, *Jerusalén,* 191–92; and Gomezjurado, *García Moreno,* X, 115–20.

52. L. Boulard to Quai d'Orsay, August 17, 1875, AMAE, 8, no #. Marianita's letters to the women of Tunja (November 30, 1875) and to Abraham Moreno, head of Catholic Society of Medellín, Colombia (also November 30, 1875), are in Proaño y Vega, *Colección.*

53. Miguel Salazar to Gobierno, August 14, 1875, ANHG, Imbabura, #51; Eguiguren to Gobierno, August 14, 1875, ANHG, Loja, #75; *El Nacional,* August 14, 1875; Francisco Javier León to Antonio, September 22, 1875, AF, #01214; and Piedrahita to Relaciones, August 18, 1875, AMRE, C.35.10, #000196.

54. Testimony of: Camilo Nolivos, ANHC, Caja 324, 26–27, and Lieutenant Darío Buitrón, same source, 40–41.

55. Andrade, *Seis de agosto,* 135–36; and testimony of: Francisco Javier Martínez, ANHC, Caja 324, 30, and Sergeant Mariano Carrión, same source, 41–42, and Gabriel Molina, ANHC, Caja 324, 17. The shooter, Manuel López, claimed he fired without orders: See Loor, *Asesinos,* 261.

56. For examples of the identification, see testimony of: Rafael Morillo, ANHC, Caja 324, 19, and Daniel Cortés, same source, 23–24; and Vicente Antonio de Sanmiguel to Gobierno, August, 1875, BAEP, reel 29.

57. Testimony of: Rafael Barba, ANHC, Caja 324, 54, and Manuel Cornejo, same source, 44–46; Andrade, *Seis de agosto*; testimony of: Manuel Polanco, ANHC, Caja 324, II, 10–13; FSC, *Defensa de Polanco,* 1–45.

58. Testimony of: Rosa Almeida, ANHC, Caja 324, 2–3, Rafael Delgado and Car-

los García, same source, 3–5, 9–10, and (fellow *pastusos*) Pantaleón León, same source, 55–56, 63–64.

59. Loor, *Asesinos*, 133–39; testimony of: Gregorio Campuzano, ANHC, Caja 324, II, 22–23, and Angela Sagú, same source, 27–28; and Juan Chiriboga to Gobierno, August 14, 1875, ANHG, Chimborazo, #77.

60. Loor, *Asesinos*, 120–27; and testimony of Manuel Cornejo, ANHC, Caja 324, 44–46.

61. Miguel Salazar to Gobierno, August 23, 1875, ANHG, Imbabura, #57; and Moncayo, *Aclaraciones*, 22–23. For petitions supporting dropping the case against Moncayo, see ANHC, Caja 324, 226–34. See also: Loor, *Asesinos*, 88–91.

62. Miguel Salazar to Gobierno, September 4, 1875, ANHG, Imbabura, #70. Andrade's extradition is in ANHC, Caja 324, 81–171.

63. Spindler and Brooks, *Selections from Montalvo*, 1–2; and Loor, *Asesinos*, 187–88, 203–5.

64. Vicente Cuesta to Bishop Remigio, August 25, 1875, *Ordóñez Cartas*, 247–59; Hamilton to London, September 4, 1875, FO, 25/65, 95–96; Christian Nullweber to Fish, December 18, 1875, RDS, T-50, reel 14, #14; RdA to Vicente Lucio Salazar, August 23, 1875, BC/JJC, File 01781; and Manuel de Ascásubi to Vicente Lucio Salazar, October 13, 1875, BC/JJC, Libro 01781.

65. Johnson, *Death, Dismemberment*, 1–26.

66. For a very complete compilation of eulogies through 1921, see Gomezjurado, *García Moreno*, X and XI.

67. Decree of Congress, August 30, 1875, BAEP, reel 29.

68. Ribadeneira, *Martirio;* José Youanen to Carlos María de la Torre, Archbishop of Quito, April 20, 1942, AARZO, Caja 117; and Paul, *García Moreno.*

69. Proaño y Vega, *Seis de Agosto*, 13–17, BC/JJC, Libro 01780, #15; and Salazar Alvarado, *Encuentro con la historia*, 12–42.

70. Gomezjurado, *Hércules cristiano*, 1, 35–37; Gomezjurado, *Mártir*, 178–200; Boletín Franciscano organo de la tercera orden, 3, No. 4, 4–9; and Valera, "Milagros de García Moreno," in *Caricatura*, 22–23.

CONCLUSION

1. Anonymous, *Batalla del monument;* and Villacís Molina, "La batalla," *Vistazo*, 74–79.

2. Andrade Moreno, *Protesta.*

3. Safford, "Politics, Ideology," III, 388–89.

4. Ayala Mora, "García Moreno y la gestación," 146.

5. Anderson, *Imagined Communities*, 4–7; and Corrigan and Sayer, *Great Arch*, 1–3.

6. Ayala Mora, "García Moreno y la gestación," 148, 160.

7. Ayala Mora, *Nueva Historia*, VII, 201; and Gardner, *Leading Minds*, 9–18, 224, 285.

8. George Earl Church to James G. Blaine, February 15, 1881, BC/JJC, Libro 01607, #1; Hamilton to London, August 8, 1877, FO, 25/68, #62; and L. Boulard to Quai d'Orsay, September 18, 1875, AMAE, 8, #83-86.

9. Meyer, *Huerta*, 231.

Bibliography

ARCHIVAL SOURCES

Manuscripts

Ecuador (Quito)

Archivo Nacional de Historia. Archivo del Ministerio de Gobierno.

———. Archivo del Ministerio de Hacienda.

———. Criminales.

———. Fondo Especial.

Banco Central del Ecuador. Archivo Histórico del Banco Central del Ecuador. Archivo del Ministerio de Hacienda.

———. Archivo Secreto Vaticano (microfilm).

———. Fondo Jacinto Jijón y Caamaño.

Biblioteca del Poder Legislativo. Actas de la Camara del Senado.

Ministerio de Defensa. Archivo General de Defensa.

Ministerio de Relaciones Exteriores. Archivo Histórico de Relaciones Exteriores.

Palacio Arzobispal. Archivo Arzobispal.

Pontificia Universidad Católica del Ecuador. Archivo Juan José Flores.

———. Diarios de Antonio Flores.

United States

Benson Latin American Collection. University of Texas, Austin. Dispatches from U.S. consuls in Guayaquil, 1826–1906 (National Archives microfilm T-209, 13 reels).

Kentucky State Historical Society. Frankfurt, Kentucky. E. Rumsey Wing Notebook. MS-98SC282.

Krueger Library, Winona State University. Winona, Minnesota. Archives du Ministère des Affaires Etrangères, France (microfilm, 4 reels).

———. Foreign Office Reports, Great Britain (British Public Records Office microfilm, 31 reels).

———. Records of the Department of State Relating to Ecuador, 1820–1906 (National Archives microfilm T-50, 19 reels).

Lilly Library, Indiana University, Bloomington, Indiana. Camilo Mutis Daza Collection. AKY 8156, 143 items.

Ohio Historical Society. Columbus, Ohio. William Coggeshall Papers. Collection MSS 115.

———. Friedrich Hassaurek Papers. Collection MSS 113.

University of Arizona. Tucson, Arizona. Biblioteca Aurelio Espinosa Pólit (microfilm 4835, 70 reels).

Published Documents

Boletínes del Ejército, República del Perú. In *Dos documentos sobre Castilla (una biografía por Juan Gualberto Valdivia y el boletín del ejército de 1859–1860)*. Lima: Editorial Huascarán, 1953.

"Cartas de García Moreno al Dr. Antonio Borrero." *Revista del Centro Histórico y Geográfico de Cuenca*. Cuenca: Tip de la Universidad, 1922, pp. 146–66.

Código militar de la república del Ecuador. New York: Imprenta de Hallet & Breen, 1871.

Colección de leyes y decretos dadas por el congreso constitucional de 1863. Quito: Imprenta Nacional, 1864.

Colección de leyes y decretos de la convención nacional. Quito: Imprenta del Gobierno, 1862.

Colección de leyes, decretos y resoluciónes dadas por el congreso constitucional de 1867. Quito: Imprenta Nacional, 1868.

Diario de los trabajos de la convención nacional reunida en la capital de la república en el año de 1861. Quito: Imprenta del Gobierno, 1861.

Dos documentos sobre Castilla. Lima: Editorial Huascaron, 1873.

Exposición del ministerio de hacienda dirigida al congreso constitucional de 1871. Quito: Imprenta de Manuel V. Flor, 1871.

Informe del ministerio del interior, 1872–1873. Quito: Imprenta Nacional, 1873.

Informe que presenta el encargado del ministerio de hacienda a las cámaras legislativas. Quito: Imprenta Nacional, 1863.

Lei orgánica de instrucción pública seguida del reglamento general de estudios dado par el consejo general. Quito: José M. Sanz, 1865.

Ley de aduanas. In *Colección de las leyes vigentes en materia de aduanas, codificada por el tribunal de cuentas de la república en conformidad con lo dispuesto en el artículo 6 del decreto legislativo del 30 de Octubre, 1873*. Quito: Imprenta Nacional, 1873.

Ley de Bancos y el informe aprobado por el senado de Ecuador en 1867. Quito: Tipográfica de Miguel Andrade Vargas, 1868.

Leyes, decretos legislativos y ejecutivos y circulares expedidos en 1869, 1870, 1871, 1872, 1873, y 1874. Quito: Imprenta Nacional, 1874.

Loor, Wilfrido, ed. *Cartas de Gabriel García Moreno*, 4 vols. Quito: La Prensa Católica, 1956.

Ordóñez Mata, Alfonso. *Cartas políticas de Gabriel García Moreno a Carlos Ordóñez Lazo, 1860–1873*, Cuenca: Tip. Alianza, 1923.

Pólit Laso, Manuel María. *Doce cartas de García Moreno a Dr. D. Antonio Flores Jijón*. Quito: Imprenta y Encuadernación del Clero, 1922.

———. *Escritos y discursos de Gabriel García Moreno*, 2 vols. Quito: Tipografía y Encuadernación Salesianas, 1923.

Recopilación de documentos oficiales de la época colonial. Guayaquil: Imprenta de "La Nación," 1894.

Reglamento de escuelas primarias compilado por el hermano Yon-José visitador de las es-

cuelas Cristianas del Ecuador y adaptado por el Supreme Gobierno para todas las escuelas de la república. Quito: Imprenta Nacional, 1873.

Reglamento de policía formado por la junta provincial de Pichincha y sancionado por la gobernación de la provincia en el presente año de 1865. Quito: Imprenta Nacional, 1896.

Villalba, Jorge, ed. *Epistolario diplomático del presidente Gabriel García Moreno, 1859–1869.* Quito: PUCE, 1976.

Newspapers (Quito)

El Diablo (1846–1848)
La Nación (1853)
El Nacional (1859–1875)
La Unión Nacional (1857)
El Vengador (1846)
El Zurriago (1846)

SECONDARY SOURCES

Bibliographies, Guides, and Aids

Alarcón Costa, César Augusto. *Diccionario biográfico Ecuatoriano.* Quito: Editorial Raíses, 2000.

Arboleda, Gustavo. *Diccionario biográfico de la república del Ecuador.* Quito: Tip. de Escuela de artes y oficios, 1910.

Cultural, Educational, Tourist, Industrial, Commercial, Agricultural, and Livestock Information Handbook of the Republic of Ecuador, 3 vols. Cuenca: Científico Latina Editores Cía. Ltd., 1980.

Hart, George C. *A Collection of Ecuadorian Laws at Indiana University.* Bloomington: Indiana University Press, 1975.

Larrea, Carlos. *Bibliografía de Gabriel García Moreno en el centenario de su asesinato: 1875–1975.* Quito: Corporación de Estudios y Publicaciones, 1975.

Norris, Robert E. *Guía bibliográfica para el estudio de la historia del Ecuador.* Austin: Institute of Latin American Studies, 1978.

Pérez Pimentel, Rodolfo, ed. *Diccionario biográfico del Ecuador*, 22 vols. Guayaquil: Litográfica imprenta de la Universidad de Guayaquil, 1987–2000.

TePaske, John J., ed. *Research Guide to Andean History: Bolivia, Chile, Ecuador, and Peru.* Durham: Duke University Press, 1981.

Vasco de Escudero, Grecia. *Guía de los fondos documentales del Archivo Nacional del Ecuador*, 2 vols. Quito: Consejo Nacional de Archivos, 1994.

Books

Agramonte, Roberto. *Biografía del dictador García Moreno: Estudio psicopatológico e histórico.* Havana: Cultural, 1935.

Ahvenainen, Jorma. *The European Cable Companies in South America before the First World War.* Jyvaskyla, Finland: Gummerus Printing, 2004.

Albornoz, Víctor Manuel. *Cantonización de Paute 1860-Febrero 26-1960.* Cuenca: Casa de la Cultura Ecuatoriana, 1960.

Anderson, Benedict. *Imagined Communities: Reflections on the Origin and Spread of Nationalism.* London: Verso, 1991.

Andrade, Roberto. *Montalvo y García Moreno*, 2 vols. Quito: Editorial el Conejo, 1987.

———. *Seis de agosto o sea muerte de García Moreno.* Portoviejo, Ecuador: Oficina Tipográfica del Colegio Olmedo, 1896.

Andrade Moreno, René. *Protesta: Monumentos a dos traidores.* Quito: El Comercio, 1983.

Andrien, Kenneth J. *The Kingdom of Quito, 1690–1830: The State and Regional Development.* Cambridge: Cambridge University Press, 1995.

Applebaum, Nancy. *Muddied Waters: Race, Region, and Local History.* Durham, NC: Duke University Press, 2003.

Arboleda, Gonzalo. *Julio Arboleda y Gabriel García Moreno.* Bogotá: Imprenta de "El Telegrama," 1888.

Arendaño, Joaquín de. *Imagen del Ecuador: Economía y sociedad vistas por un viajero del siglo xix.* Quito: Corporación Editorial Nacional, 1985.

Armijos Suárez, Julio. *Gabriel García Moreno, presidente de la república del Ecuador y Monseñor José Ignacio Eyzaguirre Portales, fundador del Pontificio colegio Pío-Latino Américano.* Quito: La Prensa Católica, 1962.

Ayala Mora, Enrique. *Lucha política y origen de los partidos en Ecuador.* Quito: Corporación Editorial Nacional, 1982.

———, ed. *Nueva historia del Ecuador*, 16 vols. Quito: Corporacíon Editorial Nacional, 1988–2005.

Ayora, Jorge A. *La primera emisión de sellos postales de Ecuador, 1865–1872.* Quito: Banco Central del Ecuador, 1972.

Backscheider, Paula R. *Reflections on Biography.* Oxford: Oxford University Press, 1999.

Barrera, Isaac J. *De nuestra América: Hombres y cosas de la república del Ecuador.* Quito: Editorial Casa de la Cultura Ecuatoriana, 1965.

Barrett, Jeffrey W. *Impulse to Revolution in Latin America.* New York: Praeger Press, 1955.

Beattie, Peter. *The Tribute of Blood: Army, Honor, Race, and Nation in Brazil, 1864–1945.* Durham, NC: Duke University Press, 2001.

Benavides, O. Hugo. *Making Ecuadorian Histories: Four Centuries of Defining Power.* Austin: University of Texas Press, 2004.

Berthe, Augustine. *García Moreno, presidente de la república del Ecuador: Vengador y mártir del derecho cristiano.* Paris: Victor Retaux é Hijo Libreros Éditores, 1892.

Blanksten, George. *Ecuador: Constitutions and Caudillos.* Berkeley: University of California Press, 1951.

Bollaert, William. *Antiquarian, Ethnological, and Other Researches in New Granada, Equador, Peru, and Chile.* London: Trubner, 1860.

Bonifaz Andrade, Diego. *Guachalá: Historia de una hacienda en Cayembe.* Quito: Ediciones Abya-Yala, 1995.

Borja y Borja, Ramiro. *Las constituciones del Ecuador.* Madrid: Ediciones Cultura Hispánica, 1951.

Borrero Cortázar, Antonio. *Refutación por A.B.C. del libro titulado "García Moreno Presidente del Ecuador vengador y mártir del derecho cristiano (1821–1875)" por RPA Berthe.* Guayaquil: Imp. de la Nación, 1889.

Bulmer-Thomas, Victor. *The Economic History of Latin America Since Independence.* Cambridge: Cambridge University Press, 2003.

Burns, E. Bradford. *The Poverty of Progress.* Berkeley: University of California Press, 1980.

Burr, Robert N. *By Reason or Force: Chile and the Balancing of Power in South America, 1830–1905.* Berkeley: University of California Press, 1965.

Bushnell, David. *The Santander Regime in Gran Colombia.* Newark: University of Delaware Press, 1954.

Bushnell, David, and Neill Macauley. *The Emergence of Latin America in the Nineteenth Century.* New York: Oxford University Press, 1988.

Carbo, Pedro. *Obras.* Guayaquil: Imprenta de la Universidad de Guayaquil, 1983.

Cárdenas Reyes, María Cristina. *Historia de la Universidad de Cuenca, 1867–1997.* Cuenca: Instituto de Investigaciones Universidad de Cuenca, 2001.

Cardoso, Fernando, and E. Faletto. *Dependency and Development in Latin America.* Berkeley: University of California Press, 1979.

Carrión, Benjamín. *García Moreno: El santo del patíbulo.* Quito: Editorial el Conejo, 1987.

Castillo d'Imperio, Ocarina. *Gabriel García Moreno: El orden de la piedad intolerante.* Caracas: Faces-U.C.V., 1998.

Castro-Klarén, Sara, and John Charles Chasteen, eds. *Beyond Imagined Communities: Reading and Writing the Nation in Nineteenth-Century Latin America.* Baltimore: Johns Hopkins University Press, 2003.

Cevallos, Pedro Fermín. *Resumen de la historia del Ecuador,* 6 vols. Guayaquil: Imprenta de la Nación, 1889.

Cevallos Salvador, Pedro José. *El Doctor Pedro Moncayo y su folleto titulado "El Ecuador de 1825 a 1875, sus hombres, sus instituciones y sus leyes" ante la historia.* Quito: Imprenta del Gobierno, 1887.

Chiriboga, Manuel. *Jornaleros y gran proprietarios en 135 años de exportación cacaotera.* Quito: Consejo Provincial de Pichincha, 1980.

Clarence-Smith, William G. *Cocoa Pioneer Fronts Since 1800: The Role of Smallholders, Planters, and Merchants.* New York: St. Martin's Press, 1966.

———. *Cocoa and Chocolate, 1765–1914.* London: Routledge, 2000.

Clark, A. Kim. *The Redemptive Work: Railway and Nation in Ecuador, 1895–1930.* Wilmington, DE: Scholarly Resources, 1998.

Clark, A. Kim, and Marc Becker, eds. *Highland Indians and the State in Modern Ecuador.* Pittsburgh: University of Pittsburgh Press, 2007.

Clayton, Lawrence. *Caulkers and Carpenters in a New World: The Shipyards of Colonial Guayaquil.* Athens, OH: University Center for International Studies, 1980.

Collier, Simon. *Chile: The Making of a Republic, 1830–1865: Politics and Ideas.* New York: Cambridge University Press, 2003.

Conservadores, Los de Pichincha. *El señor G. García Moreno y los liberales de Guayas.* Quito: Imprenta Nacional, 1868.

Cornejo, Rafael, and Federico Cornejo. *La conspiración del 6 de agosto en Quito.* Ipiales, Colombia: Tipografía de Nicanor Médicis, 1875.

Corrigan, Philip, and Derek Sayer. *The Great Arch: English State Formation as Cultural Revolution.* Oxford: Basil Blackwell, 1985.

Costales Samaniego, Alfredo. *Daquilema: Último guaminga.* Quito: Ediciones Abya-Yala, 1984.

———. *Fernando Daquilema: Último guaminga,* 2nd ed. Quito: Talleres Gráficos Nacionales, 1963.

Costales Samaniego, Alfredo, and Dolores Costales Peñaherrera. *Historia de Macas en el departamento del sur y la república.* Quito: Fondo Editorial, 1998.

Crow, John. *The Epic of Latin America.* Garden City, NJ: Doubleday Press, 1964.
Cunningham-Graham, R. B. *José Antonio Páez.* London: W. Heinemann, 1929.
D. Juan Montalvo y la verdad contra el o sea la defensa del Ecuador contra las calumnias e injurias publicadas en el folleto titulado "La dictadura perpetua." Guayaquil: Imprenta del Guayas, 1874.
Darwin, Charles. *The Voyage of the Beagle.* New York: Penguin Books, 1988.
Davis, William. *The Last Conquistadores: The Spanish Intervention in Peru and Chile, 1863–1866.* Athens: University of Georgia Press, 1950.
de Groot, C. F. G. *Brazilian Catholicism and the Ultramontaine Reform, 1850–1930.* Amsterdam: CEDLA, 1966.
de la Fuente, Ariel. *Children of Caudillos: Caudillo and Gaucho Insurgency during the Argentine State-Formation Process, La Rioja 1853–1870.* Durham, NC: Duke University Press, 2000.
Delpar, Helen. *Red against Blue: The Liberal Party in Colombian Politics, 1863–1899.* Tuscaloosa: University of Alabama Press, 1981.
Demélas, Marie-Danielle, and Yves Saint-Geours. *Jerusalén y Babilonia: Religión y política en el Ecuador, 1780–1880.* Quito: Corporación Editorial Nacional, 1998.
Denegri Luna, Félix. *Perú and Ecuador: Notes for the History of a Frontier.* Lima: Pontificia Universidad Católica del Perú, 1996.
Destruge, Camilo [D'Amecourt, pseud.]. *Historia de la revolución de octubre y la campaña libertadora de 1820–1822.* Barcelona: Imprenta Elzeviriana de Borras, Mestres y Cía, 1920.
———. *Historia de la prensa de Guayaquil,* 2 vols. Quito: Tipográfica y Encuadernación Salesianas, 1924.
Earle, Rebecca. *The Return of the Native: Indians and Myth-making in Spanish America, 1810–1930.* Durham, NC: Duke University Press, 2007.
Ecuatorianos, Los. *Mentiras y verdades.* Quito: J. Sans, 1873.
Eguiguren Valdivieso, Genaro. *El gobierno federal de Loja: La crisis de 1858.* Loja: Corporación Editora Nacional, 1992.
Espinosa Apolo, Manuel. *Los mestizos ecuatorianos y las señas de identitad cultural.* Quito: Tramasocial Editorial, 2000.
Estrada Ycaza, Julio. *Los bancos del siglo xix.* Guayaquil: Publicaciones de Archivo Histórico del Guayas, 1976.
Fels, Rendig. *American Business Cycles, 1865–1897.* Chapel Hill: University of North Carolina Press, 1959.
Flores Galindo, Alberto. *Buscando un Inca: Identidad y utopia en los Andes.* Lima: Instituto de Apoyo Agrario, 1987.
Flores Jijón, Antonio. *La conversión de la deuda Anglo-Ecuatoriana,* 2nd ed. Quito: Banco Central del Ecuador, 1979.
Gálvez, Manuel. *Vida de don Gabriel García Moreno.* Buenos Aires: Editorial Difusión, 1942.
Garcés, Enrique. *Daquilema Rex: Biografía de un dolor indio.* Quito: Editorial Casa de la Cultura Ecuatoriana, 1961.
Gardner, Howard. *Leading Minds: An Anatomy of Leadership.* New York: Basic Books, 1995.
George-Kaufmann, Amara. *Don Gabriel García Moreno, Präsident der Republik Ecuador.* Freiburg: Herderche Berlags-handlung, 1891.

Germán Pascal, Remigio. *Relación histórica del terremoto del 16 de agosto de 1868 en Imbabura.* Ibarra: Imprenta Municipal, 1972.

Goldwert, Marvin. *Psychic Conflict in Spanish America: Six Essays on the Psychohistory of the Region.* Washington, DC: University Press of America, 1982.

Gómez de la Torre, Manuel. *Refutación del impreso titulado "Para la Historia" publicado en Lima a nombre del General Guillermo Franco.* Quito: Imprenta de los Huérfanos de Valencia, 1861.

Gómez Iturralde, José Antonio. *Diario de Guayaquil,* 2 vols.,Guayaquil: Archivo Histórico del Guayas, 1999.

Gomezjurado, Severo. *Síntesis biográfica: Hércules cristiano, genio, representivo del Ecuador.* Riobamba: Imprenta Artística, 1941

———. *Mártir García Moreno?* Cuenca: Editorial Alba, 1952.

———. *Vida de García Moreno,* 13 vols. Cuenca and Quito: Various publishers, 1955–1975.

Graham, Richard. *Patronage and Politics in Nineteenth-Century Brazil.* Stanford, CA: Stanford University Press, 1990.

Guerrero, Andrés. *Curagas y tenientes políticos: La ley de la costumbre y la ley del estado (Otavalo 1830–1875).* Quito: Editorial el Conejo, 1990.

Guerrero, J. Agustín. *La música ecuatoriana desde su origen hasta 1875,* 2nd ed. Quito: Banco Central del Ecuador, 1984.

Guzmán Polanco, Manuel de. *Un Ecuatoriano Ilustre: Vicente Piedrahita.* Quito: Editorial Casa de la Cultura Ecuatoriana, 1965.

———. *Entretelones de la historia nacional: Memorias militares de José Polanco Carrión.* Quito: Private printing, 2001.

Haigh, Roger. *Martín Guëmes: Tyrant or Tool? A Study of Sources of Power of an Argentine Caudillo.* Fort Worth: Texas Christian University Press, 1968.

Hales, Edward E. Y. *Pio Nono: A Study in European Politics and Religion in the Nineteenth Century.* New York: P. J. Kennedy & Sons, 1954.

Hall, Basil. *Extracts from a Journal Written on the Coasts of Chili, Peru, and Mexico in the Years 1820, 1821, 1822,* 2 vols. Upper Saddle River, NJ: Gregg Press, 1968.

Hamerly, Michael T. *Historia social y económica de la antigua provincia de Guayaquil, 1763–1842,* 2 vols. Guayaquil: Publicaciones del Archivo Histórico de Guayas, 1973.

Hamill, Hugh, ed. *Caudillos: Dictators in Spanish America.* Norman: University of Oklahoma Press, 1992.

Hassaurek, Friedrich. *Four Years among the Ecuadorians.* Carbondale: Southern Illinois University Press, 1967.

Heiman Guzmán, Hanns. *Inmigrantes en el Ecuador, un estudio histórico.* Quito: Casa Editorial Liebman, 1942.

Heredia, José Felix. *La consagración de la república del Ecuador al Sagrado Corazón de Jesús.* Quito: Editorial Ecuatoriana, 1935.

Herrera, Pablo. *Apuntos biográficos del gran magistrado ecuatoriano señor doctor Don Gabriel García Moreno.* Quito: Tipografía Encuadernación de la Prensa Católica, 1921.

———. *Observaciones sobre el tratado del 25 de enero celebrado en Guayaquil.* Quito: Imprenta del Gobierno, 1860.

Herz, Monica, and João Pontes Nogeira. *Ecuador vs. Peru: Peacemaking amid Rivalry.* Boulder, CO: Lynne Rienner, 2002.

Hobsbawm, Eric J. *Nations and Nationalism Since 1780: Programme, Myths, Reality.* Cambridge: Cambridge University Press, 1990.

Honigsbaum, Mark. *The Fever Trail: In Search of the Cure for Malaria.* New York: Farrar, Straus, and Giroux, 2001.

Hook, Sidney. *The Hero in History: A Study in Limitation and Possibility.* New York: John Day, 1943.

Hunter, John M., and James W. Foley. *Economic Problems of Latin America.* Boston: Houghton Mifflin, 1975.

Ibarra, Hernán. *Nos encontramos amenazados por todita la indiada: El levantamiento de Daquilema (Chimborazo, 1871).* Quito: Centro de Estudios y Difusión Social, 1993.

Iglesias, Angel María. *Cañar: Síntesis histórica.* Azogues, Ecuador: Tallers Gráficos de Editorial América, 1977.

Jacobsen, Nils, and Cristóbal Aljovín de Losada, eds. *Political Cultures in the Andes, 1750–1950.* Durham, NC: Duke University Press, 2005

Jane, Cecil. *Liberty and Despotism in Latin America.* Oxford: Clarendon Press, 1929.

Jaramillo Alvarado, Pío. *Historia de Loja y su provincia.* Quito: Casa de la Cultura Ecuatoriana, 1955.

Johnson, Lyman, ed. *Body Politics: Death, Dismemberment, and Memory in Latin America.* Albuquerque: University of New Mexico Press, 2004.

Jonas, Raymond. *France and the Cult of the Sacred Heart.* Berkeley: University of California Press, 2000.

Jouanen, José. *Historia de la compañía de Jesús en la república del Ecuador 1850–1950.* Quito: Private Printing, 2003.

———. *Los jesuitas y el oriente ecuatoriano (monografía histórica), 1868–1898.* Guayaquil: Editorial Arquidiocesana, 1977.

Jurado Noboa, Fernando. *Las Quiteñas.* Quito: Dinediciones, 1995.

Karnes, Thomas. *The Failure of Union, Central America 1824–1975.* Tempe: Arizona State University Center for Latin American Studies, 1976.

Kennedy Troya, Alexandra. *Rafael Troya, 1845–1920: El pintor de los andes ecuatorianos.* Quito: Ediciones del Banco Central del Ecuador, 1999.

Klaiber, Jeffrey. *The Catholic Church in Peru, 1821–1985: A Social History.* Washington, DC: Catholic University of America Press, 1984.

Koch, Freda Postle. *Colonel Coggeshall: The Man Who Saved Lincoln.* Columbus, OH: Po Ko Press, 1985.

Kolberg, Josef. *Hacia el Ecuador: Relatos de viaje.* Quito: PUCE, 1977.

Lara, Jorge Salvador. *Quito.* Quito: Editorial Mapfre, 1992.

Larrea, Carlos Manuel. *Antonio Flores Jijón: Su vida y sus obras.* Quito: Corporación de Estudios y Publicaciones, 1974.

Larson, Brooke. *Trials of Nation Making: Liberalism, Race, and Ethnicity in the Andes, 1810–1910.* Cambridge: Cambridge University Press, 2004.

Lieuwen, Edwin. *Arms and Politics in Latin America.* New York: Praeger, 1960.

Loor, Wilfrido. *García Moreno y sus asesinos.* Quito: Editorial Ecuatoriana, 1966.

———. *Los Jesuitas en el Ecuador: Su ingreso y expulsión, 1850–1852.* Quito: La Prensa Católica, 1959.

———. *La victoria de Guayaquil.* Quito: La Prensa Católica, 1960.

López Alvarez, Leopoldo. *La batalla de Cuaspud.* Pasto: Tipografía López, 1915.
———. *La muerte de García Moreno.* Quito: Imprenta de la Universidad Central, 1922.
Loveman, Brian. *For la Patria: Politics and the Armed Forces in Latin America.* Wilmington, DE: Scholarly Resource Books, 1999.
Lynch, John. *Caudillos in Spanish America, 1800–1850.* Oxford: Clarenden Press, 1992.
———. *Argentine Dictator: Juan Manuel de Rosas, 1829–1852.* Oxford: Clarenden Press, 1981.
Lyons, Barry J. *Remembering the Hacienda: Religion, Authority and Social Change in Highland Ecuador.* Austin: University of Texas Press, 2006.
Maiguashca, Juan, ed. *Historia y región en el Ecuador, 1830–1930.* Quito: Corporación Editorial Nacional, 1994.
Malo, Benigno. *Escritos y discursos,* 2 vols. Quito: Editorial Ecuatoriana, 1940.
Malo, Benigno, and Vicente Paz. *Exposición de la legación del Ecuador en Perú confiada al excmo. Sr. Dr. D. Benigno Malo en los años de 1866 y 1867.* Lima: Diario Oficial, 1883.
Marchán Romero, Carlos, and Bruno Andrade Andrade. *Estructura agraria de la sierra centro-norte 1830–1930,* 4 vols. Cuenca: Banco Central de Ecuador, 1984.
Masur, Gerhard. *Simón Bolívar.* Albuquerque: University of New Mexico Press, 1948.
Mecham, J. Lloyd. *Church and State in Latin America: A History of Politico-Ecclesiastical Relations.* Chapel Hill: University of North Carolina Press, 1966.
Mera, Juan León. *García Moreno: Libro inédito.* Quito: Imprenta del Clero, 1904.
Meyer, Michael C. *Huerta: A Political Portrait.* Lincoln: University of Nebraska Press, 1972.
Miller, Tom. *The Panama Hat Trail: A Journey from South America.* New York: William Morrow, 1986.
Miranda Ribadeneira, Francisco. *García Moreno y la compañía de Jesús.* Quito: Imprenta y Ediciones Lexigrama, 1976.
Moncayo, Abelardo. *Aclaraciones.* Quito: Francisco E. Páez, 1909.
Moncayo, Pedro. *El Ecuador de 1825 a 1875, sus hombres, sus instituciones, sus leyes.* Quito: Imprenta Nacional, 1906.
Montalvo, Juan. *La dictadura perpetua.* Panamá: Tipografía de M. R. de la Torre e Hijos, 1874.
Mörner, Magnus. *Adventurers and Proletarians: The Story of Migrants in Latin America.* Pittsburgh: University of Pittsburgh Press, 1985.
———. *The Andean Past: Land, Societies, and Conflicts.* New York: Columbia University Press, 1985.
———. *Region and State in Latin America's Past.* Baltimore: Johns Hopkins University Press, 1993.
Murray, Pamela S. *For Glory and Bolívar: The Remarkable Life of Manuela Sáenz.* Austin: University of Texas Press, 2008.
Namier, Lewis. *The Structure of Politics at the Accession of George III.* London: Macmillan, 1929.
Nicolson, Harold. *The Development of English Biography.* London: Hogarth, 1959.
O'Conner, Erin. *Gender, Indians, Nation: The Contradictions of Making Ecuador, 1830–1925,* Tucson: University of Arizona Press, 2007.

Ordóñez Zamora, Aurelio. *Gabriel García Moreno: Verdugo a servicio de la providencia.* Cuenca: Private printing, 1969.

Orton, James. *The Andes and the Amazon, or Across the Continent of South America.* New York: Harper and Brothers, 1876.

Packenham, Robert. *The Dependency Movement: Scholarship and Politics in Development Studies.* Cambridge: Cambridge University Press, 1992.

Palomeque, Silvio. *Cuenca en el Siglo XIX: La articulación de una región.* Quito: Ediciones Abya-Yala, 1990.

Paredes Borja, Virgilio. *Historia de la medicina en el Ecuador.* Quito: Editorial Casa de la Cultura Ecuatoriana, 1963.

Pattee, Richard. *Gabriel García Moreno y el Ecuador de su tiempo,* 2nd ed. Mexico: Editorial Jus, 1944.

Paul, Augustin. *García Moreno, président de l'Equateur: Drame en 3 Actes.* Paris: Libraire Blériot, 1921.

Peloso, Vincent C., and Barbara Tenenbaum. *Liberals, Politics and Power, State Formation in Nineteenth Century Latin America.* Athens: University of Georgia Press, 1996.

Pérez Estupiñán, Marcel. *Historia general de Esmeraldas.* Esmeraldas, Ecuador: Universidad Técnica, 1996.

Pérez Moscoso, César. *El campeón de los errores: Refutación al libro de Benjamín Carrión "García Moreno, el santo del patíbulo."* Guayaquil: Instituto Nacional Garciano del Ecuador, 1960.

——— *En defensa de la verdad: Habla el hijo de Faustino Rayo, asesino de García Moreno.* Quito: Talleres Gráficos, 1958.

Pfeiffer, Ida. *A Lady's Second Journey Round the World.* New York: Harper and Brothers, 1856.

Pike, Frederick. *The United States and the Andean Republics: Peru, Bolivia, and Ecuador.* Cambridge, MA: Harvard University Press, 1977.

Pineo, Ronn. *Ecuador and the United States: Useful Strangers.* Athens: University of Georgia Press, 2007.

———. *Social and Economic Reform in Ecuador: Life and Work in Guayaquil.* Gainesville: University of Florida Press, 1996.

Pratt, Mary Louise. *Imperial Eyes: Travel Writing and Transculturation.* London: Routledge, 1992.

Proaño y Vega, Eloy. *Colección de algunos escritos relativos a la memoria del excelentísimo señor doctor D. Gabriel García Moreno, asesinado el 6 de agosto, 1875.* Quito: Imprenta de J. Campuzano y M. Rivadeneira, 1876.

———. *El seis de agosto de mil ochocientos setenta-cinco.* Quito: Imprenta del Clero, 1888.

Quintero, Rafael, and Erika Silva. *Ecuador: Una nación en ciernes,* 3 vols. Quito: Abya-Yala, 1991.

Ribadeneira, Carlos A. *El martirio de Gabriel García Moreno, presidente de la república del Ecuador.* Quito: Editorial Ecuatoriana, 1973.

Robalino Dávila, Luis. *Origenes del Ecuador de hoy: García Moreno.* Quito: Talleres Gráficos Nacionales, 1949.

Rock, David. *State Building and Political Movements in Argentina, 1860–1916.* Stanford, CA: Stanford University Press, 2002.

Rodríguez, Linda Alexander. *The Search for Public Policy: Regional Politics and Govern-*

ment Finances in Ecuador, 1830–1940. Berkeley: University of California Press, 1985.

Rodríguez O, Jaime. *The Emergence of Spanish America: Vicente Rocafuerte and Spanish Americanism, 1805–1832.* Berkeley: University of California Press, 1975.

———. *The Independence of Spanish America.* Cambridge: Cambridge University Press, 1998.

———. *La revolución política durante la época de la independencia: El reino de Quito 1808–1822.* Quito: Universidad Andina Simón Bolívar, 2006.

Rohrbacher, René François. *Histoire Universale de l'Eglise Catolique,* 29 vols. Paris: Gaumes Frères, 1850–1853.

Rolando, Carlos A. *Obras públicas ecuatorianas.* Guayaquil: Talleres Tipográficos de la Sociedad Filantrópica del Guayas, 1930.

Romero, Carlos Marchán, and Bruno Andrade Andrade. *Estructura agraria de la sierra centro-norte, 1830–1930,* 4 vols. Cuenca: Banco Central del Ecuador, 1984.

Safford, Frank. *The Ideal of the Practical: Colombia's Struggle to Form a Technical Elite.* Austin: University of Texas Press, 1976.

Salazar, Francisco Ignacio. *Defensa documentada del general doctor Francisco Javier Salazar.* Quito: Imprenta del Gobierno, 1887.

———. *La verdad contra la calumnia.* Guayaquil: Imprenta de Calvo y Cía, 1876.

Salazar Alvarado, Francisco. *Encuentro con la historia, García Moreno: Líder católico de latinoamérica.* Quito: Margarita Borja y Yanko Molina Editores, 2005.

———. *García Moreno y el general Salazar.* Quito: Editorial Ecuatoriano, 1975.

Sanders, James E. *Contentious Republicans: Popular Politics, Race, and Class in Nineteenth Century Colombia.* Durham, NC: Duke University Press, 2004.

Shafer, Boyd. *Nationalism: Myth and Reality.* New York: Harcourt, Brace, 1952.

Simson, Alfred. *Travels in the Wilds of Ecuador and the Exploration of the Putumayo River.* London: Samson, Low, Marston, Spearle, and Rivington, 1886.

Sowell, David. *The Tale of Miguel Perdomo Neira: Medicine, Ideologies, and Power in the Nineteenth Century Andes.* Wilmington, DE: Scholarly Resources, 2001.

Spindler, Frank MacDonald. *Nineteenth-Century Ecuador: An Historical Introduction.* Fairfax, VA: George Mason University Press, 1987.

Spindler, Frank M., and Nancy Cook Brooks. *Selection from Juan Montalvo, translated from the Spanish.* Tempe: Arizona State University Press, 1984.

Spruce, Richard. *Notes of a Botanist on the Amazon and Andes,* 2 vols. New York: Johnson Reprint, 1970.

Stein, Stanley J., and Barbara H. Stein. *The Colonial Heritage of Latin America: Essays on Economic Dependence in Perspective.* New York: Oxford University Press, 1970.

Tenorio-Trillo, Mauricio. *Mexico at the World's Fair.* Berkeley: University of California Press, 1996.

TePaske, John, ed. Jorge Juan and Antonio de Ulloa. *Discourse and Political Reflections on the Kingdoms of Peru and Their Government.* Norman: University of Oklahoma Press, 1978.

Terán-Guerrero, José María. *La dictadura neroniana en el Ecuador.* Ipiales, Colombia: Tipografía de Nicanor Médicis y Cía, 1870.

Thurner, Mark. *From Two Republics to One Divided: Contradictions of Post-Colonial Nation Making in Andean Peru.* Durham, NC: Duke University Press, 1997.

Thurner, Mark, and Andrés Guerrero. *After Spanish Rule: Postcolonial Predicaments of the Americas.* Durham, NC: Duke University Press, 2003.

Tobar Donoso, Julio. *García Moreno y la instrucción pública.* Quito: Editorial Ecuatoriana, 1940.

———. *El general José María Urvina: Ensayo biográfico.* Quito: Tipografía y Encuadernación Salesianas, 1920.

———. *Monografías Históricas.* Quito: Editorial Ecuatoriana, 1937.

Uzcátegui, Emilio. *Desarrollo de la educación en el Ecuador.* Quito: Editorial Casa de la Cultura Ecuatoriana, 1976.

Vacas Galindo, David. *Apuntes históricos del telegráfico nacional.* Quito: Imprenta Nacional, 1934.

Van Aken, Mark. *King of the Night: Juan José Flores and Ecuador, 1824–1864.* Berkeley: University of California Press, 1989.

Vargas, José María. *Los maestros del arte ecuatoriano,* 2 vols. Quito: Imprenta Municipal, 1955.

Veintemilla, Marietta de. *Páginas del Ecuador.* Lima: Imprenta Liberal de F. Masias y Cía., 1890.

Velarde, César Augusto. *La expedición de Castilla al Ecuador, 1858–1860.* Lima: Imprenta del Ministerio de Guerra, 1954.

Velasco, Juan de. *Historia del reino de Quito en la América Meridional.* Caracas: Biblioteca Ayacucho, 1981.

Véliz, Claudio. *The Centralist Tradition in Latin America.* Princeton: Princeton University Press, 1980.

Villacrés Moscoso, Jorge W. *Las ambiciones internacionales por las islas Galápagos.* Guayaquil: Casa de la Cultura Ecuatoriana, 1985.

———. *Historia diplomática de la república del Ecuador,* 3 vols., Vol. 3. Guayaquil: Imprenta de la Universidad de Guayaquil, 1972.

Villegas Domínguez, Rodrigo. *Vida de Abelardo Moncayo.* Quito: Editorial Casa de la Cultura, 1961.

Whigham, Thomas. *The Paraguayan War.* Lincoln: University of Nebraska Press, 2002.

Whitaker, Arthur P. *The United States and South America: The Northern Republics.* Cambridge, MA: Harvard University Press, 1948.

Wolf, Teodoro. *Geography and Geology of Ecuador,* 2nd ed. Toronto: Grand & Toy, 1933.

Woodward, Ralph Lee. *Rafael Carrera and the Emergence of the Republic of Guatemala, 1821–1871.* Athens: University of Georgia Press, 1993.

Xavier, Adro. *García Moreno, siglo xix, hispanoamérica ecuatorial.* Barcelona: Editorial Casals, 1991.

Yáñez Cossío, Consuelo. *La educación indígena en el Ecuador: Estudio introductorio.* Quito: Abya-Yala, 1996.

Zarama, Daniel. *Don Julio Arboleda en el sur de Colombia.* Pasto: Imprenta del Departimiento, 1917.

Zook, David H., Jr. *Zarumilla-Marañón: The Ecuador-Peru Dispute.* New York: Bookman Associates, 1964.

Articles

Ayala Mora, Enrique. "Gabriel García Moreno y la gestación del estado nacional en el Ecuador." *Cultura,* 4, no. 10 (May–August 1981), 141–74.

Barrera, Isaac J. "Pablo Herrera." *Boletín de la Academia Nacional de Historia,* Quito, 43, no. 97 (January–June 1961): 84–87.

Boletín Franciscano organo de la tercera orden, 3, no. 4, 4–9.

Bromley, Rosemary D. F., and R. J. Bromley. "The Debate on Sunday Markets in Nineteenth-Century Ecuador." *Journal of Latin American Studies,* 7, no. 1 (May 1975): 85–108.

Deas, Malcolm. "The Man on Foot: Conscription and the Nation-State in Nineteenth-Century Latin America." *Studies in the Formation of the Nation-State in Latin America.* London: Institute of Latin American Studies, 2002, 77–93.

———. "Venezuela, Colombia, and Ecuador: The First Half-Century of Independence." *Cambridge History of Latin America,* 3: 507–38.

Gangotena, C. de. "Los Ascásubi." *Boletín de la Academia Nacional de Historia,* Quito, 7, no. 19 (September–October 1923): 241–47.

Gold, Robert L. "Negro Colonization Schemes in Ecuador, 1861–1864." *Phylon,* 30, no. 3 (1969): 306–16.

Gruss, Louis. "The Mission to Ecuador of Judah P. Benjamin." *Louisiana Historical Quarterly,* 23 (January 1940): 162–69.

Guerrero, Andrés. "The Construction of a Ventriloquist's Image: Liberal Discourse and the 'Miserable Indian Race' in Late 19th Century Ecuador." *Journal of Latin American Studies,* 29, no. 3: 555–90.

Howe, George Frederick. "García Moreno's Efforts to Unite Ecuador and France." *Hispanic American Historical Review,* 16, no. 2 (1936): 257–62.

Kingman Garcés, Eduardo. "Del hogar cristiano a la escuela moderna: La educación como modeladora de hábitos." *Bulletin de L'Institut Français d'Ètudes Andines,* 28, no. 3 (1999): 345–59.

León, Francisco Javier. "Memorias, August 11, 1875." *El Derecho,* Quito, November 4, 1921.

Madera, Luis F. "Modesto López." *Boletín de la Academia Nacional de Historia,* Quito, 25, no. 65 (January–June 1945): 105–14.

Maiguashca, Juan. "The Electoral Reforms of 1861 in Ecuador and the Rise of the New Political Order." In Eduardo Posada-Carbo, *Elections before Democracy: The History of Elections in Europe and Latin America.* London: Institute of Latin American Studies (1996): 87–115.

———. "El proyecto garciano de modernidad católica republicana en Ecuador, 1830–1875." In Marta Irurozqui Victoriano, *La mirada esquiva: Reflexiones históricas sobre la interacción del estado y ciudadanía en los andes (Bolivia, Ecuador y Perú), siglo xix.* Madrid: Consejo Superior de Investigaciones Científicas (2005): 233–59.

Miller, Nicola. "The Historiography of Nationalism and Nation Identity in Latin America." *Nations and Nationalism* 12, part 2 (April 2006): 201–21.

Pattee, Ricardo. "García Moreno y la política internacional ecuatariana." *Boletín de la Academia Nacional de Historia,* Quito, 19 (January–June 1939): 185–208.

Robertson, William Spence. "El sueño de García Moreno sobre un protectorado en el Ecuador." *Boletín de la Academia Nacional de Historia*, Quito, 25, no. 65 (January–June 1945): 67–80.

Safford, Frank. "Politics, Ideology, and Society in Post-Independence Spanish America." *Cambridge History of Latin America.* Cambridge: Cambridge University Press, 1984, III: 347–421.

Smith, Peter. "The Image of a Dictator: Gabriel García Moreno." *Hispanic American Historical Review*, 45, no. 1 (February 1965): 1–24.

Tobar Donoso, Julio. "El ingeniero Sebastián Wisse." *Boletín de la Academia Nacional de Historia, 39* (July–December 1959); 172–211.

Valera [pseud.?]. "Los Milagros de García Moreno." *Caricatura: Seminario Humorístico de la Vida Nacional*, Quito, 32 (March 1950): 22–23.

Van Aken, Mark. "The Lingering Death of Indian Tribute in Ecuador, 1857." *Hispanic American Historical Review*, 61, no. 3 (August 1981): 429–60.

Villacís Molina, Rodrigo. "La batalla del monumento." *Vistazo,* (August 1969): 74–79.

Williams, Derek. "Assembling the 'Empire of Morality': State Building Strategies in Catholic Ecuador, 1864–1875." *Journal of Historical Sociology*, 14, no. 2 (June 2001): 149–74.

———. "Popular Liberalism and Indian Servitude: The Making and Unmaking of Ecuador's Anti-Landlord State, 1845–1868." *Hispanic American Historical Review*, 83, no. 4 (November 2003): 697–733.

Wolf, Eric, and Edward Hansen. "Caudillo Politics: A Structural Analysis." *Comparative Studies in Society and History*, 9, no. 2 (January 1967) 168–79.

Dissertations and Theses

Ackerman, Samuel. "The Trabajo Subsidiario: Compulsory Labor and Taxation in Nineteenth Century Ecuador." PhD diss., New York University, 1977.

Bustos-Videla, César. "Church and State in Ecuador: A History of Politico-Ecclesiastical Relations during the Age of Gabriel García Moreno." PhD diss., Georgetown University, 1966.

Fitzell, Jill. "Cultural Colonialism and Ethnography: European Travelers in Nineteenth-Century Ecuador." PhD diss., University of British Columbia, 1994.

Hartup, Cheryl. "Artists and the New Nation: Academic Painting in Quito during the Presidency of Gabriel García Moreno (1861–1875)." Master's thesis, University of Texas at Austin, 1997.

Helguera, J. León. "The First Mosquera Administration in New Granada, 1845–1849." PhD diss., University of North Carolina, 1958.

King, William Martin. "Ecuadorian Church and State Relations under García Moreno." PhD diss., University of Texas at Austin, 1974.

Lauderbaugh, George M. "The United States and Ecuador: Conflict and Convergence, 1830–1946." PhD diss., University of Alabama, 1997.

Wiles, Dawn Ann. "Land Transportation within Ecuador, 1822–1954." PhD diss., Louisiana State University, 1971.

Williams, Derek. "Negotiating the State: National Utopias and Local Politics in Andean Ecuador, 1845–1875." PhD diss., State University of New York, Stony Brook, 2001.

Index

Boldface page numbers indicate photographs.

www.ingramcontent.com/pod-product-compliance
Ingram Content Group UK Ltd.
Pitfield, Milton Keynes, MK11 3LW, UK
UKHW010305240525
458861UK00002B/251